The Law of Love
ENGLISH SPIRITUALITY
IN THE AGE OF WYCLIF

JOHN WYCLIF
Eighteenth-century portrait by Alexander Van Hacken

The Law of Love

ENGLISH SPIRITUALITY
IN THE AGE OF WYCLIF

Translated and Edited by
David Lyle Jeffrey

WILLIAM B. EERDMANS PUBLISHING COMPANY
GRAND RAPIDS, MICHIGAN

This book is dedicated to
my parents
Lyle E. Jeffrey and Florence L. Jeffrey

Copyright © 1988 by William B. Eerdmans Publishing Company
255 Jefferson Ave. SE, Grand Rapids, Michigan 49503

Library of Congress Cataloging in Publication Data

The Law of love: English spirituality in the age of Wyclif
edited by David Lyle Jeffrey
p.   cm.
Bibliography: p. 54
ISBN 0-8028-0299-0
1. Spiritual life—Catholic authors—Early works to 1800.
2. Spiritual life—Lollard authors—Early works to 1800.
3. Spirituality—England—History of doctrines—Middle Ages, 600–1500.
I. Jeffrey, David L., 1941–
BV4500.L37   1987
248'.0942—dc19   87-36582   CIP

57,850

Contents

Illustrations   viii
Preface   ix
INTRODUCTION   1
BIBLIOGRAPHY   54

I. CONVERSION AND THE PATTERNS OF SPIRITUAL LIFE
RICHARD ROLLE, The Amending of Life   63

II. PRAYER AND WORSHIP
WALTER HILTON, *from* The Ladder of Perfection   93
ANONYMOUS, Understanding the Lord's Prayer   102
Common Prayer
    The Lord's Prayer in Six Translations   107
    Other Scriptural Prayers   108

III. HYMNS AND SPIRITUAL SONGS
WILLIAM HEREBERT, All Glory, Laud and Honor   115
JOHN GRIMESTONE, Gold and Al This Werdis Wyn   117
JOHN GRIMESTONE, O Vos Omnes   118
ANONYMOUS, Pieta   119
JAMES RYMAN, Revert, Revert   121
ANONYMOUS, Lord, Thou Clepedest Me   123
ANONYMOUS, Adam Lay I-Bounde   124
ANONYMOUS, I Synge of a Mayden   125
ANONYMOUS, Hond by Hond   126
JAMES RYMAN, Magnificat   127
JOHN TREVISA, God Me Speed   128
JOHN TREVISA, A Pastor's Evening Prayer   130

IV. MEDITATION AND CONTEMPLATION
WALTER HILTON, *from* The Ladder of Perfection
    On Meditation   133
    Self-Knowledge and the Sight of God   135
RICHARD ROLLE, Meditation on the Passion of Christ   149
RICHARD ROLLE, The Law of Love   155

RICHARD ROLLE, Ego Dormio 162
RICHARD ROLLE, *from* The Form of Living
    Amore Langueo 168
    The Nature of Love 169
    The Seven Gifts of the Holy Spirit 174
ANONYMOUS, The Love of Jesus 175
ANONYMOUS, Dance of the Cross 177

V. MYSTICAL SPIRITUALITY

RICHARD ROLLE, *from* The Fire of Love 183
ANONYMOUS, *from* The Cloud of Unknowing 188
CATHERINE OF SIENA, *from* The Orcherd of Syon 197
BRIDGET OF SWEDEN, *from* The Revelations 207
JULIAN OF NORWICH, *from* The Showings 210
MARGERY KEMPE, *from* The Book of Margery Kempe 222

VI. THE SPIRITUALITY OF EVERYDAY LIFE

WALTER HILTON, *from* Epistle on the Mixed Life 229
ANONYMOUS, Our Daily Work: A Mirror of Discipline ... 236
ANONYMOUS, Enabling Grace 265
SIR JOHN CLANVOWE, The Two Ways 272
ANONYMOUS, Loving Our Enemies 291

VII. PREACHING AND PASTORAL CARE

JOHN WYCLIF, *from* The Duty of Pastors
    The Good Pastor 295
    The Good Husbandman 296
    Corrupt Preaching 298
WALTER HILTON, *from* The Ladder of Perfection 300
GEOFFREY CHAUCER, *from* The Canterbury Tales 304
NICHOLAS BOZON, Christ's Chivalry 317
JOHN MIRK, *from* The Festial 320

VIII. SCRIPTURE AND TRANSLATION

WALTER HILTON, *from* The Ladder of Perfection 327
JOHN WYCLIF, *from* The Authority of Sacred Scripture ... 332
JOHN PURVEY, *from* The Prologue to the Wycliffite Bible
    Scriptural Authority and Spiritual Authenticity 339
    In Defense of Translating Scripture 346

The Wycliffite Bible, *selections* 352
RICHARD ROLLE, The Song of Hannah 356
RICHARD ROLLE, The Song of Isaiah 361
ANONYMOUS, Exposition of the Ave Maria 363

IX. GOSPEL AND CULTURE

WILLIAM LANGLAND, *from* Piers the Plowman 371
ANONYMOUS, Of Servants and Lords 384
GEOFFREY CHAUCER, Gentilesse 400
GEOFFREY CHAUCER, Balade de Bon Conseil 401
ANONYMOUS, Courageous Witness 403

Illustrations

John Wyclif	frontispiece
Madonna and Child	8
St. Peter and St. Paul	10
A Forest Hermit	15
Biblia Pauperum	34
University Training	37
Margaret Beaufort	46
Richard Rolle, Hermit	62
Unknown Woman at Prayer	92
King David with Harp	114
The Throne of Mercy	132
Jacob's Ladder	182
Gentilesse	228
Geoffrey Chaucer	294
John Wyclif	326
Ploughing the Ground	370

Preface

THIS ANTHOLOGY contains some of the best spiritual writings from an age of great devotional literature. It is intended for the general reader and nonspecialist student; thus I have translated the texts from their original Medieval English, Anglo-Norman French, or Latin into modern English. In so doing I have tried to be as literal as a preservation of sense would permit, so as to retain something of the character of the medieval idiom as it is variously used by the authors. In the case of common prayer, vernacular hymns, and spiritual songs, I have left texts in their native dialects, with glosses on difficult words, except for two or three instances where a full translation seemed necessary. Where it has seemed likely to be helpful to the reader I have keyed scriptural citations in the medieval texts to modern chapter and verse references in parentheses. Although I have tried as much as possible to render the Latin and even vernacular citations from Scripture quite literally, it has been necessary on occasion to clarify potential obscurity by resorting to the familiar Authorized Version.

The fourteenth century is an astonishingly rich period in the history of English spirituality. No anthology of this scope can hope to do it justice. I have tried to be as representative as possible of the character of devotional writing in the period and have endeavored to provide complete shorter texts wherever that seemed feasible. My hope is that the resulting collection will provide an introduction to spirituality in the age of Wyclif which is both faithful and appealing. If I have been at all successful, the contemporary reader should be able to acquire a sense of the strong linkage between that period and our own time, and yet also find elements which, in their differences of emphasis, offer a challenge to our own reflection on matters of faith and life.

The general reader will want to use this book somewhat differently from the student. Having the luxury of more leisure, it should be possible for such a reader to take it up from time to time to read a selection as most were intended to be read—slowly and meditatively. For those who can do this, the volume can function in the manner of a medieval "book of hours" or devotional anthology. To all readers of this book however, I want to recommend further pursuit of those writers who seem to them most attractive. The Bibliography contains, accordingly, citations of editions and full translations of several major works.

A number of acknowledgments, finally, are due. Throughout the preparation of this book I have been conscious of my continuing indebtedness to Professor D. W. Robertson, Jr., and Professor J. V. Fleming, whose exemplary instruction made me a student of medieval spiritual literature two decades ago. I wish to thank Multnomah Press, publishers of my translation of Walter Hilton, for granting me permission to reproduce here (with minor variations and corrections) selections from *Toward a Perfect Love: The Spiritual Counsel of Walter Hilton* (1985). The translation from Wyclif's *De Veritate Sacrae Scripturae* owes much to my friend and former student Michael Treschow and derives from a translation with commentary which we have been jointly preparing of that work. Three poems appear here in translations adapted from a forthcoming edition of Anglo-Norman lyrics which Brian J. Levy and I have made for the Pontifical Institute of Mediaeval Studies Press in Toronto.

In final preparation of the manuscript, Anne Le Dressay, another student and friend, has graciously made time to help with some of the typing. The lion's share of my obligation, however, is to my dearest friend and constant collaborator, Katherine my wife, without whose patient scrutiny and determined assistance most of my projects—this book included—would surely outlast my allotted span of days.

Introduction

Luf es lyf that lastes ay, thar it in Criste es feste;
For wele ne wa it chaunge may, als wryten has men wyseste
The nyght it tournes intil the day, thi travel intyll reste.
If thou will luf thus as I say, thou may be wyth the beste.

Lufe es thoght, wyth grete desyre, of a fayre lovyng.
Lufe I lyken til a fyre, that sloken may na thyng.
Lufe us clenses of oure syn, lufe us bote sall bryng.
Lufe the keynges hert may wyn, lufe of joy may syng.[1]

*   *   *

The seruant vnderstondynge Goddis lawe is acceptable and plesant to the
kyng of heuene; and the bettere that ʒe vnderstonden what ʒe reden, the
more deuocioun ʒe schullen haue, and the more knowe ʒoure God, and the
more ʒe knowen him, the more ʒe schullen loue him, and the more ʒe louen
him, the more he schal loue ʒou.
    Amen.[2]

BOTH OF THESE PASSAGES are drawn from English spiritual literature of
the fourteenth century. The first is the opening two stanzas of a vernacular hymn written around 1345 by Richard Rolle or one of his followers. For most of us it now requires a translation to be entirely understood (see below). The second passage is the concluding portion of a
tract in defense of translating Scripture, written at the end of the century, probably in the south of England, by a student or follower of John
Wyclif. For most of us it can be read quite easily as it stands.

    Brief as they are, these two fragments are *insignia*, designs in minia-
ture on bookends to the rich and colorful library of English spirituality
in the age of Wyclif. Rolle, born about 1300, went to Oxford but fled from

---

Love is a life that lasts forever, if fixed upon Christ;
In good times or bad it remains unchanged, as the wisest man writes.
Your night it turns to day, your labor into rest.
If you will love as I say, you will dwell with the best.

Love meditates with deep desire, on a beautiful loving;
Love is like a fire that can be quenched by nothing.
Love cleanses us from sin; love shall bring us healing.
Love is what wins the heart of the King; so can love joyously sing.

academic life and the possibility of an ordinary pastoral vocation to live as a hermit. His was an enclosed and solitary calling. He was a charismatic and a mystic, and his voice was that of a poet—soft and lyrical. Yet by the fluent work of his brief life he came to be spiritual counselor to many generations through voluminous spiritual writings and scriptural translations.

Wyclif, born about 1333, went to Oxford to stay, becoming a doctor of theology, Master of Balliol, and eventually the most notable philosopher and academic theologian in the England of his day. His life was stormy, intellectual, public, and political, his voice a flint-hard preacher's voice; and even in the course of his own brief life he became a revolutionary teacher to large numbers of ordinands and clerics. Indirectly, through his prodigious theological writings and the translation of the whole Bible completed by his students, he began a reformation in spirituality that spread through John Hus to Luther and the whole of northern Europe.

Our two texts are thus quite different from each other: the first is early, the second late; the first is a hymn, the second concludes an argument. Yet each appeals to the same basic spiritual value: love. For Rolle, love fixed upon Christ is the power which transforms all of life, as Scripture says. For Wyclif, the better we understand Scripture, "Goddes lawe" (lex Cristi or lex Dei), the better we will be able to love God, and the more fully we will experience his love in our own hearts.

Love, or the "law of love," is central to the whole of English spirituality in this period—not least because it was still the central moral and religious value to which the culture as a whole made persistent appeal. The Great Commandment was to love (Matthew 22:37-40); the test of Christian character was love (1 John 2:9-11; 5:2). Love was the bond that held all society together—in theory—from the king at the top down through the serried ranks of dukes, nobles, barons, knights, and squires to peasant serfs; from archbishop down through bishops, vicars, parsons, poor curates, and those in lesser orders; from abbot general to abbot, monks, novitiates, and servants. At every level, relationships were formalized by a verbal bond of love. The feodas expressed in each act of homage was a pledge of troth resembling a marriage vow. In a solemnization, one party knelt before the other with hands pressed upright together while the other encircled those hands in his or her own as the vows were being offered; typically such a ceremony concluded with a kiss, and sometimes with an exchange of rings.[3] The association of homage with the language of love is verbally manifest in the medieval French word for serf: drû, or "lover." We see it visually reflected a century later in Albrecht Dürer's Praying Hands: this sign of prayer, developed from earlier postures with arms and hands upraised, expresses the analogy of spiritual and temporal relationships which so profoundly figured in every walk of social life.

Love bound society together not only vertically, in this way, but horizontally as well. Italian city states, for example, had charters which described civic organizations in terms of mutual bonds of charity; English craft guilds expressed in their charters the same idea. University colleges pledged students to mutual responsibility as they promised to "serve each other in charity in all things." The medieval civic ideal of "common profit," celebrated by John Gower, William Langland, and other writers in Wyclif's day, is an application of principles contained in 1 John 4 and 1 Corinthians 13 to both the body of Christ and the "body politic." It was an ideal sincerely believed in, as few ideals are today. As an ideal, however, it rested absolutely on the definition of love as charity *(caritas)*.

It is a commonplace of spiritual wisdom even in our own time that love covers a multitude of sins too often simply by becoming another name for many of them.[4] The fourteenth century knew this subtle fraud at least as well as we do. While medieval Christians ascribed all social good to charitable love, they believed equally that all social ill and personal sin came ultimately from a perversion of love—or cupidity *(cupiditas)*. Cupidity was seen as the mortal foe of charity—or, to put it in their more colloquial way, sin was the enemy of love.

Accordingly, discussions of sin in the Middle Ages make clear the profoundly social context of medieval moral theology. Because we now think of sin largely in individual terms, it is often for us essentially a psychological problem. Our medieval forebears also thought of sin as individual or self-directed in conception and action—indeed, that was for them the essential character of cupidity. Yet at the same time they thought of sin's *meaning* in social terms—its cost to others and therefore to *caritas* itself—perhaps more than we do. The graver weight that they attached to the seven deadly sins of pride, envy, wrath, covetousness, sloth, gluttony, and lechery owes to the fact that there is in each of them necessarily some damage to others, a detraction from their personal good in either psychological or material terms. The first five of the seven are always of "mortal" damage to the spirit, since in their commission the element of will is unavoidably active and inherently malicious. The other, "venial," sins may readily acquire that character if they are repeated or become habitual.[5]

Medieval society was community-oriented to a degree most of us now find difficult to imagine—unless perhaps we have lived in the country or in a small village. England in the fourteenth century was essentially a rural society. Towns and villages were small marketplaces, serving the surrounding countryside. Even London, the great capital and seat of kings, did not exceed a population of fifty thousand until the end of the century. And here, as in other middle-sized centers, society was divided into manageable groupings by parishes and guilds. Even people of the leading classes of merchants, nobles, knights, and ladies of the court knew each other's intimate lives. The ideal of a society bound together by ties of love was therefore not so unimaginable for them, and any betrayal of the ideal was experienced as a palpable loss of harmony and integrity by the whole community.

I. The World and the Church

A general loss of moral credibility in the political sphere, especially acute in the latter part of the fourteenth century, was a serious blow to Christian morale. After a series of bloody, almost annual wars against the Scots in the first part of the century, and the more militarily successful wars against the French for control of Aquitaine and other territories in mid-century, there was a brief era of triumphant and prosperous peace. The Black Prince (son of Edward III) consolidated English power in 1356 by defeating the French at Poitiers and taking John II, king of France, prisoner. Edward III established the famous Order of the Garter, and England became the European center of court chivalry. Then the Plague struck. Within a month it carried off, among thousands of others, both leading ladies of the court: Queen Phillipa and Blanche, Duchess of Lancaster, wife of John of Gaunt, the most powerful single nobleman of the time. The king did not remarry but took up with an astonishingly crude mistress named Alice Perrers, who dominated him in his dotage. With her, he soon made of himself an international disgrace.[6]

John of Gaunt, patron to both Wyclif and the poet Geoffrey Chaucer, made Chaucer's sister-in-law his open mistress, then undertook a nominal and political marriage to Constance of Castille.[7] After Edward III died in 1377—when his heir, Richard II, was a mere boy of ten—John of Gaunt, as Regent Protector, became for all practical purposes chief power in the realm. "Woe to the land whose king is a child" (Ecclesiastes 10:16) became a frequent (if whispered) refrain,[8] and then gradually, as in Langland's *Piers the Plowman,* an open lament. When Richard II came into his own at the age of twenty-two, he had been married to Queen Anne of Bohemia for more than seven years and had grown self-indulgent and insensitive to his responsibilities; in power he was an ineffective leader.

Chaucer, as chief court poet, was only one of many voices of counsel who tried to call Richard back to his coronation vows of love and fidelity. His short poem "Lak of Steadfastnesse" analyzes a society gone bad at the core, having abandoned the law of love to pursue individual lust and greed, or cupidity:

What maketh this world to be so veriable
But lust that folk have in discencioun?
For among us now a man is holde unable,
But if he can by som collusioun
Do his neyghburgh wrong or oppressioun.

Truth, he continues, is put down, reason is regarded as mere fancy, no appeal to virtue is possible, pity is in exile, no one is merciful, and greed has entirely blinded discretion everywhere one looks. It is as though the world has entirely inverted its values: wrong is now right and lies are proclaimed as truth. His conclusion, or "envoy to King Richard," pleads with him to "dred God, do law, love trouthe and worthynesse, and wed thy folk ageyn to stedfastnesse," and thus validate again the social bond of love.[9]

For Christians in the fourteenth century, both charity and cupidity were defined according to their focus or "intention." St. Augustine's classic distinction was frequently quoted:

I call "charity" the motion of the soul toward the enjoyment of God for his own sake, and the enjoyment of one's self and of one's neighbor for the sake of God; but "cupidity" is a motion of the soul toward the enjoyment of one's self, one's neighbor, or any corporal thing for the sake of something other than God.[10]

The centrality of this distinction for medieval Christianity in general is clear in St. Augustine's further observation that "Scripture teaches nothing but charity, nor condemns anything except cupidity, and in this way shapes the minds of men."[11] The law of love encoded in Scripture is thus a standard of discrimination as well as a statement of value.

The point is nicely illustrated by Chaucer's memorable Prioress in the general prologue to *The Canterbury Tales*. Revealed to us as a person of considerable religious status, she is nonetheless unhappily befuddled through a lack of scriptural wisdom. In the culminating line of her rather unflattering description, we see that she wears a large brooch with the inscription: *Amor vincit omnia*. A student of mine once mischievously translated this on an examination as "love winks at everything." The translation is, of course, wrong (it means "love conquers all"), but her point about the Prioress's unspecified love was well taken. *Amor*, as a term for love, is ambiguous and unfocused; only *caritas*, "charity," really "conquers all" in moral or spiritual terms, and a prioress, the reader hopes, will know that.[12] A central problem for fourteenth-century English society, as readers of *The Canterbury Tales* remember, is that in both church and state, each so richly represented in Chaucer's great poem, the ideal of charitable love as a law governing all of life was being undermined by perversions of love, with individuals defining themselves against the body and thus fragmenting and eroding the "common profit" which was understood to have been the goal of Christian community since the time of the apostles. Unhappily, this breakdown was nowhere as apparent as in the church itself.

It would be misleading, however, to view the English church in isolation from the Western church at large. The most dramatic public witness to the breakdown of the law of love in this period was the "Babylonian captivity," as the spiritual Franciscans called it, of the papacy. In 1309, Clement V moved the papal throne, along with the college of cardinals and curia, to Avignon. In France the papacy became almost completely dominated by French political power. Throughout the century, despite appeals by respected Italians such as Dante and Catherine of Siena to return to Rome, one French pope after another stayed in Avignon. Finally, in 1377, Gregory XI yielded, only to expire shortly after arriving in Italy.

When Urban VI was elected in 1378 to succeed him—in tumultuous and disordered circumstances—he was widely heralded in England, in part simply because he was *not* French, and in part because he had been a "diligent student of the Bible" and had a reputation for piety and justice. Wyclif in particular hailed him, thanking God for "providing our mother church with a catholic head, an evangelical man" who was living "in conformity with the law of Christ."[13] But power soon went to Urban's head, and he fell into violent struggle with his French cardinals. In July 1378, ostensibly "for reasons of health," they fled Rome, carrying with them the papal jewels. The other cardinals shortly followed. Urban, abandoned and isolated, with hardly an influential supporter in Rome other than Catherine of Siena, promptly declared twenty-four new cardinals, chosen from among his own compatriots. Two days later the deposed French cardinals elected their own pope, the Savoyard Robert of Geneva, who took the name Clement VII. The Great Schism, with rival popes at Rome and Avignon, was to last for almost forty years, until 1417.

Neither side wasted much charity on the other. Catherine wrote to Urban calling the French cardinals "devils in human form" and their pope "an antichrist." She encouraged Urban to counter the schismatics, urging him to "go without fear into the battle, with the armor of Divine

Love to cover you, for that is your sure defense." But Divine Love, as a noted historian has dryly observed, "was the last weapon in which Urban believed."[14] On the 29th of November, 1378, he excommunicated the antipope—a move applauded by the English church in general and Wyclif in particular.[15] That Clement was even less disposed to charity at first helped to make Urban's case. For many reasons the English had been disposed against the French, and the brutal character of the French pope served to justify old prejudices; if the massacre he ordered at Cesena in 1377, while still a cardinal, was not enough, his predatory material ambitions were closely enough linked to French political interests to prompt extreme English opposition.

All of Europe became divided into two opposing camps. Scotland, allied with the French against the English, went with Clement. Bohemia sided with Urban—which was to account for the marriage of Anne of Bohemia to King Richard, the coming of many Bohemian courtiers to London and Oxford, and eventually the passage of Wyclif's students under persecution to Prague. This alliance was also, of course, the basis of the connection between Wyclif and John Hus, most of whose central works were essentially copied from manuscripts of Wyclif's works and lectures.

The religious orders were also split, with some, like the Dominicans, acquiring two contesting heads. Hostilities even within religious communities were frequently intense enough to result in mayhem, bloodshed, and murder.[16] Urban, in his struggle to gain complete control, employed unscrupulous agents such as Bishop Spenser of Norwich in illegitimate "crusades" against disloyal continental cities. Spenser disgraced the church and Urban by high-handed extortion of money for a tour of rape, pillage, and arson through the lowlands.[17] While going about his grisly work he sacked a monastery and killed every man, woman, and child in the adjacent town. Yet for all his ferocity, he was eventually forced, by corruption, bad planning, and faulty logistics, to retreat to England in ignominy and disgrace.

Urban himself, whom Phillipe de Mézières called "more cruel than a serpent, Herod or Antiochus,"[18] dealt with opposition in a similarly violent way. When six of his own cardinals dared question his methods—notably a plan to make a scurrilous Neapolitan nephew pope after him—he had them flung down an old cistern, then systematically tortured and variously executed, filling their vacancies with men of less tender conscience.

One must try to imagine the effect of such events, news coming in as it were in almost every post, upon sincere Christians. Before the Schism, even Wyclif had not disputed the spiritual primacy of the papacy. He

MADONNA AND CHILD
Fourteenth-century stained glass

had, however, founded his notion of obedience to Rome on the assumption that the vicar of Christ would be "the poorest, holiest, most God-enlightened man in Christendom, who more than all others obeys God's law."[19] For a time after the Schism, Wyclif retained his support of the papacy, but eventually the evidence became too much to bear. He began to ask questions—and he was far from alone in this. What is the relationship between spiritual purity and spiritual authority? he asked in his work *On Dominion*. Are Peter's apostolic successors necessarily bishops of Rome? What is the precedent in Scripture for election by a college of cardinals, most of whom are not even priests? Who is then Christ's true vicar? Wyclif's answer—though farther reaching than those of some others—was not substantially different from the implicit or explicit conclusion of many of his contemporaries: Christ's vicar is one who truly follows Christ, who imitates him in a life of meekness, truth, and love, who is thus a servant. Surely sanctity, he reasoned, is the only sign of legitimate authority.[20]

For the ordinary faithful the Schism was profoundly disorienting. Langland mourned it as the "greatest calamity of all possible"; the village priest or person in religious vocation suddenly found not only the structures of religious life but the very foundations of its moral authority undercut. In a country known for its large numbers of genuinely pious Christians, this confounding of ecclesiastical authority did not initially prompt extreme cynicism in very many, at least openly. But it shook confidence and made people fearful. Their worry was not that such things as truth or love no longer existed but rather that these values had become almost irreparably buried under layers of falsehood, calumny, hatred, and greed. One should remember that people living at the end of the Middle Ages expected the Antichrist to come in the form of a hypocrite, a wolf in sheep's clothing. For them, a time of so much false-seeming was truly an apocalyptic age. The very existence of rival popes implied a reign of an Arch-deceiver—if only one could be sure which papal throne he occupied. By the end of the century, as graffiti in the margins and flyleaves of surviving theological books makes clear, Rome was not held to be in greater sanctity than Avignon.[21]

The actual experience of church-going in medieval England was mercifully removed from the worst elements of the papal controversy. Even in large communities, the ordinary Christian would focus spiritual life in the tranquil and beautiful sung worship of the abbey church or cathedral. Here a mass was offered in the splendor of fractured light and articulate images; the altar centered at once a moment of prayer and a pageant of history, and the beauty of holiness was figured amply in the beauty of art.

The many horrors of the Great Schism were still less apparent in rural parishes in the north or west of England. In these humbler settings—little village churches or manor chapels—even a predawn mass was remarkably well attended. Choirs were small (if they existed at all) and the service mostly "said." At the Sanctus, the "Holy, Holy, Holy" was intoned to begin the canon of the mass, and at the moment of consecration and elevation of the Host a little sanctus bell might be rung out a small window on one side of the church, so that those whose duties prevented them from attending could—whether milking in the dairy, cooking in the kitchen, starting up the blacksmith's fire, or already working in the fields—kneel down and say the Lord's Prayer.

ST. PETER AND ST. PAUL
Church wall painting, Idsworth, Hampshire

Inside the church, as indeed inside the great cathedrals as well, there were no pews, no seating at all, in fact, except in the choir and perhaps a few special misericords for the infirm. The stone floor would be strewn with rushes, changed about three times a year; one often knelt in the rustling company of rats and mice.[22] Yet despite such distractions, people in the small church tended to be more attentive to the liturgy; in the great cathedrals people strolled about talking until the sanctus bell stilled them momentarily for a Paternoster or Ave. In either sanctuary those who did not understand the Latin of the liturgy—and by the fourteenth century that was the great majority—simply watched and recited many times the familiar prayers. After the mass was over, they might came forward for a piece of the "holy bread" (a specially prepared loaf and not the consecrated wafer consumed by the priest in the mass) and then depart to their daily work.

At dusk the angelus bell (or Gabriel bell, as it was sometimes called) tolled out the knell of parting day, and parishioners hearing it would kneel to say the Ave in "gratefulness for our Lord's incarnation." After the night of rest was over, it would ring again—at 4 A.M. in summer, 5 A.M. in winter—to begin the day and call worshipers once more to divine service.

With its spire or tower lifted up over the surrounding houses, the medieval church was not merely a sanctuary for worship but a symbol reminding parishioners each and every day of God's love in Christ, of the gift of life itself, and of the value of every Christian person. For our medieval ancestors, the church was the center of life; even for a person who was not particularly spiritual, this was almost unavoidably so.

Some of this can now sound almost idyllic. There were, however, flies in the ointment. Most ubiquitous of these, by many accounts, were itinerant groups of begging and preaching friars. While fraternal spirituality had been central to the religious life of the thirteenth century and had produced a number of important devotional works, many of the early ideals of St. Francis had dissipated or become compromised out of existence. Although there were a few strong voices of Franciscan spirituality in the fourteenth century, such as that of Nicholas Bozon, one of whose Anglo-Norman verse sermons is translated in this volume, and although Franciscan lyricists such as William Herebert, John Grimestone, and James Ryman still enriched vernacular hymnody, much of the zeal and visible piety of the Franciscans slipped into decline as the century unfolded. This was especially true in the years following the first great wave of the Black Death in 1348–49, when friars closely involved in work among the poor died in great numbers.

The new fraternalism was less interested in the general welfare, but engaged in many new and impressive "ministries"—all of which required funding. Not only Franciscans but Dominicans, Carmelites, and, more rarely, Augustinians made rounds from house to house and town to town, collecting for one major project or another. Despite vows of poverty and claims of evangelical obedience, many of these men were charlatans, religious con artists who preyed on rich and poor alike, extorting from them their last farthings to further burgeoning empires. Many of the new-order friars became colorful and not very scriptural preachers. They enjoyed great success, however, both as entertainers and as substitute spiritual leaders for people who either did not hear regular preaching in their own parish churches or received only insubstantial, befuddled, or poorly prepared stuff that left them vulnerable to flashy style and glib rhetoric.[23] The friars often came with minstrels, mirth, and song; they were hard to resist. Chaucer's Friar in *The Canterbury Tales*, who plays a trendy gittern and charms the ladies with his delightful lisp, specializes in middle or upper-class clients, gives easy penance to those who will slip him some money for his trouble, and thus "steals sheep" from the local parish.

There were also other hucksters about. The summoners, who were debt collectors and tithe enforcers for the archdeacons, regularly abused their offices, taking bribes or resorting to extortion—as in the case of one of Chaucer's devilish summoners, whose specialty it is to prey on fearful widows. But summoners were notorious for other vices as well. When Chaucer's Friar says "a summoner is a runner up and down, with commandments for fornication," he implies abuse of the law of love, for which friars and summoners had both become well-known.[24]

Pardoners, who were often recruited from the fraternal orders, were also, as Langland observes, to be found everywhere. At fairs, on pilgrimages, or outside churches on feast days—anywhere they could get an audience—they sold phony bills of indulgence, offered counterfeit relics to be kissed, peddled favors for appropriate donations, and promised miraculous healings and intercession for get-rich-quick schemes.[25] The bitter intensity of Chaucer's satire against this type of "hireling" is not merely a literary posture: devout Christians came to hate such abuses and were deeply disturbed that the structure of the church, and the confusion of authority created by the Great Schism, allowed these religious peddlers to operate so freely. Chaucer, who seems to have been on the whole a rather quiet person, once had to pay a fine for beating up a friar he ran into on Fleet Street. When his fictional Host on the Canterbury pilgrimage is so enraged at the Pardoner's shameless huckstering that he threatens to make of him a literal *"eunuchus dei"* on the spot, we ought to imagine that the sentiment, at least, found fairly wide accord in Chaucer's audience.

On many fronts, then, these were hard times for the English church. If the law of love was the Christian ideal for society, it was certainly an ideal under duress. When Chaucer translated *The Consolation of Philosophy* of Boethius for those of his countrymen who knew little or no Latin, he must have identified with a yearning prayer of Boethius as well as the ideal:

Love binds together people joined by a sacred bond;
Love binds sacred marriages by chaste affections;
Love makes the laws which join true friends.
O how happy the human race would be
if that Love which rules the heavens ruled also your souls![26]

And yet, in the midst of these confusing and dark times, in a nation rocked by wars civil and foreign, riddled with ecclesiastical and political corruption, ravaged by the Black Death and successive plagues, love's still small voice was speaking.

II. Spiritual Life

One suspects more than coincidence in the fact that the three major voices in fourteenth-century spirituality—as well as many of the unknown authors who have left a rich legacy of devotional works behind them—were from the north of England, far away from the tumult of the larger southern cities and towns. From a southern point of view, Yorkshire was a kind of cultural desert, a wasteland between England and warfaring Scotland. Yet it was here, at little Thornton-le-Dale, just below the great barren moors, that Richard Rolle began his momentous life as a solitary and spiritual writer. To the west, at a place then called Wycliffe, one John of that parish was born a few years later. And Walter Hilton spent most of his life in the Augustinian priory of Thurgarton a few miles north of Nottingham, which was then also in the diocese of York. Each of these men was to become, in his own way, a signal leader in a broad movement of spiritual renewal. Two of them were to make their major contributions in English vernacular rather than in the ecclesiastical Latin or Anglo-Norman French of the previous generation, and the third was to inaugurate the first full-scale effort to translate the Bible into English. Each now represents, faithfully and richly, one of the three major streams of the medieval English spiritual tradition.

The Mystical Tradition: Richard Rolle and Spiritual Individualism

In the twelfth and early thirteenth centuries, monastic life had been the fountainhead of English spirituality. Christian communities flourished both in the north, principally in Cistercian foundations, and in the south, principally in abbeys of the Benedictines or "black monks." By the end of the thirteenth century, however, new orders of monks, canons, and friars had proliferated and had begun to dissipate the importance of the great monasteries. Within these communities intellectual life continued with modest success: St. Alban's retained its supremacy in these matters, and many monks of Durham went to Oxford and distinguished themselves as academic theologians. But the spiritual fire of previous times seems to have somehow run low on fuel. The monks turned more and more to the care of their estates, which by then had grown not only large but prosperous. At Malmesbury, for example, the great William of Malmesbury had, as Dom David Knowles succinctly puts it, "no successors in the scriptorium."[27] Abbots in the fourteenth century tended to expand their farms and harvest their forests; sometimes, in their affluence, they took up the genteel pastimes and luxuries of noblemen. The wandering Monk in *The Canterbury Tales*, a prominent member of the skeet and sherry set of his day, is, as are Chaucer's other deficient religious figures, an indicative stereotype. Knowles observes that

> abbeys had sunk into the countryside and lost forever that compelling charm which had once made them seem like outposts of Jerusalem, the vision of peace. Even the great Yorkshire abbeys, Fountains and Rievaulx, were now distinguished by little save their larger flocks and the superior magnificence of their fabric.[28]

Aelred of Rievaulx, greatest of English spiritual writers of the twelfth century, had not found comparable successors either.

Thornton-le-Dale, where Richard Rolle was born, either in the last year of the thirteenth century or the first of the fourteenth, is just a few miles from Rievaulx. When he went off to study for four years at Oxford, Rolle must have met many a monk academic from Durham and elsewhere. Evidently he was not impressed. He left Oxford at the age of eighteen to take up a solitary life, clearly reacting to feelings he had about the loss of spiritual fervor in monastic communities. And although he had been positively influenced by the Franciscans—his spirituality shows indebtedness to Franciscan spiritual writings—he resented the very idea of a strict community rule. Unwilling to be in default of a religious vow, he seems to have been seeking both freedom to exercise a certain spiritual independence—to preach and write for reform—and also an opportunity to adopt a more profound life of devotion than he observed in the religious houses he knew. He went back to Thornton-le-Dale, then to nearby Pickering, obtaining from his friend John de Dalton an "enclosure" within the Dalton family home, a kind of storeroom next to the kitchen, facing onto the stable yard.

In one of his earliest treatises, the *Melum Contemplativorum*, Rolle indicates something of the reason for his rejection of monasticism in favor of the life of a hermit. "Why do you live tepidly in a monastery?" he challenges the monks. "You might as well live *that* way in the world."[29] He goes on to examine the value of obedience to a prescribed rule of monastic life: "One can appear obedient to man and nevertheless be altogether in contradiction with the will of God. Indeed monks or others living according to an established religious habit are not holy because they obey their superiors, but only insofar as, in the zeal of holy love,

A FOREST HERMIT
Reproduced from MS Royal 19.E.iii (fol. 133) by
permission of the British Library

they seek to serve God alone."[30] Rejecting the tuneful vocal prayer of
monks in choir (which in distinctly Yorkshire accents he indelicately refers to as a "roaring" and "corporal clamor"), he chooses the silent music
of the soul in harmony with God, which, he insists

> happens in solitude, and not in a congregation. Whence in ancient days
> many of the more perfect were wont to go out from the monasteries to
> solitary places, that they might more freely give themselves to har-
> monious contemplation. Now, none go out; all have the solace of men,
> and thus without doubt lack the visitation of angels.[31]

Rolle was certainly aware of the considerable politicization of religious life in his time. Bishops and abbots, who were great landowners
and producers of much revenue, were formidable players in political
contests in London as well as at Canterbury and Rome. He despised
such pursuits and desired a life in which he would be able to focus

15

totally on God, undistracted by this sort of adulteration. He would have been furious when, at Pickering in 1323, King Edward II confirmed a grant of "pasturage" to a forest hermit "for two cows." Kings and nobles often resorted to hermits for advice, and Edward was perhaps paying for services rendered. Rolle, at least, wanted for himself no part of such a compromise.

The independent streak in Rolle's spirituality, perhaps a typical enough element of Yorkshire character, is one of its most important features for his influence on the fourteenth century. Though it alarmed many later in the period (one Carthusian critic says Rolle's followers "make men judges of themselves"), his stress on a heightened individual relationship with God captured the imagination of some of his fellow Yorkshiremen. Then all over England many, including large numbers of laypeople, began to read his writings.[32] Some of these readers, one may assume, were attracted to his critique of worldly monks and lax clergy, concerns which were to gain response from the Wycliffites, among whose writings several manuscripts of Rolle's work are to be found. Wycliffites would also have liked Rolle's brusque style—especially in his early treatises—and his disdain for "liturgical pomp," as his distinguished editor Hope Emily Allen puts it, as well as his "emphasis on Bible study."[33] They would not much have liked some of the more intensely lyrical of his mystical writings.

The goal of mystics, briefly put, is to be so carried out of the physical world in the *ecstasis* of contemplation that the soul enters into an inner and utter communion with God, an inexpressible "foretaste of eternal sweetness" as Rolle says.[34] The experience is profoundly emotional and interior: the degree of communion with God acquired by the mystic is determined by the intensity of his or her experience of love toward God. It is typical of mystics to proclaim what they aver cannot be described. The circumvention of this difficult conundrum is for some of them the language of analogy—that provided, for example, by a metaphorical reading of the Song of Songs. With his somewhat Franciscan emphasis on the involvement of the senses in mystical contemplation, this is the direction in which Rolle's writing tends; we see it in the *Ego Dormio* ("I Sleep," from Song of Songs 5:2) and especially in the *Incendium Amoris (The Fire of Love)*. Describing the mystical experience in terms of "sweetness, heat and song," he identifies two types of mystical rapture, one which occurs in the bodily senses, another which is an enrapturing *away* from the senses to a divine vision of love, which he regards as the ultimate goal of contemplation.[35]

Another way of dealing with the inexpressible heights of mystical "knowing" is the "negative way" *(via negativa)*, the "way without images." Whereas Rolle, in quasi-Franciscan fashion, makes use of the "positive way" of images, visualizing and contemplating the life and Passion of Christ as an expedient to a higher experience of Christ's love, the spirituality of the negative way desires to move more quickly toward God in the fullness of his Godhead, that glory which is essentially indescribable and utterly beyond our human power of comprehension. This negative way is implicitly founded upon the positive, to which it acts as a kind of second stage. It affirms that while God is *ultimately* unknowable—utterly beyond our limited categories of thinking about him—he is not *absolutely* unknowable; indeed, he can be reached, "known," and communed with by love. This kind of love is possible for us only because Christ has revealed it to us on the cross; yet it cannot be reached at its highest stages if the mystic remains in the realm of reason and the senses. Perfect oneness with God is finally divorced from all analytical reasoning, all analogy.

The negative way of mysticism finds its chief expression in English spiritual literature of this period in the anonymous *Cloud of Unknowing* (c. 1370). The writer who contributed most to this tradition of medieval spirituality—which has its closest counterpart in Eastern Orthodox mysticism—is Dionysius, or Pseudo-Dionysius the Areopagite, a sixth-century mystic who was greatly influenced by Neoplatonism. The author of *The Cloud* translated some of Dionysius's writings, notably in his *Deonise Hid Diuinite*, and their effect is felt also in his *Book of Privy Counselling*, the most speculative of his works.[36] *The Cloud* is an intensely affective book, describing the purgative and illuminative ways of ascent to the desired union of the soul with God. The art of recollection it teaches results in a "dark night of the senses" in which the "cloud of forgetting" obscures all manner of conscious thought even as the "cloud of unknowing" conceals God himself. The state described at the end of *The Book of Privy Counselling* is that of spiritual marriage, the unitive life which is the pinnacle of mystical experience.

Another exemplary voice of mystical spirituality in this period, Catherine of Siena (1347–1380), was born just about two years before Rolle died in the Great Plague, or the Black Death. Like Rolle, she was an enclosed solitary, but only from the time she was walled up in a room next to her father's kitchen at the age of sixteen until her first series of mystical revelations, or "spiritual espousals," three years later. Then she rejoined the life of her family while adhering to the rule of the tertiaries or lay-order Dominicans, though for another four years she maintained the enclosure or "cell" as her headquarters. She was never a nun, formally speaking, and after 1370 she traveled about quite freely in ministry to the sick and poor, as well as for the purposes of church politics.

Unlike Rolle, she welcomed her role as counselor on political as well as spiritual matters; as we have already seen she did not hesitate to give spiritual advice to popes.

Catherine's place in this volume owes principally to the fact that her *Dialogue* had wide circulation in England, especially through its partial translation into Middle English under the title *The Orcherd of Syon*. Catherine also provides an important link to continental spirituality. Hers is a strong personality, but her call is finally to extreme asceticism and obedience. There is no denying that her own self-mortification attained an extravagance which hastened her early death.[37]

The life of Bridget of Sweden (c. 1303–1373) was in many respects very different. She married, raised a family, and remained a layperson until after her husband died. By this time, however, she had acquired much "individualistic" spiritual experience of a type similar to Catherine's—recurrent revelations in which, as one historian puts it, "she believed that Christ Himself appeared to her."[38] In a remarkable vision after her husband's funeral, Bridget understood herself to be chosen the bride of Christ, and other similar visions followed, all having the character of "special revelation." She wrote these experiences down, and they were widely popularized in the Middle Ages, circulating in both Latin and vernacular versions.

Though Bridget spent most of her later years as an "individual" religious, traveling to Rome in 1349 to take up a life of pilgrimages, she also founded in Sweden a double monastery (for both men and women), which she later put under the direction of her daughter Katherine as abbess, or "sovereign." The Bridgettine Order (or the Birgittines, as they were called in England), once approved, extended all over Europe, but its most celebrated monastery was that at Syon House in London, founded in 1415 with King Henry V himself laying the foundation stone on part of his royal manor Islesworth on the Thames. These Birgittines, for whom *The Orcherd of Syon* was translated, became the most influential abbey of English female religious in the fifteenth century, by which time Bridget's *Revelations* had achieved a wide influence among female religious, including Dame Julian of Norwich and Margery Kempe.

Today, Dame Julian (1342–c. 1420) is perhaps the most celebrated of English mystics; yet in her own time she was almost unknown. There is only one surviving copy of the "short text" of her *Showings*, and only one complete copy of the "long text," which was out of sight until published for the first time in the seventeenth century. Like Bridget and some of the south German and lowland mystics whose influence was rapidly spreading in Europe from the early part of the century, Julian based her work upon special revelations, a series of visions or "shew-ings." As did many of the continental writers, she offered her revelations or allegories and her reflections upon them as a kind of direct theology. Julian clearly saw her role as prophetic. As she says,

> Everything that I saw myself I intend to be understood as having been experienced for the personal benefit of all my fellow Christians, for I have learned in the spiritual revelation of our Lord that this is how He intends it should be. And therefore I beg you all for God's sake, and I counsel you here for your own profit, that you believe the vision. . . .[39]

In our own time the aspect of Julian's visionary experience and mystical writing which has captured most attention is her imagination of the Holy Trinity as a kind of generic family, in which God the Father reveals one aspect of the divine character, while "Christ our Mother" reveals another. These passages of Julian's works never received as much circulation as, for example, the writings of Bridget or Catherine; later readers may simply have overlooked them, or perhaps they were somewhat uneasy about their content.[40] In any case, while it is not necessary to agree with Jean Leclercq that her special contribution includes "theological precision" and a "full theology of the Trinitarian life,"[41] one must certainly appreciate that Julian's individualistic vision and those of others like her now provide us an indispensable insight into English spiritual life of the fourteenth century. Julian began her religious life as a Benedictine nun; she subsequently left the convent to become an enclosed solitary, an anchoress. In some respects, both her experiences and her vocational choice create a commentary on the fortunes of contemplative community life for women in her time.

While Julian was an anchoress in Norwich she was visited by Margery Kempe (c. 1373–c. 1440). Margery is without doubt the most colorful and emotionally volatile of the figures represented in this book. Like Dame Julian, she was from Norfolk, from Lynne Bishop (now called Kings Lynne), and like her was influenced by the lowland mystics and Bridget as well as, to some lesser degree, by the writings of Richard Rolle and Walter Hilton.[42] Her *Showings* is not, properly speaking, a religious treatise but a spiritual autobiography, which was dictated to a cleric beginning in 1436. It includes revelations and direct visionary encounters with Jesus and many of the principal characters in the gospel—the Virgin Mary, Elizabeth, and others. In effect, what is recorded is a highly imaginative visualized meditative experience and the outworkings of that upon the life of Margery, her husband, and those around her.

Margery styled herself a kind of prophet, and her rebuke of a variety of religious and secular authorities takes up a significant portion of her account. Much of the rest has to do with troubles she got into because of spontaneous outbursts of weeping—which caused those nervous about continental heresies to be wary of her and, on occasion, to drive her out of town or to report her to the authorities. There is some legitimate ground for suspicion that one of the priests who followed her about on part of her journeys was, in effect, a kind of guardian against heresy: with her eruptions of public and often violent weeping, she qualified for special scrutiny. At one point she was, like almost anyone whose spiritual behavior was publicly erratic, accused of Lollardy and apprehended. If she had been an enclosed solitary and not a wandering prophet and pilgrim, this would likely not have happened. Travel she did, however—all over England while her husband was still alive, and all over Europe after he and her son died, both in 1432. She had not in fact seen much of her husband for many years. Although she was accused on that account of irresponsibility to him at the time of his death, she answered by saying that it was necessary for them to live apart, given their vow of chaste separation, in case people should suspect them of secret incontinence.[43]

Much of Margery's book is a witness to an almost desperate attempt to achieve sanctified life in the ordinary world—by the means of special revelation and prophetic witness. We must remember that Margery was not only without Latin (and French) but was illiterate even in her native English. Like many in her time, she experienced spiritual yearnings that were not met by a Latin liturgy she did not understand, and, in the absence of much substantial preaching or exposition of Scripture, her faith was frustrated for lack of doctrinal content. If her autobiography now has about it an inevitable pathos as well as much evidence of spiritual desire, it is the pathos which should help us better understand how translation and spiritual instruction in English became such a central concern for Rolle, Hilton, and finally Wyclif and his followers. Margery's spirituality, as Eric Colledge expresses it, arose from "a fervid, infinitely pathetic desire to compensate for inability to understand the liturgy by retreating into a private world, peopled with the characters of the Gospels, in which the ecstatic has her place and her office." He continues,

> It is not for us to deride such "meditations": but, just as we have seen how medieval spiritual directors feared that "ghostly favours" would induce pride in their recipients, so we cannot help observing that in such cases as that of Margery Kempe, the narrators of these astonishing apocalyptic visions often seem to emerge from them with their opinion of themselves in no way diminished."[44]

This was the danger in revelatory mysticism which carried it past the mainstream of Christian devotion in the fourteenth century. Even in their individualism, Rolle and the author of *The Cloud of Unknowing* emphasize a quiet solitude, a life of prayer and study of the Bible, and the acquisition of scriptural wisdom and spiritual discretion. If a public ministry is open to them, then it is primarily one of teaching by books and by private spiritual counsel. The later mystics lacked education in language, theological studies, and discipline. Cut off in some cases—as in that of Margery—from even an understanding of the liturgy, their desire found no comparable language of the inner life and, except perhaps in the case of Catherine, no comparable "translation" or teaching medium.[45]

The Monastic Tradition: Walter Hilton and the Claims of Community

Whether or not, as has been variously suggested, Walter Hilton began his own religious life as a recluse, later moving from solitary life to his place with the Augustinian canons at Thurgarton, the hypothesis accords with the concerns of his small but rich body of writing.[46] His life also illustrates how difficult it is to discriminate sharply between "mystics" and contemplatives in general, even though one can distinguish purely mystical spirituality from a meditative or contemplative spiritual discipline designed for life in community.

What is broadly typical of the spirituality of mystics in this time is its individualistic quality and its association with a renewal of solitary or formally reclusive life.[47] The figures we have been so far considering are not, finally, to be identified with the life of the monastery or convent. While it is clear that a number of the most eminent of these at some time considered monastic life in community, they ultimately took another path. Yet writers such as Rolle, as well as the translator of Catherine who penned *The Orcherd of Syon*, and even the author of *The Cloud of Unknowing*, seem to have sought, from without, to contribute to a spiritual revivification of monastic life. Each of them wrote works either for the use of nuns living in community or for anchoresses in smaller subgroups, and these works can be seen as guidelines for the reformation of old monastic spiritual goals and values.[48]

Walter Hilton, however, took the additional step of actually entering into a monastic community, joining himself to the Augustinian canons and living under a community rule. His own life experience was thus in many respects different from that of all the other major English spiritual writers of his time, and it is part of his special contribution to represent to us a type of spirituality and quality of vocation that has substantial links to the earlier traditions of English monastic life. As the most pastoral of those whom tradition chooses to call "the English mystics" (Hilton, Rolle, Julian, and the author of *The Cloud*), Hilton proves to be much less a mystic than "a great teaching saint," as Evelyn Underhill puts it, an intensely practical spiritual counselor.[49]

Hilton's response to a variety of requests for guidance led him to write for laypeople as well as for those living under monastic rule. Among his works are a treatise written for one Adam Horsley, Baron of the Exchequer, who ultimately became a Carthusian *reclus* at Beauvale, and two epistles to an unnamed layman whom he persuaded not to leave secular life but to strive for greater perfection in following Christ right where he was (*The Mixed Life*). His most famous work, *The Ladder of Perfection,* written in two parts separated by many years, was dedicated to a nun who eventually elected a solitary life and became an anchoress. These works spread in influence far beyond their original audience, however, and were read widely by laypersons and those in religious communities alike.

Of Hilton himself we know almost nothing. His life was, as was that of the author of *The Cloud,* one of deliberate self-effacement, a hidden life of prayer. He entirely avoids talking about his own spiritual experience and, in direct contrast to mystics like Catherine, Bridget, Julian, and Margery, he claims no special revelation for himself. Rather, he simply sets out to write a practical guide to various states and levels of spiritual life, in each case a balanced and perspicuous exposition. *The Ladder* was so successful in communicating the progress of spiritual life that even after the Lollard years, when religious authorities were disposed against the use of English, it was translated and circulated throughout Europe in a Latin version, the *Speculum Contemplativorum* (sometimes found as *Speculum Perfeccionis*). At home, it was, by the middle of the fifteenth century, the most read of all English devotional books; and in 1494, at the request of the godly noblewoman Margaret Beaufort, it became one of the first English printed books.[50]

Hilton died quietly in 1396, leaving hardly a shred of biographical witness behind him other than his books and his name. Of his life in Thurgarton Priory we can say nothing extraordinary. He was evidently never prior; his life must have been much in the way of the common round. Under the rather simple and flexible Augustinian rule, clerics would divide their time between the spiritual work of prayer and the practical life of a fairly large community. It seems that Hilton was very familiar with the business of kitchens and the raising of livestock; he may well have attended to dealings with local farmers and producers as well as the day to day running of the priory. Like others, he would have participated in the daily office—chapel services at each of the eight canonical hours—eaten with the other monks in the refectory, attended to his routine practical chores, and, when there was time left over, repaired to the library or scriptorium to take up the writing which was an expression of his pastoral care of souls. In the rehabilitated partial nave of the priory which now constitutes a parish church in Thurgarton, one can see one of the old choir stalls in which he might have sat many times a day. Outside, the sloping fields where cattle still graze and sheep still bleat offer (less a few trees) a pastoral prospect with which he would have been familiar.

These shadowy anonymous tracings, however disappointing to us, are of course no less than Hilton would have wanted: we tend to leave behind us signs of what we love. He says himself, "If you want to know what it is you love, just consider what it is you are usually thinking about." As his writings make clear, Hilton was preeminently thinking about Jesus, after that about his fellow Christians, and hardly ever about himself.

Hilton is represented in this volume chiefly by short selections from his major work. Its title, *The Ladder of Perfection,* may seem curiously unexplained in the work itself, in which there is no reference to the ladder image as such. (In the title of the Latin text the word for ladder itself disappears, being replaced by *Speculum,* "mirror.") But the concept invoked by the word *ladder* was one familiar to men and women in all walks of religious life; and since it indicates succinctly something of the hierarchical way in which our medieval forebears looked at spiritual growth and progress, it is perhaps worth pausing over here.

The first and perhaps most famous application of the image of Jacob's ladder to religious life is that found in the Benedictine Rule, which governed the life of the earliest monastic communities in Britain. Commenting on a passage which says that "everyone that exalteth himself shall be humbled, and he that humbleth himself shall be exalted,"[51] the author of the rule argues that the way to heavenly heights is along the steps of humility: the way up is the way down. He elaborates twelve "rungs" or degrees of humility, beginning with the fear of God and moving through obedience and perseverance in humility to the twelfth degree, in which "the monk's inward humility appears outwardly in his comportment," a realization of a penitent and grateful spirit which takes one to the "top, the charity which is perfect and casts out all fear."[52] This is the emphasis which had characterized the original spirituality of monastic life.

A second application of Jacob's ladder as an analogue for spiritual growth and progress comes in Alan of Lille's *Art of Preaching,* a twelfth-century book for those with prelatical or pastoral vocation. Alan commences with the paradigm on which his whole discussion of the life and work of a preacher will build:

> Jacob beheld a ladder reaching from earth to heaven, on which angels were ascending and descending. The ladder represents the progress of the catholic man in his ascent from the beginning of faith to the full development of the perfect man. The first rung of this ladder is confession; the second, prayer; the third, thanksgiving; the fourth, the careful study of the Scriptures; the fifth, to inquire of someone more experienced if one comes upon any point in Scripture which is not clear; the sixth, the expounding of Scripture; the seventh, preaching.[53]

The preacher, Alan goes on to say, is one who communicates between the top and bottom of the ladder, traveling over it regularly, as is suggested by Gregory the Great in his book *Pastoral Rule*, the greatest preacher's handbook of the Middle Ages:

> Hence Jacob, the Lord looking down from above, and oil being poured down on the stone, saw angels ascending and descending (Genesis 28:12); to signify that true preachers not only aspire in contemplation to the holy head of the Church, that is to the Lord, above, but also descend in commiseration downward to His members.[54]

According to such writers as Gregory and Alan, this is the model of spiritual life given to us in Paul and in Moses, persons whose vocation was fundamentally pastoral.

A third example may be drawn from St. Bonaventure, whose *Mind's Road to God* is a signal work of Franciscan spirituality from the thirteenth century. This work, like *The Cloud of Unknowing*, shows a strong influence of the mystical writer Pseudo-Dionysius. Here Jacob's ladder is used to figure the mystical progress of the soul toward union with God, in which, says Bonaventure,

> according to the six stages of ascension into God, there are six stages of the soul's powers by which we mount from the depths to the heights, from the external to the internal, from the temporal to the eternal—to wit, sense, imagination, reason, intellect, intelligence, and the apex of the mind, the illumination of conscience [*synteresis*]. These stages are implanted in us by nature, deformed by sin, re-formed by grace, to be purged by justice, exercised by knowledge, perfected by wisdom.[55]

The emphasis here is on climbing Jacob's ladder, not on descending it. The soul which desires spiritual growth must begin with the senses and natural means, then move by the means of grace up the ladder. The apex of the contemplative journey is the wisdom known in silence, when the mind of the contemplative, finally suffused with eternal wisdom, passes beyond itself. Then, in mystical transport, a direct vision of God is obtained—as, for example, in the case of St. Francis's vision of the seraph nailed to the cross. Bonaventure says that at such a moment of utter self-transcendence, in which all fetters of the world fall away, "another Jacob is changed into Israel, so through him all truly spiritual men have been invited by God to passage of this kind and to mental transport by example rather than by word."[56] Jacob's ladder is thus a model for spiritual aspiration in those practitioners of the contemplative life we call mystics, of whom the author of *The Cloud*—for whom the highest "knowing" of God is "unknowing"—is a most noteworthy example.

Hilton, in Book 1 of *The Ladder of Perfection*, is squarely within the traditions of monastic spirituality. His emphasis is on growth through humility, on the way up being the way down. In Book 2 he freely incorporates elements drawn from the other two traditions, pastoral and mystical, so that the exercise of repentance, confirmed in prayer, then grows through meditation and contemplation to a fullness of charitable love. This then leads to an understanding of Holy Scripture, an understanding of the various types and states of spiritual life, and an inward recognition of Jesus as at once both God and man, transcending all things. The end of the contemplative life for Hilton is thus "only to think on Jesus," to enter into the fullness of his love, and by that means to acquire humility and all other virtues.[57] In this respect, Hilton, as an Augustinian canon, can be viewed both as a voice for the continuity of monastic spirituality and as a reformer of Christian spirituality in general. By drawing together the three ladders in this fashion, then refusing to systematize them in a way which might privilege one vocational choice over the others, he uplifted the goal of spiritual maturity, turning his readers consistently toward the end at a time in which many were merely squabbling about the means. In all of this he was acting the part of a spiritual counselor in the widest sense—a kind of spiritual bishop to all walks—and we may be sure that this had much to do with the wideness of his witness in medieval times.

Richard Rolle's witness was similarly wider than his original reclusiveness might seem to suggest. Although he remained an anchorite or hermit and, as we have seen, began his career in criticism of the monks, he nevertheless had an important role to play in *coenobitic* or contemplative life in community. His contribution came largely through the works he wrote for the community of nuns at Hampole and is further exemplified in his *Ego Dormio*, written for a nun of Yeddingham, and his *Commandment of Love to God*, written for another Yorkshire nun (probably while Rolle was himself at Hampole).

Rolle's spirituality, with its radical emphasis on poverty, owes much to the Franciscans, and his style of living—periods of seclusion broken by wanderings from place to place with intermittent preaching—resembles that of the spiritual Franciscans, that is, it was erratic. But in his meditative works, such as the *Meditation on the Passion of Christ*, and in his *Commentaries on the Psalms* he was providing teaching which would find its most frequent use in community contemplative life.[58] That he always favored the solitary life himself is beyond dispute, and it is clear that Margaret Kirby, one of the nuns of Hampole for whom he wrote several of his later works, including *The Form of Living*, became an anchoress under his influence.[59] In this much he presages Hilton; Book 2 of Hilton's *Ladder* is addressed to the same nun as the first, but she had evidently become by this time an anchoress as well. Thus though there are other devotional writings which spring from the contemplative communities of the fourteenth century—or which, like the two Anglo-Norman poems "The Love of Jesus" and "The Dance of the Cross," are probably written for them—Rolle's example illustrates how the characteristic energy of this period is still moving away from monasticism and the spirituality of enclosed communities toward a greater and persistent emphasis on the individual spiritual life.

An unusual book which appeared sometime between 1382 and 1410 indirectly helps us to understand from quite another point of view why the quality of monastic spirituality was on the wane. This book, called *The Chastising of God's Children*, was composed for a specific house of nuns, probably by a monk of the Carthusians, and extant copies were owned by Augustinian nuns in Suffolk, by Birgittine nuns at Syon, by Carthusian nuns in Yorkshire, and by Benedictine nuns in Sussex. Among these several convents were apparently "two of the worst-conducted nunneries in fifteenth century England."[60] Deeply indebted to several continental writings, including notably Jan van Ruysbroek's *Spiritual Espousals*, *The Chastising* seeks to call its readers back to a life of community rule and discipline. It takes a strong position against charismatism—"private" religion—and it rebuts claims for "perfection" among solitary religious.[61] Its four chief concerns are the recognition and combat of heresy, the repression of "enthusiasm" or charismatic experience, the discernment of spirits, and an insistence on use of the Latin liturgy in preference to private devotions in English.[62] It is evident that the author viewed all the conditions being opposed as symptoms of spiritual sickness. *The Chastising* is thus a treatise which sets itself over and against the trend toward spiritual individualism in the fourteenth century, and in so doing it helps to indicate the seriousness of that challenge to traditional monastic life.

In criticizing the behavior of those who counterfeit "spiritual favors,"

The Chastising clearly has in mind followers of Rolle and some of the more evidently charismatic mystics. Of the behavior he finds offensive the author writes:

> Sum men in þat tyme bien plenteuouse of teeris: sum men in þat tyme bien stired wiþ al þe membris of her bodi, so þat þei must skippe, ren or daunce: summe for ioie bete her handis togidre: summe crien aloude wiþ an hiȝ uoice; summe bien stille and mow nat speke. . . .[63]

The text goes on to say that some persons "in such a time" think the whole world shares their kind of experience; others cannot understand why, apparently, all other Christians do *not* share their experience. The description itself is impartial; the observations follow from a discussion of possible manifestations of that laudable condition in which "our Lord Jesus is lifted up in our hearts above all other things," when in gratitude and worship of him "sometimes there comes a sweet rain of an inward beholding, and a heavenly dew of sweetness of the Godhead" which is "a special working of our Lord Jesus in the hearts of those who love Him, all who are his beloved children."[64] Yet at the beginning of his next chapter the author goes on to warn that such personal visitations—or the seeking of them—can be dangerous, easily leading those who receive them to celebrate them vaingloriously for their own sake and not for the sake of God from whose love they derive, and implicitly to regard them as credits to themselves. The devil, moreover, can too easily counterfeit this type of emotional *ecstasis*—one must be very discerning about the nature of the spirit which produces such manifestations. Finally, excessive dependence on such intensive emotional experience can lead, if ever the experience ceases for a time, to periods of prolonged spiritual aridity and even despair.

In this light, chapter 19 of *The Chastising* emphasizes the need for spiritual discretion on the part of superiors—abbots, priors, and prioresses. Does the visionary have the fruits of the Spirit described in Galatians 5? Has he or she humility and obedience to superiors? Eric Colledge has noted that the author of *The Chastising*, in his editing and rearranging of various works he has translated, suppresses approving references to St. Bridget, commending only "her strict observance of spiritual obedience"—characteristics not so prominent in her actual life as this commendation suggests. For him, it appears, Bridget (and others, like Julian and Margery) actually provides fair examples of a visionary spirituality which might prove extremely problematic if multiplied in the convent.[65]

The Chastising of God's Children thus offers us excellent insight into attempts from within the monastic tradition to check and contain the strong drift toward spiritual individualism in the fourteenth century and to reclaim such spiritual energy for a quiet channeling under the established rules of monastic community. But by its choice of means to accomplish this purpose, it proves to be at least as valuable for helping us understand why the clock could not be turned back.

Central to the purpose of *The Chastising* is its author's desire to direct his audience of nuns away from the use of prayers and devotional literature in English toward exclusive use, at least for the daily office, of Latin. In this it is typical of Roman ecclesiastical interests at the end of this period, and echoes of the same concerns are abundant in a variety of continental writers, on many of whom, indeed, *The Chastising* draws heavily.[66] The problem was this: even in houses of monks and communities of friars, illiteracy—the inability to understand or read Latin— was commonplace. While there were always some literate members in the community, lay brothers were typically unable to understand the words of the Latin office or mass. They were required, as the regulations of the Benedictines at Canterbury make clear, to memorize some of the basic prayers in Latin, *pro more laycali,* "whether they understand them or not." If they could not do this well, they were to substitute repeated Aves and Paternosters as the service progressed. In either case, it is evident that little or nothing would be understood by the participants; yet it was typical both to legislate that lay brethren should not be allowed to say their prayers in English, and even, if they should possess devotional books or psalters in the vernacular, to confiscate them.[67]

The situation was much worse in houses for female religious: even fewer professed nuns knew any Latin. If they could use Latin in the office at all it was often merely because they could "read" just well enough to pronounce the words; actual comprehension of the liturgy was extremely minimal. This was not new. One can perceive it in the *Ancrene Riwle* of the twelfth century, in which the author found it necessary, as Rolle and Hilton also did, to translate each Latin citation he quotes, whether from Scripture or from other sources. At Syon Abbey in the early fifteenth century, lay brothers were permitted to use English prayers (if they recited them in whispers) during the Latin office recited by the regular monks, whereas

> in the corresponding chapter of the sisters' rule there is no such distinction made between those who can read and those who know Latin: instead, we are told that "sustres vnlettred" are to stand in front of the choir stalls, rising, bowing, prostrating themselves with the choir whilst the hours are sung: their recitation either of Paters and Aves or of "our lady matens after secular vse," which is defined, is presumably to be done at another time.[68]

Simply put, most nuns had almost no knowledge of what they were saying or listening to in worship. Yet they were regularly forbidden to use prayers in their mother tongue, especially in the latter part of the fourteenth century. We can hardly fail to appreciate the enormous spiritual vacuum that must have resulted from this situation, nor is it difficult to imagine the appetite that must have existed for the vernacular devotional treatises and guides for female religious which were being composed by writers such as Rolle and Hilton.

Even ordinary laypeople in some parts of the country received much better instruction in the content of their faith. *The Lay Folks' Catechism* of John Thoresby, Archbishop of York, for example, was designed to allow parents to teach their families the central prayers of the church in their native tongue.[69] The use of vernacular prayer and private books of devotion was especially prevalent among the upper classes, those who could afford books. Here, where even a woman might learn Latin and own her own *Book of Hours*—a collection of Latin offices, psalms, and prayers—there was the additional benefit of free access to the best vernacular spiritual literature of the time. Hence a signal irony, that "by the fourteenth century great lords and ladies were saying their devotions in English or French, whereas nuns, if they could read, had to recite the office in Latin which, almost invariably, it would seem, they did not understand."[70] That the upper classes, especially the families of "grete lordis," should have provided the most fertile seedbed for the evangelical spirituality of John Wyclif is, in this light alone, no surprise.

Among those responsible for the nuns, however, this increasing availability of English devotional books and translations was much feared. The monastic author of *The Chastising of God's Children* tells a curious anecdote of St. Hildegard, whose Latin prayers were answered, even though she did not know for what she was praying, and then states that the tendency to seek after "sweetness of devotion" in private prayer is in fact a temptation of the devil, since it draws the nuns away from attention to their Latin devotions. His argument is typical: even though the Latin liturgy is not understood, it is possible to obtain merit for "uncomprehended" prayer. The liturgy was ordained in Latin, not in the vernacular; and to use it shows humility and obedience. Latin is superior to English, which has no "grammar,"[71] and Scripture is not properly translatable into English. English translation focuses on the literal sense, whereas the spiritual, mystical, allegorical, and anagogical senses, which are accessible in Latin, are much more profitable. Wyclif, as we shall see, had already voiced a strong preference for the literal level of Scripture, and it is noteworthy that the arguments here raised against English prayer are virtually identical to those soon to be raised against the English Bible.

The Chastising of God's Children is an important document in the study of the monastic tradition in the fourteenth century. Though not itself a devotional work, it shows a distinct and subsequently characteristic attempt to revivify monasticism under the pattern of original Latin rules and the current aegis of Rome. Hilton's attempt in this direction had been less disciplinary and more spiritual in its intention and effort. But while Hilton was read and venerated long after his death, he was most valued for his emphasis (in *The Ladder of Perfection*) on the life of the spirit that transcends traditonal vocational boundaries, as well as for his recognition (in *The Mixed Life*) that the sanctification of ordinary life was also God's calling, and that individuals had to work out their own salvation not merely "in fear and trembling" but also in love and meek truthfulness where God had placed them. Both the author of *The Chastising* and Hilton wrote in English, the one (ironically) to argue against spiritual individualism and the use of English, the other simply to urge a growth of individual spiritual maturity and service by whatever means God had made available.

The "Mixed" Tradition: John Wyclif and Reform Spirituality

Almost every major work of English spirituality written in this period was composed in the mother tongue, not Latin. In contrast, almost every surviving piece of writing which can be certainly identified with John Wyclif was composed in Latin. This may be surprising to contemporary readers who associate Wyclif above all with the English translation of the Bible which has persistently borne his name. Actually, in his early career he was, more than anything else, an academic theologian and scholastic philosopher. As such, he wrote and taught in Latin, the language of the universities. In the course of his theological research, however, he grew to be much more interested in the study of Scripture itself than in questions of method and disputes about sources. He began to mount ambitious and systematic explorations of the text of the Bible, and in so doing became the first professor at Oxford ever to give lecture courses on the whole of the Bible. In his later years, as a teacher of young ordinands, he directed his energies toward the preparation of pastors who would be biblically literate. Finally, he came to believe that access to the Scriptures was essential for every Christian—layperson and clergy alike. It was in this connection that he initiated the translation which still bears his name, though the bulk of the work was actually carried out by his students and colleagues.

Wyclif may have developed his interest in translation—at least in the matter of prayers, psalms, and devotional extracts—quite early in his academic career. Although the earliest record of him at Oxford shows that he was in 1356 a young probationary fellow at Merton, his connection with the university was quite likely first as a student at Balliol, perhaps as early as 1350. In 1360 he became master at Balliol, a college with strong connections to Yorkshire.[72] As one who hailed from the north, it would have been possible for him to have had contact with some of the works of his fellow Yorkshireman Rolle, which were already circulating widely during Wyclif's student years. Perhaps he was even familiar with Rolle's translated *Psalter*, which later on would circulate with tracts by Wyclif's followers attached.[73] He would have known *The Lay Folks' Catechism* of Archbishop Thoresby, who in 1357 had had the "fourteen articles of belief," the Ten Commandments, the seven sacraments, seven works of mercy, seven virtues, and seven deadly sins all translated and set to English verse by John Gaytrik, a Benedictine monk of St. Mary's, York.[74] In 1361 Thoresby ordered parish priests to have their congregations memorize it, and since Wyclif was himself a priest of the diocese of York, in all probability ordained by Thoresby's license, he would certainly have seen the translations by that time. Indeed, with modest expansion, this type of catechism would have sufficed for Wyclif's own purposes; he did not at first dedicate himself to translation of the whole Bible. In a tract ascribed to John Purvey, one of Wyclif's assistants, we likely have a fair notion of Wyclif's own early objectives in translation for the parish level: "The Ten Commandments, the Paternoster, the Creed and Ave that all Christian people ought to know, [and] common things of Holy Writ [such as] Gospels and Epistles read in church [ought to be] well translated and truly, sentence for sentence, with good exposition."[75] Except that the projected service book was intended primarily for the clergy and for members of the upper classes, what it amounted to, in effect, was something very like Cranmer's *Book of Common Prayer* of 1564. Only later was Wyclif driven to make his case for a translation of the entire Bible and for its dissemination to an even wider public.

Among the *doctores* or schoolmen of Oxford (*clerkis*, in Middle English), most of whom were monks or friars, the Bible was not only much neglected, it was sometimes attacked as illogical under the conventions of the Aristotelian method and thus found "impracticable" as a basis for contemporary theology. Others simply avoided the Scriptures altogether. It was in the university much as it was in the convent or parish: "Few there be who are willing to be taught, few who know how to teach, and extremely few who are willing to teach, and so God's Word and God's Law are nearly forgotten in the land."[76] Some, if we take Wyclif at his word, went so far as to accuse the Scriptures of heresy; and it was common for *doctores* merely to catalogue what they took to be weaknesses and defects in the logic and content of biblical texts.[77] Wyclif confesses that he began his own career tending in much the same direction.

An alternative to the Scriptures as a foundational authority for doing theology and establishing doctrine had by then, of course, been fairly well developed. At least since the *Decretum* of Gratian (1148), the growth of canon law had served the church as a means of synthesizing and codifying its temporal decisions as a witness to the "development" of church doctrine.[78] By the time of the Great Schism the prestige of canon lawyers had greatly increased, and their influence began to overshadow that of the theologians. Because of the increasing ascription of authority to the political structure of the Roman church and its temporal pronouncements, this teaching or "magisterium" became ever more important. Scripture, meanwhile, drifted into a shadowy antiquity. If one studied theology at Paris or Oxford in the fourteenth century, one would write a thesis on a doctrinal "question"; if the thesis was exegetical it typically attended not to the text of Scripture itself but to the standard textbook for university lecture courses, Peter Lombard's *Sentences on the Gospel*. Exegetical work was thus increasingly a matter of commentary upon commentary rather than a fresh encounter with the scriptural text.

Two traditions concerning the idea of authority had developed in the medieval church. One of these emphasized the role of Scripture as the foundation for all spiritual understanding and took further guidance from the understanding of Scripture reflected in the commentaries of the fathers and doctors of the church. In case of any dispute, Scripture itself would have the final authority. This tradition, which included figures such as Anselm, Hugh of St. Victor, and, in Wyclif's time, Thomas Bradwardine, saw itself as basically Augustinian.[79] The second tradition, which had gradually become more dominant, perhaps owed its origins to Basil the Great. In his book *On the Holy Spirit*, Basil discussed the relationship of Scripture to tradition and put forward the idea that the individual Christian owes obedience to ecclesiastical traditions as much as to Scripture.[80] As this view developed in canon law, it became evident that in cases of dispute, ecclesiastical tradition, expressing itself in the voice of papal decree, would have the final authority. This view is strongly represented in disputes over the papacy in Wyclif's time, and it governed most of the assumptions of medieval university learning.[81] For the young Oxford student Wyclif, this assumption probably went unquestioned. But as he saw (with many others) the unhappy dissolution of papal credibility and the rampant ethical corruption of ecclesiastical office in every sphere, questions certainly started to arise.

For whatever reasons, Wyclif turned his energies away from administrative and political options to the study of Scripture during these years. In 1371 he took his doctorate in theology and gave his *Principium,* or inaugural lecture. In this work we see that his approach to Scripture focuses on two key points: the authority of the divine author and the spiritual preparedness required of one who wants to study the Scriptures with the intention of hearing them speak.

Wyclif always impressed his colleagues—even those who most bitterly opposed him—with the sanctity of his personal life. He was evidently a deeply spiritual man, possessed of a profound interior life of devotion and a scrupulous, charitable outward behavior.[82] He undertook his academic prelature in much the spirit advocated by Walter Hilton, who, in his discussion of the "mixed life," gives full spiritual value to a consecration of active duties in the workaday world—the sort of life, Hilton says, which is most appropriate to lords of the realm and priests.[83] Wyclif, in contrast to many of the *doctores possessionati,* the academic theologians from monastic or fraternal orders who were most often his Oxford opponents, seems earnestly to have sought this vocation of the "mixed" or middle way and approached his profession in an utter dedication of spiritual effort.

Wyclif's inaugural lecture provides a clear reflection of his spirituality; here, at least, the academic question of authority is made subservient to an examination of the scholar's conscience. He argues that one who wishes to interpret Scripture so as to acquire the Author's intention must have three prerequisites. First is a sound moral disposition—an inclination of the heart to spiritual truth. After that comes the more predictable requirement of philosophical training. But the third requirement is the actual practice of virtue—an obedient life of faith. Without these, he argues, we cannot oppose the world, the flesh, and the devil in disposing our soul to acquire spiritual wisdom.[84] It is quite clear that heretics, infidels, and persons in mortal sin can all study theology, he says, but they do not, in that state, gain true wisdom by it. The first condition for students of Scripture, then, exceeding in value any capacity they may have for disputation or logical analysis, is a basic godly morality such as will prompt them to seek a just interpretation of the text.[85] What this comes to is a thoroughgoing extension, to the whole of the theological task, of Augustine's goal of reading "charitably": it is the law of love expressing itself as an attitude of the heart, dedication of the soul, and formation of the mind. It is, effectively, the foundation of everything Wyclif stands for.

BIBLIA PAUPERUM
Page from a "poor folks' Bible"—really a Bible picture book designed to assist those unable to read
the Latin text. Rubrics are quotations from the
Scriptures, which are arranged in typological
sequences relating the life of Christ to events in the
Old Testament. Here the Resurrection is contextu-
alized between depictions of Samson tearing the
gates off the city and the whale's expectoration of
Jonah.

What we can begin to see is how clearly Wyclif's life and thought are
rooted in a spiritual emphasis. His most controversial applications of
these spiritual principles follow soon afterward. His theory of dominion, basic to all his later theological thought, is pursued out of a concern
for appropriate spiritual credibility in those who hold pastoral or civil
office. In two lecture courses of 1374–76 that dealt with the civil and religious spheres respectively, he set forth his convictions that what en-
titles anyone to hold office—be it the office of priest, bishop, or pope—

is a quality of spiritual life requisite to the duties of that office.[86] If a quality of virtuous obedience to the word and example of Christ is not present in one who proclaims the gospel or administers the church, that person ought properly to be stripped of his duties. Only one who is in a state of grace has "true dominion." This idea was unavoidably linked to the larger questions of the power of the church to levy tithes, or tax, and the wealth of the higher clergy. It responded to a widely shared view already clearly expressed in Langland's *A* text of *Piers the Plowman* (1362) that the church ought to imitate Christ in a life of evangelical poverty if it wants to speak with Christ's voice.

Given the outrage many felt at the corruption of ecclesiastical office in Wyclif's time, we can well imagine that this position was attractive. Its initial appeal, however, was not, as we might expect, to people such as Langland and other voices speaking for the poor, but rather to lords of the realm and even the king, who were convinced that the rapacious demands of the Avignon papacy were in direct aid of their French enemy. But the corollary of Wyclif's argument, the right of the laity to pass judgment on priests and the obligation to disendow those who corrupt their office, struck alarm into the hearts of those who could foresee the implications. Fear soon turned to anger.

Wyclif was put on trial in 1377 at St. Paul's after Pope Gregory XI sent a bull to Oxford condemning "errors and heresies" which he had heard Wyclif was teaching. The questions at issue all had to do with dominion. When the results of this first trial were inconclusive, especially from the papal legates' point of view, a second was held at Lambeth in 1378. The trial at Lambeth ended in a fiasco, not least because a huge crowd of common partisans to Wyclif's cause gathered around the archbishop's palace and then, after Sir Lewis Clifford intervened to protect Wyclif, surged into the chambers to join in defending the theologian from his attackers.

Such controversy only served to fix for Wyclif the course of his own prophetic calling. During 1377 and early 1378 he devoted his energies to two signal works. His *De Ecclesia (On the Church)*, like his seminal work *De Veritate Sacrae Scripturae (On the Authority* [or *Truth*] *of Sacred Scripture)*, codifies all his earlier ideas about dominion as a spiritually validated right to hold office. *De Ecclesia* was likely finished just after arrival of the news of the Great Schism; *De Veritate* had been prepared as a course of lectures during 1377 and was probably finished just before *De Ecclesia,* or almost simultaneously with it.

In *De Ecclesia* Wyclif defines the church as the *universitas praedestinorum,* the body of the elect; that is, those who "shall be saved" and who "cannot be lost even though they sin, for they have the grace of perseverance to the end."[87] The basis of the church in his view, as it was for Augustine and Bradwardine, is divine election. God alone decides who is a member of Christ's body; the institution has no power to determine whether or not one is actually in genuine relationship with God.[88] Why should we assume the pope's indisputable primacy in authority, Wyclif asks, if we are unable to know even if he is, in God's eyes, a member of Christ's body?[89] A pope's right to authority is determined not by his institutional office but by his conformity to the will of God revealed in Scripture. With current examples in mind, he suggests that the Christian community must continually ask whether the edicts of the papacy are consistent with the gospel. This is why, he continues, "every catholic ought to know the sacred scriptures" and why "the life and teaching of Christ are the best mirror" by which we may distinguish a true child of God from one who is really Christ's enemy.[90]

The implications of such a position for much of contemporary church "business" was, of course, sweeping. Wyclif was not alone in opposing indulgences or the veneration of saints for example; Langland and Chaucer, among a host of others, had voiced attacks on the former; and a variety of English spiritual writings of the fourteenth century (including the anonymous *Our Daily Work* from the north of England, translated in this volume) reject the idea of the saints as "intercessors" or objects of veneration. What Wyclif did was give a basis for testing these matters. How his argument applied to the question of indulgences, such as Langland's and Chaucer's pardoners so arduously peddle, can readily be inferred from his position that only personal spiritual obedience on the part of the pope provided the criterion of his right to hold office. As Herbert Workman observes, "the whole system of indulgences . . . rests upon the false basis of supererogatory merit at the disposal of the pope."[91] On the matter of saints, how can we evaluate their sanctity from this distance? We can be more sure about the apostles and martyrs, but what about "modern saints who are canonized for family reasons, gain or reward," or for "favor of parties" (that is, various orders or communities of interest)?[92]

For Wyclif, sacred Scripture, God's law *(lex Dei, lex Cristi)*, is entirely sufficient for the guidance of the body of Christ;[93] canon law is of a distinctly secondary order. This is the central argument of his *On the Authority of Sacred Scripture*. If the Scriptures had always received the attention due them, he argues, the confusion of modern times would not pertain. The Scriptures are perfectly logical when studied in their own terms and in context, and the unique logic and voice of Scripture would not have grown alien to modern ears if the Bible itself—and not questions of method and scholastic gamesmanship—were at the heart of the

UNIVERSITY TRAINING
MS illustration from the late fourteenth century showing magisterial instruction. Note that the "professor" holds both a pen and a scraping knife to the page, indicating the process of revision and emendation. Reproduced from MS Royal 17.E.iii (fol. 209) by permission of the British Library.

curriculum. Wyclif even dates the diminishment of the study of Scripture from the time of the *Decretals*—the beginnings of canon law.[94]

In this assertion of the authority of Scripture, Wyclif, as we have seen, was neither unprecedented nor entirely alone in his own time. Nor was he the first in his time to take an interest in making parts of the gospel available to laypersons. The Franciscans, by whom he was much influenced in his youth, had made various efforts in that direction. Translations of the Bible into the vernacular had been available in France for more than a century. But in his argument that everyone, whether a cleric or a layperson, ought to examine the Bible for himself—really study it as the standard by which all other religious information should be tested—he opened a new focus for the emerging individualism already so marked in fourteenth-century English spirituality. "The New Testament," he wrote, "is of full authority, and yet open to the understanding of simple persons in all points necessary for salvation."[95] While God has ordained the various vocational responsibilities of priests, knights, and commoners in every walk of life, as a later Wycliffite translates him, "it helps all Christians to study the Gospel in that language in which they may most fully grasp Christ's message."[96]

What is the control on this astonishing openness of the ordinary individual to scriptural authority? The same standard of spiritual life which alone can validate the interpretation of the academic theologian or ecclesiastical pontiff: "Whoever lives in meekness and charitable love will have the true understanding, and perfection of all Holy Writ," for "Christ did not write his laws on tables, or on the skins of animals, but in the hearts of men."[97] If we are faithful in the beginning, the Holy Spirit will teach us the meaning of Scriptures, even as Christ taught its meaning to the apostles.

No one before him had opened the way to lay spirituality so widely as did Wyclif.[98] Given his notion that each person held his or her "dominion," in a spiritual sense, directly from God and could lose it if not responsible to the "law of God," it was necessary for every person to have unambiguous access to Scripture. A Wycliffite tract in defense of the translation makes the case succinctly:

> Every Christian person takes on the binding authority of God as a condition of his membership in faith, to be a disciple of Holy Writ and a real teacher thereof in all his life upon the peril of damnation [if he does not do it] but for the sake of attaining the joy of heaven [if he does]. What Antichrist would dare, to the shame of Christians, prevent those who do not know Latin from learning even their holy obligations so strictly commanded of them by God? Each person is bound to do so, in order that he may be saved, and each person who shall be saved is a real priest made of God, as Holy Writ and holy doctors plainly declare.[99]

The right, and responsibility, of individual interpretation—in which all Christians come into a direct "living" relationship with the law of God, binding them in covenant service to their Lord—must be unimpeded by institutional filters and the "glossing" of dubious lesser authorities. It virtually demands, therefore, translation of the whole of Scripture into the vernacular. Who would read this translation? It soon became evident that the readership would include not only those in contemplative vocations—nuns, monks, anchorites, anchoresses—but also parish priests and ordinary layfolk.[100]

Wyclif made many calls for a translation of the entire text of Scripture into English,[101] and his call did not fall on deaf ears. The first portion of the task fell to Nicholas Hereford, who by 1382 had completed about half of the Old Testament. During that summer, Wyclif again came under public attack, with many holding him partially responsible for the Peasants' Revolt of the previous year. In a sermon preached at St. Mary's, Oxford, his followers were, perhaps for the first time, denounced as "Lollards," a term which previously had been associated only with groups of pious students of the Bible from the Low Countries and with wandering charismatics. On May 17, the bishops and friar theologians met in London under Archbishop Courtenay to condemn several points of Wyclif's teaching deemed to be heretical and to enact a formal suppression of the teaching of his views at Oxford. On May 21, in the midst of this conclave, the nation was rocked by a great earthquake. Church steeples fell and towers crumbled to the ground in many parts of the south of England. The session panicked and several of the bishops urged an immediate adjournment, but Courtenay's inflexible will and clever rationalization prevailed upon the gathering to conclude its judgments against Wyclif and his followers. Notaries were sent to Oxford to shadow all theologians and theological students known to be of Wyclif's persuasion and particularly to record any official statements by Nicholas Hereford. They attended Hereford's Ascension Day sermon and found him "exciting the people to insurrection and excusing and defending Wyclif." Under considerable pressure, it seems, Hereford went into his scriptorium and wrote on his manuscript, beneath the last line he had penned, "Here ends the translation of Nicholas of Hereford." Then he left town, probably for the Continent.

This early Wycliffite translation is rough, excessively literal, and syntactically disjointed. The balance of the first draft was completed by others, possibly including Wyclif himself. As an initial attempt it was a major accomplishment, but it is greatly inferior to the subsequent version traditionally ascribed to John Purvey and a committee of unspecified collaborators.

Purvey, who seems to have acted as a kind of secretary to Wyclif, was certainly a well-educated scholar and had an excellent command of English idiom. His version, and the General Prologue which accompanies it, are fluent and effective. Finished along with the text in 1395 or 1396, this prologue recapitulates much of Wyclif's argument for making Scripture available in translation to common people. That it was also intended for the use of priests is implicit, both in Purvey's prologue and in Wyclif's own writing. The average English parish priest could not manage in Latin very well—some not at all[102]—and for most of those who could come by a copy, Purvey's translation would have been the first opportunity to read the whole of the Bible in any language or version.[103] But the majority of early copies of this manuscript, which could be produced only slowly and laboriously, must have gone to those who could most afford them, such as the nobles known as "Lollard knights." One copy was presented to Queen Anne, and Purvey, evidently present at her funeral at Westminster Abbey, notes to his satisfaction that Archbishop Arundel—a bitter opponent of Wyclif and Bible translation—was obliged, against his wishes, to say in the funeral sermon that the queen's copy of *Gospels in English* was her daily companion.[104]

Many of the earliest attempts at translation of the Bible in this period seem to have been made in the north or north-midland dialect.[105] Rolle's *Psalter* and Thoresby's *Catechism* might perhaps have led to a translation of the Scriptures even if Wyclif had not gotten involved. Perhaps some other translator such as John Trevisa, Wyclif's sometime colleague at Queen's College, would have produced one. The point is that it finally did happen because of a compelling need for faith to find understanding and for spirituality to acquire content and authority larger than uninformed personal experience. What the translators of Scripture desired, Rolle had already put succinctly enough in the prologue to his *Psalter:* "The intent is to confirm those who have fallen in Adam, that they may be joined to Christ in newness of life." Rolle's principles in translation likewise set the pattern for Wyclif and his followers:

> In þis werk I seke no strange Inglis, bot lightest and comunest and swilke þat es mast like vnto þe Latyn, so þat þai þat knawes noght Latyn be þe Inglis may cum tille many Latyn wordes. In þe translacioun I folow þe letter als mekil als I may, and þare I fynde na propir Inglys I folow þe witte of þe word, so þat þai þat sal rede it, þam thar noght dred errynge. In expounynge I folew haly doctours, for it may cum into sum envyouse mans hand þat knawys noght what he suld say, þat wille say þat I wist noght what I sayde, and so do harme tille hym and tille other if he despise þe werk þat es prophetabil tille hym and other.[106]

Purvey's General Prologue restates the same basic goals and principles. His achievement, and that of his unknown colleagues, had a tremendous impact upon those who could gain access to the translation. As we in our own time read its old cadences and hear through them the powerful direct address of the gospel, we can imagine the great excitement the first copies must have caused.

The "Lollard knights," men of considerable political power in the reign of Richard II, were familiar with Wyclif's ideas and, in some cases at least, with Purvey's Bible. While John of Gaunt, patron to Wyclif, would not have been so identified (he was not in any case a notably spiritual person), a large number of the powerful noblemen of the day came to share many of Wyclif's concerns and to reflect his view of a scripturally informed laity.

Wyclif, like Hilton, urged these people to a consecrated secular vocation, a kind of "mixed" life. One of his more widely circulated documents was a letter to a young "friend in God," evidently a layman, urging him as Hilton does his correspondent to pursue his vocation as a spiritual responsibility. He talks about the law of love as a motivation for all of life.[107] The layperson may well have been one of the knights in whom he and his followers took comfort. Among these were Sir Thomas Latimer of Northamptonshire, who loaned copies of Wyclif's works to young Bohemian scholars attached to the retinue of Queen Anne; Sir Lewis Clifford, a Knight of the Garter and member of the Order of the Passion of our Lord, who intervened on Wyclif's behalf in the Lambeth trial; Sir Richard Sturry, a close friend of Clifford and Chaucer and notable adherent to Wyclif's views, also a member of the Order of the Passion; Sir John Montague, Deputy Marshall of England and a leader in the Lollard demonstration of 1395; Sir William Neville; Sir William de Beauchamp; Sir Phillipe de la Vache; and others. These knights helped keep persecution of Wyclif at bay during his lifetime, and, as leaders who endeavored to use Scripture as a guide to more active spiritual life, they were among the principal fruits of Wyclif's labors. A Wycliffite homily against persecution of those who try to spread the gospel says that institutional forces oppose the idea that men should know about the life of Christ because it inevitably shames the life of many priests and bishops. Indeed, the author continued, the persecutions are so great that it seems like the time of Antichrist, but "on coumfort is of knyghtes, that they saueren muche the gospel, and haue wylle to rede in Englysche the gospel of Cristus lyf, for afterwarde, ʒef God wul, the lordeschype schal be taken fro prestes, and so the stafe, that maketh hem hardy aʒeynus Crist and hys lawe."[108]

It is laypeople of this class in the fourteenth century who offer our first distinctive examples of devotional works written by English laymen since the time of King Alfred. Among the most eminent of the knights, the "grete lordis" who would later be tarred with the name Wycliviani, was Sir John Clanvowe, who in addition to his worldly work and his military accomplishments was, like his friend and fellow poet Geoffrey Chaucer, evidently a deeply spiritual man. His devotional treatise, *The Two Ways*, is a fine example of the maturity reached in lay spirituality of the fourteenth century.[109] As such, it bears comparison in content, style, and tone with the spiritual writings of Chaucer, which include not merely some of his lyrics but certainly his Parson's Sermon in *The Canterbury Tales*.[110] Clanvowe, who is willing to refer to himself

as a "loller" in his treatise, shows his affiliation with Wyclif's teaching
in the primacy he gives to Scripture, in his equation of the "narrow way"
with the way of God's law, and in his emphasis on the way of love being
the way of obedience to Scripture, the center of which is the Great Commandment to love. He shows on every page an intimate familiarity with
Scripture and a love for it, and when he invokes the scriptural standard
by which men and women are to know whether they are pilgrims on
the narrow way that leads to life, he proclaims what Wyclif often proclaimed:

> Christ, who cannot lie, says this, "Whoever loves me will keep my words
> and my commandments, and my Father shall love him and we shall come
> unto him and make our dwelling with him. And those who do not love
> me do not obey my words" (John 14:23-24). Christ also says, "He who has
> my commandments and who keeps them—that is the one who loves me"
> (John 14:21).[111]

Geoffrey Chaucer was not a knight like Clanvowe but a squire, an important civil servant before 1386 as Clerk of the King's Works, and,
under John of Gaunt's patronage, the court poet of England. Few readers think of him today in terms of the whole canon of his works, which
includes much spiritual as well as secular wisdom. But he, too, is an example of the "mixed" life, a Christian in, but not entirely of, the world,
and much of his writing in the years after his *House of Fame* (1378) can
be seen as a call for renewal of spiritual values in obedience to scriptural
authority. Chaucer wrote *The House of Fame* just as Wyclif was publishing *De Ecclesia* and was giving the lectures which form the substance of
De Veritate. Like Wyclif's treatises, Chaucer's poem explores the bank-
ruptcy of traditional sources of authority and the unreliability of history
itself as a vehicle for the transmission of truth. It appeals—beyond the
text of the poem—to a "man of grete auctoritee" who can cut through
the morass of conflicting proclamations with the word of truth.[112]

The Canterbury Tales can be viewed, I think, as a larger, fictional companion to Clanvowe's *Two Ways*. In Chaucer's poem the pilgrimage
begun by representatives of sinful men and women in all walks of English society reflects much inclination to the "broad way" and "wandering by the way." The tales told by some of the tellers, though internally
critiqued by a scriptural standard they abuse, can be as vulgar or perverse as the intention of their fictive tellers would make them. Chief
among the obstacles to the pilgrimage's becoming the "narrow way"—
"of thilke parfit glorious pilgrymage / that highte Jerusalem celestial,"
as Chaucer's Parson puts it—are monastics and contemplatives who
have forsaken their spiritual calling. The Pardoner, Summoner, Friar,

Monk, and Prioress serve as modern-day "scribes and Pharisees," religious counterfeits who distort and abuse the gospel even when, like the Wife of Bath, they can quote it in fragments to their own ill purposes.[113] But Chaucer makes clear his own purposes in his last and greatest poem. He begins to do so in the person of the Knight, who commences the tales, who loved "trouth, honour, fredom and curtesye," and whose tale proclaims an order of divine providence in a manner both worthy and wise; in the Oxford Clerk, the young theologian who earnestly pursues his philosophy and theology for right ends, who "wolde gladly lerne and gladly teche"; in his own pilgrim tale of scriptural wisdom, "The Tale of Melibee"; and in the evangelical example of his anonymous Second Nun with her tale of the many conversions wrought by faithful St. Cecilia. But lastly, in his model Parson, Chaucer tells us about his own dedication of heart. This Parson, a "lollere in the wynd,"[114] as he is judged to be, is a lively example of the sort of priest Wyclif prayed for. "In the end is every tales strengthe," Chaucer says in *Troilus*. Here, the strength of his longest and most comprehensive cultural criticism is a sermon on repentance followed by a personal confession. *The Canterbury Tales* is, as a whole, a prelatical exercise. Closely following the form of the *ars praedicandi*, it begins with "the progress of the catholic man" and moves toward the expounding of Scripture and a preaching which is faithful and exemplary. Chaucer himself, not ordained a priest, offers a good example of priestly spirituality in action.[115]

The fourteenth century was a difficult time for anyone to sort out problems of spiritual authority. The conditions described by Langland in *Piers the Plowman*—a striking Christian critique of an avaricious culture—are a nightmare of confusions, distortions, and outright perversions of scriptural values. But in the midst of it all, with institutional credibility more undermined than defended by the church's ferocious attacks against spiritual individualism seeking a direct encounter with the Scriptures, the beginnings of a new age were being forged.

It must have been hard for a man like John Purvey, great optimist and soldier of faith that he was, to see the new age coming. He, like many of his friends, thought that he was in the last days, that perhaps the year 1400 would signal the apocalypse. When the burning of Lollards started, justified in 1401 by the parliamentary statute *De heretico comburendo (On the Burning of Heretics)*, the times became for many a dark tribulation indeed. After 1407 it became illegal to own a Bible in English without a prodigiously expensive license, and one might be burned with the Bible if caught. Wealthier families did sometimes keep copies, as records suggest, but it was dangerous: one could be arrested on suspicion of Lollardy even for being found in possession of a copy of Chaucer's *Canterbury Tales*.[116]

One thinks of Purvey with a certain mixture of admiration and regret.[117] He was an able and scholarly man and fiercely loyal to his old master. He was a good translator and a fair exegete. Some of his views, controversial enough in their own time, would be of interest today. We gather, for example, that in a book now lost he argued that women should be allowed to preach—a position not, so far as we know, explicitly anticipated by Wyclif.[118] He wrote a book on marriage, also lost to us, in which he seems to have argued for marriage, in certain situations, of the clergy. In the petitions to Parliament of 1395, he and his Wycliffite colleagues declared themselves opposed to war and to the death penalty—opinions which were not likely to improve his hearing with either king or pope, or to gain him much of a following beyond the immediate ranks of the Lollard knights.

Purvey, as was typical for him in these years, was sagging under a burden of leadership too great for any one person to bear. Philip Ripingdon, one of Wyclif's star pupils, had recanted his "heretical" views and become abbot; he was soon to be made a bishop for his troubles. Nicholas Hereford, after a few years in the pope's prison in Rome, had also recanted, along with other potential Oxford leaders. And the exiled Wyclif himself had, of course, already died: on December 31, 1384, the great theologian had suffered a stroke just as the eucharistic Host was being raised in consecration in his Lutterworth parish church. Though one exhausted man had thus escaped further persecution, those he left behind lost in him their most powerful intellectual and moral leader. In 1400, after years of flight and hiding, Purvey too was arrested and placed in Archbishop Arundel's foul prison at Saltwood. After being tortured there,[119] he was brought on Monday February 28, 1401, before Convocation in the chapter house of St. Paul's and charged with heresy. The proceedings went slowly. On March 2, another Lollard, William Sawtre, was burned at the stake. On Saturday March 5, when Purvey appeared before the bishops, he recanted.

For a time Purvey was allowed to hold a modest church, but only under close observation. Then in 1403 he wrote a little treatise defending moderate Wycliffite views reminiscent of Wyclif's own earlier teaching. In 1408 Arundel suppressed Hereford's and Purvey's translations of the Bible. Purvey supported some of the Lollard knights in a failed attempt at legal disendowment of the institutional church, and in 1410 he was once again thrown into prison. He was still there in 1421, possibly as late as 1427. No one knows for sure when or how he died. He may have heard, in his cell, of the order of the Council of Constance in 1415 that Wyclif was at last to be judged a heretic, and that his bones would be dug up and burned. But it was not until 1428 that popular support for Wyclif and his followers had died down to the point that the council's orders for his remains could be carried out in safety. Forty-two years after Wyclif's death, the sentence was performed and his ashes thrown into the river Swift, thence to flow, as historians have been fond of noting, into the Avon, then the Severn, and from the Severn out into the sea and all over the world as a fit, if unintended, token of the impact of his and his students' work. By that time Purvey himself was almost certainly beyond hearing of it; and perhaps he never knew, either, that in 1415 John Hus, whose paraphrases and copies of Wyclif were to influence Luther, had already been burned in Bohemia—in his case, alive.

The first three decades of the fifteenth century were times of terrible persecution for the "later Lollards," as they have been called. By no means all of these people were direct disciples of Wyclif or his early followers; many had simply expressed concern about corruption in the church, had worked out a strong individual faith, and were desirous of a biblical foundation for their religious life. Not only priests but many laypersons were imprisoned, deprived of office and property, and even burned at the stake for failing to recant. After the martyrdom of Sir John Oldcastle, a scholar, knight, and friend of King Henry V who was finally captured and burned in 1417, and after the failure of Jack Sharpe's Rebellion against wealthy church endowments and the tenure of immoral prelates in 1431, new leadership failed to materialize, and those who identified with many of Wyclif's goals were driven underground. Bibles were still being copied, and small meetings were held in out-of-the-way places, but politically speaking, the ecclesiastical establishment had regained firm control.[120]

English spirituality in the fifteenth century beyond this point offers little to compare with the powerful devotional writings of the fourteenth century. The great northern figures, Rolle, Hilton, and Wyclif himself, had no successors of like magnitude. No writer of comparable power in probing interior life succeeded the author of *The Cloud of Unknowing*. Lay spirituality acquired no talents comparable to Clanvowe or Chaucer. And the English women mystics were swallowed up in oblivion; if there were others of their striking character in the subsequent generations, they have remained hidden from the record. Part of the reason for all this, of course, may be the very success Rome achieved in curbing spiritual individualism in a variety of spheres.

That we do not have great books to show for this later period is not,

MARGARET BEAUFORT
Painting by Rowland Lockey, reproduced by per-
mission of the Master and Fellows of St. John's
College, Cambridge.

of course, to be taken as evidence that the Spirit had fled. Nor does the
thinning of the record indicate that the light of the gospel had been entirely extinguished. The fifteenth century produced a number of able
preachers, some of whose sermons remain, and there were important
developments in English-language common prayer and vernacular
hymnody: it was during this period that James Ryman, the Canterbury
Franciscan, did much to transform the English carol from a dance song
to a hymn of the church and to bring about the association of the carol
with Christmas, which is now so familiar to us.[121]

But the great days were over. Perhaps the most visible evidence of
devotion to Christ was to be found in the lives of some of the nobility,
that class of "gentils" on whom Wyclif and his followers had so much
depended. Quietly but persistently, noble lay men and women of
genuine piety kept on reading the Scriptures—often copies of the
banished Wycliffite version—as well as devotional books by Rolle and

Hilton, among others. The nuns of Syon Abbey had one of the Wycliffite Bibles given to them in the bequest of a noble family in 1517; other copies appear to have been seen and read approvingly even by Thomas More, who did not know their origin.[122] Other copies were held by the royal family, one of them by Henry VI.

One of the most eminent protectors of the fourteenth-century tradition was Margaret Beaufort (1443–1509), a descendant of John of Gaunt and his mistress Catherine Swynford, and queen mother of Henry VII. A genuinely devout woman, she established Christ College Cambridge and founded St. John's College Cambridge to be institutions of Christian learning. She also persuaded the printer Wynkyn de Worde to print for the benefit of a new era some of the English devotional works of the fourteenth century, among them Walter Hilton's *Ladder of Perfection* in 1494. At the beginning of the sixteenth century, then, just when it seemed to some that the light of faith had almost gone out, sparks from an already distant past began to kindle new spiritual life in the English church.

Notes

1. "A Song of the Love of Jesus," included in *English Writings of Richard Rolle, Hermit of Hampole,* ed. Hope Emily Allen (1931; reprint, Oxford: Clarendon, 1963), 43. These are the first two of twenty-four stanzas.

2. From MS Cambridge University Library, Ii.6.26, printed in *The Holy Bible, containing the Old and New Testaments with the Apocryphal Books . . . made from the Latin Vulgate by John Wycliffe and His Followers,* ed. Rev. Josiah Forshall, F.R.S., and Sir Frederic Madden, K.H., F.R.S., 4 vols. (Oxford: Oxford University Press, 1850), 1: xiv.

3. See the description of these ceremonies in Marc Bloch, *Feudal Society,* 2 vols. (Chicago: University of Chicago Press, 1963).

4. C. S. Lewis, in *The Four Loves* (New York: Harcourt, Brace, Jovanovich, 1960), offers an extended reflection on the subject.

5. A good book on this general subject is Mary Flowers Braswell, *The Medieval Sinner* (London: Associated University Presses, 1983); see also Morton Bloomfield, *The Seven Deadly Sins: An Introduction to the History of a Religious Concept, with Special Reference to Medieval English Literature* (East Lansing: Michigan State College Press, 1952).

6. D. W. Robertson, Jr., *Chaucer's London* (New York and London: John Wiley & Sons, 1968), 46, 130-36.

7. This marriage was terminated by the early death of Constance; by 1381 Gaunt was already trying to legitimize his children by his mistress, Catherine Swynford, whom he finally married in 1396.

8. Chaucer's "Tale of Melibee" is an almost verbatim translation of Jean de Meun's version of the tale (which was originally told by Albertanus of Brescia,

a thirteenth century judge). Yet while this line is found in both these texts Chaucer significantly omits it.

9. See *The Complete Poetry and Prose of Geoffrey Chaucer*, ed. John H. Fisher (New York: Holt, Rinehart and Winston, 1977), 701.

10. Augustine, *On Christian Doctrine*, 3.10.16, trans. D. W. Robertson, Jr., The Library of Liberal Arts (Indianapolis: Bobbs-Merrill, 1958), 88.

11. Ibid., 3.10.15, p. 88.

12. The Prioress's Tale, in fact, suggests a spiritual understanding governed less by charity than by sentimentality; she tells a sensationalist and morbid legend of the type specifically condemned by both Gregory the Great and Pope Innocent III.

13. Wyclif, *De Ecclesia*, ed. J. Loserth (London: Wyclif Society, 1886), 37. This work was finished in 1378. References to Urban VI early in Wyclif's *De Veritate Sacrae Scripturae*, also 1378, are respectful as well. The *De Ecclesia* of Hus, which takes this same point of view, is largely an abridgment of Wyclif's work of the same title.

14. Herbert B. Workman, *John Wyclif: A Study of the Medieval Church*, 2 vols. (Oxford: Clarendon, 1926), 2: 57-58.

15. See Wyclif's *Sermones*, ed. J. Loserth, 4 vols. (London: Wyclif Society, 1887–90).

16. See Workman, *John Wyclif*, 2: 61-72.

17. Henry Knighton observes that

The bishops collected an incredible sum of money, gold and silver, jewels and necklaces, mugs, spoons and ornaments, especially from noble ladies and other women. . . . Men and women, rich and poor, gave according to their estate and beyond it, that both they and their dead friends might be absolved from their sins. For absolution was refused unless they gave according to their ability and estate. Many recruited men-at-arms and archers at their own expense, or set off by themselves on the "crusade." For the Bishop [Spenser] had wonderful indulgences, with absolution from punishment and guilt, conceded to him for the purposes of the crusade by Pope Urban—on whose authority the Bishop, on his own or through one of his commissioners, absolved both the living and the dead on whose behalf a large enough contribution was forthcoming.

Knighton, *Chronicon*, ed. J. R. Lumby, 2 vols. (London: Rolls Series, 1895), 2: 198-99.

18. Workman, *John Wyclif*, 2: 71.

19. Ibid., 2: 73. This was a position widely adopted by later Wycliffites.

20. *De Potestate Pape*, ed. J. Loserth (London: Wyclif Society, 1907), 360. This position accords firmly with Wyclif's doctrine of dominion.

21. Since the thirteenth century, antifraternal literature had connected corrupt religious, such as errant friars, with apocalyptic troubles. This is apparent already in the writings of Archbishop Richard FitzRalph *(Defensio Curatorum)* and William of St. Amour. In vernacular literature it can be seen in the characterization of Faux-Semblaunt in Jean de Meun's *Roman de la Rose*. Typical of the surviving antifraternal graffiti was the acrostic gloss: *Radix Omnium Malorum et Avaritia* ("the root of all evil and avarice"). See Marjorie Reeves, *The Influence of Prophecy in the Later Middle Ages* (Oxford: Clarendon, 1968), 61-63.

22. Abbot Gasquet, *Parish Life in Medieval England* (London: Methuen, 1906), 61-62.

23. See Penn R. Szittya, *The Anti-Fraternal Tradition in Medieval Literature* (Princeton: Princeton University Press, 1986); also G. R. Owst, *Literature and Pulpit in Me-*

dieval England (Oxford: Blackwell, 1966). For the friars' earlier spirituality and their use of the vernacular, see D. L. Jeffrey, *The Early English Lyric and Franciscan Spirituality* (Lincoln: University of Nebraska Press, 1975).

24. The Friar's Prologue, lines 1283-84.

25. See Langland's description of a pardoner in his *Piers the Plowman*, excerpted below.

26. Boethius, *The Consolation of Philosophy*, 2.m.8, trans. R. Green, The Library of Liberal Arts (Indianapolis: Bobbs-Merrill, 1962), 41. Note how the marriage metaphor governs this passage.

27. Dom David Knowles, *The Religious Orders in England,* 2 vols. (Cambridge: Cambridge University Press, 1955; 1961), 1: 308-19, quote from 316; cf. W. Pantin, *The English Church in the Fourteenth Century* (London: Cambridge University Press, 1955; Notre Dame: University of Notre Dame Press, 1962), 18-21.

28. Knowles, *The Religious Orders in England*, 1: 316.

29. Rolle, in Hope Emily Allen, ed., *Writings Ascribed to Richard Rolle, Hermit of Hampole, and Materials for his Biography* (New York: Modern Language Association, 1927), 267.

30. Ibid., 328.

31. Ibid., 128.

32. Allen observes in *English Writings of Richard Rolle* that there are over four hundred manuscript volumes of his work still extant.

33. Ibid., lvii.

34. Allen, *Writings Ascribed to Richard Rolle*, 256.

35. Richard Rolle, *Incendium Amoris*, ed. Margaret Deanesly (n.p.: London, 1915), chap. 37.

36. *The Cloud of Unknowing and the Book of Privy Counselling*, ed. Phyllis Hodgson, Early English Text Society, O.S. 218 (London: Oxford University Press, 1944).

37. Catherine's extremism has received recent treatment by Rudolph M. Bell in *Holy Anorexia* (Chicago: University of Chicago Press, 1985); one difference between English and southern European spirituality is indicated by the fact that the more spectacular evidences of sanctity, as her biographers imagine it, are suppressed in English translations and accounts.

38. Msgr. J. P. Kirsch, "St. Bridget of Sweden," in *The Catholic Encyclopedia* (New York: The Encyclopedia Press, 1907; 1913).

39. See the full selection in Part V below.

40. Edmund Colledge, O.S.A., and James Walsh, S. J., try to find parallels or precedents for Julian's views in such authors as St. Mechtild of Hackeborn. Jean Leclercq, O.S.B., in his preface to Colledge and Walsh's translation tries to set her in the tradition of the church. See Colledge and Walsh, *Julian of Norwich: Showings* (New York: Paulist, 1978), 6-8. It seems, however, that Julian is at best awkwardly related to traditional Catholic teaching in these respects.

41. Leclercq, in ibid., 9-10.

42. She was actually present for Bridget's canonization in Rome. See Kirsch, in *The Catholic Encyclopedia*.

43. See W. Butler-Bowden, trans., *The Book of Margery Kempe* (New York: Devin-Adair, 1944), 164.

44. Eric Colledge, in *The Chastising of God's Children and the Treatise of the Perfection of the Sons of God*, ed. Joyce Bazire and Eric Colledge (Oxford: Blackwell, 1957), 81.

45. Catherine learned to write very late in life; most of her works, like those of

other female mystics in the fourteenth century, were dictated. However, because they were quickly perceived as supportive of the Roman see, they were widely influential.

46. For this hypothesis see Rotha Mary Clay, *The Hermits and Anchorites of England* (London: Methuen, 1914), 177; also Alaphrido C. Hughes, *Walter Hilton's Directions to Contemplatives* (Rome: Pontifica Univ. Gregoriana, 1962), 6-7.

47. A renewal of solitary life had characterized the religious revival of the twelfth century.

48. One should keep in mind that we typically associate the term *monastic* with only one of the two legitimate classes of persons living the monastic life, that is, with the *coenobite*—the person living in a monastic community. Yet anchorites—solitaries like the Carthusians living in loose groups of huts or simply alongside a monastic house or chapel—were regarded as monastics as well, and they also lived under a rule, indeed, often a more severe rule than that governing those within a community. Having separated themselves still further from the world, they were often seen as spiritually exemplary.

49. Evelyn Underhill, *Mixed Pasture* (London: Methuen, 1933), 188.

50. Ibid., 193. Margaret Beaufort (1443–1509) was Countess of Richmond and Derby.

51. Luke 14:11; Psalm 131:1-2; for the Rule of St. Benedict on this, see *Western Asceticism*, trans. and ed. Owen Chadwick, Library of Christian Classics, vol. 12 (Philadelphia: Westminster, 1958), 301-5.

52. Chadwick, *Western Asceticism*, 304.

53. Gillian R. Evans, trans., *Alan of Lille: The Art of Preaching*, Cistercian Studies Series, no. 23 (Kalamazoo: Cistercian Publications, 1981), 3.

54. Gregory the Great, *Pastoral Rule*, ch. 5, in Nicene and Post-Nicene Fathers of the Christian Church, ed. Philip Schaff and Henry Wace, second series, vol. 12, part 2 (reprint, Grand Rapids: Eerdmans, 1969), 13.

55. *St. Bonaventure: The Mind's Road to God*, trans. George Boas, The Library of Liberal Arts (New York: Bobbs-Merrill, 1953), 9.

56. Ibid., 44.

57. Underhill, *Mixed Pasture*, 205.

58. See Marjorie Orchard Collins, "Psalms from the *English Psalter Commentary* of Richard Rolle" (Ph.D. diss., University of Michigan, 1966), which focuses on Rolle as a commentator and translator of Scripture and patristic exegesis.

59. *The Form of Living* was written in 1348 for her enclosure.

60. Bazire and Colledge, *The Chastising of God's Children*, 38.

61. "In this regard they say that as long as a person busies himself to improve and acquire virtue he is [obviously] not yet perfect. They, on the other hand, by their own lights, are already in perfection above all saints and angels and any reward that any other person might deserve. Accordingly they feel they can no longer add to their virtue of life or obtain more blessing, and believe that they are no longer capable of sin . . ." (my translation).

62. Bazire and Colledge, *The Chastising of God's Children*, 47.

63. Ibid., 103. This passage follows Ruysbroek verbatim, as does the quotation following.

64. Ibid., 102; see also chaps. 4, 19-20.

65. Ibid., 57, 64-65. Jean Gerson complained a century later about "the voluminous and repetitive *Revelationes* of St. Bridget," concerned that so much might be piled on top of scriptural revelation that, as he said, the New Law which

God wished to be a light burden and easy yoke could become by such additions more burdensome than the Old Law and dicta of the Pharisees which it replaced.

66. These include, besides Ruysbroek's works, Henry of Suso's *Horologium Sapientiae,* and the twelfth-century English *Ancrene Riwle.*

67. The regulation is from general Dominican guidelines for the training of lay brethren of the mid-thirteenth century, but it is also found elsewhere. See Bazire and Colledge, *The Chastising of God's Children,* 66-67.

68. Ibid., 70.

69. *The Lay Folks' Catechism,* ed. T. F. Simmons and H. E. Nolloth, Early English Text Society, O.S. 118 (New York: Kraus Reprints, 1973).

70. Bazire and Colledge, *The Chastising of God's Children,* 71-72.

71. I.e., no case endings, the inflections of Anglo-Saxon having largely disappeared by the fourteenth century.

72. J. A. Robson, *Wyclif and the Oxford Schools* (Cambridge: Cambridge University Press, 1961).

73. Allen, *English Writings of Richard Rolle,* 2-4; see also Collins, "Psalms from the English Psalter Commentary," 2: 15-17.

74. See *The Lay Folks' Catechism.*

75. Margaret Deanesly, *The Lollard Bible* (Cambridge: Cambridge University Press, 1920), 272.

76. MS Cambridge University Library, Ii.6.26; printed in Forshall and Madden, *The Holy Bible,* xiv.

77. Workman, *John Wyclif,* 2: 150n.

78. For a concise and helpful discussion of the growth of common law from Gratian through the *Decretals* (the second stage of common law) in the papacy of Gregory IX to the *Liber Sextus* of Boniface VIII, see Margaret Deanesly, *A History of the Medieval Church 590–1500* (1925; reprint, London: Methuen, 1965), 138-42.

79. Bradwardine, the authority on predestination and election cited by Chaucer's Nun's Priest in *The Canterbury Tales,* was briefly Archbishop of Canterbury before dying in 1349 in the Black Death. He is one of Wyclif's favorite authorities.

80. See the discussion by Heiko Oberman, *The Harvest of Medieval Theology: Gabriel Biel and Late Medieval Nominalism* (Grand Rapids: Eerdmans, 1967), 369ff.

81. These were the assumptions of even some of the signal figures upon whom Wyclif was himself to draw, including William Occam, the Franciscan philosopher-theologian who was Wyclif's great predecessor at Oxford early in the century.

82. Even at the height of his philosophical and theological struggles, his worst enemies did not call into question "his excellent piety." See John Stacey, *Wyclif and Reform* (London: Lutterworth, 1964), 13-14.

83. Hilton, *Epistle on the Mixed Life;* see text below. This idea is reflected also in the anonymous *Abbey of the Holy Ghost,* included in Carl Horstman, *Early Yorkshire Writers: Richard Rolle of Hampole . . . and his Followers* (London: Swan Sonnenschein, 1895), 321-37.

84. See Beryl Smalley, "Wyclif's *Postilla* on the Old Testament and His *Principium,*" in *Oxford Studies Presented to Daniel Callus, O.P.* (Oxford: Oxford University Press, 1964), 276.

85. For a more extensive discussion, see David L. Jeffrey, "John Wyclif and the Hermeneutic of Reader Response," *Interpretation* 39 (1985): 272-87.

86. The key work is *De Civili Dominio*, ed. J. Loserth, 3 vols. (London: The Wyclif Society, 1900–1904).

87. Wyclif, *De Ecclesia*, 74, 111, 140.

88. Ibid., 3-5, 29, 130, 464.

89. Ibid., 29, 464.

90. Ibid., 34, 38-41, 88.

91. Workman, *John Wyclif*, 2: 115.

92. Wyclif, *De Ecclesia*, 44-45, 67, 465.

93. *De Veritate Sacrae Scripturae*, ed. Rudolf Buddensieg, 3 vols. (London: Trubner, 1905; New York: Johnson Reprints, 1966), 1: 55, 148, 183, 245, 296.

94. *De Veritate*, 1: 343; for reference to more extensive discussion see D. L. Jeffrey, "John Wyclif and the Hermeneutic of Reader Response."

95. *De Veritate*, 2: 201.

96. Quoted by Workman, *John Wyclif*, 2: 151n.2. A Wycliffite tract, MS Cambridge University Library, I.i.6.26, divides Christian people into three categories: those who are university educated, for whom "ben ordeyned" books of Hebrew, Greek, and Latin; those who are illiterate ("lewid"), who must be content with the book of creation; and finally,

summe ther ben that kunnen rede but litil, or noȝt vnderstonde, and for hem ben ordent bookis of her moder tongue, to Frensche men bokis of Frensche, to Ytaliens bokis of Latyne corrupte, to Duche men bokis Duche, to Englische men bokis of Englische; in whiche bokis thei mowen rede to konne God and his lawe, and to fulfille it in worde and dede, and so to slee synne in hem silf and ech in other, bi ther power and kunnynge, wher thorouȝ thei mowe desserue eendeles blisse.

97. Wyclif, *De Veritate*, 3: 132, 242.

98. Rudolf Buddensieg, in *John Wiclif's Polemical Works in Latin* (London: Wyclif Society, 1882–83), 1: xv.

99. Forshall and Madden, *The Holy Bible*, xv.

100. While Wyclif does not advance any further the argument for "real priesthood" in each individual, John Purvey was to see it as leading naturally to the equal right of women to preach. See p. 44.

101. See, for example, *Polemical Works*, 1: 126, 128; 2: 711; *Opus Evangelicum*, 2: 36; *Opus Minorum*, 9, 74.

102. Deanesly, *Lollard Bible*, 161, 195, 204. See the priestlike rooster Chaunticleer in Chaucer's "Nun's Priest's Tale," whose comical misconstrual of *in principio mulier est hominis confusio* suggests the problem at large.

103. See Deanesly, *Lollard Bible*, 139, 214, 217-19, 222.

104. Ibid., 445.

105. Workman, *John Wyclif*, 2: 172-75.

106. Allen, *English Writings of Richard Rolle*, 7.

107. David L. Jeffrey, "Chaucer and Wyclif: Hermeneutic and Narrative Theory in the Fourteenth Century," in *Chaucer and Scriptural Tradition*, ed. D. L. Jeffrey (Ottawa: University of Ottawa Press, 1984), 114n.28.

108. Forshall and Madden, *The Holy Bible*, xv. See Trevisa's translation of Occam's *Dialogus inter Militem et Clericum*, ed. Aaron Jenkins Perry, Early English Text Society, O.S. 167 (1925; reprint, London: Oxford University Press, 1971), which indicates that some knights were disposed to these opinions already before Wyclif came along.

109. An earlier work, the Anglo-Norman *Livre de Seyntz Medicines*, was written by the nobleman Henry of Lancaster—father to Blanche, the first Duchess of John of Gaunt—and has been published by the Anglo-Norman Text Society. Though for lack of space it is not included in this volume, it is of considerable interest.

110. Clanvowe also wrote a long courtly poem, "The Boke of Cupide." His works have been collected in *The Works of Sir John Clanvowe*, ed. V. G. Scattergood (Cambridge: Cambridge University Press, 1975).

111. See the full text of Clanvowe's *Two Ways* in Part VI below.

112. I have discussed this text from this point of view in detail in "Sacred and Secular Scripture: Authority and Interpretation in *The House of Fame*," in *Chaucer and Scriptural Tradition*, 207-28.

113. See Russell A. Peck, "St. Paul and *The Canterbury Tales*," in *Chaucer and Scriptural Tradition*, 143-70.

114. Epilogue to "The Man of Law's Tale," in Fisher, *Complete Poetry and Prose of Geoffrey Chaucer*, 101, lines 1173-77.

115. Paul A. Olson's recent book, *The Canterbury Tales and the Good Society* (Princeton: Princeton University Press, 1987) should do much to clarify Chaucer's position as a reformer in fourteenth-century society. Unfortunately, this work appeared too late to be more than noted here.

116. J. A. F. Thomson, *The Later Lollards: 1414-1520* (Oxford: Oxford University Press, 1965), 243.

117. Purvey has been widely regarded as—and himself claimed to be—the main translator of the second version of the Wycliffite Bible. Yet some have suggested that there is an absence of hard evidence to support that assumption and that the attribution derives largely from the work of eighteenth-century scholars. See Anne Hudson, "John Purvey: A Reconsideration of the Evidence for His Life and Writings," *Viator* 12 (1981): 355-80. There has not, however, been any positive evidence to dismiss Purvey's claim, and so I have elected to let the traditional identification stand. The events of Purvey's life which follow here are not in dispute. It will be understood, I think, that he and his friends would have had every incentive to remain silent if he had done the translation himself or even if he had been only an amanuensis for his declining master, Wyclif.

118. Workman, *John Wyclif*, 2: 179-80.

119. Ibid., 2: 167.

120. See, however, the collection of Wycliffite sermons edited by Anne Hudson, *English Wycliffite Sermons*, vol. 1 (Oxford: Clarendon, 1983), and her *Selections from English Wycliffite Writings* (Cambridge: Cambridge University Press, 1978); see also Thomson, *The Later Lollards*.

121. David L. Jeffrey, "James Ryman and the Fifteenth Century Carol," in *Fifteenth Century Studies: Recent Essays*, ed. Robert F. Yeager (Hamden, Conn.: Archon, 1984), 303-20.

122. Workman, *John Wyclif*, 2: 187-90.

Bibliography

Primary Works

Alan of Lille. *The Art of Preaching*. Trans. Gillian R. Evans. Cistercian Studies Series, no. 23. Kalamazoo: Cistercian Publications, 1981.

Augustine, Saint. *On Christian Doctrine*. Trans. D. W. Robertson, Jr. The Library of Liberal Arts. Indianapolis: Bobbs-Merrill, 1958.

Boethius. *The Consolation of Philosophy*. Trans. Richard Green. The Library of Liberal Arts. Indianapolis: Bobbs-Merrill, 1962.

Bonaventure, Saint. *The Mind's Road to God*. Trans. George Boas. The Library of Liberal Arts. New York: Bobbs-Merrill, 1953.

Bridget of Sweden. *The Revelations of St. Birgitta*. Ed. W. P. Cumming. The Early English Text Society, O.S. 178. London, 1929. Reprint. New York: Kraus, 1971.

Brown, Carleton, ed. *Religious Lyrics of the XIVth Century*. 2d ed. Oxford: Clarendon, 1965.

Chadwick, Owen, ed. and trans. *Western Asceticism*. Library of Christian Classics, vol. 12. Philadelphia: Westminster, 1958.

The Chastising of God's Children and the Treatise of Perfection of the Sons of God. Ed. Joyce Bazire and Eric Colledge. Oxford: Blackwell, 1957.

Chaucer, Geoffrey. *The Complete Poetry and Prose of Geoffrey Chaucer*. Ed. John H. Fisher. New York: Holt, Rinehart and Winston, 1977.

Clanvowe, John. *The Works of Sir John Clanvowe*. Ed. V. G. Scattergood. Cambridge: Cambridge University Press, 1975.

The Cloud of Unknowing and The Book of Privy Counselling. Ed. Phyllis Hodgson. Early English Text Society, O.S. 218. London: Oxford University Press, 1944.

Deonise Hid Diuinite and Other Treatises on Contemplative Prayer Related to "The Cloud of Unknowing." Ed. Phyllis Hodgson. Early English Text Society, O.S. 231. 1955. Reprint. London: Oxford University Press, 1958.

Hilton, Walter. *The Scale of Perfection*. Ed. Evelyn Underhill. London: John M. Watkins, 1948.

————. *Toward a Perfect Love: The Spiritual Counsel of Walter Hilton*. Ed. and trans. David L. Jeffrey. Portland, Oreg.: Multnomah, 1986.

The Holy Bible, containing the Old and New Testaments with the Apocryphal Books . . . made from the Latin Vulgate by John Wycliffe and his Followers. Ed. Josiah Forshall, F.R.S., and Sir Frederic Madden, K.H., F.R.S. 4 vols. Oxford: Oxford University Press, 1850.

Horstman, Carl, ed. *Early Yorkshire Writers: Richard Rolle and His Followers*. 2 vols. London: Swan Sonnenschein; New York: Macmillan, 1895.

Hudson, Anne, ed. *Selections from English Wycliffite Writings*. Cambridge: Cambridge University Press, 1978.

————, ed. *English Wycliffite Sermons*. Vol. 1. Oxford: Clarendon, 1983.

Hurlbut, Stephen A., ed. *The Liturgy of the Church of England Before and After the Reformation, Together with the Service of Holy Communion*. Grand Rapids: Eerdmans, 1941.

Julian of Norwich. *Showings*. Trans. Edmund Colledge, O.S.A., and James Walsh, S.J. Classics of Western Spirituality. New York: Paulist, 1978.

Kempe, Margery. *The Book of Margery Kempe*. Trans. W. Butler-Bowdon. New York: Kevin-Adair, 1944.

Knighton, Henry. *Chronicon*. Ed. J. R. Lumby. 2 vols. London: Rolls Series, 1895.

Langland, William. *Piers the Ploughman*. Trans. J. F. Goodridge. Baltimore: Penguin, 1959.

————. *Langland's Piers the Plowman and Richard the Redeless*. Ed. Walter W. Skeat. 2 vols. 1886. Reprint. London: Oxford University Press, 1961.

The Lanterne of Li3t. Ed. L. M. Swinburn. Early English Text Society, O.S. 151. London, 1917. Reprint. New York: Kraus, 1971.

The Lay Folks' Catechism. Ed. T. F. Simmons and H. E. Nolloth. Early English Text Society, O.S. 118. Reprint. New York: Kraus, 1973.

The Lay Folks' Mass Book . . . and Offices in English According to the Use of York. Ed. Thomas F. Simmons. Early English Text Society, O.S. 71. 1879. Reprint. London: Oxford University Press, 1968.

The Lives of Women Saints of our Contrie of England. Also Some other Lives of Holie Women Written by Some of the Auncient Fathers. Ed. C. Horstman. Early English Text Society, O.S. 86. London: Trubner, 1886.

Loomis, Roger Sherman, and Rudolph Willard, eds. *Medieval English Verse and Prose in Modernized Versions*. New York: Appleton-Century-Crofts, 1948.

Mechtild of Hackeborn. *The Booke of Gostlye Grace of Mechtild of Hackeborn*. Ed. Theresa A. Halligan. Toronto: Pontifical Institute of Mediaeval Studies, 1979.

Michel, Dan. *Dan Michel: Ayenbite of Inwyt, or Remorse of Conscience*. Ed. Pamela Gradon (revising R. Morris). Early English Text Society, O.S. 23. London: Trubner, 1866. Reprint. Oxford: Oxford University Press, 1965.

Mirk, John. *Mirk's Festial: A Collection of Homilies*. Early English Text Society, E.S. 96. London: Oxford University Press, 1905.

————. *John Myrc: Instructions for Parish Priests*. Early English Text Society, O.S. 31. London, 1868. Reprint. New York: Kraus, 1973.

Pecock, Reginald. *The Donet*. Ed. E. V. Hitchcock. Early English Text Society, O.S. 156. London, 1921. Reprint. New York: Kraus, 1971.

The Prymer or Lay Folks' Prayer Book. Ed. Henry Littlehales. Early English Text Society, O.S. 105. London: Kegan Paul, Trench, Trubner, 1895.

Robertson, D. W., Jr., ed. *The Literature of Medieval England*. New York: McGraw-Hill, 1970.

Rolle, Richard. *English Writings of Richard Rolle, Hermit of Hampole*. Ed. Hope Emily Allen. 1931. Reprint. Oxford: Clarendon, 1963.

————. *The Fire of Love*. Trans. Clifton Wolters. London: Penguin, 1972.

————. *The Fire of Love and the Mending of Life*. Trans. Richard Misyn. Ed. Ralph Harvey. Early English Text Society, O.S. 106. London, 1896. Reprint. New York: Kraus, 1973.

————. *The Fire of Love and the Mending of Life*. Trans. M. L. del Maestro. New York: Doubleday, 1981.

————. *Incendium Amoris*. Ed. Margaret Deanesly. London, 1915.

————. "Psalms from the *English Psalter Commentary* of Richard Rolle." Ed. Marjorie Orchard Collins. Ph.D diss. Ann Arbor: University Microfilms, 1967.

————. *Selected Works of Richard Rolle, Hermit*. Trans. G. C. Heseltine. London: Longmans, Green, 1930.

————. *Writings Ascribed to Richard Rolle, Hermit of Hampole, and Materials for his Biography*. Ed. Hope Emily Allen. New York: Modern Language Association, 1927.

Trevisa, John. *Dialogus inter Militem et Clericum, Sermon by FitzRalph, and þe Bygyunnyng of þe World*. Ed. Aaron Jenkins Perry. Early English Text Society, O.S. 167. London, 1925. Reprint. New York: Kraus, 1971.

Upland, Jack. *Jack Upland, Friar Daw's Reply, and Upland's Rejoinder*. Ed. P. L. Heyworth. Oxford: Oxford University Press, 1968.

Wyclif, John. *De Ecclesia*. Ed. J. Loserth. London: Wyclif Society, 1886.

————. *De Potestate Pape*. Ed. J. Loserth. London: Wyclif Society, 1907.

————. *De Veritate Sacrae Scripturae*. Ed. Rudolf Buddensieg. 3 vols. London, 1905. Reprint. New York: Johnson Reprints, 1966.

————. *The English Works of Wyclif Hitherto Unprinted*. Ed. F. D. Matthew. Early English Text Society, O.S. 74. 2d and rev. ed. New York: Kraus, 1975.

————. *John Wiclif's Polemical Works in Latin*. Ed. Rudolf Buddensieg. 2 vols. London: Wyclif Society, 1882–83.

————. *Johannes Wyclif Sermones*. Ed. J. Loserth. 4 vols. London: Wyclif Society, 1887–90.

Secondary Works

Aston, Margaret. *Lollards and Reform: Images and Literacy in Late Medieval Religion*. London: Hambledon, 1984.

Bennett, J. A. W. *Poetry of the Passion: Studies in Twelve Centuries of English Verse*. Oxford: Clarendon, 1982.

Bloomfield, Morton. *Piers Plowman as a Fourteenth Century Apocalypse*. New Brunswick, N.J.: Rutgers University Press, 1961.

————. *The Seven Deadly Sins: An Introduction to the History of a Religious Con-*

cept, with Special Reference to Medieval English Literature. East Lansing: Michigan State College Press, 1952.

Braswell, Mary Flowers. *The Medieval Sinner*. London: Associated University Presses, 1983.

Clay, Rotha Mary. *The Hermits and Anchorites of England*. London: Methuen, 1914.

Dahmus, Joseph. *The Prosecution of John Wyclif*. New Haven: Yale University Press, 1952.

———. *William Courtenay: Archbishop of Canterbury 1381–1396*. University Park: Pennsylvania State University Press, 1966.

Deanesly, Margaret. *A History of the Medieval Church 590–1500*. 1925. Reprint. London: Methuen, 1965.

———. *The Lollard Bible*. Cambridge: Cambridge University Press, 1920.

Fowler, David C. *The Bible in Middle English Literature*. Seattle: University of Washington Press, 1984.

Gasquet, Abbot. *Parish Life in Medieval England*. London: Methuen, 1906.

Hughes, Alaphrido C. *Walter Hilton's Directives to Contemplatives*. Rome: Pontifica Universitas Gregoriana, 1962.

Jeffrey, David Lyle, ed. *Chaucer and Scriptural Tradition*. Ottawa: University of Ottawa Press, 1979.

———. *The Early English Lyric and Franciscan Spirituality*. Lincoln: University of Nebraska Press, 1975.

———. "James Ryman and the Fifteenth Century Carol." In *Fifteenth-Century Studies: Recent Essays*. Ed. Robert F. Yeager, 303-20. Hamden, Conn.: Archon, 1984.

———. "John Wyclif and the Hermeneutics of Reader Response," *Interpretation* 39 (1985): 272-87.

Joliffe, P. S. *A Check-List of Middle English Prose Writings of Spiritual Guidance*. Toronto: Pontifical Institute of Mediaeval Studies, Subsidia Mediaevalia 2, 1974.

Kenney, Anthony, ed. *Wyclif in His Times*. Oxford: Oxford University Press, 1986.

———. *Wyclif*. Oxford: Oxford University Press, 1985.

Knowles, Dom David. *The English Mystical Tradition*. New York: Harper, 1961.

———. *The Religious Orders in England*. 2 vols. Cambridge: Cambridge University Press, 1955.

Leclercq, Dom Jean. "Les traductions de la Bible et la spritualité medievale." In *The Bible and Medieval Culture*. Ed. W. Lourdaux and D. Verhelst. Mediaevalia Lovaniensia Series 1, Studia 7. Louvain: Louvain University Press, 1979.

Leclercq, Dom Jean, Dom Francois Vandenbroucke, and Louis Bouyer. *La Spiritualité du Moyen Age*. Vol. 2. Paris: Aubier, 1961.

Levy, Brian J. *Nine Verse Sermons by Nicholas Bozon: The Art of an Anglo-Norman Poet and Preacher*. Medium Aevum Monographs, N.S. 11. Oxford: Society for the Study of Mediaeval Languages and Literature, 1981.

Mallard, William. "Clarity and Dilemma: The Forty Sermons of John Wyclif." In *Contemporary Reflections on the Medieval Christian Tradition. Essays in Honor of Ray C. Petry.* Ed. George H. Shriver, 19-38. Durham: Duke University Press, 1974.

Manning, Bernard Lord. *The People's Faith in the Time of Wyclif.* Cambridge: Cambridge University Press, 1919.

Milosh, Joseph E. *The Scale of Perfection and the English Mystical Tradition.* Madison: University of Wisconsin Press, 1966.

Moorman, John R. H. *A History of the Church in England.* 1953. Reprint. London: Adam and Charles Black, 1958.

Oberman, Heiko Augustinus. *The Harvest of Medieval Theology: Gabriel Biel and Late Medieval Nominalism.* Grand Rapids: Eerdmans, 1967.

Olson, Paul A. *The Canterbury Tales and the Good Society.* Princeton: Princeton University Press, 1987.

Owst, G. R. *Literature and Pulpit in Medieval England.* Oxford: Blackwell, 1966.

Pantin, W. A. *The English Church in the Fourteenth Century.* London: Cambridge University Press, 1955. Reprint. Notre Dame: University of Notre Dame Press, 1962.

Pepler, Conrad, O.P. *The English Religious Heritage.* London: Blackfriars, 1958.

Reeves, Marjorie. *The Influence of Prophecy in the Later Middle Ages.* Oxford: Clarendon, 1968.

Robertson, D. W., Jr. *Chaucer's London.* New York: John Wiley & Sons, 1968.

———. *A Preface to Chaucer: Studies in Medieval Perspective.* Princeton: Princeton University Press, 1963.

Robson, J. A. *Wyclif and the Oxford Schools.* Cambridge: Cambridge University Press, 1961.

Sitwell, Gerard, O.S.B. *Spiritual Writers of the Middle Ages.* New York: Hawthorn, 1964.

Smalley, Beryl. *The Study of the Bible in the Middle Ages.* Notre Dame: University of Notre Dame Press, 1964.

———. "Wyclif's *Postilla* on the Old Testament and His *Principium.*" In *Oxford Studies Presented to Daniel Callus, O.P.* Oxford: Oxford University Press, 1964.

Stacey, John. *Wyclif and Reform.* London: Lutterworth, 1964.

Szittya, Penn R. *The Anti-Fraternal Tradition in Medieval Literature.* Princeton: Princeton University Press, 1986.

Thomson, J. A. F. *The Later Lollards: 1414–1520.* Oxford: Oxford University Press, 1965.

Thomson, Williell, ed. *The Latin Writings of John Wyclyf: An Annotated Catalogue.* Subsidia Mediaevalia 14. Toronto: Pontifical Institute of Mediaeval Studies, 1983.

Tuma, George Wood. *The Fourteenth Century Mystics: A Comparative Analysis.* 2 vols. Salzburg: Salzburg Studies, 1977.

Underhill, Evelyn. *Mixed Pasture.* London: Methuen, 1933.

Workman, Herbert B. *John Wyclif: A Study of the Medieval Church*. 2 vols. Oxford: Clarendon, 1936.

————. *The Evolution of the Monastic Ideal from the Earliest Times Down to the Coming of the Friars*. Boston: Beacon, 1962.

PART ONE

Conversion and the Patterns of Spiritual Life

RICHARD ROLLE, HERMIT
Reproduced from MS Cotton, Faustina B.VI.ii (fol. 8b) by permission of the British Library.

RICHARD ROLLE

The Amending of Life

The name of this treatise in the original Latin text, *Emendatio Vitae,* means literally the "amending" or "emending" of life. Written about 1340, it was evidently extremely popular; there are ninety or more surviving manuscripts in Latin as well as at least five Middle English translations. The present translation is based upon the versions found in MS Egerton 671 and Misyn's Middle English Rendition.

The *Emendatio* describes a progress from conversion through growth in the spiritual life to mystical contemplation and, finally, a rich indwelling of God's spirit and a self-abandoning pursuit of God's presence. Although its purpose is thus clearly defined as an invitation to the deepest kind of spiritual and contemplative life, it was evidently read by large numbers of men and women who desired a more profound spirituality in the midst of the responsibilities of ordinary living.

I. Of Conversion

DO NOT BE SLOW to be converted to our Lord, nor put it off from day to day, for frequently the agony of death seizes an unregenerate person, and bitter pains suddenly devour those who seek to avoid conversion. We cannot imagine how many worldly people have been led astray by sinful presumption, toying with God's grace.

It is truly a great sin to trust in God's mercy and yet not to cease from sin, believing His mercy to be so great that He will not give to sinners the punishment they deserve. Christ Himself urges us to work "while it is day; the night cometh when no man can work" (John 9:4). "Light" or "day" is what he calls this life, in which we ought never to cease from good works, knowing that our death is certain, even though the hour of its approach is uncertain. By "night" he refers to death, in which our limbs grow stiff and knowledge is laid aside, and we can no longer do any good work, but only receive joy or torment according to our deeds. We live only for a moment of time—indeed, less than a moment—for our life is nothing when compared to life everlasting.

How our life is wasted through love of vanity, as all the day we stand idle without repentance! Lord, turn us and we shall be turned; heal us and we shall be healed (Jeremiah 17:14).[1] Many are not healed and their

---

1. In the original Latin there is evident wordplay between *turn (vertere)* and *convert (convertere)*. See St. Augustine's *Confessions,* book 8, for the model on which this popular wordplay was based.

wounds turn to decay; for today they are turned to God and tomorrow away from Him, today they do penance and tomorrow turn back to sin. Of such it is written: "We would have healed Babylon, but she is not healed" (Jeremiah 51:9), for she is not truly turned to Christ.

What else is turning to God but turning away from the world and sin, from the devil and flesh? What is turning from God but turning from unchangeable good to changeable good, to the pleasant beauty of creatures, to the works of the devil, to the lust of the flesh and to the world? We do not go toward God with physical footsteps but by following his example in love, and in good disciplines and habits.

Our conversion is also accomplished as we give the attention of our minds to God, and continually ponder his counsel and his commandments, so that they may be fulfilled by us. Thus, wherever we are, whether sitting or standing, we keep the fear of God in our hearts. (I speak not of that fear which is a painful experience but that which is the outcome of love, with which we give reverence to the presence of so great a majesty; we fear lest we should offend in any way, however small.) In such a condition we are truly turned to God, since we have turned away from the world.

Now, to be truly turned from the world is nothing else but putting behind us all lust,[2] gladly suffering the bitterness of this world for God. It is forgetting all idle occupations and worldly affairs so that the soul, wholly turned to God, dies utterly to all things which we might love or seek in the world.

Being thus given to heavenly desires the converted have God ever before their eyes and behold Him without weariness; as the Psalmist bears witness: "I have set the Lord always before me" (Psalm 16:8), which is to say, "In my sight I saw our Lord forever before me." Forever. Not only for the space of an hour, like those who set the fair or lovely things of earth before their inward eye (which they behold, and in which they delight and desire, for their love's sake, to find rest).

Later the Psalmist says, "Mine eyes are ever toward the Lord; for he shall pluck my feet out of the net" (Psalm 25:15). By this is meant that unless our heart is ceaselessly fixed on Christ we shall not escape the snare of temptation.

And there are many things which prevent the heart from being thus fixed on God, of which I will name three: the abundance of riches, the flattery of women, and the fairness and beauty of youth. This is a "triple-

---

2. *Lust* in Rolle, as in other fourteenth-century writers, refers not only to sexual sin but to any type of carnal or worldly appetite.

braided rope" that can scarcely be broken (Ecclesiastes 4:12); yet it must be broken and despised if Christ is to be loved.

Those who desire to love Christ truly, not only negatively (without regret) but positively (with untold joy) cast away everything that may hinder them. They spare neither father nor mother nor themselves; they receive no-one's hospitality; they are violently opposed to all that would hold them back; they break through all obstacles. The most they can do seems but a small thing for the love they bear to God. They flee from vices, and seek no worldly solace. Since they are absolutely and entirely turned towards God, they have almost forgotten the outward things of sense. They are wholly lifted up and drawn into Christ, so that when outwardly they seem to be in sorrow, they are actually wonderfully glad.

There are many who say they would turn to God, but they are held back by this or that occupation. Their lack of love we reprove with sorrow. Without doubt, if they were touched with the least spark of Christ's love, they would busily seek how they might do God's service, and they would not cease to seek until they had found the way. Often the excuse they make serves to accuse them more.

Riches draw many away, and the flattery of women beguiles many more; even those who for a long time have done well are sometimes drowned in the worst ditches. For it is all too easy to fall in love with beauty, and when such beauty feels itself loved it is all the more readily encouraged to hope for more. At last the one who is tempted by love is cast down and is made worse than he was before his conversion. His name is blackened and, from being once accounted worthy, is now despised and abhorred by all. I knew a man once of whom it was said that he disciplined his body with great severity for fifteen years and afterwards lapsed into sin with his servant's wife, refusing to be parted from her until his death. At his death, it was told how he cursed the priest who came to him, and refused to receive the sacraments.

The newly converted ought to flee the occasion of sin and with steadfast will avoid words, deeds and sights that provoke sinful thought. The more unlawful a thing is the more rigorously must it be avoided. The devil actively reproaches those whom he sees turned away from sin and converted to God, endlessly kindling fleshly and worldly desires in them. He brings to their mind the delight that they once had in sin; he makes evident the harshness and bitterness of repentance in order to make them weary of it; he raises numberless visions of evil, new thoughts and affections which hitherto were quiet and dormant. In the midst of these attacks, the penitent must rouse himself up and take arms against the devil and all his suggestions. He must subdue fleshly appetites and desire the love of God; he must depart not from God, but despise the world. Of this last point we will now speak.

II. Of the Despising of the World

To "despise" the world is, in effect, to pass through this life without giving our love to temporal and passing things: to seek nothing in this world but God, to care nothing for vainglory and comfort, to take with us the barest of essentials and, if at times we lack the necessities of life, to bear such deprivation with good will. This is "the despising of the world." Keep this standard in mind lest you perish through love of the world.

All that we love we worship.[3] It is foul to worship dirt—that is, to love earthly things. Rich men bind themselves as slaves to corruptible things, and rejoice to be called "lords of men," though they may actually be "servants of sin." If a man is a "lord of men," his position is a matter not of nature but of fortune. But if evil rule in his heart, that is the fault of his own perverse will. Put away, therefore, your wicked will, and you shall be free from the devil and from sin, and made a servant of that righteousness which teaches you not to love earthly things.

Worldly covetousness and the love of God are contraries, and cannot remain together in one soul. The place is so narrow that one or the other must be dislodged. The more you cast out covetousness the more you experience the love of God. The more you have of covetousness, the less of love.

O wretched soul, what do you seek in this world where all things are deceitful and passing away? The things that most flatter you are the quickest to deceive. Why do you busy yourself to acquire temporal possessions? Why do you yearn with great desire for things that will perish? Do you not see that they perish even before they are possessed? "I know . . . where thou dwellest, even where Satan's seat is" (Revelation 2:13). The devil himself has blinded your eyes and by his falsehoods deceived you so that you incline your heart to ephemeral things, loving that which is hateful, despising that which is abiding, and being drawn to that which perishes. Thus, you build your life on a false foundation; and when you think yourself to be standing firmly, you fall into the fire.

People who live in affluent circumstances are prone to be deceived by five things which they love: riches, dignity, independence, power and honors. They are thus enslaved to sin and imprisoned in wickedness. Indeed, they are never freed from these desires except by death.

3. *Worship* is here used in its root sense: "to ascribe worth or value to."

To be set free at the last, when only remorse is left, is to be set free too late.

These desires hinder such folk from properly despising the world, from experiencing God's love, from gaining self-knowledge, and from seeking the kingdom of heaven. No one can be saved unless he ceases to love the world with all that is in it. Cease therefore while life is yet in the body and the beauty of youth remains to you.

What things delight those who set themselves to love Christ? They will despise the rampant appetites of youth and preserve their strength for God. They will disregard riches. They will remember that favor is deceitful and beauty is vain (Proverbs 31:30). Need I write more? They will despise all things that in this world pass away as a shadow.

O lover of the flesh, what do you find in your body to cause you to take so much delight in it? Does the form or shape of it please you? Do you find your joy in a skin? Why do you not heed what is hidden under the skin? Do you not know that bodily beauty is the covering of defilement, the spark of corruption, and that it is often itself a cause of damnation? Therefore let it suffice you, all else being despised, to love God, and not depart from Him, but to cleave to Him with uncompromised desire.

The world itself leads us to despise it, since it is so full of unhappiness. We see in it continual malice, destructive persecution, increasing wrath, consuming lust, false accusations of sin, and the bitterness of slander. Here all things are confused and without order: righteousness is not loved nor truth approved; faithfulness becomes unfaithful and friendship cruel, often enduring only in prosperity and failing us in adversity.

There are still other considerations that should move us to contempt of the world—the fickleness of the times, the shortness of this life, the certainty of death's coming (and yet the uncertainty of the hour), the security of eternity, the emptiness of things present, and the prospect of the joys which are to come.

Choose what you will. If you love the world, you shall perish with it; if you love Christ, you shall reign with Him.

III. Of Poverty

"If thou wilt be perfect, go, sell all that thou hast and give it to the poor," and come and follow Christ (Matthew 19:21). In the forsaking of worldly things and in the following of Christ there is perfection. Not all people who have forsaken their goods follow Christ, for many end up worse than they were before. There are some who give themselves to back-biting, and are fearless about detracting from the good reputation of their neighbors. They swell with envy and malice; they rank themselves before all others; they praise themselves and condemn others. Think how the devil has deceived such persons. They possess neither the world nor God, while the devil leads them by various temptations into endless torment.

If you have understood what I have said, you might perhaps now consider your poverty from another point of view. When Christ says, "Go and sell," He indicates a basic change of thought and desire. He who was proud is made humble; he who was angry becomes meek; he who was envious learns charity; he who was covetous becomes generous. He who was once given to excess in meat and drink now makes amends by fasting. He who loved the world too much now gathers himself altogether into the love of Christ, and turns all the waywardness of his heart into a singleness of desire for things eternal. It is no wonder that voluntary poverty should be profitable to a person, and the harm that he suffers for God be a glorious crown. As Scripture tells us, "Blessed are the poor in spirit for theirs is the kingdom of heaven" (Matthew 5:3).

What is poverty of spirit but a meekness of mind whereby a person recognizes his own weaknesses? Since one cannot achieve steadfastness of heart except by the grace of God, he forsakes anything that might withhold that grace from him, setting his desire only on the joy of his Maker. As from a single root spring many branches, so from voluntary poverty, considered in this light, proceed virtues and wonders almost beyond conception. Yet there are some who change only their clothes and not their souls; they forsake riches, yet do not cease to gather innumerable vices.

What is worse than a proud poor man? What more cursed than an envious beggar? If you want truly to forsake all things for God, concentrate more on what you should be despising rather than merely on that which you have denied yourself. Pay diligent heed to follow Christ in your daily life. "Learn of me," he says, "for I am meek and lowly in heart" (Matthew 11:29). He says not "Learn of me for I am poor." In itself poverty is not a virtue but merely a misfortune. It is not to be commended for its own sake, but rather as an instrument of grace, and because it leads to blessedness and causes many to shun occasions of sin. For this reason, then, poverty is to be praised and desired. It is true that it prevents some from being honored, though they are virtuous, and actually causes them to be despised and oppressed and cast out by worldly people. But it is necessary for us to suffer such things for Christ's sake.

Christ, to set our example, led a life of poverty in this world, since He knew how hard it is for those who abound in riches and pleasures to enter the kingdom of heaven. In order that men should the more earnestly desire poverty, He has promised high honor and even the task of judging the world to those who forsake all material things for his sake, saying, "Ye that have [forsaken all things and] followed Me . . . shall sit on twelve thrones, judging the twelve tribes of Israel" (Matthew 19:28).

Nonetheless, those who have embraced holy poverty and still lack the meekness and lowliness that Christ teaches are more wretched than those who have plenty of riches. They shall not share the apostles' place in the day of judgment, but shall be covered with confusion, to the damnation of their body and soul, while those who shine in meekness and lowliness, even though they possess great riches, shall be set at the right hand of Christ.

Some people say, "We cannot abandon everything, we are sick, we must keep the essentials in order to live"—and this is lawful. These folk are, to be sure, less worthy, since they dare not suffer anguish, poverty and need for Christ's sake. Yet by the grace of God they may reach the height of virtue, lifting themselves to the contemplation of heavenly things, if they forsake worldly occupations and without weariness continue in meditation and prayer. And they ought not to love the goods they have, but, having them, they should draw away from them in their spirit.

Be careful to recognize that seeking more than is necessary for you is gross covetousness. To hoard up necessities for yourself is weakness. To forsake all things [for Christ's sake] is perfection. So long as you set your eyes on high things that you cannot reach, you will be prevented from pride or presumption concerning the small things which you have. In this attitude, one can attain to the right ordering of life, the subject to which we now turn.

IV. Of the Right Ordering of Life[4]

In order that one's life may be rightly directed to the worship of God,

4. This section is heavily marked by numerical patterns of arrangement, rhetorical devices often used by medieval writers (with scriptural precedent—see especially Proverbs 30) to make a text easier to remember in detail.

and to his own profit and that of his neighbor, four things must be considered.

First: What is it that defiles us? There are three sins, or three kinds of sin, namely sins of thought, word, and deed. We sin in thought when we think anything against God. Further, if we do not employ our mind with the praise and love of God, but allow it to be disturbed with other thoughts or to become empty, we have sinned in thought. We sin in word when we lie, when we swear falsely, when we curse, when we slander, when we use foolish or foul speech, or when we speak vain or idle words. We sin in deed in many ways: by lust, by sinful embraces and kisses, by willful defilement, or by allowing, without great cause, occasions to arise in which we know we may be defiled. Sins in deed also include robbing, stealing, deceiving or smiting others, and other similar actions.

Secondly: What are the things that cleanse us? These are three also, and counter the three sources of defilement.[5] The first is contrition of thought, and a rooting out of all desires that have no reference to the praise and worship of God and his love. The second is confession of the mouth, that ought to be early and complete. The third is satisfaction of deed, which has, in turn, three parts: fasting (because the sin is against oneself), prayer (because the sin is against God), and almsgiving (because the sin is against one's neighbor). Alms must never, however, be given out of someone else's goods; anything that has been taken from another must be restored, for sin is not forgiven unless restoration is made for that which has been taken.

Thirdly: What things make for cleanness of heart? There are three. The first is a consistent awareness of God, so that there is no moment when you do not think of Him, except in sleep which is common to all. The second is a careful guarding of your physical senses, so that tasting, hearing, and seeing may be wisely restrained, bridled and governed. The third is honest occupation, such as reading the Scripture, speaking of God, writing, or other similarly good activity.

There are three things also that preserve cleanness of word: consideration in speech, avoidance of excessive talking, and a hatred of lying.

And three things help us keep purity in work: moderation in food and drink, avoidance of bad company, and constant remembrance of our mortality.

Fourthly: What things are they which lead us to conformity with the will of God? These also are three. They are: the example of creatures,

---

5. The three actions of repentance were typically described as contrition (sorrow of heart), confession (admission of guilt), and satisfaction (doing something to remedy the wrong).

which is learned by observation; familiarity with God, which is reached by meditation and prayer; and awareness of the joy of heaven, which is felt in part by contemplation.

The godly person, living in this way, shall be as a tree that is planted by the waterside—that is, the stream of grace—so that he shall always be green in virtue and never dried up by sin. Moreover he shall bring forth fruit in due season (Psalm 1)—that is, he shall do good works as an example, and speak good words to the worship of God, and not for personal vainglory. (When he says "in due season," the Psalmist speaks against those who fast when they should feast, and feast when they should fast, as well as against covetous men who delay to give their fruit until it is rotten, or until they die.)

It is wise for us to pray thus: "Teach me thy good judgment and knowledge" (Psalm 119:66). For what is the effect of good judgment but a correcting of behavior? At first we are taught righteousness, and corrected by discipline; later we come to know what we should do and what we should shun. In the end we delight not in earthly things, but in things eternal, heavenly, and divine.

When someone in all diligence has set himself to do the will of his Maker and has so grown in virtue that he has overtaken another person in the spiritual life, both in steadfastness of purpose and in longing for Christ, he ought not on that account to rejoice or praise himself, or consider himself better than the other person. Such a person should rather esteem himself worse, and his performance more miserable.

You should judge no one but yourself, and esteem all others before yourself. You should not desire to be called holy by other people but rather to be despised by the world. When you come among other folk you should seek to be the last and least thought of, for the greater your position the more you should make yourself meek in all things. So shall you find grace in the sight of God, and be made high. The power of God is great and held in honor by the meek; it is therefore despised by the proud, who seek not the worship of God but only their own satisfactions.

If you receive with great pleasure the favor of people and the honor of men for your holiness and good reputation in this life, truly you have received your reward. If you appear to be exceptional in penitence and chastity, and find yourself on this account rejoicing more with the joy of men than of angels, in the time to come nothing but torment awaits you. What you should rather do is to learn utterly to despise yourself, forsaking the pleasures of the world, and to think and do nothing except for the sake of God's love, so that the whole of your life, inward and outward, may voice aloud the praise of God.

In food and drink be sparing and wise. In eating or drinking, do not forget that it is God who feeds you. Praise, bless, and glorify Him in every morsel, so that your heart is more concerned with the praise of God than with your food; your soul will not then be parted at any moment from Him. So doing, in the sight of Jesus Christ, you shall be thought worthy of a crown, and shall avoid the temptations of the devil that wait to deceive so many in the matter of food and drink.

By taking too much food, many are cast down from the height of virtue; others, by excessive abstinence undermine that virtue. You will have observed persons who are wildly irregular in their eating habits, so that they always take either too little or too much, never acquiring a reasonable balance but imagining first one style and then the other to be better. The ignorant and unlearned, who have never felt the sweetness of Christ's love, imagine that holiness consists in extravagant abstinence, and they believe that they cannot be worthy of the praise of God unless they be known by everybody to be remarkable for their frugality and asceticism.

Abstinence of itself is not holiness; it is only virtuous when it helps us to be holy. If it is unwise, it actually prevents holiness, because it undermines mature discipline, without which virtues become vices. Anyone who wishes to be markedly abstemious ought to shun the presence of other persons and their praises lest he become proud and so lose everything, for people too readily consider the most frugal to be the holiest, whereas they are often the greatest sinners. Whoever has really tasted the sweetness of God's eternal love will never consider himself to exceed anyone in abstinence. Ironically, the more apparent his lowly estimation of himself the more remarkable is he likely to be esteemed by others.

The best thing and, I suppose, the most pleasing to God, is simply to conform your practice in eating and drinking to the time, place, and condition of those you are with. Then you will not be considered condescending or hypocritical.

You can be sure that if one or two think well of such a person as I have described, there will be others who call him a hypocrite or a deceiver. Some people are indeed so desirous of flattery that they refuse to be regarded as ordinary. They either eat so little that they occasion comments or they make a fuss about procuring unusual foods in order to appear different from others. May any such folly and stubbornness be far from me!

It is, however, a wholesome thing for those who fast little to give preference to those who fast much, and to grieve inwardly that they cannot practice such abstinence. Those who fast much should likewise respect others whose virtues are more hidden. For such virtues may indeed exceed those of their own abstinence, which readily earns the praise of many. Unless it is clothed with meekness and charity, austerity is of no account with Christ.

The virtue of some people is truly the greater in that it is not readily seen. Who can tell how much love a person has towards God, or how much compassion towards his neighbor? The work of charity exceeds beyond all comparison the mere practice of fasting or abstinence, and all other works that may be seen by others. Indeed, it often happens that one who in the sight of others is seen least to fast, is inwardly and before Christ most fervent in love.

A healthly constitution is required of anyone who wants to exercise the love of God in a mature way. Often a person is actually prevented from praying because the body is so weakened; he is thus less able to lift himself up to high things even with fervent desire. I would rather a person failed for the extravagance of love (as even the bride of the Canticles said of herself, "I am sick with love" [Song of Solomon 5:8]) than from too much fasting.

Therefore, be steadfast in all your ways, and order your life according to the model which has been set before you. If you do not obtain your desires at first, do not fall into doubt, but be patient; for with time and experience you will progress toward perfection.

Perhaps you are a pilgrim, or perhaps you rest by the way. Whatever you do in this life, have an eye to God. Do not let your thought go from Him, and count as wasted that time in which you have not kept Him in mind. Praise Him and seek his love during the night, so that sleep may find you occupied in prayer and meditation upon Him. See that your mind is not filled with vain thoughts or occupied with other considerations, but strive to attain and hold fast this purity of focus, so that you neither dread the misery of this world nor desire immoderately to possess its good things. Whoever is afraid to suffer adversity has not yet learned properly to despise the world, and whoever rejoices in worldly things is far from things eternal.

It is proper to the grace of abstinence to give more thought to eternal life than to adversity or prosperity, or indeed to death itself. True love is the desire for heavenly things alone. A perfect lover rejoices to die, and patiently suffers in this life. If, by the grace of Christ, you reach such perfection in love, you will not, of course, be without tribulation and temptation. This we will consider in the next chapter.

V. Of Tribulation

When the devil sees one person out of thousands completely turned to

God, following in the footsteps of Christ, despising this present world, loving and seeking only things unseen, being utterly repentant, and cleansing his life from its evils of mind and body, he prepares a thousand deceptions to harm that person and a thousand means to bend him away from the love of God. He seeks to entice such a person into love of the world, to fill him again with the wickedness of sin so that at the very least by unclean thoughts he should be made an offense to God. He brings against this person persecution, tribulation, slander, false accusations of sin, and all kinds of hatred so that pain may wound and slay him, even if he is above being tempted by prosperity.

At one moment Satan puts before him life's adversities, at another luxury, or he brings to mind the remembrance of carnal appetites. He gathers together visions of sin. He recalls old wickedness, and the delights of past love. He enflames heart and body with sexual fire. He begins with the least but goes on to the greatest flames of wickedness. With great energy he tries to bring against us all kinds of temptation, torment and tribulation; and he is sorrowful if we, by the mercy of God, have escaped his designs. He does not do anything which is not intended to separate us from the spiritual embrace, most sweet and chaste, of everlasting love, and then to defile us in the pit of degradation. And that fate is more wicked than tongue can tell.

Who would not think a person mad who left the delicacies of the king's table for swine's food? Yet he is even more demented who forsakes the delicious meat of uncreated wisdom and lowers himself to the filthiest order of the flesh. Are not gluttony and lust like the husks which the swine eat, and those who indulge in such things effectively eating the devil's food?

Therefore patience must teach us how to resist the tribulation and temptation of our enemies and to stand against them. Of this we will now speak.

VI. Of Patience

God's children disdain to eat the food of irrational animals, despising unlawful appetites and worldly comfort for the love of Christ. One who is truly being fed with the bread that comes down from heaven in no way desires the inferior things offered him by the devil. And when temptation or tribulation arise, he sees that spiritual armor must be put on, for it is time to go to battle.

Temptations are overcome by steadfast faith and love, tribulation by patience. What is patience but the voluntary suffering of adversity?

One who is patient does not murmur at grievances but finds profit in every circumstance, always praising God. The more patient a person is under provocation the more glorious shall he be in heaven.

Tribulation is to be endured cheerfully, whether it comes to us as adversity, annoyance and bitterness, or pain, sickness and thirst, for by these experiences and others like them our sinful nature is made clean, and our reward increased. We must either be consumed with the fire of God's love and accept tribulation in this life or else be most bitterly crucified and punished in the fires of hell in the next. Choose therefore: you must endure one or the other. Here and now with relatively little pain—indeed, with joy if we cleave to God—we may escape all pain to come.

Tribulations are sent to us, therefore, to call us from the love of the world, so that we will not be sorely punished in the life to come. By sorrow we must be cleansed from the stains of lust. If sinners "plow upon our backs and make long furrows" (Psalm 129:3), they do not trouble us so much as themselves, if we are able to endure with patience. If they put us to a little pain they lay up a crown for us, but torment for themselves.

The wicked are often allowed to pass through this life without great tribulation, but in the time to come no joy is left for them. Therefore godly persons welcome tribulations for they know that through such experiences they will win endless life. On the other hand, the lost always murmur under adversities, and flee from them as much as they can. As long as they are given overly much to the things of this life, they are deprived of the hope of things eternal. Only in outward circumstances can they find comfort, since they have entirely lost the desire for heavenly things.

There is no soul on earth that does not love either creatures or the Creator. If it loves the creatures it loses God and goes down with the creature it has loved to death. All such love is, in the beginning, labor and foolishness; in the middle of things it passes into weariness and unhappiness, and it ends in hatred and pain.

One who truly loves his Maker forsakes all that is in the world, and counts it all joy and sweetness to speak of Him and with Him; his refreshment is the thought of God. He restrains his outward senses lest death should enter by the window, and he become unprofitably occupied in vain concerns. Sometimes despising, reproof, scorn and slander are raised against him; in such cases, he takes up the shield of patience and is more ready to forget than to remember wrongs. Such a person will pray for the conversion of those who hate and attack him, and will not concern himself with pleasing man, but rather fear to offend God.

If you are tempted in the flesh, learn to discipline your body so that the spirit will not be undermined. Temptation to which we do not consent results in the strengthening of virtue. For no one knows whether he is weak or strong until he is tested. Likewise no one is called patient when all goes well, but only when he is oppressed by misfortune; then he shall know if he possesses the grace of patience. Many seem patient as long as they are not pricked, but when a soft wind—not of misfortune but only of correction—touches them, their minds turn at once to bitterness and wrath. If they hear a single word uttered against them they give back two even more ungodly in return. I pray that my own soul may withstand this temptation.

The fiery darts of the enemy are to be quenched with the meekness and sweetness of Christ's love. Nor is it proper to give place to temptation, however grievous it may be. For the greater the battle the more worthy the victory and the more noble the crown, for it is written: "Blessed is the man that endureth temptation: for when he is tried, he shall receive the crown of life which the Lord hath promised to them that love him" (James 1:12).

Rest assured that you are progressing toward a perfected life if contempt has become to you almost like praise, poverty like riches, hunger like having plenty to eat, and if you suffer these things with an even disposition. Flee, and hate as much as you can the praise of men, for you are most truly praiseworthy if your praiseworthiness is not celebrated by others. Flatterers' tongues beguile many, just as by the tongues of backbiters many are destroyed. Despise therefore the currying of favor, the worship of men, and all vainglory; endure with meekness wrath, hatred and all detractions, so that whether by slander or by good report you are not impeded in traveling toward the kingdom of heaven.

Often we fall in order that, taught by many a hard experience, we may stand more firmly. The strong do not fear, nor are the patient made sorrowful, in adversity. It is in this sense that the Scriptures say, "There shall no evil happen to the just" (Proverbs 12:21). With such a disposition, it will be no wonder if you overcome all temptations and quench all malice. You will see that your detractors are far less happy than you are. For yourself, with all your mind cleave to Christ.

VII. Of Prayer

When you are set upon by temptation or tribulation, have recourse at once to prayer. If you pray fervently you shall have help. Sometimes you will be troubled by distractions and waverings of heart, and thoughts of different kinds will fill your mind, getting in the way of your praise of God. At such times it is good to meditate upon holiness, until your mind becomes more stable and your prayers thus become more effectual.

If any have left all worldly occupations for the love of God and are continually given to holy prayer and meditation, within a short time, by the grace of God, they will find their heart established in love and prayer. They will no longer waver between this and that, but remain in rest and lasting peace.

It is a source of great strength to have a steadfast heart occupied in frequent prayer and the singing of psalms. By diligent prayer we overcome our adversary, weakening his attacks and provocations. He is enfeebled and without power as long as we continue unwearied in strong prayer.

Those who have made it their custom to pray for a long time sometimes find in their prayers a greater sweetness and more fervent desire than usual. While that sweetness and warmth last it is good for them not to cease from prayer. And when they cease—as sometimes happens because the flesh is weak—they should turn to the reading of Holy Scripture or do some other profitable thing so that they do not allow their thoughts to wander from God. Thus, when they turn to prayer again, they may be more alert than they were before.

We truly pray well when we think of nothing else, but have all our thoughts turned toward heaven, and our soul inflamed with the fire of the Holy Spirit. In this way a wonderful abundance of God's goodness will be found in us; for from the innermost depths of our heart the love of God shall rise, and all our prayer will be fervent and effectual. We will not hurry over the words but with great conviction and urgency offer every syllable to the Lord.

Our heart being thus kindled with the fire of love, our prayer will also be kindled and offered by our lips with great sweetness in the sight of God, so that it becomes a great joy to pray. And when this great sweetness is given to one who prays, his prayer is transformed into songs of praise.

Some people are foolish, paying more heed to meditation than to prayer, not realizing that God's "speech" is a consuming fire; so that as we use it in prayer the wickedness of sin is burnt up, and the mind inflamed with love.[6] They say that they will first meditate and so estab-

6. See "On Prayer," the selection from Walter Hilton's *Ladder of Perfection,* and the section on common prayer, both in Part Two below.

lish their hearts; but such folk are actually established more slowly, since they are not first strengthened by prayer.

Although we cannot compose our hearts as perfectly as we should like, we should not cease from trying. Little by little, we should steadily grow in prayer so that Jesus Christ may establish us at the last. To this end, meditation is indeed a help, if it is not over-indulged in measure or manner.

VIII. Of Meditation

It is good to meditate upon the passion and death of Christ, and frequently to remember how much pain and grief He freely endured for our sake in his earthly life, as he went about preaching in the midst of hunger, thirst, cold, heat, reproaches, cursings and sufferings. If we remember this, it ought not to grieve his unprofitable servants to follow their Lord and King.

One who says he dwells in Christ ought to walk as He did. Christ says (speakingthrough Jeremiah):[7] "Remember mine affliction and my misery, the wormwood and the gall" (Lamentations 3:19)—that is to say, that sorrow and bitterness by which He went from the world to the Father.

This concentration or meditation upon the passion and death of Christ overcomes the devil and destroys his crafts; it quenches the temptations of the flesh and kindles the soul with the love of Christ; it raises, cleanses and purifies the mind. It is the most profitable subject of meditation for those who are newly converted to Christ. It sets forth the perfect manhood of Jesus Christ in which we should always rejoice, and in which the Christian has occasion both for joy and for sorrow. The joy, of course, is for the certainty of our redemption; our sorrow is for our sinful wickedness, for which so extravagant a sacrifice was offered. The superficial and carnal soul is not enraptured by the contemplation of the perfect Godhead until all fleshly hindrances are done away with through meditation and contemplation.

When someone begins to have a clean heart, and no vision of earthly things can any longer beguile him, then he is admitted to higher things, so that in the love of God he may be made wonderfully glad. Some think about the joy of the blessed angels and holy souls rejoicing with Christ; and this is a part of true contemplation. Some meditate upon the misery of man's condition and his sin, and in their thought thus counter

7. This passage was read typologically, much like Psalm 22, as referring to Christ's suffering.

our human tendency to forget unseen joys, being preoccupied instead with the vanities of this present life.

Others despise their thoughts in such a way as to want nothing but the praise and desire of their Maker, so that they may love Him as much as is possible for us in this life. To such a meditation no one comes except one who is well versed in those things I have already mentioned. But this last is the best type of meditation and makes a person most truly contemplative.

We see that as the lives and habits of the saints vary, so also do their styles of meditation. Yet, as they all spring from one source in Christ, all reach the same goal and happiness. They may go by different routes, yet all through that same charitable love, even though it can seem more evident in one person than another. For this reason the Psalmist writes, "He shall lead me in the paths of righteousness" (Psalm 23:3), as if to say that while there is one righteousness, there are many paths by which we are led to the joy of everlasting life. Though all are one in being, we are different in needs and are led to God by various means. Some go by a low path, some by a middle, and some by a high. The higher path is given to one who is ordained to love Christ more intensely, not because he works more than others, or gives or suffers more, but because he loves more. Yet this love is a warmth and sweetness which seeks a dwelling in everyone.

No one may set his own feet in any of these paths, except that it be the one which God has chosen for him. Sometimes those who seem to be in the higher path are actually in the lower, and the lower in the higher, for the journey of the soul toward God is an interior one and does not consist in any outward form of living which a person may practice. According to the disposition and desire of one's meditation he is prepared for one path or another. But no one's place in the sight of God may be judged by outward works. Therefore it is foolish to attempt to judge who are the elect of God and to say "So-and-so surpasses another," or "This one's merits are far below this other's," when plainly we do not see into their minds. If we did, we might legitimately judge.

It is God's will, therefore, to keep these things hidden, lest people despise some too much or pay too much honor to others. For doubtless if they could but see into the human heart they would despise many whom they now honor, and others whom they do not much esteem or desire to see, they would honor as most worthy of love; indeed, they might honor them as much as the holy angels.

The good thoughts and meditations of the elect are a gift of God, which He provides to each in accordance with his state and condition. Therefore I can tell you how I meditate, but I cannot say what would be the best method for you, since I do not see your inward desires. I am sure that those meditations are most pleasing to God and profitable to you which God in his mercy sends you.

Nevertheless, at first you may make use of the words of others: that I know by experience. If you despise the teaching of learned and saintly people, imagining that you can find something better yourself than they teach you in their writings, then know of a certainty that you shall not taste the love of Christ. It is foolish to say, "God taught them, why should He not teach me?" I answer, "Because you are not such as they were." In such a mood you are proud and obstinate, and they were meek and lowly; they asked nothing of God in presumption but, humbling themselves, took knowledge from the saints before them. He taught them so that we might be taught by them in turn through their books.

If you truly desire the love of Christ in your meditation, or yearn to sing his praises, then you are in the right disposition. But exercise in those meditations in which you feel the most sweetness in God is by far the most profitable for you. For to meditate well, but without this presence of his Spirit, profits you little.

IX. Of Reading

If you want to experience the love of God and are afire for the joys of heaven, and if you would learn to shun earthly things, do not be negligent in reading and meditating on the Holy Scripture, especially those parts where it teaches godly behavior and the means of escaping the wiles of the devil. Read also where it tells of the love of God and speaks about the spiritual life. Hard sayings may be left to arguers and to intelligent persons well trained in doctrine.

Reading of the Holy Scriptures helps us greatly to acquire habits of holiness. By it we learn to distinguish between our faults and our good deeds, occasions in which we sin and those in which we do not, what we should do and what we should avoid; the most subtle deceits of our adversary are also laid open before us. The Holy Scriptures kindle within us the fire of love and move us to penitence. If we delight in them, as in all manner of riches, they spread before us a veritable banquet of delights.

But let it not be that desire for honor, favor or the praise of others incites us to the study of Holy Scripture, but rather a pure intention to please God. Our purpose should be to know how to love Him, and to teach our neighbors the same. We ought not to seek to be reputed wise by others; we should prefer to hide our knowledge rather than exhibit it for the sake of praise. Consider the Psalmist, who said, "Thy word have I hid in my heart, that I might not sin against thee" (Psalm 119:11); and you can be sure that sin includes empty or vain expositions.

The sole cause of our speaking should be the praise of God and the edification of our neighbors, that the saying of the Psalmist may be fulfilled in us: "His praise shall continually be in my mouth" (Psalm 34:1). That happens only when we are not seeking our own honor, or speaking in a manner which contradicts praise of Him.

X. Of Purity of Heart

By the nine degrees of spiritual progress I have already touched upon one may attain to that purity of heart wherewith he may enjoy a vision of God. Yes, I am speaking of purity which may be had in the pilgrimage of this life.

You may ask: how may perfect purity be reached here where so often man is defiled at the very least by venial sin? Even the feet of the saints need to be washed, since they draw upon themselves the dust of the earth. Who can truly say, "I am free from sin"? No one in this life; for as Job says, "If I wash myself with snow water, and make my hands ever so clean; yet shalt thou plunge me in the ditch, and mine own clothes shall abhor me" (Job 9:30-31). "If I wash myself with snow water" speaks of true repentance; "and make my hands ever so clean" of works of innocence. "Yet shalt thou plunge me in the ditch" is a reminder of venial sins that cannot be avoided. By "mine own clothes shall abhor me" is meant "my flesh makes me loathe myself, and my sensual nature, which is so frail, slippery and ready to love the beauty of this world, often makes me sin." The Apostle said, "Let not sin reign in your mortal body" (Romans 6:12), which is to say, "Sin is bound to be present in us, but it need not rule over us."

What purity therefore can one have in this life? Truly we may have great purity if we accustom ourselves to reading Scripture, prayer and meditation as we have said before. Though we sometimes commit a venial offence, yet quickly, because our whole heart is turned to God, that sin is destroyed. The flame of love in us burns off all the rust of sin as if it were a drop of water cast into a blazing fire.

The character of a renewed and cleansed soul is therefore a mind which is set upon God, for in this state all thoughts are directed toward Christ and our whole heart spread out before Him, ready to be ordered according to his Word. In a clean conscience nothing is bitter, sharp or hard, but all sweet and lovely, and out of a pure heart rises the song of joy, sweet melody and joyful mirth. A wonderful joy toward God is offered up, and heavenly melodies are poured out in the soul. In this state one can know that he is in a state of love which he need never lose. Henceforth he fears not that he might suffer torment, but only that he might offend his Lover. I hesitate to say more, since I know myself to be so great a sinner: too often my own flesh is attacked and assailed.

Now, though much that pertains to the love of God and a contemplative life is included in the things already said, yet there is somewhat more to be added for the reader's profit.

XI. Of the Love of God[8]

"O my Maker unmade, uncircumscribed who all things dost circumscribe, most sweet and pleasant light, enlighten the keenness of my spiritual sight with eternal brightness of perspective, so that my mind, being cleansed from all uncleanness and made marvellous in gifts of the Spirit, may swiftly pass to the joyful heights of love. There let me be kindled by thy love, that I may sit and rest at thy feet, rejoicing in thee, Lord Jesus. Thus enraptured with divine sweetness and established in the vision of things unseen, I shall be never made glad except by thy Spirit."

"O everlasting Love, enflame my soul with the love of God, so that nothing but his embraces may set my heart on fire. O good Jesus, who shall make me to feel thee here, who may not now be either felt or seen? O pour out thy very self into the depths of my soul! Enter into my heart and fill it with thy sweetness. Refresh my mind with the strong wine of thy love, that, forgetting all ills, scornful of vain imaginations, and having only thee, I may be glad and rejoice in Jesus my God. Leave me not, most sweet Lord, but stay with me forever; for in thy presence alone is my comfort, and apart from thee I am heavy with sorrow."

"O Holy Spirit, thou who dost breathe upon whom thou wilt, enter into me and draw me up to thyself. Transform the nature which thou hast made with heavenly gifts that my soul, filled with thy joy, may despise the things of this world and cast them off. May she receive spiritual gifts from thee, the Giver, and entering by happiness into light unspeakable be all consumed by holy love. Burn up my inward parts and all my heart with thy fire, and my heart will burn forever on thine altar!"

"O sweet, true Glory, I pray thee come! Come, most sweet and most

---

8. This section is really less a guide to or discussion of its subject than itself a kind of spiritual exercise, a series of ecstatic prayers to God often addressing Christ as "Love," as in the hymn, "Love Divine, All Loves Excelling." I have deleted some of the prayers from this and the next section simply because they tend to be repetitive.

desired! Come, my Beloved who art all my comfort! Enter into this soul that longs for thee. Kindle with thy warmth new health in my heart; with thy light lighten my inmost parts; feed me with heavenly songs of love until I want no more."

You should rejoice your heart in this sort of meditative prayer, so that you may thus attain to the heart of love. Love suffers no loving soul to dwell alone but draws it to its Lover, so that the soul is more at home in that place where it loves than the body ever is.

Now there are three degrees of the love of Christ: the first is called "all-surpassing"; the second, "undivided"; and the third, "solitary."[9]

Love is "all-surpassing" when it cannot be overcome by any other desire, when it casts away hindrances and quenches all temptations and fleshly lusts, when it patiently suffers all hardships for Christ and is not overcome by any flattery or indulgence. Every labor is light to a lover, nor can one labor more effectively than for the sake of love.

Love is "undivided" when the mind is on fire with a great love, and cleaves to Christ with unswerving attention. It suffers Him not to depart for an instant, but as if bound in heart to Him, thinks and sighs after Him, crying out to be held by His love alone and loosened from the fetters of mortality, to be alone with Him who is the joy of our desiring. So much does such a heart worship and love the name Jesu that this name is constantly informing each thought.

Where the love of Christ is so firmly fixed in the heart of one who loves God and despises the world that no other love can root it out, it may be called "high" [or "all-surpassing"]. When a person holds unswervingly to Christ, ever remembering and never forgetting Him, it may be called "everlasting" or "undivided." If indeed such love is high and everlasting, you may ask, what could be higher or greater?

Yet there is a third stage of love. It is called singular or "solitary." It is one thing to be high, and another to be alone. If you seek or receive any comfort apart from God, though you perhaps love Him in the highest of degrees, such is not yet a truly singular love. You see then to what heights you must attain before you are alone. Love reaches the solitary degree only when it excludes all comfort but that which is in Jesus and when nothing but Jesus can suffice.

The soul has achieved this degree when it loves Him alone. She yearns for Christ and desires only Him. She waits and sighs for Him; in Him she is on fire; in Him alone she is warmed and set at her rest. Noth-

---

9. In Rolle's text, the terms are *insuperable, inseparable,* and *singular,* the meanings of which are clear enough in Latin but which now require a less latinate translation.

ing is sweet to her, nor does anything have savor for her except it be made sweet in Jesus, whose presence in the mind is as a song of music in a feast of wine. Whatever the soul has to offer or brings to mind is immediately spurned and despised unless it accords with the will of Jesus. She suppresses all habits that do not bring her to the love of Christ. Whatever she does seems to be unprofitable and unendurable unless it leads to Christ, the goal of her desire. When she has learned to love Christ she knows that she has all that she desires, and without Him all things are distasteful to her. Because she desires to love Him eternally she remains steadfast and does not grow weary in body or in soul. Rather, she loves with perseverance and suffers all things gladly. The more she thus lives in Him, the more will she burn with love and the more like Him she will become.

Such singular intensity of love is well suited to one who finds few close companions among men and women. The more enraptured such a person is with inward joy, the less he is concerned with outward things; nor is he likely to be held back by the temptations and cares of this life. It seems almost as if the soul could become immune to pain, since she rejoices in God forever. Such charitable love is the noblest, the most excellent, the sweetest of all virtues, that brings the lover to the Beloved and joins Christ to his elect. It forms in us again the image of the Holy Trinity, and makes the creature resemble the Creator.

O gift of love, how worthy it is, that reaches to the highest place the angels have! The more love we receive in this life the greater and higher shall be our place in heaven. O singular joy of everlasting love that ravishes all those who are in Christ to the heavenly places, holding them there fast and secure!

"O dear Charity! No one is yet a finished creation, whatever else he may possess, unless he has thee. One who is occupied in rejoicing in thee is at once raised above earthly things. You alone enter into the bedchamber of the Everlasting King. You alone, Charity, are not ashamed to receive Christ, since you have sought and loved Him. Christ is yours; you can hold Him, since Christ cannot fail to receive her whose desire is to obey Him. Without charity no work is pleasing to God. She makes all things delightful to Him. Charity is a seat in heaven, in the fellowship of the angels, a marvellous holiness, a blessed vision, and the true state of everlasting life."

"O holy Love, how sweet thou art and full of comfort; thou dost make whole again that which was broken. Thou restorest the fallen and settest the captive free; thou makest mankind to be equal with angels. Thou liftest up those who are downtrodden, and those who are raised thou dost endow with sweetness."

In this degree love is chaste, holy and freely given, loving that which is loved for its own sake and not for any advantage, and uniting itself to that which is loved. Seeking nothing outward, content with itself, burning, fragrant, it draws love in itself in a manner passing all description. Rejoicing in the loved one, despising and forgetting all else, reaching upward in desire, overwhelmed in his love, continuing in embraces, overcome by his kisses, the soul is altogether consumed in the fire of love.

So then, the lover of Christ keeps no check upon his love and covets no position in the heart of God, because however fervent and joyful he is in the love of God, in this life, he wants only to love Him more and more. Yes, and if such a one might live evermore in this life, he would never stand still or fail to make progress in love; the longer he lived, the more he would burn with love.

God is truly of infinite greatness, more than we can think. He is of unspeakable sweetness, unknowable by created things, and can never be comprehended by us as He is in Himself. But even here and now, whenever the heart begins to burn with a desire for God, she is made able to receive that uncreated light and, inspired and fulfilled by the gifts of the Holy Spirit, she tastes the joys of heaven. She transcends all visible things and is raised up to the sweetness of eternal life. When the heart is filled with the sweetness of the Godhead and the fire of creating light, she offers herself in sacrifice to the everlasting King, and, being accepted, is wholly consumed.

"O joyous love, strong, ravishing, burning, freely offered, courageous, unquenched, that subdues all my heart to thy service and suffers it not to think of anything except thee: thou claimest for thyself all my life, my delight, and my very being."

Let Christ, whom we love for Himself, be the beginning of our love. So shall we love appropriately whatever claims our love, for the sake of Him who is the well of love. Into His hands we commend all those we love and those who love us. Herein truly is perfect love; when all the intents of our mind, all the secret workings of our heart are lifted up into the love of God, so that the power and joy of true love is so great that worldly happiness and material possessions are no longer defended because they are "lawful," nor do they seem any longer even pleasant.

"O Love that will not let us go! O unique and solitary love!"

Even if there were no torments for the wicked nor rewards for the chosen, you ought not to be separated from God's holy love. It would be better for you to endure untold grief than once to fall into deadly sin. Love God for Himself and for no other reason, and it follows that nothing but God Himself will satisfy you. How can God be all in all, if there is worship in our hearts for any other?

"O pure and perfect Love, come unto me and take me into thee, and so present me before God. Thou art pleasant to the taste, a sweet-smelling fragrance, a cleansing fire, and an everlasting comfort. Thou makest hearts to be contemplative; thou openest the gate of heaven; thou shuttest the mouths of accusers; thou makest God to be seen; and thou coverest a multitude of sins. We praise thee, we preach thee, by thee we overcome the world. In thee we rejoice and by thee we ascend the ladder of heaven. In thy sweetness enter into me; I commend me and my house to thee forever."

XII. Conclusion

Let me then summarize. Contemplative life, or contemplation, has three parts: reading, prayer and meditation. In the reading of Scriptures God speaks to us; in prayer we speak to God. In meditation, it is as if angels come down and teach us in order that we not go wrong; in prayer, they ascend and offer our words to God—acting, thus, as messengers between ourselves and Him.

To reading belongs intellectual activity and the search for truth, which is the light of the soul. To prayer belongs praise, song, vision, and wonder; and thus the contemplative life and contemplation itself is founded upon prayer. Meditation is concerned with God's immediate inspiration, with understanding, wisdom and desire.

Contemplation itself is harder to define. Some say it consists in the knowledge of things hidden and to come, or the withdrawal from worldly occupation, or the study of God's Word. Others maintain that contemplation is an open vision of spiritual wisdom when the heart is lifted up in wonderment. Others say that a contemplative life is like an open book, spread with blank pages on which the Spirit may write—a kind of openness of the soul. Some say, and say well, that contemplation is joy in heavenly things. And still others say, and say best of all, that contemplation is the death of all carnal desire through the joy of an uplifted heart.

To me it seems that contemplation is the joyful song of God's love sounding in one's mind and heart. This rejoicing is the end of perfect prayer and the highest devotion in this life. This is the spiritual joy of the heart towards its eternal Lover, which breaks forth into loud rejoicing. This is the richest and most perfect of all the actions of this life. Therefore the Psalmist says, "Blessed is the people that know the joyful sound: they shall walk, O Lord, in the joy of thy countenance" (Psalm 89:15), that is, in heavenly contemplation.

Anyone who dwells apart from God cannot rejoice in Jesus, or taste the sweetness of his love. If we yearn to be forever kindled with the fire of everlasting love, and to be made fair, with all purity of body and soul, and to be touched with the anointing of the Spirit, then we need to be lifted up in all patience, humility, and gentleness to contemplation.

Let us, without ceasing, seek for virtues, by which we are cleansed from sin in this life: then in another life, free from all pain, we may forever rejoice in the life of the blessed. Moreover, in this present exile also, we will be counted worthy to feel the joyful gladness of God's love. Do not be slow to discipline yourself with prayer and vigils, and make use of holy meditation, for with these spiritual labors, and with sorrow and weeping from inward repentance, the love of Christ is kindled and all the virtues and gifts of the Holy Spirit are shed abroad in your heart.

Begin therefore with voluntary poverty. When you are no longer desirous of anything in this world, you will be able to live in sobriety, chastity and humility before God and man. In the course of things it happens to some of us that we have nothing in this world; for all of us, however, the desire to have nothing is a great virtue. We may have many needs. Even so, we will be in the state of desiring to have nothing so long as we are using what we do have only to supply our needs and not our appetites. Someone who seems to have many things may, in this way, really possess nothing for he does not love what he has, but only uses it for his bodily needs. Even those who are most perfected in love must have necessities. To refuse to take the essentials of life can, indeed, be a contradiction of perfection.

The rule of life for those who desire perfection should be first of all to despise all worldly goods for God's sake and yet, of course, to accept from the world both food and clothing. If these are lacking at any time we are not to murmur but to praise God, and as far as possible, we should refuse all excess. The warmer we grow with the fire of everlasting light, the more meekly we will behave in times of adversity.

One who is meek and without any pretense considers himself to merit contempt, and is not provoked to wrath by harm or reproof. Such a person, giving himself to continual meditation, is permitted to ascend to the contemplation of heavenly things. His inward vision being cleansed by his bodily sufferings, it is granted him to sing sweetly and ardently with spiritual joy. Even when he is concerned with outward things, the humble person does not go about his tasks with a proud step, but is made glad, enraptured as in an ecstasy, with the sweetness of God's love, and wondrously happy.

Such is the contemplative life when it is approached in the right way. By constant practice of spiritual disciplines we come to the contemplation of eternal truths. The eyes of the mind are occupied with the vision of heavenly things, though not, of course, with perfect clarity. So long as we walk by faith we see, as it were, only shadowy reflections in a mirror. Yet if our inward vision is turned toward that spiritual radiance, even though we see it not as it is in itself we may nevertheless detect its presence, since we receive within ourselves the fragrance and heat of that unknown light.

There is a psalm which says, "The darkness and the light are both alike to thee" (Psalm 139:12). Although all the truly dark things of sin are cleansed from a sanctified soul and unclean things have passed away, and although the heart is purified and enlightened, yet so long as we dwell in this life that wonderful light is not seen by us in its heavenly perfection. Holy and contemplative people behold the face of God through revelation. That is, either their minds are opened and made sensitive through an understanding of the Scriptures or else the door of heaven is opened to them in a direct revelation of the Spirit. This latter experience may be explained as one in which all hindrances between themselves and God are put away, their hearts are cleansed, and they behold the citizens of heaven. Some have experienced both these kinds of special joy.

As we see nothing if we stand in the darkness, so when contemplation enlightens the soul there is no visible light. Christ makes the darkness his resting place and speaks to us out of the midst of a cloudy pillar. Nevertheless, that which is experienced is full of heavenly delight.

This is the perfection of love: when a person, dwelling in the flesh, can rejoice only in God, and wills and desires nothing but God, or for God's sake. By this it is clear that holiness does not consist merely in heartfelt crying or tears [of penitence], or in outward works, but in the sweetness of perfect charity and heavenly contemplation. Many are momentarily full of tears and crying, and afterwards will turn away to do evil; but no one defiles himself with worldly concerns if he has learned to rejoice in everlasting love. Tears and sorrow belong to the newly-converted, to beginners and those who are making progress; but to sing with joy and to proceed to contemplation is the mark of those who have attained greater perfection.

Contemplative sweetness is only reached with great effort. To be sure, it is not of man's merit, but God's gift. Yet do not be deceived. From the earliest moment until the present day no one has ever attained to the contemplation of everlasting love unless he has first utterly forsaken the vanity of the world. In this perspective, then, we ought to accustom ourselves to meditation and devout prayer before we expect to arrive at a full contemplation of heavenly joys.

Contemplation is sweet and desirable work. It makes the believer glad and hurts him not at all. No one pursues it save in joy; he is not weary when it comes but when it goes. O health-giving labor to which mortality must set itself! O noble and wondrous working which those who sit still may do the more perfectly! He must be still in mind and body whose heart the fire of the Holy Spirit has truly enflamed. Many do not know how to be quiet in mind, nor how to put away empty and unprofitable thoughts, and they cannot carry out the counsel of the Psalmist: "Be still and know that I am God" (Psalm 46:10). People who pray only with their lips and whose minds wander are not worthy to taste and see how sweet our Lord is, or how wondrous the heights of contemplation.

Every truly contemplative person loves to be alone, so that he may more fervently, frequently, and unceasingly be employed in his heart's delight. When one knows that for him the contemplative life is higher and richer in reward than the active life, truly he will be drawn by God to live a solitary life, and because of the sweetness of contemplation he will be especially fervent in love.

It would seem as if solitary persons, raised by the gift of contemplation, are highly exalted and reach the greatest perfection. But they may be exceeded by some who attain the heights of contemplative life and yet continue to fulfill their office of preaching or teaching others. Such persons excel all solitaries who are given only to contemplation and not to the needs of their neighbors. Being in the same inward state of contemplation they are, for their preaching's sake, worthy of a special crown.

A contemplative person is turned toward the unseen things of God with so great a longing that people often consider him a fool or madman, because his heart is so on fire with the love of Christ. Even his bodily appearance is changed, and he is so far removed from other people's style of life that it might seem as if God's child were a lunatic. Yet all the while the contemplative soul gathers up all of herself into the endless joy of love. Withdrawing herself inwardly she does not go out to seek worldly delights. Because she is fed inwardly with such delicacies, it is no wonder that she at last exclaims, "O that I may kiss thee, my brother!" (Song of Songs 8:1, Vg.)—which is to say, "May I be allowed to discover you, freed from the limitations of my flesh, and seeing you face to face be joined to you forever."

Nothing is more profitable, nothing more full of happiness, than the grace of the contemplation that lifts us up from this order of things and offers us to God. What is this grace but the beginning of joy? And what is perfect joy but the fulfillment of grace? In this fulfillment there is laid up for us a joyful happiness and a happy joy, a glorious eternity and an eternal glory, to live with the saints and dwell with the angels. And yet there is one thing more, above all else: to know God truly, to love Him perfectly, to behold Him in the glory of his majesty and, with wonderful jubilation and melody, to love and praise Him forever—to whom be worship and joy with thanksgiving forever and ever.

Amen.

PART TWO

Prayer and Worship

UNKNOWN WOMAN AT PRAYER
By an unknown artist. Reproduced by permission of the National Portrait
Gallery, London.

WALTER HILTON

from
The Ladder of Perfection

Walter Hilton was one of the great spiritual writers of his time. The first part of this work, variously catalogued as *Speculum Contemplativorum, Speculum Perfeccionis,* or *Ladder of Perfection,* was written about 1380, when he would have been about fifty years old. This selection from that work was composed with a certain anonymous enclosed nun in mind as primary reader. She evidently showed it to others, and Book 1 of the *Speculum* was copied many times and widely circulated. Under pressure to develop his counsel further, Hilton wrote Book 2 sometime before his death in 1396 as a kind of sequel. A reflection on the use of Scripture from Book 2 appears later in the present volume. Hilton's work rapidly grew in popularity with lay readers, and it was one of the first English books to be printed, appearing in 1494 from the press of Wynkyn de Worde. I have based my text on the version found in MS B.M. Harley 6579.

On Prayer

PRAYER IS A MOST PROFITABLE and expedient means of obtaining purity of heart, the eradication of sin, and a receptiveness to virtue. Not that you should imagine that the purpose of your prayer is to tell the Lord what you want, for He knows well enough what you need. Rather, the purpose of prayer is to make you ready and able to receive as a clean vessel the grace that our Lord would freely give to you.

Now this grace may not be experienced until you are tried and purified by the fire of desire in fervent prayer. For though it is true that prayer is not the cause of our Lord's grace being given, it is nevertheless a channel by which that grace freely flows into a soul. But it may be perhaps that what you really want to know is how you should pray, and upon what things you should focus your mind as you pray. Also, you may wonder what forms of prayer are best for you to use.

I. The Spirit of Prayer

As far as the first matter is concerned, in order to answer the question I would like to begin with that first moment of consciousness, when you awaken from your sleep. Though you may be ready to pray, you are likely to feel yourself to be sensually minded and drowsy, lapsing downward into vain thoughts, either of dreams or fantasies, or irrational imaginations of worldly activity or pursuits of the flesh. That is precisely when it is a good idea to quicken your heart by prayer, and stir it as much as you can to a spirit of devotion.

In beginning your prayer itself you should not be setting your heart on earthly concerns, but all your effort should be directed toward turning your mind away from the world of things, so that your desire might be, as it were, stripped naked of even the appearance of worldly encumbrances, ever striving upward unto Christ. For you may neither see Him physically as He is in his divine nature, nor contain Him, by a picture of his bodily likeness, in your imagination.[1]

You may, however, through devout and continuous beholding of the meekness of his incarnate humanity, feel his goodness and the grace of his divinity. This may come when your desire is somewhat reshaped, aided and liberated from all carnal thoughts and appetites. Then, when your heart is mightily uplifted by the power of the Holy Spirit into a spiritual apprehension and delight in Him, and is held there continuously through the time of your prayer, you will have little concern for earthly things, and your mind will pay little attention to them.

If you pray in this spirit, then you pray well. For prayer is nothing if not an ascending desire of the heart unto God, with a corresponding withdrawal of the heart from all earthly thoughts. And so prayer is likened to a fire, which of its own nature leaves the earth and strives ever upward, ascending into the air. Just so, desire in prayer, when it is touched and lit by that spiritual fire which is God Himself, is ever ascending unto Him from whom it comes.

Not all those who talk about the "fire of love" well understand what it is. Indeed, *what* it is I cannot tell you myself, except this much: it is not of the body, nor is it experienced physically. A soul may feel it in prayer, or in devotion, and that soul will still be, of course, in the body. But it does not feel this fire by any physical sense. For even though it is possible that it will work so fervently in a soul that the body feels the heat and becomes, as it were, burning for a sympathetic travail within the spirit, nevertheless the fire of love is not itself a physical sensation. It lives only in the spiritual desires of the soul.

1. Hilton encourages, as in his selection "On Meditation" in Part Four below, meditation on the life and Passion of the Savior. Like Wyclif, he is at pains to distinguish between a spiritual contemplation of these things and a naive imagination that receiving a "picture" of the physical Jesus is a plausible or legitimate aspiration.

Now this is not a matter of perplexity to anyone who experiences real devotion. But some folk are simple and imagine that because it is referred to as "fire" it should be a physical feeling, hot in the way that a physical fire is hot. And it is for their sake that I am at pains to make the distinction.

II. Types of Prayer

Now for the second question, concerning what types of prayer are best to use: let me offer a considered opinion.

You should understand that there are three broad categories of prayer. The first is spoken prayer uniquely created for our use by God Himself, such as the Lord's Prayer, and also, more generally, those prayers which have come down to us by the ordinance of his Holy Church—such as we have in morning prayer, evensong, and other services at their various hours. Some prayers of this type we have also from devout persons as special sayings and forms of address to our Lord, to Mary his mother, and the saints.[2]

Common Prayer

As for this first kind of prayer, which is also called vocal, or spoken, it seems to me that for those of you who have a religious calling and are responsible by custom and obligation for the saying of liturgical prayers, it is most expedient that you say them with all the devotion in your power.

When you recite your morning prayers, you say the Lord's Prayer principally among them. Beyond this, to stir our hearts in faithful devotion it has been ordained for us to say psalms, scriptural hymns and other songs of praise which are also authored by the Holy Spirit. Therefore you should not say them speedily and recklessly, as if you who are bound to say them got little personal benefit from the praying, but rather you should concentrate your affection and focus your mind so as to pray these prayers more soberly and more devoutly than any other special individual prayer. Know truly that since this is prayer which has been hallowed through use by all of Christ's Holy Church, there is no

2. All medieval Christians used not only the Ave and Magnificat in daily worship but also, on various feast days of the saints, invocations and apostrophes which, in effect, constitute a "remembrance" of the special spiritual virtues associated with that saint. One of these, for the feast of the conversion of St. Paul, is found in John Mirk's sermon for that day and is included below.

prayer so profitable for you to use vocally, and in community, as is this common prayer. By the means of this kind of prayer, you shall overcome all your heaviness of heart, and by grace turn your feeling of need into good will toward others, and your sense of bondage into great freedom, so that whatever burdens you bear shall not be able to hinder you in your spiritual life.

After these good prayers you may use others of their kind. Of them, choose those in which you feel most spiritual heightening and comfort: these things, in my opinion, should be discovered by personal experience in prayer.

This kind of common prayer is often also expedient for someone who is just in the beginning of his spiritual life, and more appropriate, perhaps, than any other type of spiritual occupation. For a new convert is still superficial, rude and carnal. Until such a person has a fuller experience of grace, he cannot readily think sound spiritual thoughts in meditation, for his soul is not yet fully cleansed from old, sinful habits. Therefore, I believe it is especially expedient for the new convert to use this type of prayer, saying the Lord's Prayer, the *Ave* and other prayers of this kind, and reading the prayers of the Psalter.

He who cannot run lightly in the path of Spirit-directed prayer, because his two feet (of love and understanding) are crippled with sin, will need to have a secure staff to hold him up. This staff can be those special spoken prayers ordained of God and his Holy Church for the aid of our soul's progress. By this type of prayer, the soul of a carnal person which is always stumbling down into worldly thoughts and fleshly affections shall rise up again, and be held to its course as by a staff. Fed with the sweet words of common prayer as is a child with milk (cf. 1 Peter 2:2), he may also be governed by it in such a way that he does not fall into errors or fantasies by immature meditations. For in this kind of scriptural prayer there is no deceit. Who so will, let him steadfastly and humbly learn to pray effectually in this way.

Let me add a note on this subject. You may have seen examples of folk who, at the beginning of their conversion or shortly after, as soon as they feel a little spiritual growth in love or understanding but before they are yet grown stable, leave off spoken common prayer too soon. Sometimes they drop other compatible spiritual exercises as well, giving themselves entirely to meditation. They are not wise.

For often in the tranquility of their meditation such persons imagine and think of spiritual things according to the inclinations of their own wit, and follow their emotions when they have not received sufficient grace to do so. By indiscretion they often outrun their wits or even exhaust the strength of their bodies, so that they fall into fantasies and singular conceits—even into open theological errors. So doing, they can for the sake of vanities easily abandon the grace that God has given them.

The cause of all this can be a private pride and presumption. For example, some will, when they have experienced a little of God's grace, imagine that it is so extraordinary and superior to that given to others that they will fall right into the trap of vainglory. And so they will abandon the common prayer of all Christians. If only they knew how flimsy it is, this feeling of theirs about what God has given or may give to them, they would be ashamed to speak openly of it except by necessity.

We should all, then, remember the model of vocal prayer which David offers to us in the Psalter, stirring us to prayer in this way both with our heart and our understanding: "With my voice I cried to God, and with my speech besought the Lord" (Psalm 77:1; 142:1).

Personal Prayer (Vocal)

The second general type of prayer is also spoken, but not according to any special model. This kind of prayer occurs when a man or woman experiences grace of devotion by the gift of God, and in this devotion speaks to Him as if He were bodily present in the same place. Here words are used which most accord with one's feelings at the moment of prayer—things which come to mind spontaneously according to sundry considerations which have been on the person's heart. This kind of prayer can involve the confessing of our sins and personal sinful disposition, or expressing concerns about the malice and slights of our enemy; or else it may praise the goodness and mercy of God.

In this kind of prayer a person may cry out with the desire of his heart and the speech of his lips to our Lord, seeking his help and sustaining aid. It may seem almost like the voice of a man in peril amongst his enemies, or in sickness, showing his sores to the physician, saying as David said, "Deliver me from my enemies, O my God" (Psalm 59:1) or "Lord, be merciful unto me: heal my soul, for I have sinned against thee" (Psalm 41:4), or making other utterances like this that come to mind.

But this type of prayer is also well suited to a person who finds so much goodness, grace, and mercy in God that he wants simply and with heartfelt affection to express his love for Him, giving Him thanks by such personal words and psalms as accord to the loving and praising of God. As David said: "O give thanks unto the Lord; for He is good: for his mercy endureth forever" (Psalm 136:1).

This kind of prayer pleases God greatly, for it springs exclusively from the affection of the heart. On this account it is never offered without some measure of grace. It is a type of prayer which belongs to the second stage of contemplation, as I have said elsewhere.[3] Whoever has this gift of fervent prayer from God ought when he prays to flee the company of others and get off alone that he might not be hindered in praying.

And whoever has this prompting of the Spirit to pray, let him exercise it while he has it, for the true fervor of it does not last very long at a time. For if such a fullness of grace to pray comes in abundance it is exceedingly taxing to the spirit, however exhilarating, and it takes considerable toll on the physical nature of those who experience it frequently. For when grace comes in such power it makes the body sway back and forth in ecstasy, much like that of a man who is drunk and cannot steady himself. This is effectively an intense focusing of the passion of love, which by a kind of violent overpowering breaks down all carnal appetites, wounding the soul itself with the blissful sword of love. In such a case the body may even fall down, unable to bear it.

This "touching" of the Spirit is of such great power that the most vicious and carnal man alive, if he were once mightily touched with this sharp sword, would become serious and quietly sober for a long while afterward. And he would loathe all the appetites and lusts of his flesh, and all the earthly things which up to that point had provided him his chief delight.

Of this kind of experience in prayer the prophet Jeremiah seems to have been speaking when he said: "His word was in my heart as a burning fire shut up in my bones" (Jeremiah 20:9), for as a physical fire burns and consumes all physical things where it burns, just so spiritual fire, the love of God, burns and consumes all carnal affections and appetites in a person's soul. And this fire is well stoked up in my bones, says the prophet of himself. By this he means to say that his love fills up the capacities of his soul, his mind, reason and will, with grace and spiritual sweetness just as marrow fills up the core of his bones. That is, the fire is within, and not produced outwardly, by means of the senses.

Nevertheless this force is so mighty within that it strikes out into the body, so that all the body may quake and tremble. And because it is so far from bodily conditions which resemble it, and so unfamiliar, a person in such a state cannot control it by reason, and may not be able to bear the force of it—even falling down, as the prophet Jeremiah says, who was himself at last overcome in this way (Jeremiah 20:9).

Therefore our Lord tempers the intensity, and withdraws the fervor, permitting the heart to fall into a sobriety of softness and tranquility.

---

3. See Hilton's "On Meditation," below.

But whoever can pray in this way frequently will be much blessed, and that very speedily. He may acquire more spiritual growth in a short time than another, who is just as spiritually sound, obtains in a much longer time, despite all the disciplines of prayer that such a person may undertake. Indeed, whoever has this special gift of God in prayer will not need to overcharge his physical nature with extremes of restraint and penitential exercise.

Personal Prayer (Silent)

The third type of prayer I have in mind is that which is only of the heart. It is without speech, and is experienced in great rest and quietude of the body and soul.[4]

One who wishes to pray well in this fashion needs to have a pure heart. It comes to those men and women who, by dint of extended physical and spiritual effort, or such strong seizures of love as I have described, then come into a restedness of spirit. Here their affection is turned utterly toward things which have the taste of heaven, so that they may be in a state of unceasing prayer in their hearts, loving and praising God with a minimum of temptation and distraction.

Of this kind of prayer St. Paul has said: "For if I pray in an unknown tongue, my spirit prays, but my understanding is unfruitful"; that is, the mind is not fed. What then shall I do? Paul says, "I will pray with the spirit, and I will pray with understanding also: I will sing with the spirit, and I will sing with the understanding also" (1 Corinthians 14:14-15); in the sweetness of the love and the sight of God he was thus able to pray.[5]

By this habitual prayer the fire of love should never be extinguished in the souls of godly men and women, which are an altar of our Lord. And let priests of the Lord each day lay to this fire fresh fuel and kindle it (cf. Leviticus 6:12). Let the people of the Lord by holy psalms, clean thoughts and fervent desires nourish the fire of love in their hearts, so that it never goes out.

III. Effectual Prayer

I can imagine that by now you are saying that I have been setting goals

---

4. Almost no one in the Middle Ages was capable of reading silently. Similarly, people did not "pray silently" in the way in which we are accustomed to now. Hilton is referring to a "spirit of prayer" in which one offers his or her thoughts as a kind of continuous prayer.

5. The phrase in 1 Corinthians ("in an unknown tongue") is here understood to refer not to glossolalia but to an "unvoiced" mystical prayer, distinct from (but not opposed to) a more intellectual form of prayer.

for your prayer life that are far too high, and that it is relatively easy for me to talk about such things, but much harder for you to do them. You may be saying to yourself that it is just not possible for you to pray so devoutly or in so utterly heartfelt an abandon as I am suggesting. When you would have your mind's eye turned upward to God in prayer you simply feel too many vain thoughts of what you have been doing before, or what you will be doing, or what other people are doing, and the like. You may feel that these things get so much in your way that you can experience neither the sweetness nor the restedness, nor even devotion in your attempts to pray. Indeed, you may be saying that often the more you struggle to keep your heart in a spirit of prayer, the more this spirit eludes you. Sometimes you can hardly concentrate in a time of prayer from one end of it to the other, so that you think all that you have been attempting to do in prayer is nothing but lost effort.

Well, as to your suggestion that I have been setting goals for your prayer which are too high, I am willing to admit that I speak of levels of intensity that I am unable myself to achieve. Nevertheless I say these things to this end: I want you to know how we ought to pray if we really are to do well in our prayer. And to the degree that we are unable to measure up then we are humbly aware of our feebleness and may call upon God's mercy.

Our Lord commanded us to seek a *totality* of commitment when He said: "Thou shalt love the Lord thy God with all thy heart and with all thy soul and with all thy might" (Luke 10:27). It is impossible for any person alive to completely fulfill this commandment, yet our Lord commanded that we should love Him in this way. St. Bernard suggests that He did so for this intent, that we should know by this standard the state of our own frailty and so be moved to cry humbly upon his mercy— and his mercy we shall have!

Let me tell you, nevertheless, what I think myself. When you pray, direct your will and intention as purely and completely toward God as you may in short compass of your thought. Then begin and do what you can. And though you be ever so frustrated in your first intention, do not be too much depressed, or too angry with yourself. Nor should you be impatient with God because He does not seem to be giving you that same quality of spiritual sweetness that you imagine He gives to others. Simply recognize your own feebleness, and bear it easily, holding before you your own prayer, simple as it is, with meekness of heart. And trust also securely in the mercy of our Lord that He shall make your prayer good, and far more profitable for you than you know or feel.

For you should understand that you satisfy by this endeavor the debt of prayer you owe Him, and you shall have reward for it as for any other good deed which you have done in love, even though your heart was not as fully concentrated as you would have liked upon the actual doing of it. Therefore do what is yours to do, and wait upon the Lord to do what *He* will do, and do not try to predict his response. And though you think yourself reckless and negligent, or in great default for your inadequacies in these things, just treat them like any other inadvertent sin which may not be entirely eschewed in this life, and lift up your heart to God! Acknowledge your failures, and ask Him for mercy, with confidence in his forgiveness. And then stop struggling, and stop being hard on yourself, as if you could by sheer self-control overcome your feelings of inadequacy.

Leave this off then, and go to some other good activity, bodily or spiritual, and set yourself to make more progress another time. And even if you fail the next time in a similar way, or even a hundred or a thousand times fail to reach your goal, yet do as I suggest, and all shall be well. And remember this: a soul that is never able to achieve real contentment of heart in prayer, but spends her whole life long struggling with errant thoughts, distracted and troubled by them, still, if she keeps herself in humility and love in other respects, she shall have a bountiful reward in heaven for all of her good endeavor in the Lord.

ANONYMOUS

Understanding the Lord's Prayer

This tract was first attributed to Wyclif, but its authorship is impossible to fix. It is a good example, however, of Wycliffite emphasis on the Paternoster as model prayer. Its assignment of a particular virtue to each of the seven petitions is typical; untypical is the depth of its application of the prayer to issues of practical morality, Christian "economics," and social theory. The text that follows is from MS Corpus Christi College, Cambridge, 296.

Oure fadir þat art in heuenes, halwid be þi name. þi reume or kyngdom come to þe. be þi wille don in herþe as it is doun in heuene. ʒeue to vs today oure eche dayes bred. & forʒeue to vs oure dettis, þat is oure synnys, as we forʒeuen to oure dettouris, þat is to men þat han synned in vs. & lede vs not in-to temptacion, but delyuere vs from euyl. amen, so be it.

WHEN WE SAY, "Our Father that art in heaven," we reflect that we have already been taught to love each other as brethren of one father and one mother physically. So much more then, since God is our heavenly Father who has made us out of nothing, we are being taught here to live in meekness with each other, to desire heavenly things, virtues of a holy life, and to do all our business both private and public for the honor of God and the bliss of heaven. Indeed, our own life ought to be fixed upon heaven by a holy and continuous desire. Thus, at the very beginning of this prayer we are obliged, by our family obligation, to be meek and in charitable love with all persons, both Christian and non-Christian, both friends and enemies. Otherwise we are not worthy to pray the Lord's Prayer.

When we say, "Hallowed be thy name," we are actually praying that we who say this will be sanctified and brought to spiritual maturity by the holy name of God and his grace and mighty works, and that we will become sanctified by his grace—for our Father is already holy in and of Himself. In this petition we are asking devoutly for sincerity of faith, without which faith we may not please God. We are also praying for ourselves that every kind of pride, whether of thought, deed, speech, bearing or countenance may be put away, for such pride makes us into the children of Lucifer. And also, when we pray this we are effectively asking that every aspect of true meekness be grounded in us as an antidote to pride, for it is true meekness before Him that makes us God's children.

When we say, "Thy kingdom come," we are praying that all men and women living in this world who are to be saved, and all those saved now departed may come to the bliss of heaven as soon as it is God's will, to see there our blessed bridegroom Jesus Christ, and have endless joy with Him and all his saints and angels. For all the angels and all men and women who are to be saved constitute God's kingdom and his holy church. And our Lord Jesus is King of this realm and head of his holy church. On the other hand, all those who shall be damned in hell are the devil's church and the devil is their false prince and king, or rather their dictator. In this petition we are praying for true and everlasting confident hope of the bliss of heaven, by the mercy of God and through a good life concluding in perfect charity. In this phrase we pray, in effect, that all accursed envy and hate be put away from us, and that a fullness of burning love toward God and our fellow Christians be so thoroughly rooted in us that it will not wither away in this life, come what may.

When we say, "Thy will be done in earth, just as it is in heaven," we pray that we may do the will of God unceasingly and without error, even as the blessed angels do in heaven, and that we may do this will of God out of a rich and full understanding of it, and with great desire, joy and good pleasure, not with moroseness and grumbling. In this petition we are asking, in effect, that in all things our will may be conformed to the will of God, that nothing may alienate our will from the will of God, or our love from his love, which is eternal and just.

And here, by the same token, we are praying that we may obtain the high virtue of charitable love, without which all other things are of no avail to bring us to heaven. So our prayer implies in that request that God will preserve us from a wicked acquisitiveness after material possessions, and that we offend neither the commandments of God nor good conscience by efforts to acquire or display our worldly goods. For whoever obtains or holds his neighbor's goods by the means of breaking God's commandments—whether that is a matter of false claims, false weights and measures, or any form of shortchanging, not only fails to do God's will but, according to the law of God, is a thief and traitor to God and his neighbor both.

When we say, "Give us today our daily bread," we are praying for the necessary sustenance of our body, and to have an understanding of God's word and obedience to it, and especially of his promises, which are the spiritual sustenance of our soul. Also, that we may obtain our physical sustenance honestly and not by plundering, extortion, or any false means, and that it be used in the service and fear of God, and that we thank God humbly for all his grace and gifts which He grants to us out of his great goodness. In this petition we are praying, by implication, to have the virtue of prudence by which to recognize what sort of sustenance is necessary and reasonable for us, and how therefore we ought to handle the matter before God, consuming it in such a way as to banish every kind of gluttony and drunkenness, as well as fastidiousness or wastefulness of meat and drink. For this tendency to excess of food and drink causes people to love their belly and gullet more than they love almighty God—their "[false] god is their belly," as St. Paul says (Philippians 3:19).

When we say, "Forgive us our debts"—that is, our sins—"as we forgive our debtors"—that is to say, people who have trespassed against us—we are praying that God will have mercy on us even as we have had mercy on those who have angered us. Assuredly, if we have no mercy on those who have trespassed against us, then we are praying to God in such a way as to ask that his judgment against sin be brought down on our own heads. What is meant here is that people should forgive the rancor, hate, or ill will of their neighbor; they may, of course, lawfully pursue the matter of worldly debts as long as they do this by just means, and preserve patience and charity in so doing. And if some persons are poor but they are just in their manner of living and truly want to repay, if they are industriously and honestly working to manage their debt and are not wasters of their own small means, then this prayer implies that such poor folk be not prosecuted or imprisoned, but that you in patience and mercy will persevere with them until they are able to pay. In this petition, then, we are praying for righteousness sufficient to extinguish unreasonable wrath and vindictiveness, and to keep us steadfast in true mercy and in patience, countering melancholy and an irrational spirit, so that reason and mercy may govern all our stirrings of heart and speech and action.

When we say, "And lead us not into temptation," we pray that God will not permit us, through a withdrawal of his help and grace, to be overcome by temptations of the devil, the world, or by fleshly lusts and foul pleasures. It is profitable to be tempted and withstand the temptation by help of God and his angels, for by this means is our joy and reward restored to us; but it is an evil thing to be overcome by temptation which is merely the result of our negligence, sloth and false pleasure in sin. Therefore in this petition we pray to have the virtue of spiritual strength, to become strong through the help of the Holy Spirit to withstand all temptations, and not to become hardened in sin, but that we live a life of devout prayer and good use of our time, our mind focused steadfastly on the shortness of sin's pleasures and on the bitter pains of purgatory and hell. And if we will, by such a mind and disposition (since God's grace and help is available), we shall be able to overcome all our temptations and obtain our eternal crown in heaven.

When we say, "But deliver us from evil," we are praying that God will deliver us from all evil consequences of sin, and its pains both of body and soul in this life, but especially from the pains of hell, and that we not fall into despair of God's mercy through rootedness in old sinful habits. This petition also implies prayer for the virtue of temperance, so as to use material things and pleasures that we forget not God in heaven above, and so temper the appetites of the flesh that we have no sexual dealings with any woman except it be in true and lawful matrimony, and even there in reverence of God and not as unreasoning beasts who are completely obsessed with lust to the forgetting of God and all his creative purposes. Remember what the archangel Raphael taught Tobias: that the devil has power over all those who thus contaminate the order of marriage and do everything merely for the sake of their own lusts, so forgetting to reverence God and acting as animals, without discretion (Tobit 6:27, Vg.).

May God deliver us all from sins both secret and open, and especially from persisting in sin and in despair of the mercy of God, and from war, revenge and suffering, both in this life and in purgatory and hell, granting us by a just and true faith and by perfect charity to obtain the blessedness of heaven. May it be, Lord Jesus, in your great mercy.

We may be assured that the "Our Father" surpasses all other models of prayer in authority, in richness and in profit to body and soul. It is of highest authority because our Lord Jesus Christ, God and man, made it and commanded Christian persons to say it. Other prayers have been composed by men, but they contain nothing which departs from the "Our Father" in essential order and meaning unless by way of error. Therefore, since Jesus Christ is more worthy than other persons, who are sinful, so the Lord's Prayer has more authority than prayers composed by other persons, even though those may be good. The "Our Father" is more rich than other prayers in that it is composed of the eternal wisdom and love of Christ, and comprises all the considerations necessary for the good of body and soul, both in this world and the next. Our Lord Jesus made it of short words filled with much meaning, that no one should be obtuse to it or able to give an excuse for not understanding what it means, and what it means to say it. And it is the most profitable of prayers, for if a person prays it well he shall not fail in anything that is necessary and profitable for this bodily life, nor in that which is virtuous for bringing us to heaven, there to have bliss in body and soul eternally.

Lord, how much to be blamed are those who fuss themselves over prayers made by sinful men to the neglect of this Paternoster, the "Our Father" that is best of all and most ordained, and which comprehends all things good for us both in body and soul.

Blessed be this eternal good Lord, who of his wisdom and love taught us this short prayer.

Amen.

Common Prayer

The Lord's Prayer (Luke 11:2-4)

Of all prayers employed in Christian worship, this is the most basic and, of course, the most frequently used. Although the Paternoster was said universally in Latin versions closely following that of St. Jerome, translations were also made into various European languages from the earliest period of Christian missionaries down through the Reformation. Several vernacular versions are printed here for comparison. All of them, except the Old High German, were used in England.

I. Latin (eighth century, following the fifth-century Vulgate)

Pater noster qui es in caelis, sanctificetur nomen tuum, adueniat regnum tuum, fiat voluntas tua sicut in caelo et in terra; panem nostrum supersubstantiale da nobis hodie, et demitte nobis debita nostra sicut nos demittimus debitoribus nostris; et ne inducas nos in temtationem, sed libera nos a malo.

II. Old High German (c. 830)

Fater unser thu thar bist in himile, si giheilagot thin namo, queme thin rihhi, si thin uuillo so her in himile ist so si her in erdu; unsar brot tagalihhaz gib uns hiutu, inti furlaz uns unsara sculdi, so uuir furlazemes unsaren sculdigon; inti ni gileitest unsih in costunga, uzouh arlosi unsih fon ubile.

III. Old English (c. 1000)

Faeder ure thu the eart on heofonum, si thin nama gehalgod; to-becume thin rice; gewurthe thin willa on eorthan swa swa on heofonum; urne gedaeghwamlican hlaf syle us to daeg; and forgyf us ure gyltas, swa swa we forgyfath urum gyltendum; and ne galaed thu us on costnunge, ac alys us of yfele, sothlice.

IV. *Middle English (Wycliffite, late fourteenth century)*

Our fadir that art in heuenes, halwid be thi name; thi reume or kyngdom come to the. Be thi wille don in herthe as it is doun in heuene. Geue to vs to-day oure eche dayes bred. And forgeue to vs oure dettis, that is oure synnys, as we forgeuen tu oure dettouris, that is to men that han synned in vs. And lede vs not in-to temptacion, but delyuere vs from euvl. Amen, so be it.

V. *Renaissance (William Tyndale, 1534)*

O oure father which arte in heven, halowed be thy name. Let thy kyngdome come. Thy wyll be fulfilled, as well in erth, as it ys in heven. Geve vs thisdaye oure dayly breede. And forgeve vs oure treaspases,[1] even as we forgeve our trespacers. And leade vs not into temptacion; but delyver vs from evell. For thyne is the kyngedome and the power, and the glorye for ever. Amen.

VI. *The Authorized, "King James," Version (1611)*

Our father which art in heauen, hallowed be thy name. Thy kingdome come. Thy will be done in earth, as it is in heauen. Giue vs this day our daily bread. And forgiue vs our debts, as we forgiue our debters. And lead vs not into temptation, but deliuer vs from euill. For thine is the kyngdome, and the power, and the glory, for euer. Amen.

Other Scriptural Prayers

The *Lay Folks' Prayer Book,* from which these prayers are taken, is an example of service books of common prayer which came into use in England in the fourteenth century, particularly in the north. Following scriptural models for prayer—indeed, praying the "prayers of David" or the words of Job and the prophets—was (as we have seen in Hilton's "On Prayer") considered to be appropriate not only in church but also in the private devotionals of new Christians not yet strong in their faith.

I have here chosen to retain the original texts, with annotations, so that readers can obtain a flavor of these translations. (Note that *j* was written as *i* in Wyclif's time—hence the "ioie of the Lord"—also that *v* and *u* were frequently reversed—thus, "vnserteyn & pryue thingis of thi wisdom.")

1. In an earlier edition (1525) Tyndale translated ". . . them which trespas vs."

I. Prayers of Penitence

Job 10:8-12

THYNE HONDIS MADEN ME, & han formed me al in cumpas; & thou castist me doun so sodeynli! y biseche thee haue thou mynde that thou madist me of cley, & schalt brynge me agen in-to poudur. Whether thou hast not softid me as mylk; and hast cruddid me to-gideres as chese? Thou hast clothid me with skyn & flesch; & thou hast ioyned me to-gideres with bones & synewes. Thou hast goue liyf and merci to me; & thi visitacioun hath kept my spirit.

Responses: Lord, whanne thou schalt come to deme[2] the erthe, where schal y hide me fro the face of thi wrathe? for y haue synned ful myche in my liyf.

I drede my trespassis, & y am aschamed to-fore thee: whanne thou schalt come to iugement, nyle thou condempne me.

Ffor y haue synned ful myche in my liyf.

Psalm 51

God, haue thou merci on me! bi thi greet merci, And bi the mychelnesse of thi merciful doyngis, do thou awey my wickidnes! More, waische thou me fro my wickidnesse, and clense me fro my sinne! For y knowleche my wickidnes; & my synne is euere agenes me. I haue synned to thee aloon; & y haue don yuel befire thee, that thou be iustified in thi wordis, & ouercome whan thou art demed.

For, lo! y was conseyued in wickidnessis; and my modir conseyuede me in synnes. For, lo! thou louedist treuthe; thou hast schewid me the vnserteyn thingis & pryue thingis of thi wisdom. Lord! sprynge thou me with isope, & y schal be clensid; waische thou me, & y schal be maad whiyt more than snowe. Gyue thou ioie & gladnesse to myn heryng; & bones maad meke schulen ful out make ioie. Turne awei thi face fro my sunnes; & do a-wey alle my wickidnessis!

God! make thou a clene herte in me; & make thou newe a rightful spirit in myn entrailes. Caste thou not me awey fro thi face; & take thou not fro me thin hooli spirit! Gyue thou to me the gladnesse of thin helthe; & conferme thou me with the principal spirit! I schal teche wickid men thi weies, & vnfeithful men schulen be conuertid to thee.

God! the god of myn helthe! delyuere thou me fro bloodis, & my tunge schal ioiefuli synge thi rightfulnesse. Lord! opene thou my lippis, & my mouth schal telle thi preisyng. For if thou haddist wolde sacrifice,

2. *deme:* "judge."

y hadde ynoue; treuli thou schalt not delite in brent sacrificis. Sacrifice to god is a spirit trublid: god! thou schalt not dispise a contrit herte, & maad meke. Lord! do thou benyngneli in thi good wille to sion; that the wallis of ierusalem be bildid. Thanne thou schalt take plesauntli the sacrifice of rightfulnesse, offringis & brent sacrificis; thanne thei schulen putte calues on thin auter.

II. Prayers of Commendation

Psalm 119:1-16

Blessid ben men in the weie with-outen wem,[3] that gon
    in the lawe of the lord.
Blessid ben thei that seken hise witnessyngis, seken hym
    in al herte!
For thei that worchen wickidnesse, yeden not in hise weies.
Thou hast comaundid, that thin heestis be kept gretli.
I wolde that my weies be dressid to kepe thi iustifiyngis!
Thanne y schal not be schent, whanne y schal biholde parfitli
    in alle thin heestis.
I schal knouleche to thee in the dressyng of herte, in that that y
    lernede the domes[4] of thi rightfulness.
I schal kepe thi iustifiyngis; forsake thou not me in ech side!
In what thing amendith a yonge wexinge man his weie?
    in kepynge thi wordis.
In al myn herte y soughte thee; pute thou not me awey
    fro thin hestis!
In myn herte y hidde thi spechis, that y do not synne
    agenes thee.
Lord, thou art blessid! teche thou me thi iustifiyngis!
In my lippis y haue pronounsid alle the domes of thi mouth.
I delitide in the weie of thi witnessyngis, as in alle richessis.
I schal be occupied in thin hestis, & y schal biholde thy weies.
I schal bithenke in thi iustifiyngis; y schal not forgite thi wordis.

Psalm 119:105-112

Thi word is a lanterne to my feet, & light to my pathis.
I swoor, & purposide stidefastli, to kepe the domes
    of thi rightfulnesse.

3. *wem:* "error"; "blemish"; "sin."
4. *domes:* "judgments."

I am maad low bi alle thingis, lord; quykene thou me bi thi word!
Lord, make thou wel plesynge the wilful thingis of my mouth;
    & teche thou me thi domes!
Mi soule is euere in myn hondis; & y forgate not thi lawe.
Synneris settiden a snare to me; & y erride not
    fro thi commaundementis.
I purchaside thi witnessyngis bi eritage withouten ende;
    for tho ben the ful ioiynge of myn herte.
I bowide myn herte to do thi iustifiyngis, with-outen ende,
    for yelding.

III. *Prayers of Praise and Desire for God*

Psalm 19

Heuenes tellen out the glorie of god; & the firmament tellith
    the werkis of hise hondis.
The dai tellith out to the dai a word; & the nyght schewith
    kunnyng to the nyght.
No langagis ben, nether wordis; of whiche the voicis of hem
    ben not herde.
The sown of hem yede out in-to alle erthe; & the wordis of hem
    yeden out in-to the endis of the world.
In the sunne he hath set his tabernacle; & he as a spouse
    comynge forth of his chaumbre.
He fulli ioiede as a giaunt to renne his weie; his goyng out was
    fro the higheste heuene.
And his goynge agen was to the higheste ther-of; & noon is
    that hidith him-silf fro his heete.
The lawe of the lord is with-out wem, & conuertith soulis;
    the witnessyng of the lord is feithful,
    & gyueth wisdom to little children.
The rightfulnessis of the lord ben rightful, gladinge hertis;
    the commaundement of the lord is cleer, lightnynge iyen.
The hooli drede of the lord dwellith in-to the world; the domes
    of the lord ben trewe, iustified in-to hem-silf.
Desiderable more than gold & a ston myche preciouse, &
    swettere than hony & hony-combe.
For whi thi seruant kepith tho; myche yelding as in tho
    to be kept.
Who vndurstondith trespassis? make thou me clene
    fro my pryuy synnes; and of alien synnes spare thi seruant.

If the forseid defautis ben not lord of me, thanne I schal be
　　with-outen wem; & y schal be clensid of the most synne.
And the spechis of my mouth schulen be that tho plese;
　　& thenkynge of myn herte euere in thi sight.
Lord, myn helpere, & myn agenbier!

Psalm 42

As an hert desirith to the wellis of watris, so thou, god,
　　my soule desirith to thee.
My soule thirstide to god, that is a quyk welle: whanne schal y
　　come, & appere bifore the face of my god?
My teeris weren looues to me, bi dai & nyght,
　　while it is seid to me ech dai: "where is thi god?"
I bithoughte of these thingis, & y schedde out in me my soule;
　　for y schal passe in-to the place of this wondurful tabernacle,
　　til to the hous of god,
In the vois of ful out-ioiyng and of knouleching, is the sown
　　of the etere.
Mi soule, whi art thou sorie? & whi disturblest thou me?
Hope thou in god, for yit y schal knouleche to him;
　　he is the helthe of my chere, & my god.
Mi soule is disturblid at my silf; therfor y schal be myndeful
　　of him, fro the lond of iordan, & fro the litil hil of
　　hermonyim.
Depthe clepith depth, in the vois of thi wyndowis.
Alle thin highe thingis & thi wawis passiden ouer me.
The lord sente his merci in the dai, & his song bi night.
At me is a preier to the god of my liuf; y schal seie to god:
　　thou art my taker-up.
Whi forgitest thou me? and whi go y soreuful, while the enemy
　　turmentith me?
While my boones ben brokun to gidere, myn enemyes
　　that trublen me dispisiden me,
While thei seien to me bi alle daies: "where is thi god?"
Mi soule, whi art thou sorie? & whi disturblist thou me?
Hope thou in god, for yit y schal knouleche to him;
　　he is the helthe of my chere, & my god.
Antem: Mi soule thirstide to god, that is a quyk welle!
　　whanne schal y come & appere bifore the face of the lord?

PART THREE

Hymns and Spiritual Songs

KING DAVID WITH HARP
Carved choir stall decoration of the mid-fourteenth century.

WILLIAM HEREBERT

All Glory, Laud and Honor[1]

Wele, heriȝyng, and worshype boe to crist þat doere ous bouhte,
To wham gradden "osanna!" chyldren clene of þoute.
þou art kyng of israel and of Davidþes kunne,
Blessed kyng, þat comest tyl ous wyþoute wem of sunne.

Al þat ys in heuene þe heryȝeth under on,
And al þyn ouwe hondewerk and euch dedlych mon.

þe volk of gywes wyth bowes comen aȝeynest þe,
And woe wyht boedes and wyth song Moeketh ous to þe.

Hoe kepten þe wyth worsȝyping aȝeynst þou shuldest deyȝe,
And woe syngeth to þy worshipe in trone þat sittest heyȝe.

Hoere wyl and here moekynge þou nome þo to þonk;
Queme þe þoenne, mylsful Kyng, oure ofringe of þys song.

Wele, heriing and worshipe boe, &c.

* * *

All glory, praise and worship to Christ who us has bought,
To whom proclaim "Hosanna!" his children clean of thought.
You are the king of Israel and David's royal kin,
Blest king who comes unto us without a stain of sin.

All the hosts of heaven now praise you every one,
And all your own creation and every mortal man.
You are the king of Israel . . . (etc.)

The people of the Jews came bearing boughs to you,
And we with fronds, also with song, do our obeisance too.
You are the king of Israel . . . (etc.)

They surrounded you with honor in hopes you would not die;
While we sing in your worship unto your throne on high.
You are the king of Israel . . . (etc.)

1. This hymn is a Middle English translation by the Franciscan friar William
Herebert of the first twelve lines of a Latin hymn by Bishop Theodulphus, a work
which was regularly sung in the procession for Palm Sunday. My own translation
of Herebert follows.

Their good will and their honor you took and thanked the
throng;

Receive then, king of mercy, our offering of song.
You are the king of Israel . . . (etc.)

All glory, praise and worship to Christ who us has bought,
To whom proclaim "Hosanna!" his children clean of thought.
You are the king of Israel and David's royal kin,
Blest king who comes unto us without a stain of sin.

JOHN GRIMESTONE

Gold and Al This Werdis Wyn

Gold and al this werdis wyn[1]
Is nouth but cristis rode;°   *Christ's cross*
I wolde ben clad in cristes skyn,[2]
That ran so longe on blode,
& gon t'is herte and taken myn in—
Ther is a fulsum fode.
Than yef i litel of kith or kyn,[3]
For ther is alle gode.[4]
    Amen.

1. *Werdis* can mean both "of words" and "of the world"; *wyn* can mean both "wine" and "joy." Here all combinations of meaning and nuance are apropos of the balance of the poem. John Grimestone was a Franciscan friar who collected a large number of lyrics in a commonplace book of 1372. Therefore, it may be that the poem is not his.

2. This metaphysical image is a striking anticipation of seventeenth-century lyricism, but it is consistent with the style and content of Franciscan spirituality as it influences the medieval lyric.

3. The allusion is to Matthew 10:37.

4. *Gode* can signify both "good" and "God"; *alle* can mean both "all" and "wholly,"—occasionally "very."

JOHN GRIMESTONE

O Vos Omnes

Ye that pasen be the weyȝe,[1]
Abidet a litel stounde!°   *few moments*
Beholdet, al mi felawes,
Yif ani me lik is founde.
To the tre with nails thre
Wol fast I hange bounde,
With a spere al thoru mi side
To min herte is mad a wounde.

---

1. The text upon which this is based, "O vos omnes qui transitis per viam," comes from Lamentations 1:12, which by established tradition was interpreted as the speech of Christ and used by the church in the Easter liturgy.

ANONYMOUS

Pieta

Sodeynly affrayed, half wakyng, half slepyng,
And greetly dismayde, a womman sat wepyng.

Wyth favour in hir face fer passyng my resoun,
And of hir sore wepyng this was the enchesoun:°   *occasion*
Hir sone in hir lappe lay, she seyde, slayn by tresoun.
If wepyng myghte ripe ben, it semed than in sesoun.
    "Jhesu!" so she sobbed,
    So hir sone was bobbed°   *beaten*
    And of his lyf robbed;
Seying thise wordes, as I seye thee:
"Who can not wepe, come lerne at me."

I seyde I coude not wepe, I was so hard-herted.
She answerde me wyth wordes shortely that smerted:
"Lo, nature shal meve° thee, thou most be converted.   *move*
Thyn owene fader this nyght is deed,"
    lo, thus she thwarted,°   *retorted*
    "So my sone is bobbed
    And of his lyf robbed."
For sothe than I sobbed,
Verifying the wordes she seyde to me:
Who can not wepe may lerne at thee.

"Now breek, herte, I thee preye! This cors lieth so rewely,° *ruefully*
So beten, so wounded, entreted so Jewely,
What wight may me biholde and wepe not? Non, trewely,
To see my dede dere sone lie bledyng, lo, this newely."
    Ay stille she sobbed
    So hir sone was bobbed
    And of his lyf robbed,
Newyng the wordes, as I seye thee:
"Who can not wepe, come lerne at me."

On me she caste hir eye, seyde, "See, man, thy brother!"
She kiste him and seyde, "Swete, am I not thy moder?"
In swownyng° she fil ther, it wolde be non other.   *swooning*

I not° which more deedly, that oon or that other.   *know not*
  Yet she revived and sobbed
  So hir sone was bobbed
  And of his lyf robbed.
"Who can not wepe"—this was the laye°—   *refrain, song*
And wyth that word she vanisht awey.

JAMES RYMAN[1]

Revert, Revert

Revert, revert, revert, revert!
O synful man, yif me thyn herte.

Have mynde how I mankynde° have take   *human form*
Of a pure mayde, man, for thy sake,
That were most bounde most free to make.
   O synful man, yif me thyn herte.

Have mynde, thou synful creature,
I took baptesme in thy nature
From filthe of synne to make thee pure.
   O synful man, yif me thyn herte.

Have mynde, man, how I took the feeld,
Upon my bak beryng my sheeld;
For peyne ne deeth I wolde not yelde.
   O synful man, yif me thyn herte.

Have mynde, I was put on the rode
And for thy sake sheede myn herte blood;
Bihold my peyne—bihold my mood!
   O synful man, yif me thyn herte.

Bihold me, hed, hond, foot, and side!
Bihold my woundes five so wide!
Bihold the peyne that I abide!
   O synful man, yif me thyn herte.

Have mynde, man, how faste I was bounde
For thy sake to a piler rounde,
Scourged til my blood fil to grounde.
   O synful man, yif me thyn herte.

Have mynde how I in forme of breed
Have left my flessh and blood to wedde°   *as a covenant*
To make thee quik whan thou art deed.
   O synful man, yif me thyn herte.

1. James Ryman was a fifteenth-century Franciscan of Canterbury, author and compiler of a large collection of carols found in MS Cambridge University Library Ee.I.12.

Have mynde, man, how I have thee wroght,
How wyth my blood I have thee boght,
And how to blisse I have thee broght.
   O synful man, yif me thyn herte.

O synful man, bihold and see
What I have don and do for thee,
If thou wylt be in blisse wyth me.
   O synful man, yif me thyn herte.

Bothe for my deeth and peynes smerte
That I suffred for thy desserte
I axe namore, man, but thyn herte.
   Revert, revert, revert, revert.

ANONYMOUS

Lord, Thou Clepedest Me[1]

Lord, thou clepedest me
And I noght ne answerde thee.
But wordes slowe and slepy:
"Thole° yet! Thole a litel!"   *be patient*
But "yet" and "yet" was endeles,
And "thole a litel" a long weye is.

---

1. *Clepedest:* "called." This poem recalls the story of Samuel, called by God in the night to listen to divine prophecy for his life (1 Samuel 3). It is in the form of a direct translation of certain lines from *The Confessions* of St. Augustine (8.5), whose book immediately precedes this little poem in the manuscript.

ANONYMOUS

Adam Lay I-Bounde

Adam lay i-bounde
    Bounden in a bond;
Foure thousand wynter[1]
    Thoghte he not to longe.
And al was for an appel,[2]
    An appel that he took,
As clerkes fynden writen
    In here book.

Ne hadde the appel take ben,
    The appel take ben,
Ne hadde nevere oure lady
    A ben hevenes quene.
Blessed be the tyme
    That appel take was,—
Ther-fore we mowen synge
    "Deo gracias."[3]

1. It was thought that the harrowing of hell, when during the three days of his death Christ delivered the captive souls of godly men and women of the past, took place approximately four thousand years after humanity's fall from Eden.

2. The Bible does not specify the fruit the serpent offered, but because of the similarity between the Latin words for evil *(malus)* and for apple *(malum)* the association was imaginatively irresistible.

3. This is the notion of the *felix culpa*, or "fortunate fault": if human beings had not first sinned, there would not have been the joy of their redemption.

ANONYMOUS

I Synge of a Mayden

I synge of a mayden
That is makeles:[1]
Kyng of alle kynges
To hir sone she ches.°   *chose*

He cam also stille°   *as silently*
Ther° his moder was   *where*
As dewe in Aprill
That falleth on the gras.

He cam also stille
To his modres bour
As dewe in Aprill
That falleth on the flour.

He cam also stille
Ther his moder lay
As dewe in Aprill
That falleth on the spray.°   *branch of buds*

Moder and mayden
Was nevere non but she:
Wel may swich a lady
Goddes moder be.

---

1. One of the most beautiful of extant nativity lyrics, this poem makes striking use of double entendre. Here the maiden is understood to be both "matchless" and "mateless"—i.e., without carnal knowledge of a man.

ANONYMOUS

Hond by Hond[1]

Hond by hond we shullen us take,
And joye and blisse shullen we make,
For the devel of helle man hath forsake,
And Goddes Sone is maked oure make.

A child is born amonges man,
And in that child was no wam;°   *blemish*
That child is God, that child is man
And in that child oure lyf bigan.

Synful man, be blithe and glad,
For youre mariage thy pees is grad°   *peace is proclaimed*
   Whan Crist was born!
Com to Crist—thy pees is grad;
For thee was his blood i-shad,
   That were forlorn.

Synful man, be blithe and bold,
For hevene is bothe boght and sold
   Everich a foot!
Com to Crist—thy pees is told;
For thee he yaf a hundredfold
   His lyf to boot.°   *as compensation*

1. "Hand by Hand." This poem (c. 1350) is in the genuine carol, or round dance, form and may have been sung and danced to at the same time.

JAMES RYMAN

Magnificat

Thus seide Mary of grete honoure:
"My soule my lord dothe magnifie,
And in my god and sauyoure
My spirite reioyseth, verily.

For he the mekenes hath beholde
Of his handemayde, that lorde so good.
That I am blessed manyfolde,
Alle kynredes shall sey of myelde moode.

For he, that is so full of myght,
So grete thingis to me hath done.
Holy his name is ay of right,
By whome oure goostly helth is won.

And in alle tho, that hym doth drede
(Truly, thus seithe holy scripture),
His mercy dothe bothe spring and sprede,
And of heven they be fulle sure.

This myghty lorde of grete renowne
By his swete sonne the helthe hath wrought
Of meke people and hath put downe
Prowde people onely with a thought.

Tho, that desireth that lorde, oure helth,
That king of grace soo goode and swete,
Fro whome cometh alle goodenes and welth,
With alle vertue they be replete.

Of his grete mercy havyng myende
He toke nature in Ysraell
And became man to save mankynde,
To oure faders as he did telle."

Ioye be to god in trinitie,
Fader and sonne and holigoost,
That was and is and ay shall be,
Bothe iij, and one, of myghtis moost.

JOHN TREVISA[1]

God Me Speed

A Croys was maad al of reed
In the bigynnyng of my book
That is clepid° god me speed,[2]   *called*
In the first lessoun that I took.

Thanne I lernede A and B.
And other lettris by her names:
But alwey god spede me
Thoughte me needful in alle games.

If I pleyede in feeld or medis°   *meadows*
In stillnesse either with noys,
I praiede helpe in alle my deedis
Of him that dyede on the croys.

Now dyuerse pleyes° in his name   *various pleasures*
I shal lete passe forth, and fare
And auenture to pleye o, long game:[3]
But yit also I schal spare.[4]

Both wodis, medis, and feeldis,
Places that I haue pleyed inne:
And in his name, that al thing weldis,°   *controls*
This game I schal bigynne.

1. John Trevisa, vicar of Berkeley Castle Chapel in Gloucestershire, was born in Cornwall and went to Oxford, where he was for some time a colleague of Wyclif and from which, in 1379, he was temporarily expelled during some of the university's troubling controversies. A considerable scholar, he translated many Latin texts into English, among them works by Occam and FitzRalph upon which Wyclif had drawn. Something of his own spiritual character is revealed in the poems here. This one Trevisa put at the head of his translation of the great medieval dictionary of Bartholemaeus Anglicus, *De Proprietatibus Rerum*.

2. He calls the "boke" of his life *God Me Speed*—"God has helped me," or "may God help me." He sees his life as a history of God's blessings and provident care.

3. This refers to the dictionary of Anglicus, the major work of translation which followed this poem in its original setting.

4. "Although I shall take a rest from time to time in my labors"—i.e., go back, as the next line says, to the woods, meadows and fields, which he has played in, by God's grace, since he was a little boy.

And pray help, counseil and reed,°   *spiritual wisdom*
To me that he now wil sende,
And this game wel rule and leed,
And bring it to a good ende.

JOHN TREVISA

A Pastor's Evening Prayer

A douout prayere toward thy bedde at nyght

Now Ihesu lord, Welle of all goodnes,
For þy gret pyte I the pray
Foryeue me all my wykkydnes,
Wherewith I have greuyd the to day.

Honoure & praysyng to the be,
And þankyng for þy yeftys° all,   *gifts*
That I thys day receuyd of the
Now, curteyse Cryst, to þe I call.

Thys nyght from parell thow me kepe
My bodyly reste whyle that I take,
And as long as myn eyen slepe
Late my hert in þy seruyce wake.

For feryng of þe fende oure fo
Foule dremes, and fro fantasies,
Kepe me this nyght fro syn also
In clennes þat I may vpryse.°   *rise up*

Saue my good doers[1] fro greuaunce,
And quyte° hem þat þey on me spende,   *reimburse*
Kepe myne enemyes from noyaunce,°   *hampering me*
And yeue hem grace to amende.

Mercy, Ihesu, and gramercy,[2]
My body and soule I the beken,
In nomine patris & filii
Et spiritus Sancti, Amen.

---

1. He prays not only for protection for his faithful parishioners but also that the Lord will make up to them the tithes and offerings they spend in his support.
2. "Have mercy on me, Jesus, and grant me to be merciful."

PART FOUR

Meditation and Contemplation

THE THRONE OF MERCY
A familiar motif in medieval churches, here represented by a small
(about 30 cm. [12 in.] high) English ornamental brass of the mid-
fifteenth century.

WALTER HILTON

from
The Ladder of Perfection

On Meditation

This selection follows Hilton's chapter "On Prayer" in Book 1 of the
Speculum Perfeccionis. It is concerned with showing that an imaginative
and authentic identification with the cross of Christ leads to a perfection of love for God.

NOW I WANT TO SAY a little about meditation as I understand it. You
should recognize that in the matter of meditation there is no universal
rule which can be established for everyone to keep in every situation.
These things are, by nature, a free gift of our Lord, and are directed to
the various dispositions of his chosen souls according to their particular state and condition. And according to each person's growth in virtue
and spiritual estate He increases opportunities of meditation, both for
their spiritual knowledge and love of Himself.

For one who has always been ardent for the *knowledge* of God and of
spiritual things, it can sometimes seem that he increases after a certain
point relatively little in *love* for God. And that may be. But consider what
is revealed to us in the life of the Apostles. When they were filled with
burning love of the Holy Spirit at Pentecost they were not made fools
or dolts, but they were made wonderfully wise—enriched in knowing
and speaking of God and spiritual things—as much as any one might
be in this life. And thus Holy Writ says of them: "And they were all filled
with the Holy Spirit, and began to speak with other tongues . . . the
wonderful works of God" (Acts 2:4, 11). But all that "knowing" became
theirs as they were being ravished in love by the Holy Spirit.

There are a variety of meditations that our Lord puts in a person's
heart. Some of these I shall tell you as they occur to me. My intent in
this is your edification. If you experience any of these things, I would
that you might more effectively take advantage of them because of what
I am teaching you.

I. The Good of Meditation

In the first stages of the conversion of a person who has been greatly befouled by worldly or carnal sins, his or her thought is commonly directed toward those sins. With great compunction and sorrow of heart, great weeping and many tears, he meekly and diligently asks God's mercy and forgiveness. And if he is touched sharply because our Lord desires to purify him quickly, he is likely to be so overcome with the perception of his sins that he can hardly live with himself. And it can be that though he repent ever so sincerely, yet for all that he will still experience a kind of fretting and nagging of the conscience, so that he may even think that he has not properly repented and been cleansed from his burden. A person in such a state can hardly rest for anxiety and stress unless our Lord of his mercy comforts him in such time as He wills. This comfort can be obtained by intense devotions or meditations on his Passion, or some other profitable meditation as He chooses to grant it.

In this manner our Lord moves in some people's hearts, more or less, as proves necessary. And all this is part of the great mercy of our Lord, that He will not only forgive our sins and trespasses, but relieve also the purgatorial suffering for them, honoring generously what is after all a matter of only a little anguish of conscience on our part.

We see that if God chooses to prepare someone to receive any special gift of his love, He first scours and cleanses that person by fires of compunction for all of his great sins previously committed. Of this kind of purging David speaks in many places in the Psalter, but especially in the psalm *miserere mei Deus,* "Have mercy upon me, O God, according to thy loving kindness: according to the multitude of thy tender mercies blot out my transgressions" (Psalm 51:1).

II. The Gift of Meditation

Some time after this sort of travail and wrestling with the effects of sin, such a person (or else another who by the grace of God has lived in relative innocence) may be given by our Lord a meditation on his manhood, or his birth, or his Passion, or his compassion for his Virgin mother, Saint Mary. When this kind of meditation is led by the Holy Spirit then it is most profitable and an instrument of grace.

You shall recognize it as such by this token or pattern. When it happens that you are stirred up to a meditation in God, and quite suddenly your thought is drawn away from worldly concerns and in their place it seems as though you are looking at our Lord Jesus in a bodily likeness as He was on earth, this is a gift of meditation. If it is suddenly as though you were seeing or reliving how He was captured by the Jewish leaders and bound as a thief, beaten and scorned, scourged and condemned to death; how lowly he bore the cross on his back, and how cruelly he was nailed upon it; or you see the crown of thorns upon his head and the sharp spear that stung Him to the heart; and if in this spiritual vision you feel your heart stirred to such great compassion and weeping with every fiber of your being: then you will find yourself amazed at the goodness, love, patience and meekness of your Lord Jesus, that He would—for so sinful a wretch as you—suffer this much.

And if in all these things you experience a profound fullness of the goodness and mercy of our Lord welling up in your heart in love and joyful gratitude to him with many sweet tears, and you find yourself in deep trust that your sins are forgiven and that your soul is saved by the virtue of his precious Passion on your behalf, then you are indeed being blessed. For when the remembrance of Christ's Passion or any part of his human life is thus impressed upon your heart by such a spiritual quality of insight, and your own affection is responding to it, know for sure that this is not something produced by your own effort, nor a counterfeit of some wicked spirit, but it is a gift of God by the grace of his Holy Spirit. Here you will have an opening of your spiritual eyes into the life of Christ.

This may be thought of as a sort of corporeal love of God, as St. Bernard calls it, inasmuch as it is focused on the corporeal nature of Jesus Christ. And it is a great good, and of a major help in the mortification of serious sin, and a good means to come to a virtuous imagination, and so in time to contemplation of the Godhead. For no one can come to spiritual delight in the contemplation of Christ's Godhead except by coming first in imagination to a painful identification [with his Cross] by compassion and steadfast thinking on his humanity.

Consider the example of St. Paul. First he says: "For I determined not to know anything among you, save Jesus Christ and him crucified" (1 Corinthians 2:2). This is as if he said: My knowing and my trust is only in the Passion of Christ. And to the same end he says also: "God forbid that I should glory, save in the cross of our Lord Jesus Christ" (Galatians 6:14). And further he says: "We preach Christ crucified . . . Christ the power of God and the wisdom of God" (1 Corinthians 1:23-24), telling us thus that first he preached the incarnate humanity and the Passion of Christ; then he preached the deity of Christ and power and eternal wisdom of God.

Self-Knowledge and the Sight of God

This passage, from Book 1 of the *Speculum Perfeccionis*, falls into the category of spiritual discipline called "examination of conscience." In it Hilton deals perceptively with the psychology of sin.

A SOUL THAT DESIRES SPIRITUAL KNOWLEDGE needs first to have self-knowledge. For one does not obtain understanding of a kind which is above the self unless first there is some self-understanding. And this can only happen when the soul is at peace with itself and appropriately distanced from a preoccupation with worldly things and the senses. It is only then that the soul recognizes itself in its own integrity, undistracted by the body's demands. Accordingly, if you really desire to know and see your soul for what it is you will not introvert your imagination toward your physical body to discover and experience your soul there, as if it were somehow hidden within your reflective heart in the same way that your heart is hidden and enclosed by your body. If you seek it in this way you shall never find it in itself. The more you seek to discover and experience the soul in the way you would imagine experiencing a physical thing, the further you will be from it. For your soul is not material, but a life unseeable. It is not hidden and enclosed within your body as a smaller thing is hidden and enclosed within something larger; it is, in fact, enclosing and giving life to your body, and is much greater than your body in strength and power.

I. Spiritual Self-Understanding

So, if you want spiritual self-discovery, withdraw your mind from all external physical distractions, even from your five senses as much as you are able, and from remembrance of your own bodily experience as well. Think instead about the rational and spiritual nature of the soul, in the same way you would think about any virtue such as honesty or humility.[1] In precisely this manner imagine that a soul has a life of its own, deathless and invisible, and has capacity in itself to recognize and know the sovereign truth, and to love the sovereign goodness that is God. When you have grasped this, then you will be beginning to understand something of your own true nature. And look for your self in no other place; for the more fully and clearly you are able to reflect on the nature and worthiness of your rational soul, and come to know it, the better you will see your real self.[2]

It is hard going for a soul that is still crude and carnal to have much

1. That is, think conceptually, not as you would about physical entities. The soul, as St. Augustine and others point out, is a real entity, but not, of course, a physical one.

2. See St. Anselm: "The more earnestly the rational mind devotes itself to learning its own nature, the more effectively does it rise to a knowledge of that Being, while the more carelessly it contemplates itself, the further does it descend from a knowledge of that Being." *Monologion,* book 16.

perspective on itself, let alone to imagine an angel or God. Right away it falls into the imagination and memory of bodily shapes, naively expecting in this way to obtain self-perspective, as well as a vision of God and of spiritual things! Clearly that cannot be, since all spiritual things are recognized and known by understanding in the soul, and not by the carnal imagination. Just as the soul "sees" that the virtue of righteousness exists in submission to those qualities which are proper to righteousness, so in the same manner the soul comes to "see" itself by submitting to its own proper means of understanding.

My point is not that your soul should content itself with this kind of self-understanding, but rather that it should by means of this step pursue a higher kind of knowing, above itself, of the nature of God. For your soul is really just a mirror in which you are enabled to see God spiritually. But for this reason you need first to find your "mirror" and then keep it bright and clean from carnal rubbish and worldly vanity, holding it well up from the earth so that you can see it and our Lord in it. In this life all souls which are elect are to work to this purpose, in their intention and desire, even when they are not especially conscious of doing so.

In this light you will remember my remarking how it is that many souls in the first stages of their Christian life have plenty of fervent moments and powerful experiences of sweet devotion, as they seem to be completely consumed by their first love. And yet they do not have that perfect love, nor a true spiritual consciousness of God. For as you well know, however great a fervor a person feels, even if it is so strong that he thinks his body cannot bear it, and though he be perpetually melting away in tears, as long as his thinking and his experience of God are mostly a matter of emotion and not understanding, he has not yet come to effective contemplation or to perfect love.

II. Growth in Love

Think of the love of God as having three stages. All are good, but each successive degree of love is better than the former.

The first comes only through faith, without there yet being a grace-filled imagination or spiritual knowledge of God. This love is in the least soul that is reformed in faith, and on the lowest plane of charity. And it is good, for it is sufficient for salvation.

The second stage of love occurs when a soul by faith and imagination apprehends Jesus in his manhood. This love, when the imagination is stirred by grace, is better than the first, since the eye of the spirit is opened in the beholding of our Lord's human life.

The third stage of love attains, through the manhood of Jesus as it may be seen here, a spiritual apprehension of the Godhead itself. This love a soul will not feel until it is reformed in spiritual consciousness.

Souls which are just beginning to come to life and first growth do not have this love, for they cannot yet think about Jesus or love him in a godly way, but rather, as it were, in a human and natural fashion according to the conditions of his human likeness. Upon that conception of Him they shape all their effort, in their thoughts and in their affections. They respect Him as a man, and worship Him and love Him for the most part according to the human imagination and go no further. For example, if they have done wrong and trespassed against God, they think then that God is angry with them in the same way that a great person would be against those who had trespassed against him. Therefore they fall down as it were at the feet of our Lord with sorrow of heart and cry mercy. And when they do this they have a reasonable expectation that our Lord will of his mercy forgive them their trespasses and sin. Now this kind of behavior is very good, but it is not as spiritually mature as it might be.

Such persons, when they worship God, are inclined to present themselves in their thought as if before our Lord's face in a bodily likeness, and to imagine a wonderful light where our Lord Jesus is. Then in this imagination they reverence Him, worshiping and honoring Him, fully putting themselves in his mercy to do with them according to his will. When they love God consciously they behold Him, worship Him and honor Him as they would a man, not yet as God *in* man but focusing on his Passion or some other event of his earthly life. In this imagination they feel their hearts much stirred up in the love of God.

All this type of worship is good and a channel for grace, but it remains much more limited and at a lower stage than the effort toward spiritual understanding which occurs when the soul by grace really beholds *God* in man.

In our Lord Jesus are two natures: his manhood and the Godhead. Just as the Godhead is more sovereign and more worthy than is manhood, even so our spiritual beholding of the Godhead incarnate in Jesus the man is more worthy, more spiritual, and more necessary to us than is the beholding of his manhood alone, whether we conceive of that manhood as mortal or as glorified.

By the same token, the love that a soul feels when considering and reflecting upon the Godhead in human form, when it is revealed by grace, is worthier, higher, and more spiritually valuable than the fervor of devotion a soul experiences in imagination only of his humanity, no matter how much outward emotion that experience produces. After all, the manhood of Jesus is itself already a concession to our humanity. For our Lord does not show Himself to the imagination as He is, nor in what He is, for the soul in such a stage of development is not, because of the frailty of our fleshly nature, able to bear it.

Nevertheless, this human imagination is given unto souls that cannot yet really think of the Godhead spiritually, in order that they should not err in their devotion, and that they should be comforted and strengthened through some manner of inward beholding of Jesus. They need this to encourage them in fleeing sin and the love of the world. Therefore our Lord Jesus tempers the invisible light of his Godhead, clothing it under the bodily likeness of his manhood, and showing it only to the inner eyes of the soul. Here He feeds us with spiritual love of his precious body. And this love is of such great power that it slays all wicked loves in the soul, strengthening it to endure bodily constraint and distress in times of need, all for the love of Jesus.

This experience of love is like a shadowing of our Lord Jesus over a chosen soul. In this overshadowing the soul is protected from being burned, for just as a shadow is formed by the relationship of light and a body, just so this spiritual shadow is made by the blessed unseeable light of the Godhead and the manhood of Jesus joined to it, as that is revealed to a devout soul. It is of this shadow that the prophet speaks when he says: "Our Lord before our face is a spirit; under His shadow we shall live amidst humanity" (Lamentations 4:20).[3] We are to recognize that our Lord Jesus in his deity is a spirit, and may not be seen by us through the medium of human flesh as He is fully in his blessed light. Therefore we shall live under the "shadow" of his manhood as long as we are here.

Though it is true that this kind of love achieved in the imagination is good, a soul ought nevertheless to desire to have spiritual love achieved in understanding of the Godhead. It is this height of love which is the final goal and fullness of joy for the soul: all other bodily perceptions are but a means leading us to it. I am not at all saying that we should separate God from the man in Jesus, but that we should love Jesus both as God and as man—God in man and man in God—loving Him in a fully spiritual and not a merely fleshly way.

III. Discerning the Object of Love

This is what our Lord was teaching Mary Magdalene, the contempla-

---

3. Hilton may here be remembering the phrase from Lamentations from its context as a gloss on the angel's salutation to the Virgin Mary: "The Holy Spirit shall come upon you, and the power of the Most High overshadow you . . ." (Luke 1:35).

tive one, when He said to her, "Touch me not, for I am not yet ascended to my Father" (John 20:17). We are reminded how Mary Magdalene loved our Lord ardently before the time of his Passion, but her love was perhaps more directed to his physical nature and less to the spiritual. She knew well enough that He was God, but she concentrated little on that fact for she was not able for it then, and so permitted all her affection and her reflection to be directed toward Him as she found Him in human form. Nor did our Lord blame her for this at that stage, but praised her greatly.

But afterward, when He was risen from death and had appeared to her, and she would have worshiped Him with exactly the same type of love as she had before, then our Lord forbad her, saying, "Touch me not." That is to say, "Do not put your confidence or the love of your heart in that form of man which you see with your fleshly eyes only, to be content with that, for in that form I am not ascended up to my Father. That is, I am not at the same level with the Father, for in the form of man I am less than He is. Touch me not in this way then, but rather set your thought and your love on that form in which I am united with the Father, the form of the Godhead. So love me, know me, and worship me as God, and God in man—not as a godly man after the human fashion. So shall you rightly touch me, for since I am both God and man, and the whole reason I am worthy of love and worship is that I am God and yet took upon myself the nature of man, therefore allow me to be God in your own heart. In your love worship me with your understanding as Jesus, God in man, sovereign truth, sovereign goodness and blessed life. For this is what I am." This, then, is what I understand our Lord to have been teaching her, as well as all other souls that are disposed to contemplative understanding and made able for it.

Notwithstanding all that I have been saying, it remains good for other souls who are not yet discerning or made spiritual by grace to keep on directing their love toward God by means of their imagination and human affection until such time as more grace comes freely to them. It is not sound to leave off any good entirely until we perceive and experience a higher good.

This principle applies also to other experiences which involve bodily feeling: for example, the hearing of delightful music, a sense of warmth and well-being, a perception of light or of sweetness or any physical sensation. These are not in fact spiritual feelings, for truly spiritual feelings are felt in the inner faculties of the soul—principally in love and understanding—and less in the imagination. These other emotions are related to the imagination and are therefore not, in themselves, spiritual experiences. Yet when they are most true and reliable they are outward tokens of the inward grace which is experienced in the recesses of the soul.

The distinction is clearly maintained by Holy Writ in the passage which says that the Holy Spirit apeared to the Apostles in the day of Pentecost in the likeness of burning tongues, enflaming their hearts, and "sat upon each of them" (Acts 2:3). Now the Holy Spirit—God Himself invisible—truly was not the fire or the tongues that were seen or the burning sensation that was felt bodily. He was invisibly experienced in the depth of their souls, where He lightened their reason and kindled their affection through his blessed presence so clearly and ardently that they had suddenly a spiritual consciousness of truth and the perfection of love. This was even as our Lord had told them, saying of the Spirit of Truth: "He will guide you into all truth" (John 16:13). The fire and the burning were nothing more than a physical manifestation, outwardly witnessing to an experience of grace which was profoundly inward.

And just as it was for the Apostles so it is in other souls that are visited and inwardly lightened by the Holy Spirit, experiencing a similar outward feeling as a comfort and witness to the inward grace. But this type of manifestation is not found, I think, in all souls that are being perfected, except where the Lord specifically wills it so. Other imperfect souls can have such an emotional experience outwardly without having received the inward grace. It is not good for them to depend on such feelings too much, but rather to value them only as they help the soul to greater stability of thought in God, and to more charitable love. For some of this kind of experience may be true and some of it feigned, as I have said before.

IV. The Reformation of Consciousness

Now I have spoken to you a little already of our reformation in faith, and also touched lightly upon the progress from that initial reformation to the higher reformation that occurs in our experience and spiritual consciousness. I do not at all intend that by these words I should in any way set God's works under a model of my own exposition, as if to say "this is the way God works in a soul and in no other." No, I mean nothing of the kind. Rather, I am saying according to my own simple sense of it that our Lord Jesus seems to work in this way in some lives. I certainly anticipate that He works otherwise also, in ways which surpass my own understanding and experience.

Nevertheless, whether He works in this or another fashion, by whatever means, over a longer or shorter period, with much or little effort, if it all comes to one end—that is, to the perfect love of Him—then it will do as much good for that soul as if the person had been examined, made to endure suffering, mortified and purified over a period of twenty winters.

Accordingly, take what I have said in the spirit in which it is offered, and especially try to grasp my intent. For now, by the grace of our Lord Jesus, I shall try to speak a little of my thoughts on the reformation of our whole manner of perception: what it is, how it occurs, and what kind of spiritual experiences a soul receives in the process.

So that you do not take my speaking concerning the reformation of the soul in spiritual consciousness as some kind of invention or fantasy on my own part, I want to ground it in St. Paul's words where he says: "Be not conformed to this world, but be ye transformed by the renewing of your mind" (Romans 12:2). That is, "you that are by grace reformed in faith, do not henceforth conform yourselves to the manners of this world in pride, covetousness and other sins. Rather, be reformed in newness of spiritual consciousness." Now here you may see that St. Paul speaks of a reformation of experience and consciousness, and what the character of that new consciousness is he develops elsewhere in this way: "For this cause we also . . . do not cease to pray for you, and to desire that ye might be filled with the knowledge of his will in all wisdom and spiritual understanding" (Colossians 1:9). This is what reformation in spiritual consciousness is all about.

You should think of the soul as having two modes of consciousness. The one is external, via our five physical senses. But there is another which is internal, and employs our spiritual senses. These, properly understood, are those special faculties of the soul—memory, intellect and will.[4] When these faculties are by grace fulfilled in all understanding of the will of God and mature in spiritual wisdom, then the soul will have a new and gracious character of perception. That this is true he shows us elsewhere, when he says: "And be renewed in the spirit of your mind; and . . . put on the new man, which after God is created in righteousness and true holiness" (Ephesians 4:23-24). To be renewed in the "spirit of your mind" is not to be transformed merely in bodily feelings or imagination, but in the core of your intellect. When St. Paul says "put on the new man," he means that we should shape ourselves after God in righteousness, holiness and truth.

To explain this further: your reason, which is intended to become the

---

4. See St. Augustine, *On the Trinity*, which is the *locus classicus* for a description of the trinitarian image of the soul's faculties as memory, intellect, and will. *On the Trinity*, 11.12.

image of God through grace of the Holy Spirit, shall be clothed in a new light of truth, holiness and righteousness. Then it will be properly reformed in consciousness. For when the soul has a perfect knowing of God, then it is "reformed." So St. Paul says: "Put off the old man with his deeds; and . . . put on the new man, which is renewed in knowledge after the image of him that created him" (Colossians 3:9-10). Suppress in yourself "the old man with all his deeds"—that is, cast off the love of the world and all worldly manners. And "clothe yourself in the new man"—that is, be renewed in the knowing of God after the likeness of Him who made you.

By these same words you understand that St. Paul would have all souls reformed in a perfect knowing of God, for this is the new consciousness that he speaks of everywhere. And therefore, following his words, I want to say something more fully concerning this reformation, as God gives me grace.

We see that there are two species of consciousness of God. One of these is had principally in the imagination and consists relatively little in real understanding. This kind of knowing is found in chosen souls who are just beginning and growing in grace. These are the souls that love Him humanly and not spiritually, with natural affections according to his bodily likeness, as I have explained before. This kind of knowing is good, and it is likened to the milk by which such souls are tenderly nourished as children until they are able to come to the Father's table and receive at his hand whole bread (1 Peter 2:2). Another kind of spiritual consciousness exists, which is principally experienced in the understanding as it is comforted and illumined by the Holy Spirit; this is relatively obscure at the level of the imagination. For understanding here is the lady, and imagination only her maidservant, serving the understanding as is necessary. It is this higher sort of knowing which is our whole bread, meat for the soul's perfection, and it constitutes a reformation of the whole character of our perception.

V. Spiritual Insight

When a soul is called from love of the world, after it is set upright, mortified and purified, then our Lord Jesus in his merciful goodness reforms it in perception as He sees fit. He opens the inner eyes of the soul when He lightens the reason through a touch of his blessed light, in order that the soul may see Him and know Him. This does not happen all at once, but little by little at different times as the soul permits Him access.

Such a soul sees Him not for *what* He is, for that is not possible for any creature in heaven or on earth. Nor does he see Him *as* He is, for that sight comes to us only in the bliss of heaven. But he does see *that* He is, recognizing in Him unchangeable being, sovereign power, truthfulness and goodness, blessed life and endless bliss. And the soul sees this, and all that comes with it, not blindly, nakedly and blandly in the fashion of a student who learns to define Him according to his professional instruction and on the strength of mere reason. Rather, the soul sees Him in understanding that He really is eternal God, is comforted thereby and lightened by the gift of the Holy Spirit in a wonderful reverence and secret burning love, and with spiritual savor and heavenly delight this soul knows Him more clearly and more fully than ever it could be written or said.

This kind of vision, though it be brief and fleeting, is so worthy and powerful that it entirely ravishes the affections of the soul away from the consideration and remembrance of earthly concerns. One's desire is to dwell in such a state forever. And for this kind of perception and knowledge the soul comes to direct all of its affections. Then it reverences God-in-man in his wisdom, marvels over Him in his power, and loves Him in his goodness.

This sight and knowledge of Jesus with the joyous love that comes of it may be thought of as the reformation of a soul in faith and spiritual consciousness of which I have been speaking. It is a matter of faith in that it remains cloudy by comparison with that full revelation of Him which we shall have in heaven. For then shall we see not only *that* He is, but as St. John says: "Then shall we see Him *as* He is" (1 John 3:2). And yet it is also a matter of enriched spiritual consciousness by comparison with that blind knowing to which a soul is limited when it first stands in faith alone. For this second kind of soul now knows something of the nature of Jesus as God through his gracious maturity of insight; the first does not yet know it in experience but merely believes that it is true.

In order that you may better grasp what I am saying, I shall try to illustrate these three species of the soul's reformation by an example of three persons standing in the light of the sun. Of these three, one is blind, another is able to see but his eyelids are still sealed, and the third has full use of his eyesight. The blind person has no way of knowing that he is in the sun, but he believes this to be true if a trustworthy person says so. And we can take this person to signify a soul that is only just reformed in faith, and believes in God as the Church teaches, but beyond that knows little. Yet what he has is sufficient for salvation.

The other person sees the light of the sun, but not clearly, either in what it is or as it is, since his sealed eyelids prevent him from seeing more. But he does see the glimmering of a great light. This person can be taken to signify one who is reformed in faith and in spiritual consciousness, and so is contemplative. For he is seeing something of the divinity of Jesus through grace—not fully or clearly, since the lids of his bodily nature form a barrier between him and the character of Jesus our God, screening the person from a clear vision of Him. But inasmuch as he sees through this screen by grace, he sees that Jesus is God, sovereign goodness, sovereign being and that blessed life from whom all other goodness comes.

All this the soul perceives by grace, notwithstanding the impediment of bodily nature. And the more pure and discerning the soul is made and the more separated from carnality, the sharper is his sight and the stronger his love of the divinity of Jesus. This perception becomes strong enough that even if no other person alive would believe in Jesus or love Him, he would never believe or love Him the less, for his faith has been reinforced by such true insight and perception that he could not disbelieve it.

The third person, who has full sight of the sun, does not need to believe in it because he actually sees it fully. And this person we may take to signify a blessed soul who without any impediment of physical nature or sin can see openly the face of Jesus in the bliss of heaven. This is no longer a matter of faith, the person having been completely recreated in perception and spiritual consciousness.

There is no condition above the second that a soul may have in this life. The second, however, is an experience of being perfected and brought on the way toward heaven. Not all souls in this state are alike in their experience of vision. Some have it little, have it briefly, and have it seldom; other have it longer, clearer and more often. Some have by grace an outstanding quality of spiritual vision. Yet all have what we have called the gift of contemplation—of looking toward the Sun of Righteousness.

The soul does not acquire a perfect vision of Jesus all at once. First there comes a little glimmer, after that some growth and development of spiritual consciousness, waxing more mature in the knowledge and love of Jesus as long as life goes on. Truly, I know not what more joy can be imagined by someone who has enjoyed a little of this growth in vision of Him; everything else seems paler and paler by comparison with a clearer sight and love of Jesus, in whom we see all the blessed Trinity.

This kind of vision of Jesus, as I understand it, is like an opening of heaven to the eyes of a pure soul, of which holy men speak in their writings.[5] It is not, as some imagine, that the heavens open, as if a soul could see by the faculty of imagination through the skies above the firmament to where our Lord Jesus sits in majesty in a physical light as great as a hundred literal suns. No, it is not like this. Though you could see ever so far out into the firmament in that manner, truly you would not see into the spiritual heaven. And the higher you would ascend above the sun to see Jesus by such imagination, the lower you would actually fall beneath the Sun. Nevertheless, I suppose this kind of imagination is permitted to simple souls who know no better way to seek Him Who is invisible.

VI. Things Seen and Unseen

What is heaven to a rational soul? Truly nothing else but Jesus, our God. For if heaven is that which is above all other things then is God alone heaven to man's soul. For He alone is above the nature of the soul. Accordingly, if a soul is enabled through grace to have a knowledge of the blessed nature of Jesus, truly he sees heaven, for he sees God.

Many people err in their understanding of some things spoken of God, not understanding them in a spiritual way. Godly authors indicate that the soul wishing to find God should lift up the inner eyes and seek Him above themselves. Then, trying to follow the injunction, some are led to imagine the words "above themselves" in a literal sense, as indicating a higher standing or worthiness of physical place, thinking that one planet in the cosmos is above another in worth or position, and so on. This is not a spiritual understanding. For the soul itself is above all physical creation, not by physical placement, but in the intricacy of its nature. In the same fashion God is above every physical and spiritual creation, not in a physical sense, but in the discernment and worthiness of his unchangeable blessed nature.

Therefore whoever will wisely seek God and find Him ought not to run out in his thought as if to climb above the sun and probe the universe, imagining the majesty of God, perhaps, as the light of a hundred suns. Rather, he should in his thought draw down the sun and all the cosmos, as it were, and forget it, casting it beneath even his own small standing place, and setting all creaturely things as insignificant beside the God he seeks. One needs to be thinking in a spiritual manner, both of the self and of God. And if this happens it becomes possible for the soul to "see" above itself, and so "see" heaven.

5. See 2 Corinthians 12; Acts 7:56. The image is reflected in medieval mystical writers with whom Hilton would have been familiar.

You should also understand the word "within" in this same way. It is commonly said that a soul ought to see our Lord within all things and within itself. And it is true that our Lord is within all creatures, but not in the way a kernel is hidden within the shell of a nut or in the way that any small physical thing may be contained within one which is greater. Rather, He is within all creatures maintaining and preserving them in their being by the intricate, ingenious powers of his own blessed invisible nature.

Just as something which is most precious and pure is kept in the innermost place of protection, one speaks of the nature of God, most precious, pure and spiritual, and furthest removed from physical nature, as hidden within all things.

Therefore, whoever will seek God within ought first to forget material things, because of their externality, and to forget also his own body. And he ought to try to forget his preoccupation with his own soul, thinking instead about that uncreated nature which is in Jesus. It is this uncreated nature which has created us, and now enlivens and preserves us, and which gives us our intellect, memory and will. All of these are inward things, granted through his power and sovereign ingenuity. This is the direction in which the soul should move when grace prompts it to look for the Lord Jesus. Otherwise it avails little to hope to find Him within the self and in his creation—at least as far as I can tell.

It is told to us in Scripture that "God is light" (1 John 1:5). This light should not be understood as physical light. God is light in the sense that He is truth and integrity, for truth is spiritual light. Thus it is that whoever most graciously knows truthfulness best "sees" God. The light of truth is likened to physical light for this reason: just as the sun reveals itself to our physical eyes and reveals all other physical things by its light, so the truthfulness of God reveals itself to the rational soul first and then by this light reveals all other spiritual things that are necessary for the soul to know. And so the prophet says: "In thy light shall we see light" (Psalm 36:9). That is—we shall see the truth that is in You by the light which is Yourself.

In the same manner it is said that God is a fire: "Our God is a consuming fire" (Hebrews 12:29). This is, of course, not to say that God is the element called fire, which heats a physical body and burns it. Rather, it is another way of saying that God is love, for just as a fire consumes every physical thing that is combustible, just so the love of God burns and consumes all sin and dross from the soul, refining and purifying it, like an intense fire purifying metal.

This sort of language—along with any other figures of speech pertaining to our Lord in the Scripture—is to be understood spiritually; otherwise there is no value in it. There is, however, a good reason for such language being used in Holy Writ to speak of our Lord. We are ourselves so physically oriented that we cannot speak of God or understand his character unless at least initially such language is employed. But when the inner eye is opened by grace to receive a glimpse of Jesus, then shall the soul easily enough refer the metaphors to their appropriate spiritual understanding.

This spiritual opening of the inner eye is what I have called our reformation in faith and spiritual consciousness. For at this level the soul experiences something in conscious understanding of what it had previously only in naked belief. This extra dimension is the beginning of contemplation, of which St. Paul says: "We look not at the things which are seen, but at the things which are not seen: for the things which are seen are temporal; but the things which are not seen are eternal" (2 Corinthians 4:18). To this kind of vision every soul should desire to come, here in part and then fully in heaven. For in that sight and knowledge of Jesus the bliss of our rational soul and endless life are fully known.

"And this is life eternal, that they may know thee, the only true God, and Jesus Christ, whom thou hast sent" (John 17:3).

RICHARD ROLLE

Meditation on the Passion of Christ

This particular meditation on the Passion of Christ takes the form of a discipline of prayer. It is heavily influenced by Franciscan and pseudo-Bonaventuran meditations. This translation is based on the version found in MS Cambridge University Ll.i.8.

DEAR LORD JESUS CHRIST, I thank you and acknowledge the graciousness of that sweet prayer and holy intercession that you made for us on the Mount of Olives before your holy Passion. And I beseech you, dear Lord, that you hear my prayer.

Adoramus te, Christe, et benedicimus tibi. Pater noster. Ave Maria.

Dear Lord Jesus Christ, I thank you and acknowledge the graciousness of that great concern you had for us, when you had become so filled with anguish that an angel from heaven came to comfort you as you sweated blood: I beseech you Lord, praying for your sweet mercy, that you be my help through my own anguish and temptations, and send me, Lord, your angel of counsel and comfort in all my needs, that I might through that bloody sweat pass through all my spiritual sickness into a life of health, even in my body.

Adoramus te, etc. Pater noster. Ave.

Dear Jesus, I thank you and acknowledge the graciousness with which you bore the hurt, anguish, shame and cruelties which men did to you so treacherously. Men bound you up as a thief without mercy or pity. Lord, I thank you for those precious and pitiable footsteps that you trod, for love of us, toward your own pain and death. I pray to you Lord, and beseech you, that you unbind us from the bonds of all our sinfulness, on account of which you suffered yourself to be bound out of love for us.

Adoramus. Pater noster. Ave.

I thank you, dear Lord Jesus Christ, for the wounds and shame that you suffered before the bishops and magistrates, at the hands of your enemies—the beatings and blows on the neck and many other shameful things that you suffered. And among other things, I thank you for that look wherewith you regarded the disciple who had forsaken you, St. Peter. You looked on him with a look of mercy, showing openly the love and charity you had toward us, and that no hurt or shame, however great, could draw your heart away from us. Dear Lord, full of

149

mercy and compassion, grant that through your blessed compassionate regard we may turn toward your grace and repent of our trespasses and misdeeds so that we too might come with St. Peter unto your mercy....

Alas, that I should live and see my gracious Lord, so meek in his suffering, who never trespassed, so shamefully arrayed! This moaning and groaning, sorrow and sighing, in pity for his injured countenance—I would it were my own death. The crown of all bliss, who is crown of all the blessed, King of kings and Lord of lords, is here crowned with thorns by hell-hounds. The worship of heaven is despised and befouled; He who made the sun and everything that is good in the earth, all of which we have as his gift, and who had nowhere even to hide his head, became so poor for the purposes of making us rich that He goes naked in the sight of all people.

Ah, Lord, your sorrow—why was it not *my* death? Now they lead you forth as naked as a worm, with torturers around you and armed knights. The press of the crowd was incredibly intense as they threw things and harried you so shamefully, kicking at you as if you had been a dog. I see in my soul how ruefully you walk, your body so bloody, so raw and blistered. The crown on your head is so sharp, and your hair, blown in the wind, is all matted with blood. Your lovely face is so pale and swollen with the blows and beatings, and covered with spittle and phlegm. And down runs your blood; it horrifies me to see it. So loathesome have the Jews made you that you appear more like a leper than a healthy person. The cross that they hung on your back, strapped so tightly, is heavy, long, and so rough.

Ah, Lord, the groaning that you made, so hard and painfully it pressed to your bones. Your body is so sick, so feeble and weary from the fasting you have undertaken and from being kept awake all night without any rest, and from the beatings and whipping you are so broken down that you walk all stooped over and in grim countenance. Your flesh, where the cross moves against it, is all raw, your bruises and blisters are black and blue, and the pain of that burden sits so sorely upon you that with each footstep you take I am stung to the heart. Thus in moaning and great pain you go out of Jerusalem toward your death.

The city is so festive, the crowd is so great—with people coming running out of every street—that everything is choked to a standstill, and there is such a great cloud of dust that everyone must wonder what is happening. No thief was ever led to death in such a parade of worldly curiosity-seekers. There were some of the common people who sighed sorely and earnestly over your plight, and who knew that it was you being tortured, and that it was on account of envy. (For the princes and bishops who had direction of the law were putting you to death for speaking the truth, when you reproved them for their errors.) These common folk knew it was outrageous injustice that you were suffering, and followed you, weeping and sighing sorely. You then said something that afterward came to pass: you bid them weep for themselves, for the great vengeance that should fall upon them on account of your death, and upon their children and all the city, and vengeance that for their guilt would cause them to be exiled.

Ah, Lord, the sorrow that must have fallen on your heart when on your mother you cast your eyes. You saw her following along among the great crowd; as a woman beyond herself she wrung her hands; weeping and sighing she flung her arms about, and her tears dropped down to her feet. She even fainted dead away more than once out of sorrow for your suffering, which smote her to the heart. The sorrow and great grief she was experiencing aggravated in manifold fashion all your other torments, so that when she realized this, then it was similarly worse for her, and you also then wept for her. So your sorrow, each for the other, was in this way multiplied and heaped up. The love of your hearts, that was beyond other loves, without peer, was in sorrow unlike any other woe; it stabbed into your hearts like death itself.

Ah, Lady, mercy! Why were you so courageous, among so many deadly enemies, to follow so close? How was it that natural timidity or maidenly reserve did not cause you to draw back? For it was not seemly for you to follow such a rout, so vile, grisly and shameful to see. But you had no regard for the opinions of men, nor for anything else that would hinder you, but were beside yourself for grief, your heart set utterly on the Passion of your son. Your love for each other was so keen and so burning, your sighings so extreme, that the grief in your countenance was a deadly woe. The love and sorrow that stabbed into your breast bereft you of concern for physical harm, shame, or any kind of hindrance so much that you were out of your mind with it.

Ah, Lady, for the sorrow that you suffered in your son's Passion—which would have been my own, since I deserved it, and much worse, and was the cause of it all while he was guiltless, his dear wounds being rightfully my own—out of thy mercy grant me a touch of that pain in my own heart, and a drop of that pity by which to follow Him. If all that woe was mine by rights, do not withhold from me an identification with his experience. . . . Let me share in your own sore sighings, that I may identify with you in your sorrow also. I do not ask, dear Lady, for castle, towers or worldly wealth, nor for the sun, moon or stars so bright, but rather wounds of sympathy are all my desire, the suffering and compassion of my Lord Jesus Christ. Worst and least worthy in men's eyes, I have a yearning to participate in his suffering, and beseech my Lord for a drop of his red blood to bloody my own soul, as a drop of that water to wash it clean.

Ah, Lady, for the sake of that mercy, you who are mother of mercy, focus for all sorrow and remedy for our misfortune, who have been made the mother of wretches and the sorrowing, harken to this wretch and visit your child. Sow in my heart as hard as stone a glimmer of compassion for that dear Passion, a wound out of that pity to make it soft again.

Ah, Lord, such pain, sharp and cruel, with which the wicked Jews tormented you on the mount of Calvary without mercy! They cast down the cross flat on the ground and with strong ropes bound you to it hand and foot. They pulled and stretched you out both ways, and drove in the nails, first hard through one hand, then the other. The nails were blunted in order the more to burst skin and flesh; they pierced your hands and feet through with blunt nails in order to increase your pain.[1]

> Glorious Lord, so grievously spattered,
> so ruefully stretched upright on the cross,
> in your great mercy, your meekness and power
> you conquer my woe with the balm of your blood.[2]

Ah, Lord, the pitiful sight I now see! Your wounds gape so widely, your limbs under the nails are so tender, so raw and red you lie stretched on the cross, with that sharp crown sitting so painfully on your head. Your face is so blackened that once was so fair. Your sinews and bones are stretched out so starkly that your bones may be numbered. The red streams of your blood run down in a flood; your bleeding wounds are grisly to behold, and the sorrow of your mother increases your woe.

> Ah Lord, King of might, who have chosen to lay aside your might,
> becoming weakness, my wrongs to right,
> What good is it for me to speak and beat the wind?
> Here I am talking about your feelings, and not really touching
>   the matter.
> I blunder in my efforts, as one who is blind.
> I analyze my thoughts, and find them wanting,
> symptoms of my death and the filth of my sin
> that has already slain my soul, fastening itself
> so that my sensitivity is blocked, and I can't honestly identify—
> I who have been your unfaithful betrayer.

1. The text has a gloss at this point to Psalm 22:16.
2. Rolle was a poet and hymnist, and he often inserts portions of poems or hymns into his meditative texts.

Even my words can become a kind of prison, glorious Lord, shutting me out of the sight of your Godhead—this stink of my shame, sorrow of my soul and filth of my mouth. When my lips form these words, they defile your name. No wonder I cannot appreciate such comforts; I have no sense of the sweetness of taste I have lost through sin, for I cheerfully blunder on, lusting after a diversity of sinful things.

> But you, glorious Lord, you bring the dead back to life,
> And many have you transformed and brought to eternal reward,
> Those born blind you gave sight, as in your Book I have read,
> All signs of spiritual transformations, I have no doubt.

Quicken me, Lord Jesus Christ, and grant me grace to experience some taste of spiritual sweetness. Lend me your light, that I may have insight concerning the quality of my spiritual thirst. I know well, and have read, that whosoever desires and seeks aright, even though he has no strong feelings, already possesses more than he realizes by love of your Godhead. So this kind of speaking, and others like it, are actually able to be a matter of preparation. If a person experiences nothing profound, and thinks himself fit for exclusion, rebuke, and reviling on account of his weakness, judging himself to be on a level of devotion too unworthy to have any such special gift of our Lord God because he can achieve no spiritual intensity, at that very point he may yet obtain a gift of his grace. . . .

Lord, often in my imagination I put my arms around the foot of the cross, lying flat as you lay there on the ground, with the stench of dead men's blood that was there so loathesome under your nose. But nothing then shall grieve me or change my heart, I take such comfort in this pleasant imagination. I will not cast my eye upward to see the glorious sight of your wounds, since I am, glorious Lord, so full of guilt and, as cause of it all, unworthy to look.

I would rather be lying among the dead, stinking so foul, and even lower if possible, if it helped me remain in the virtue and grace of your blood. I will not rise up from this place nor leave it until I am red with your precious blood and thereby marked as one of your own, and my soul softened in that dear bath. So may it be, Lord, that my heart, now hard as stone, may open up and grow tender and alive to your sufferings.

Lord, your sweet Passion raised the dead out of their graves, so that they walked about; it opened hell's gates, the earth trembled, the sun went out, and yet my sorry heart in its devilish nature is harder than the stones which were broken open at your death. It is not able to feel even a little bit of your Passion, nor do I rise with the dead in pity of it, nor tear in two as the temple veil, nor tremble with the earth, nor does the door open that has been shut so tightly.

My Lord, is the malice of my leathery heart greater than the virtue of your precious death, which wrought such wonders and many more than these, that the memory of it does not move me? Why Lord, a drop of thy blood fallen upon my soul in the remembering of your Passion may heal all my wounds, softening and making supple again by your grace that which had grown so hard, so that I am willing to die according to your will. I know well enough, gracious Lord, my heart is not worthy that you should enter into it; it has no dignity like the holy sepulchre in which your humanity was enclosed. But you, Lord, deigned to visit hell[3] to set things to rights, and in that same manner I ask you to come into my heart.

I know well, glorious Lord, that I have never been worthy to be a companion of your mother, to stand at your Passion beside her and John. But in that spirit, Lord, if I may not be there to see that blessed sight on account of my great unworthiness, I do count myself worthy on account of my great trespass to hang by your side as did the thief. So Lord, although I may not be there as one who merits it, I plead, as one guilty of your death, that while I am not worthy that my heart be visited, my need and wickedness cry out that you make it right.

Come then, according to your will, heavenly physician, and light upon me soon, for you know my need. A glimmer of your passion of love and pity kindles in my heart to quicken it, so that burning completely in love I may yet forget the world and wash myself in your blood. Then shall I bless the time that I felt myself so stirred up in your grace that all worldly well-being and appetites of the flesh lost their appeal by contrast to meditation upon your death.

3. The reference is to the harrowing of hell. Rolle here invokes Christ's deliverance of the saints to ask for an analogous deliverance of his own spirit.

RICHARD ROLLE

The Law of Love

This treatise, ascribed to Richard Rolle, is found in the same northern manuscript as some of Rolle's meditative works which appear elsewhere in this volume (MS Cambridge University Library Bd.v.64). Its subject is the importance of loving God in everything we do. The first part of the text builds on Matthew 6:24-34 as a reflection on the Great Commandment. The dedication at the end of the manuscript is to "the sisters at Hampole."

THE COMMANDMENT OF GOD is that we love our Lord with all our heart, with all our soul, and with all our thought—that is, in all our understanding, without erring; in all our will, without objecting; and in all our thought, so that we think about Him and forget Him not. This is the way of a true and faithful life, and it is a work which must be effected as a response of the will.

Love, after all, is a willed motion of the heart toward God, so that it accepts nothing which opposes the love of Jesus Christ, and it is that perseverance in sweetness of devotion toward Him which is the perfection of life. The enemy of love, and its opposite, is mortal sin—more so than venial sins, sins of the flesh. (This is because venial sin does not drive away charitable love, but only prevents its exercise and its flourishing.[1]) For this reason all those who wish to love God perfectly will want to be free from not only every kind of mortal sin, but also, as much as they can, all venial sin, whether of thought, word, and deed. To this end they will guard their speech, for when silence is employed in the business of good thoughts it greatly assists us in the love of God. Gossips and backsliders, who diminish the lives of other persons with wicked words, and all those who love their own estate before that of everyone else, or who despise the position in life in which any other person is able to be secure and happy—they have no more vision of the love of God in their soul than the "eye" in your backside has of the sun.

---

1. Medieval theologians located malice in each of the five "spiritual" or "mortal" sins and accordingly counted them as a more serious breach of both the social fabric and divine law than "venial" sins—an order corresponding roughly to that of the Ten Commandments. As a result, they tended to locate the obscene in sins like pride, envy, wrath, greed, and even sloth. After the Reformation, this order tended to be inverted, so that lechery especially became associated with obscenity, while the "spiritual" sins sometimes received less attention.

Empty speech and diseased words are signs of a vain and sick heart, one that is devoid of God's grace. By contrast, one who always speaks of the good, and regards every other person as better than himself, demonstrates clearly that he is mature, with good health in his heart, and full of charitable love toward God and his neighbor.

That you may be able to envision the way to arrive at an experience of the sweetness of God's love, I am setting out for you three degrees of love in which you ought always to be growing. The first of these is called "insuperable," the second "inseparable," and the third "singular."[2]

Your love is of the "insuperable" kind when nothing may overcome it—neither prosperity nor adversity, ease nor anguish, lusts of the flesh nor pleasures of the world. Instead, it endures ever in good thoughts, even when tempted severely, and hates all sin, so that nothing may diminish that love.

Your love is "inseparable" when all your thoughts and intentions are gathered together and focused entirely on Jesus Christ, so that at no time do you forget Him, but have Him always in your mind. And this is the reason such love is called inseparable, since it cannot be separated from thinking about Jesus Christ.

Your love is "singular" when all your delight is in Jesus Christ, and you feel joy and comfort in none other. In this degree love becomes as strong as death.

Therefore, if you wish to love anything, love Jesus Christ, who is the fairest, richest and most wise of lovers, and whose love lasts forever in eternal joy. All earthly love is transient, and soon fades away. . . . If you are desirous after the good, love Him, and you shall have all good. Desire Him truly, and your soul will want for nothing. If pleasures attract you, love Him, for He grants delights to his lovers which will never perish, while all the delights of this world are superficial and deceptive, and will let you down in your hour of greatest need; they begin sweetly enough, but their end is more bitter than gall. If you cannot live without fellowship, lift up your eyes to heaven, that you may find comfort with all the saints and angels, the which will help you toward God, and not stand in your way, as do some of your carnal friends.

Restrain your will for a while from all the lusts and appetites of sin, and you shall afterward have all your will, for it shall then be cleansed and made so free[3] that you will want to do nothing except what accords

2. See Rolle's *Amending of Life* above.
3. *Free* here has its medieval meaning of "generous" or "unselfish," which is of course almost opposite to some of our own uses of this word, which can emphasize autonomous liberty to the point of selfishness. It was thus somewhat easier for the medieval Christian to associate "freedom" with obedience than it is for our contemporaries.

with God's purpose. If you feel like speaking, check yourself at the beginning for the sake of God's love, for when your heart finds its delight in Christ you will not care to speak or even chat except about Christ. If you cannot bring yourself to sit alone, set yourself steadfastly in his love and He shall make you so stable of heart that all the solace of the world shall not cause you to be removed, simply because it will not have any appeal to you.

When you have decided to go off by yourself, stick with it until bedtime, either in prayer or godly meditation. And order your prayers, vigils, and fasting that they be conducted with discretion, neither to excess nor stintingly. Remember that what God wants most of all is the love of our hearts and, accordingly, let your concern be more to love Him than to perform any spiritual exercise.[4] Irrational or ill-advised penance is worth little or nothing. Love, on the other hand, is always the best thing you can offer, whether you do much in the way of spiritual exercise or little. Let your energies be turned completely around, so inwardly directed to the love of Jesus Christ and so replete with spiritual joy in your soul that nothing people do or say can make you sorry. And let your inward thought be fed exclusively on the sweetness of Christ's love, not taking delight in comfortable living or in the affections of people, even when they begin to say good things about you in a spiritually glib manner. Trust in God, and for what He will give, until you learn to praise Him in a reasonable way.

For Christian souls, reasonable prayer is that which night and day seeks and asks for the love of Jesus Christ, that the soul may love Him truly and experience its comfort and delight in Him, casting out worldly thoughts and sinful preoccupations. And you may rest assured that if you covet his love truly and persistently—so that neither carnal love nor anger with the world, nor the speech or hatred of men draw you down again, casting you into preoccupation with bodily things—you shall have his love, and discover that it becomes more delightful in one hour than the whole world of visible wealth even if you had it all until doomsday.

Should you fail and fall into temptation, or yield to anger or begin to love your friends in an excessive manner, it ought not to surprise you if He withholds from you that which you do not truly desire. He says that He loves those who love Him, and that those who seek Him early shall find Him. You who rise up early often enough, why is it that you do not find Him? Certainly, if you seek Him in the right way you shall find Him. But while you are still in the midst of pursuing earthly pleasures,

4. Middle English *penance*, here translated "spiritual exercise," is to be understood in the broad sense of "actions of a penitent life."

no matter how early you wake up you will not find Christ—for He is not to be found in the place of a people who live only for appetites of the flesh. His mother, when He was directed away from her, sought Him weeping, early and late, calling among his kindred and her own. But for all her hunting she did not find Him until at last she came into the temple, and there she found Him sitting among the teachers, listening and answering questions. You would do well to follow her example: seek Him inwardly, in the truth, hope and charity of Holy Church, casting out all sin and hating it with your whole heart because it keeps Him from you, standing in the way so that you cannot find Him.

The shepherds who sought Jesus found Him lying in a manger between two beasts—that you know. If you seek Him truly it will take you in the way of poverty, and not in the path of riches. The star led three kings into Bethlehem, where they too found Christ swaddled in simple cloths, as a little poor-boy. Understand from this that while you are living in pomp and vanity you will not find Him. How can you, who are merely his servant yet dressed in many rich garments, follow without shame your bridegroom and lord who has nothing but a simple wrap, while you have nearly as much excess trailing behind you as He has altogether on?

If this is the way things are, I would advise you to leave off following before you and He meet, so that He does not reprove you for this outrage; for it is his will that you have that which is sufficient for you and no more. He said to his disciples that they should not have as many clothes as two persons could be sustained with, for to invest work in such stuff is an outrageous business that He forbids.

The love of Jesus Christ is the worthiest of treasures, the one wholly delightful joy and most trustworthy. Accordingly, He doesn't give it out to fools who are unable to handle it and guard it tenderly. But those to whom He gives the gift of his love will not let it pass out of their hands come good times or bad; they would rather die than give offense to Jesus Christ.

No wise person puts precious liquor in a stinking vessel, but only in one which is clean. Neither does Christ pour his love into a foul and sinful heart which has willfully bound itself in lusts of the flesh, but rather into a heart which is fair, pure and virtuous. Nonetheless, a foul vessel may be washed out so cleanly that a most precious thing may be safely stored in it. So Jesus Christ many a time purges sinful human souls, making them fit through his grace to receive the delectable sweetness of his love, and to be his dwelling-place in holiness; and the cleaner the vessel becomes, the more excellent joy and solace of heaven does Christ pour into it.

When a person has first been converted to God he may not be aware of that sweet liquor—not until he has become well used in God's service and had his heart purged through prayer, repentance, and godly thought. For even someone who loses his life in the service of God may not necessarily be burning with that love, unless he has given himself to it with all his might, working day and night to fulfill the will of God. When that love is in a person's heart it will not admit idleness, but is always stirring that person up to do some good to God's good will and pleasure, whether in prayer, profitable activities, or in speaking of Christ's Passion, but above all as a matter of thought-life, that the mind of Jesus Christ remain present. For if you love Him truly, you will be glad in Him, and pride yourself in nothing else, and you will focus your thought on Him, casting away the interference of other thoughts. But if you are false and take pleasure in something other than Him, delighting yourself instead in earthly things against his will, know for certain that He will forsake you even as you have rejected Him, and condemn you for your sin.

Wherefore, that you may love Him truly, understand that his love is proved in three areas of your life—in your thinking, in your talking, and in your manner of working. Turn your thought away from the world and cast it wholly[5] upon Him, and He shall nourish you. Turn your mouth away from vanity and worldly talk, and speak about Him, and He will give you comfort. Turn your hands away from works of vanity and lift them up in his name, and work in everything for the sake of his love, and He shall receive you [unto Himself]. Do this, and you will be loving truly, and walking in the way of perfection.

Delight yourself in Him, so that your heart admits neither joys nor sorrows of the world, and be not afraid of any anguish or joy which may beset you in your own body or that of any of your friends. Rather, accept all these things as God's will and thank Him always for what He sends, so that you may have the peace and health of his love. For if your heart is preoccupied with either fears of the world or the world's sort of comfort, you are going to be a very long way from the sweetness of Christ's love.

And see to it that you do not seem to be one sort of person on the outside and entirely another within, as do hypocrites, who are like a whitened sepulchre—richly painted without but on the inside rotting with stinking bones. If you take pleasure in the name of religion, see to it that you take a lot more pleasure in the actions of life which are the responsibility of a religious life. Your abbot says that you have forsaken

---

5. ME *haly*, a play on words that here means both "holy" and "wholly."

the world, that you are committed to the service of God, that you take no pleasure in things of the world: good. Now see to it that it is in your heart as it seems in the eyes of others, for nothing can make you truly spiritual except true virtue and purity of soul in charitable love. If your body is externally clothed according to the habit of your order, be careful that your soul is not left naked within. . . .

Fear the judgments of God, and fear to incur his anger. Let your heart find its stability in his love, and so hold sin at bay. Reject sluggishness, conduct yourself humanely in good living; be courteous and meek toward all persons and let nothing provoke you to anger or envy. Deck out your soul beautifully, making there a tower of love for God's Son, and prepare your will to desire to receive Him as gladly as you would greet the one you love most dearly in all the world. Wash your thought with the tears of love and burning desire so that He finds in you nothing foul, for his joy is that you be fair and lovely in his eyes. Beauty of soul—that is what he looks for. And it requires that you be chaste and meek, mild and patient, never resentful in doing his will and always despising wickedness. So in all you do think always of coming to a vision of his beauty, and set all your intent on that end, for that ought to be the proper goal of all our endeavor, that evermore, while we live here, we desire that sight with all our heart and reflection of our mind.

So then, fasten in your heart the memory of his Passion and of his wounds. Great joy and spiritual sweetness will be yours when you meditate on the pain Christ suffered on your behalf. If you labor uprightly in his love and desire Him with a burning heart, you will be able to overcome all temptations and fears of evil, and through his grace, triumph over foulness. And everyone He sees endeavoring with godly purpose to love Him, He helps against their enemies, and raises their thought above earthly things so they may enjoy the consolation and sweetness of heaven.

Betake yourself to the well of weeping, and cease not until you have Him, for in the heart where tears spring up, there will the fire of the Holy Spirit be kindled. And the fire of love that will then flame in your heart will burn until there is nothing left of the rust of sin, and purge your soul of all filth, making it as pure as gold which is refined in a furnace. I do not know of anything that will so prepare your heart inwardly to desire God's love—to desire that joy and to despise the vanities of this world—as steadfast meditation on the abuses and grievous wounds Jesus Christ suffered for us in his death on the cross. Such reflection will lift up your own thought above earthly pleasure and make your heart burn with love for Christ, infusing your soul with anticipatory delights of heaven.

But perhaps you will say, "I don't know how to despise the world, and I cannot find it in my heart to deprive my body, and I am constrained to love my carnal friends and take it easy whenever I get the chance." If you are tempted by such thoughts I beg you to counter them with this reflection: since the very beginning of the world, where do you think the lovers of this world are now, and where are those who have been lovers of God? Certainly they were all men and women such as ourselves; they ate and drank and laughed. But what of those poor wretches who loved this world, pursued creature comforts and lived as their appetites led them, pleasing their wicked intentions and living out their days in lust and pleasure? To put it plainly, they fell into hell.

Now you may see that they were fools and greasy gluttons who in a few short years wasted the endless joy which was ordained for them if only they had repented of their sins. You can see that all the riches and pleasures of the world vanish away and come to nothing. And truly, so it goes with all who love these things. For no one can stand with any stability on false ground. Their bodies are given over to worms in the earth, and their souls to the devils of hell. But all who forsake the pomp and vanity of this life and stand courageously against all temptations conclude their life in the love of God. These are the ones who are now joyful, having received an eternal heritage, there to live eternally, at peace in the delightful sight of God. For here they sought no more rest or creature comforts than they had need of.

I counsel you this: never forget the name of Jesus, but keep it in your heart day and night, as our most special and precious treasure. Love it more than your own life, and root it in your mind. Love Jesus, for He it is who made you, and who bought you back again at so expensive a price. Give your heart to Him, for it belongs to Him.[6] And set your affection on his name, Jesus, which means "health."[7]

No evil thing can hold sway in the heart of one who keeps Jesus faithfully in mind. For his name chases away devils and destroys temptations, puts away wicked fears and vices, and cleanses the thought-life. Whoever loves this name truly is full of God's grace and spiritual virtues, enjoying spiritual comfort in this life, and when such persons die they are taken up into the orders of angels, there to look upon Him whom they have loved in joy that has no end.

6. ME *for it es his dette*—i.e., his "duty"—a feudal term meaning the service or "rent" owed by a servant to his master.

7. See Matthew 1:21; this is a connection widely observed, and which may be found in Hilton and in Chaucer below.

RICHARD ROLLE

Ego Dormio

Richard Rolle, in one of his four extant letters, sends spiritual counsel to a Yorkshire woman, who may, later in her life, have joined a contemplative order. This letter, written in 1343, is an especially interesting example of a letter of spiritual friendship exchanged between Christians of the fourteenth century. Its title, *Ego Dormio (I Sleep)*, derives from the opening words of the Song of Solomon 5:2 ("I sleep, but my heart waketh"), and its use of amatory imagery and allegory of the biblical text, while entirely traditional since the second century, has here a particularly Cistercian character.

In the original manuscript, *Ego Dormio* contains three poems of good intention but indifferent quality. I have omitted these in my translation.

EGO DORMIO et cor meum vigilat. Let those who desire love hearken, and hear of love. In the Song of Love it is written: "I sleep, and yet my heart awakes." Great love is shown by the one who is never weary of love but—whether standing, sitting, going, or working—is always thinking, and often indeed dreaming, of his love. Because I love, I woo you, that I might have you as I would, not to myself but to my Lord.[1] I would like to become, as it were, that messenger who will bring you to his bed, He who has made you and redeemed you—Christ, the son of Heaven's king. For his will is that you dwell with Him, if indeed you will love Him: He asks of you no more than your love. And so, my dear sister in Christ, you do my will too if you choose to love Him. What Christ covets is your spiritual beauty, and desires that you give Him wholly your heart. I preach nothing else, except that you do his will, and I would encourage you day and night to leave all fleshly love and all desires that interfere with your loving Jesus Christ truthfully.[2] For surely, as long as

1. This rather striking image derives from John 3:29-30, where John the Baptist speaks of himself as the "friend of the bridegroom" who, in effect, "woos" the bride—not for his own sake but for Christ's, and whose "joy is fulfilled" when that marriage is realized. The biblical passage, both lovely and provocative, was popular in the Middle Ages as it was seen as providing a kind of male correlative to the image of the "handmaiden"—the submissive attendant whose love prompts the attitude: "He must increase but I must decrease."

2. *Verraly* (*Verily*, in the language of the King James Bible) means not only "truly" in our sense of "faithfully" but also "truthfully," without dissimulation or affectation.

your heart is beholden to the love of any bodily thing, you may not perfectly be joined to God.

To you I write especially, for I have hope of more godliness[3] in you
than in some others—that you will give your mind to fulfill in deed[4]
that which you have said is most profitable for your soul and offer that
life until such time as you may be able to offer your heart to Jesus Christ
utterly, being as little as possible given to the business of this world. For
if you firmly establish your love, and yet are truly burning in that love
while you live here, then without doubt your seat will be ordained full
high at his table in heaven and you will be joyful before God's face
among his holy angels. For in that same degree from which proud devils fell, meek men and women, Christ's doves, are set to have rest and
joy without end, rewarded for a little short penance and travail that
they have suffered for the sake of God's love.

You may perhaps think it hard to turn your heart away from all
earthly things, from all idle and vain speech, from all fleshly love, and
alone to work and pray, and to think instead of the joy of heaven and
the Passion of Jesus Christ, and to imagine also the pain of hell ordained
for sinful men. Well truly, once you are accustomed to it, you will think
it lighter and sweeter than any earthly thing or pleasure. As soon as
your heart becomes touched with the sweetness of heaven, you will
have little desire for the mirth of this world; when you feel the joy there
is in Christ's love, then you will be disgusted with the counterfeit joy
and comfort of this world, and all the games people play.[5] For all the
melody, riches, and delights that all people in the world can ordain or
think up sounds like mere discord and irritation to the heart of one who
is truly burning in the love of God. Why? Because such a person has
mirth and joy and melody in the songs of angels, as you may already
well know.

If you leave behind all those things which your fleshly love desires
for the sake of God's love, and have no thought for your gossipy friends,
but forsake all this for God's love, giving your heart only to coveting his
love and attending upon Him, you shall find and have more joy in Him
than I can begin to describe. How can I then write of it? I cannot tell if
there are many in such a state of love, because the higher the love is, of

3. *Godenes* depends upon an equivalence (not merely a pun) in Middle English
whereby "goodness" and "godliness" are the same word. Thus the greeting "Gode
day" implied both an acknowledgment that the day was the Lord's and a blessing
or benediction upon the one who received the greeting.

4. *In deed* is much stronger than the modern *indeed;* not merely a token of emphasis, it stresses the aspect of will in action.

5. *Erthly games,* i.e., "worldly games."

course, the fewer followers it has here. All too many things draw us from God's love—that you may hear and see for yourself—but God comforts his lovers more than those who love Him not could ever imagine. Thus, even when we seem outwardly to be suffering we have great joy within us, granted that we have ordained ourselves wisely to God's service, and set upon Him all our thoughts, forsaking the vanity of this world.

Turn your intent to the understanding of this writing, and if you have set all your desire on loving God, there are three degrees of love by which you may rise from one to the other until you reach the highest. (For I will not conceal from you that it is my hope to turn you toward the path of holiness.)

The first degree of love is when a person adheres to the ten commandments, keeps himself from the seven deadly sins,[6] and is stable in the truth of Christ's holy church. It is when a person will not for any earthly thing invoke the wrath of God, but truly stands at his service, and remains therein unto the end of his life.

It behooves each person who will be saved to have this degree of love; for no one may come to heaven except he love God and his neighbor—without pride, ire, envy, backbiting—and live without all other venomous sins, such as gluttony, lechery, and covetousness. For these vices slay the soul, causing it to depart from God, without whom no creature can live. Just as a man poisoned by some sweet morsel takes into himself the venom which slays his body, so also does a sinful wretch in indulging the appetites and lusts of the flesh: his soul is destroyed and brought to eternal death.

People think it sweet to sin, but the reward that is ordained for them is more bitter than gall, more sour than the adder's venom, yes, worse than all the woe we ever see or feel in this life. Only when you have lived well according to the ten commandments of God, vigorously separated yourself from all deadly sin, and are paying God that appropriate degree of respect, are you ready to begin thinking about how to please God more and move your soul toward a more perfect love.

At this point you will enter into a second degree of love, which is to forsake all the world, even your father and mother and all your kin, in order to follow Christ in poverty. In this degree you shall study to know how pure you are in heart, and how chaste in body, and give yourself to humility, suffering and obedience. Here you will examine yourself to

---

6. For a relatively typical fourteenth-century analysis of the seven deadly sins, see the discussion in the treatise of Sir John Clanvowe, "The Two Ways," in Part VI below.

learn how you may make your soul more fair in virtues, hating all vices, so that your life becomes genuinely spiritual and not carnal.

Nevermore then speak evil of your neighbor, or answer one evil word with another. Whatever people say to you, evil or good, suffer it meekly in your heart, without being stirred up to wrath. Then shall you be at rest within and without, and so come readily into a spiritual quality of life that you shall find sweeter than any earthly thing.

A perfectly spiritual life is to despise the world and covet the joy of heaven, and to destroy through God's grace all the wicked desires of your flesh. Forget the solace and affections of your family and friends, and love no one except as they are in God. Whether they die or live, whether they be poor or rich, sick or healthy, thank God always, and bless Him in all your works. For his judgments are known only to Himself, and no creature can comprehend them.

It often happens that folk have their own will and heart's desire in this world, and hell in the other. Some others are in pain, persecution and anguish in this life, and have heaven for their reward. Accordingly, if your friends are always at their ease, healthy, and wealthy in this world's goods, you and they both ought to be concerned that they do not lose the eternal joy of heaven. On the other hand, if they are in suffering and sickness, and yet live righteously, they may securely hope to come to bliss.

Since in this highest degree of love you shall be filled with the grace of the Holy Spirit, you shall have no sorrow or complaint except as it pertains to spiritual things—for example, anguish over your own sin and that of others, or repentant sadness for the love of Jesus Christ as you think of his Passion. And I would, indeed, that you have his Passion much in mind, for it will kindle your heart to regard as nothing all the pleasures and goods of this world, and to have a burning desire for the light of heaven with all the saints and angels.

When your heart is wholly ordained to the service of God, and all worldly thoughts extinguished, then you should steal away by yourself alone to think on Christ and to be much in prayer. For through good thoughts and holy prayer your heart shall be made, as it were, burning in the love of Jesus Christ, and then shall you feel true sweetness and spiritual joy both in your prayer and in meditation. And when you are alone by yourself, give yourself over to saying psalms, the Lord's Prayer, and the Ave. The point is not that you say many prayers but that you pray effectually, with all the devotion of which you are capable, lifting up your thoughts to heaven.

It is better to recite seven psalms with a keen spirit of desire for Christ's love than to say seven hundred thousand while suffering thoughts of worldly vanity to pass through your mind. What good do you imagine can come of that, if you let your tongue babble over your book while your heart is running about various parts of the world? Therefore, set your thought on Christ, and He shall conform it to Himself and keep you from the venom of worldly distractions.

I pray you, as you covet to be a lover of God, that you love the name of Jesus, and keep it in your heart, so that you never forget it wherever you are. You shall truly find in it great joy and comfort. And for the love with which you love Jesus, so tenderly and so singlemindedly, you shall be fulfilled of his grace on this earth and shall be Christ's beloved servant in heaven.

Nothing pays so much respect to God as true love of the name of Jesus. If you love his name persistently, never ceasing for the sake of anything that anyone may do or say, you shall be received into a higher life than you know how to imagine. His goodness is so great that when we ask Him for one measure, He gives five, if we have set our love on Him.

In this degree of love you may overcome those old enemies, the world, the flesh and the devil, no matter how they struggle with you during your life. Until your life's ending it behooves you to stand firm, so that you do not fall into evil thoughts, words, or actions. For this reason you ought to be yearning fervently for a true love of Christ.

... If you will think on his Passion this day, you will find a sweetness that will draw your heart up in great longing for Jesus. With your thought completely on Him, it will be carried beyond all the things of earth, even above the firmament and the stars, so that the eye of faith may look into heaven. Then you will have entered into the third degree of love by which, if you have grace to come to it, you shall have great delight and comfort.

I am not suggesting, of course, that you or anyone else who reads these words will necessarily do all of this, for it is a matter of God's will to choose whom He will. As He gives grace we may have one experience of contemplation or another. For to different persons God distributes the grace of our Lord Jesus variously; but the end of all who love Him is to be set in the joy of heaven. Whoever achieves this third degree of maturity in love, however, acquires wisdom and discretion, learning to love what God wants him to love, and according to his will.

This degree is called the contemplative life. It is a life that finally loves to spend time alone, away from the sound of ringing bells or the din of people singing or weeping. At the beginning, when you come to this state, your spiritual eyes will be lifted up to a heavenly plane, there to be enlightened with the light of grace and kindled with the fire of

Christ's love. Then shall you feel the burning of his love in your heart, ever more and evermore, lifting you heart to God. And you shall feel love, joy, and sweetness so intensely that no sickness, anguish, shame or burden of guilt shall grieve you, but all your life shall turn into an experience of joy.

Then for the very elevation of your heart your prayers will be transformed into joyful songs, and your thoughts into melody. Then will Jesus be all your desire, all your delight and joy, your solace and your comfort. Of Him will your song be ever, and in Him all your rest. Then may you also sing: "I sleep, and yet my heart is awake. What shall I to my beloved say? For his love I yearn both night and day."

All who love novelty and the world's entertainment and set their heart on things other than God cannot arrive at this degree until they have come through the other stages I have mentioned. Therefore, it behooves you to forsake all forms of worldly solace in order that your heart not be bound to the love of any creature or to any worldly business. In this way, being in silence before God, you may be made stable and stalwart, your heart steadfast in the love and fear of God.

Our Lord does not grant beauty, riches and delights of this world to men and women in order that they may set their hearts on those things and spend themselves in sin. No, He does this so that they should come to know Him and love and thank Him who is the giver of these gifts. All the more shame it is, then, if they provoke Him to wrath who has given these gifts, by abusing them in body and in soul. We ought to be moved by our fear of God's judgment to restrain ourselves entirely from lusts, appetites, delights, and wicked accommodation of this world. We ought also to ensure that we do not allow self-pity and complaints about the world to preoccupy us, but that we hold fast to our hope in Jesus Christ, and courageously withstand all temptations that come our way.

RICHARD ROLLE

from
The Form of Living

Amore Langueo

This text is from the seventh chapter of Rolle's *Form of Living*. It is addressed to the person who adopts the vocation of hermit or anchoress and is characteristic of Rolle's writing in saying that it is love, not acts of penance, that determines our closeness to God.

AMORE LANGUEO: these two words are written in the Book of Love, which is also called the Song of Love or Song of Songs. For those who love much like often to sing about that love, for the joy they have when thinking of the one they love, particularly if their beloved is faithful and loving. And the English translation of these two words is: "I languish for love."

Different people on this earth have differing gifts and graces from God, but the special gift of one who is called to lead a solitary life is exclusively to love Jesus Christ. You say to me, "All love Him who keep his commandments." That is true enough. But not all who obey his bidding also keep his counsel, and not all who keep his counsel are fulfilled in the sweetness of his love, nor feel the fire of that love burning in their heart.

For this reason, the diversity in the experience of love makes for a diversity of holiness and spiritual richness. In heaven, the angels which burn most brightly in love are nearest to God. In the same way, men and women who have the greatest experience of God's love, whether they do acts of penance or not, shall attain the highest degree in heaven; those who love Him least shall be in a lower order of relationship.

If you love Him greatly, you will feel a great burning of joy and sweetness in his love for you, and it will be comfort and strength to you day and night. If your love is not burning toward Him, your delight will be small. For no one may experience Him in joy and sweetness unless he or she is a clean vessel filled up with his love. And yet you may come to this condition with great travail in prayer and thought, having such meditations as are focused entirely on the love of God and the loving of Him in return.

When you sit down to eat, express your love for God continuously by taking thought of Him at each morsel, saying something like this in your heart:

> Love be to you, my King,
> and thanks be to you, my King,
> and blessed be you, my King,
> Jesus, all my rejoicing,
> so good in all your gifts
> who for me shed your blood
> and died on the cross.
> Give me grace to sing
> a song of your love.

And think this way not only when you are eating, but also before and afterward—indeed, whenever you pray or speak. Or if you have other reflections which draw you to more profitable devotion than this I teach you, think those thoughts. What I hope is that God will bring such thoughts into your heart as are pleasing to Him, and such as you are ordained by Him to have.

When you pray, do not worry about how much you say, but how truly you say it, so that the love of your heart might be directed steadily upward, and your thought fixed on what you are saying as much as possible. If you are engaged in prayer and meditation all the day long, I know that you will be able to grow greatly in the love of Jesus Christ, and that within a short time you will experience much spiritual delight.

The Nature of Love

This brief selection is taken from the tenth chapter of *The Form of Living*.

I. What Is Love?

BUT NOW YOU QUESTION ME, and say, "You speak so much of love. Tell me, what is love?"

And I answer, Love is a burning desire for God, with a wonderful experience of delight and sense of assurance.

Now God Himself is a burning light. Light clarifies our knowledge; burning kindles our appetites, until we desire nothing but Him.

Love is a life joining together the lover and the beloved. For meekness makes us sweet to God, and purity joins us to God; love makes us one with God.

Love is the beauty of all virtues.

Love is the thing by which God loves us and we Him, and each of us one another.

Love is desire of the heart, always thinking of the one it loves; when it has the one it loves then it rejoices, and nothing can make it sorry.

Love is a stirring in the soul that prompts us to love God for Himself, and all other things for the sake of God. This love, when it is ordained of God, obliterates all inordinate love for anything that is not good. (Now all mortal sin is inordinate love for something that is nothing; so then, it is love that extinguishes all mortal sin.)

Love is a virtue, the most proper affection of the human soul.

Truth may exist without love, but it cannot be of any help without it.

Love is the perfection of poetry, the virtue of prophecy, the fruit of truth, the healing in the sacraments, the establishment of intellect and learning, the riches of the poor and the life of those who are dying.

See how good love is. If we suffer ourselves to be slain; if we give away everything we possess and take up a beggar's staff; if we know as much as man can in this earth, and all this is without love, it will prove nothing but our lot of sorrow and torment.

If you want to ask how good a man or women is, ask how much love he or she has (although that, of course, no one can know for sure; indeed, I hold it but folly to pass judgment on someone's heart, which no one knows truly but God).[1]

Love is a righteous turning away from all earthly things, being joined to God forever, and being kindled with the fire of the Holy Spirit, far removed from failings, far from corruption, obliged to no vice of this life, high above all carnal lusts, and ready always and anxious for the contemplation of God.

Love is through all things victorious, the sum of all good affections, the health of good manners, the goal of God's commandments, the death of sinfulness, the life of virtues, chief virtue while the fighting lasts, the crown of those who overcome, and the merriness of holy thoughts. Without it no one can satisfy God; with it no one sins. For if we love God with all our heart, nothing is left in us through which we may fall into sin.

True love cleanses the soul and delivers it from the torments of hell,

---

1. The standard of Augustine for determination of character was provided by the question, "What does a person love, and how does he or she express that love?" Everything one needs to know about a person, Augustine felt, is contained in an accurate answer to this question. Rolle is typically reluctant to apply this psychology in a shallow or dismissive way.

as from foul bondage to sin and the ugly fellowship of devils. It makes of a child of the devil a child of God and partner in the heritage of heaven.

We should endeavor to clothe ourselves in love, even as the iron or coal does with the fire, or as the air clothes itself with the sun, or as wool does likewise with the dye. The coal so wraps itself in the fire that everything is fire; the air so clothes itself with the sun that everything is light; the wool so substantially takes in the hue of the dye that they become indistinguishable. A true lover of Jesus Christ ought to do likewise. His heart should so burn in love that it is transformed into the fire of love, and become, as it were, totally on fire, and he shall so shine in virtues that no part of him is left in the shadow of vices.

II. Where Is Love?

The answer is that love is in your heart, and in the human will, not in one's hand or mouth. That is, it is not to be identified with works but is a matter of the soul itself. Many there are who speak good and do good, but do not in fact love God—hypocrites, for example, who endure great penances and seem holy in the eyes of men. But because they seek praise and honor from the world and its favor, they have lost their reward, and in the eyes of God are children of the devil and rapacious wolves. But if someone is charitable in almsgiving, living in poverty and penitence, it is a sign that he or she loves God. This only becomes true of such a person, however, if they have truly forsaken the world for the love of God and set all their thought on God, loving all others as themselves. Then all their good deeds are undertaken with the intent of pleasing Jesus Christ and coming at last to the rest of heaven. It is God who is being loved, and the place of that love is in the soul; good deeds are merely an external witness to it. If you speak and act according to what is good, people will suppose that you love the good; therefore be at pains to direct your thoughts toward God, or else you will be deceiving both yourself and others. Nothing I do externally proves that I love God.

A wicked person might do just as much bodily penance as I do, engage in as much early rising and fasting. How then may I imagine that I love or that I am somehow better on account of that which anyone else might do? Certainly it is my heart, which no one but God knows, that determines whether I really love God or not, whatever people may see me doing. We see, therefore, that love is truly a matter of the will, not of work, which is only a sign of love. Yet [if you know] any who say that they love God and yet will not do what they can to demonstrate that love, tell them that they are lying. Love will not be idle; it is always working out some good thing. If it ceases to be exercised, know well that it cools and at last goes out altogether.

III. How Shall I Truly Love God?

My answer here is that true love is to love Him with all your might stalwartly, in all your heart wisely, in all your soul devoutly and sweetly.

Nobody can love Him stalwartly who is not strong and courageous. That person is stalwart who is meek—for all spiritual strength comes from meekness. On whom does the Holy Spirit rest? On a meek soul. Meekness governs us and keeps us through all our temptations so that we are not overcome. But the devil deceives many who are meek through tribulations, reproofs and backbitings. Beware: if you are all worked up through anguish of this world, or for anything that people say to you, you are not meek, nor may you love God stalwartly. For love is as stalwart as death, which slays every living thing on earth, and as irresistible as hell that will not let go of those who die in their sins.

One who loves God perfectly does not grieve Him, whatever shame or anguish he or she may suffer. Rather, this occasions delight, in that such a person desires to be counted worthy of suffering torment and pain for the sake of Christ's love, and can actually rejoice when people are reproving and trying to blacken his name. Just like a corpse, whatever people do or say, does not answer back, so it is with one who loves God perfectly; he does not get worked up on account of any word that a person might say. For a person cannot love who cannot suffer pain or the anger of the crowd for the sake of his Friend's love. To the one who really loves, this is no burden.

Proud men or women do not love in this stalwart way, for they are so weak that they fall over in the slightest breeze of temptation. They evidently seek a higher place than Christ, for what they want is that their own will should be done, whether right or wrong, whereas Christ wills that nothing be done but what is good and without harm to other persons. Those who are truly meek will be seeking not to have their own way in this world, in order that they may have fulfillment in the next.

There is no means whereby we may sooner overcome the devil than by meekness, which he thoroughly hates. After all, he can keep vigils, fast and endure pain more readily than any other creature, but meekness and love are entirely beyond him.

It behooves you also to love God wisely. That you cannot hope to do unless you are wise. You are being wise if you are poor without longing after the things of this world, if you can despise yourself for the love of Christ, and are expending all your intelligence and strength in his service. Some who seem wise are in fact the biggest fools of all, sacrificing all their wisdom to greed and concern for material things. If you saw someone with jewels enough to purchase a kingdom, yet who traded them for an apple as a child might do, you could fairly say he was not wise at all but a great fool. By the same token we have, if we want to, precious gems; they are poverty, penitence and spiritual travail, with which we may "purchase" the kingdom of heaven. If you love poverty and despise the riches and delights of this world, regarding yourself as vile and a poor thing defined by nothing except your own sin, on account of this poverty [of spirit] you will come to have eternal riches. And if you have genuine sorrow for your sins and, because you are so long exiled from your true country, you forsake the comforts of this life, you shall receive for this sorrow the joy of heaven. And if you are in travail, and punish your body temperately and in discretion by vigils, fasts, prayer and meditations, and endure heat, cold, hunger, thirst, privation and anguish all for the sake of the love of Jesus Christ, then for these burdens you shall come unto the rest that lasts forever and sit in a couch of joy with angels. But there are some folks who do not love wisely; they are like children who love an apple more than a castle. [In fact], there are many like this. They trade the joy of heaven for a little delight of the flesh which is not worth a plum.

Now you can see that whoever wants to love wisely should love lasting things everlastingly, and passing things passingly, with a heart settled and focused on nothing but God Himself.

And if you would love Jesus truly, you should not only love Him stalwartly and wisely, but also devoutly and sweetly. Love is sweet when your body is chaste and your thoughts pure. Love is devout when you are offering your prayers and thoughts to God with spiritual joy and a heart burning with the warmth of the Holy Spirit. If people think your soul is, as it were, drunk with delight and solace in the sweetness of Jesus, and your heart is so aware of God's present help that people might imagine that you never think of anything else, then you are coming into such a rest and peace of soul and tranquility of heart—beyond vain thoughts and vices—that it is as if you were quietly asleep, gently berthed in Noah's ark,[2] where nothing at all may hinder you from devotion and sweet love. For you will have obtained his love, and your whole life, until death comes to take you away, will be an experience of

2. The MS has *shyppe* here.

his joy and comfort. Here you are truly Christ's lover, and He rests in you, whose dwelling place is made a place of peace.

The Seven Gifts of the Holy Spirit

This is one of numerous works in medieval devotional literature which follow a septenary schema. Others include the petitions of the Lord's Prayer, the Beatitudes, the seven last words from the cross, the seven deadly sins, and the seven virtues. This list of seven gifts derives from Isaiah 11:2 (Vg.).

LET US CONSIDER the seven gifts of the Holy Ghost which are given to men and women who are ordained to the joy of heaven, and who lead their lives in this world righteously. They are: Wisdom, Understanding, Counsel, Strength, Knowledge, Piety, and the Fear of God. With these seven gifts the Holy Ghost teaches each person individually.

Let us begin with Counsel, for there is need of counsel at the beginning of our work so that we mistake nothing afterwards. Counsel is doing away with the world's riches, and with all delight in things that may entangle us in thought or deed, so that we may be drawn into contemplation of God.

Understanding is the knowledge of what is to be done and what is to be left alone; it shall be given as a gift to those who have need of it, not to others who have no need.

Wisdom is the forgetting of earthly things and thinking of heaven, and the use of discretion in the ordinary activities of life. In this gift contemplation shines, for it is, as St. Augustine says, a spiritual direction of fleshly affections through the joy of uplifted thought.

Strength is endurance in fulfilling good intentions, perseverance so that they not be abandoned through either good fortune or bad.

Piety is a condition of mildness which prevents us from gainsaying Holy Writ when it condemns our sins, whether we understand it or not. It allows us with all our might to purge the meanness of sin in ourselves and in others.

Knowledge is that which nourishes good hope, not so that one boasts of his own righteousness, but so that he grieves for his sins. Such a person gathers earthly goods only for God's honor, and for the advantage of others.

The Fear of God is that by which we refrain from turning again to our sins, despite any evil encouragement to do so. And this fear [of God] is perfected in us, and truly spiritual, when we dread to anger God by the smallest sin that we are aware of, and when we flee from it as from poison.

ANONYMOUS
The Love of Jesus

"Cuard est k'amer n'ose" comes from the same large manuscript book as the verse sermon of Nicholas Bozon included later in this volume (British Library MS Additional 46919), but this selection is in fact a re-working of a thirteenth-century versified exhortation to meditation on the Savior. It was perhaps given the form translated here by the Franciscan friar William Herebert, a collector, translator, and reviser of devotional literature who died in 1333.

He is faint-hearted who dares not love and base who does not
    wish to:
Without love there is no rest for the heart of men,
    nor peace of mind.
Yet folly it is to love something that cannot endure;
it flatters for awhile, but afterward crumbles away,
    unable to afford solace.

Fleshly love is such foolishness: he who wishes to love wisely
should avoid it, for life's brevity grants it no permanence.
The body doesn't exist, however appealing, that will not descend
    to decay.
Lechery offers but brief delight; hell's torments last forever.

Whoso wishes to love without regret, I will show to him
    a true Friend,
one who is so powerful that none can measure up.
He is a king of noble birth, in beauty without a peer
and of unfailing goodness, a very courtly and gentle-hearted
    lover.

I speak of the winsome Jesus: what could be more loving
than to rescue us from the devil's clutches, redeeming us
    by his precious blood?
If you but look on his handsome face, his fair, delightful
    countenance,
the world will not seem worth much beside the desire you feel
    for Him.

Gentle Jesus, so delightful, teach us of your love!
Grant us a steadfast heart fit to serve you day and night

and prepared to reject the world with its vanities
    and false promises of sweetness;
its beauty is but passing and withers like the flower.

Jesus our redemption, our love, our desire:
a proper way of life please grant me before I die,
that my soul may not be damned, but come to you
where there is naught but joy and all that a true heart may
    delight in.

Amen.

ANONYMOUS

Dance of the Cross

This Anglo-Norman poem is from MS Lambeth 522, a large mid-century anthology of religious writings, most of which are meditative works on the life and Passion of Christ or poems in honor of the Virgin. "Venez dames" is both a prayer and a song of invitation to worship, perhaps for the use of nuns. It inverts the familiar motif of the "dance of death," making of life's pilgrimage a dance of joy toward union of the bride of Christ—including, representatively, the nuns who are singing this song—with the beloved Bridegroom. It is possible that this lyric was intended for use in liturgical dance.

Come, ladies, come along;
    step out on the path of righteousness:
arise, arise with singing;
    arise without delay!
The cross is now raised on high,
    and there lies our path:
let us go in rain or shine,
    for Love leads the way.

Jesus goes this way to die for us,
    to reveal to us great joy:
let us go to Him with great desire,
    for Love leads the way.
True love cannot lie sleeping,
    whether in sorrow or joy:
let us go to Him with all our will,
    for Love leads the way.

The mother goes following her Son
    on the one true path:
Let us go, let us go, let us go on,
    For Love leads the way.
Her sweet Son goes to die on the cross,
    in deep sorrow, bereft of joy:
let us go to the cross with God to die,
    for Love leads the way.

Willingly He mortifies Himself, and suffers
   in expectation of joy:
let us go, then, let us go on,
   for Love leads the way.
All the others have left Him alone,
   He who was their joy:
let us go to die on the cross with Him,
   for Love leads the way.

But the most noble of ladies goes before
   and shows us the way.
Let us follow after,
   for Love leads the way.
It would be bad should He die alone,
   He who is our joy:
let us follow after,
   for Love leads the way.

His head has been made all bloody
   by a crown of thorns:
let us go, let us go, let us go on,
   for Love leads the way.
From his hands and feet the blood runs down,
   horribly riven by nails:
let us go to Him with all our will,
   for Love leads the way.

The spear of Longinus pierces his heart;
   the blood wells heavily out:
let us go with Him with all our will,
   for Love leads the way.
This death He there endures
   through courtly love and true:
let us go to Him with all our will,
   for Love leads the way.

Alas that Jesus suffered so,
   so we might come to bliss:
let us go, let us go, let us go on,
   for Love leads the way.
When there is one who wishes to love and serve,
   is this love not well placed?
Then let us go to Him with all our will,
   for Love leads the way.

Now let us pray and sing
   for it is right and joyous:
Come, come, come on ahead,
   for Love leads the way!
That at our death He may give to us
   life, rest and joy,
let us go to Him with all our will,
   for Love leads the way.

Let us sing AMEN;
   and may Jesus grant our prayer.

PART FIVE
Mystical Spirituality

JACOB'S LADDER

Miniature from the *Rutland Psalter*, Add. MS 62925 (fol. 83v) in the mid-thirteenth century. Reproduced by permission of the British Library.

RICHARD ROLLE

from
The Fire of Love

The Fire of Love (Incendium Amoris) was probably the best known and most widely disseminated of this prolific writer's Latin works during his own lifetime (c. 1300–1349). A translation from the Latin was made by one Richard Misyn, a Carmelite friar, as early as 1435.[1] The work as a whole is a long, rambling discussion of various difficulties attending the faithful pursuit of a contemplative life, but the opening section, included here, reflects on the process of conversion and early spiritual growth. It is written from the perspective of one who has had a dramatic encounter with the Holy Spirit; Rolle shares this experience with his reader in the prologue, thus providing an autobiographical context for his subsequent observations. Rolle's lifelong spirituality is accented by an evidently passionate nature which is seeking the controlling form of a disciplined life. These pages, written about 1343, serve as an introduction to much of his more mature work, several examples of which are included in this collection.

CONCERNING WHAT I AM ABOUT TO TELL YOU—about the time I first felt my heart begin to warm—I have been amazed more than I am able to say. I felt it truly, not simply in my imagination, but just as though my heart was burning with a physical fire. I marvelled, you may be sure, at how this burning in my soul leapt up, and at its unanticipated comfort. It was so vivid an experience that often I put my hand against my chest just to see if I could feel any cause for the heat outwardly! But once I knew that it was purely a matter of inward, spiritual nature, and that the burning sensation was not from carnal love or concupiscence, I realized it had to be a gift from my Creator. Accordingly I was glad, and melted with a desire for a greater experience of love, especially on account of the inflow of the sweetest pleasure and spiritual delight with which that spiritual flame comforted my mind. Before this comforting warmth came to me, shedding its sense of devotion within, I frankly believed that no such experience could come in our present state of

1. Misyn's text, MS Corpus Christi College, Oxford, 236, was included in *The Fire of Love and the Mending of Life*, ed. Ralph Harvey, Early English Text Society, O.S. 106 (London: Early English Text Society, 1896). The Latin text of the *Incendium Amoris* exists in more than forty MSS and has been edited by Margaret Deanesly (London, 1915). The most readable modern translation of the whole work is that of Clifton Wolters, *The Fire of Love* (London: Penguin, 1972).

exile, for truly it enflames the soul just as if a real fire were burning there.

Now there are people who we say are "on fire" with love for Christ, because we can see them despising the world, utterly given over to the service of God. Yet [this of which I speak is an inward burning]—just as when you put your finger in the flame it is enveloped in a burning sensation, so it is for the soul enflamed by this love: it feels a most palpable heat—sometimes more intensely, sometimes less so, according to the frailty of our flesh.

Who is there who could bear for long this great heat in his mortal body in all its intensity? . . . [I am so taken up in it that] even sleep seems to me to be an enemy, for the only empty time I have is that in which I am constrained to sleep. Awake, I am busy warming up my soul when it is seems numb with cold. For when it gets a little too complacent in its devotion I know quite well how to set a fire under myself, and how to be quickly lifted up above all earthly attachments with intense desire. Truly, the overflowing of this eternal love does not come to me when I am unoccupied, nor do I feel its spiritual heat when I am physically weary from my work or, as seldom happens, intertwined with worldly mirth or given immoderately to argument. In fact, I have usually at such times felt myself growing cold, at least until I was able to put all those things behind my back so that I could make a real effort to be in the Savior's presence, there again to dwell in this inwardly burning love.

Wherefore I offer this book to be read not by the philosophers or wise persons of this world, nor to great theologians who are all wrapped up in infinite questioning, but to simple and unlearned people who are more zealous to love God than to acquire knowledge. For what is here is not learned by debate or disputation but rather is known by loving experience. I believe that matters of theological debate are, of all forms of knowledge, the most preeminent, but the love and law of Christ is not finally a matter of intellect.

So I have not written for these people unless they have forgotten and put behind themselves already those things which really belong to the world, and desire to direct their love only to our Maker. First, then, they must flee from every kind of earthly dignity, hate all pride of intellect and vainglory and finally conform themselves to a life of great poverty, in prayer and meditation giving themselves industriously to the love of God. It will then be no wonder if they discover in themselves that fire of uncreated charitable love, conditioning their hearts to handle the heat in which all darkness is consumed, lifting them up in that lovely and most merry burning fire. Then temporal concerns will pass away from consciousness, and they shall know themselves set in eternal peace. The more knowledgeable they are, the more capacity they have to love by this law, as long as they are glad to be despised by others and cheerfully to despise themselves. . . .[2]

In this wretched dwelling place of our exile here, most people realize that no one may be taught to love eternal life or be anointed with heavenly sweetness unless he is first genuinely turned to God. Indeed, he must be truly converted, with a mind unambiguously turned away from earthly matters, before the love of God can be experienced even in small doses.

It is by a rightly directed love that this turnaround is effected, so that one loves what is worthy of being loved and learns to burn more fervently in love for those things which are most worthy, less for what is less worthy. God is to be loved most of all. Heavenly things are greatly to be loved after that, while earthly things are to be loved no more than is necessary and little or not at all by comparison. A person can be absolutely sure he or she has been turned toward Christ when nothing else is desired but Christ alone. In turning away from the "good things" of this world which actually deceive and do not protect those who love them, one experiences an absence of fleshly desires and a hatred of all kinds of wickedness, so that there remains no appetite for worldly things, nor any desire to hang on to more of these than is strictly necessary. Those who heap up riches (for whom?) take their comfort in riches, and are not on that account worthy to have their hearts gladdened with heavenly mirth—despite all their feigned devotion and phony piety— though they imagine they are experiencing in their temporal prosperity some anticipation of the felicity that is to come. In fact it is just this sort of presumption which has precipitated their downfall from that true spiritual sweetness with which God's lovers are rewarded, for they have armed themselves against it by their incompatible ambition for worldly wealth.

All love which is not God-directed is, in fact, wickedness, and corrupts those who are possessed by such love. This is why those who are devoted to what the world regards as excellent are ignited with a different sort of fire, and become further separated from the heavenly heat than heaven itself is from the earth. Assuredly, they take on the characteristics of the things they love, becoming conformed to a wanton concupiscence; persisting in old and wretched appetites for the vanities of this life, they exchange a holy love for this love, so exchanging the incorruptible joy of purity for a wanton "beauty" that cannot last. And truly they could not do this unless they were blinded by the fire of su-

---

2. This section is both preemptive of censure for Rolle's not being "theological" in his approach, and an advertisement that the kind of spirituality advocated is, in its own way, a challenge to the professional "religious" of his day.

perficial love which both destroys virtue at its source and nourishes the roots of every kind of vice.

Many there are who, because they are not prey to the beauty of women, nor to lechery, assume that on this account they are assured of their salvation. Because of an external chastity they fancy that they are saints surpassing all others. But this is a wicked presumption, and entirely vain, if at the same time they do not weed out greed, which is the root of all sin. Truly, as it is written, there is nothing worse than the love of money (see 1 Timothy 6:10),[3] for while the heart is occupied with the love of temporal things it admits no kind of devotion. Love for God and for the world cannot exist together in the same soul; whichever love is the stronger puts the other out, so that it becomes quite clear who is a lover of the world and who a follower of Christ. Lovers of Christ set their behavior against the world and the flesh, while lovers of the world set themselves against God and their own soul.

Those who are truly chosen of God—whether they eat or drink, or whatever they do—turn their mind to heavenly things; they seek only what is necessary, not the lusts of the flesh. When they have to speak about worldly things they do it with anguish of heart and pass over it quickly, turning their minds back toward God as quickly as possible so that whatever time remains can be put to God's service. They do not stand around in idleness, nor go to plays or spectacles—which are a token of the reprobate— but rather conduct themselves honestly in the things which pertain to God, and do not hesitate about it, either in speech or thought.

The reprobate, on the other hand, conduct themselves in the things of God altogether casually. They hear God's words with "hard" ears, they pray without real affection, and when they think of God it is without desire. They go to church alright, and even pack it out to the walls, and beat their breasts and sigh aloud, but this is plainly a counterfeit of spirituality, intended for the eyes of other people and not for the eyes of God. Truly, even though their bodies are in the church they find their minds easily distracted to worldly goods they possess or desire to possess, so that their hearts are actually far from God. They eat and drink, not because they need to, but to gratify a lustful appetite, and can only be satisfied with exotic foods.[4] Though they give bread to

3. The word of the Vulgate is *cupiditas*, "cupidity," or self-aggrandizing love of any kind. Rolle here anticipates early translations of the Bible, down to the King James Version, in narrowing *cupiditas* down to "money."

4. A charge directed not only (perhaps not even primarily) at wealthy laypeople but at vocational religious in well-endowed communities who were abusers of the table. William Langland, in *Piers the Plowman,* makes the same charge.

the poor and even, perhaps, clothing to those who are cold, they are doing their alms in mortal sin and vainglory, giving sometimes out of ill-gotten gains. Small wonder it is if this sort of thing does not please our Redeemer, but rather provokes our Judge to vengeance.

The character of the elect is such that even when they are required to be occupied with things of the world or the flesh, they are watchful, turning their mind always toward God. The reprobate, by contrast, even when they seem to be occupied in the service of God, are preoccupied with things of the world and with those things that pertain to the world and the flesh, and their heart is entirely ravished away. And while the chosen do not displease God in the way they handle life's necessities, the reprobate fail to please God even in the good deeds that they are seen to perform, for their actual good deeds are few, and badly compromised with more deeds that are evil.

The devil has hold of many folk whom we consider "good"—even alms-givers, chaste persons and meek, self-confessed sinners who punish themselves with hairshirts and penances. Under a cloak of spiritual health, alas, deadly spiritual wounds lie often hidden. The devil has control over more than a few who are hasty in spiritual work and busy to preach, but over none, doubtless, who are truly warmed by the fire of charitable love and dead to the world's vanity. The inwardly wicked, on the other hand, incline to self-gratification, always greedy for gain and dead to real spiritual self-discipline, and weakened by extreme flabbiness. Their love is ever inordinate, for they love temporal goods more than the things of eternity, love more their bodies than their souls.

ANONYMOUS

from
The Cloud of Unknowing

The Cloud of Unknowing was written about 1370 by a priest, probably a country parson of the northeast midlands of England. He seems to have chosen deliberately to remain anonymous in his very successful writings, and although he apparently had a fairly large flock for which he was responsible as spiritual director, there is no evidence to suggest that even those under his immediate pastoral care knew him as an author of spiritual books. Six other works have been attributed to this priest: loose translations of both the *Mystica Theologica* (a work ascribed in the Middle Ages to Paul's convert Dionysius)[1] and the famous *Benjamin Minor* of Richard of St. Victor,[2] as well as four shorter pieces, *The Book of Privy Counselling, An Epistle on Prayer, An Epistle on Discretion Regarding Stirrings in the Soul,* and *A Treatise on the Discerning of Spirits.*[3]

The Cloud shows the influences of the writings of Richard of St. Victor, especially his *Benjamin Minor,* as well as the works of Pseudo-Dionysius. It is further undergirded with a basic theology which can be traced to St. Augustine and St. Gregory the Great. Its debt to the biblical theology of Augustine and Gregory is found in its major premises and pastoral purpose; its indebtedness to the mystical writers governs its vocabulary, style, and themes. This is a spiritual book which emphasizes the *via negativa,* the apophatic or "negative" way of pursuing a relationship with God. That is to say, it begins with the insistence that human nature and the nature of God are so far removed from each other that God, who is "wholly other," cannot be understood by the mortal intellect. Accordingly, the author suggests, our approach to God must proceed through a complete resignation of any notion that such knowledge can be acquired by the means of study and rational analysis. Rather than being a subject of human knowledge, God's glory is utterly beyond the grasp of the intellect. It is accessible only through God's own disclosure of

---

1. See *Deonise Hid Diuinite,* ed. Phyllis Hodgson, Early English Text Society, O.S. 231 (1955; reprint, London: Oxford University Press, 1958). While attributed in the Middle Ages to Paul's convert (Acts 17:34), *Mystica Theologica* was actually written around the sixth century by the author we now know only as Pseudo-Dionysius the Areopagite. It was first translated into Latin shortly thereafter.

2. "A Treatyse of the Stodye of Wysdome at Men Clepen Benjamin." See Hodgson, *Deonise Hid Diuinite,* 11-46.

3. *Deonise Hid Diuinite* includes all of these texts except *The Book of Privy Counselling,* which can be found in Hodgson's edition of *The Cloud of Unknowing,* Early English Text Society, O.S. 218 (London: Oxford University Press, 1944). The works are found all together in a number of manuscripts; see Hodgson, *Cloud of Unknowing,* for a list and descriptions.

himself as Presence to a soul which has by disciplines of the will—not the intellect—learned to lay aside every self-generated impediment to that revelation and to become passive, an empty vessel waiting to be filled.[4]

As is typical of such spiritual writing, this work is directed to those well established in faith who have been introduced to faith in Jesus, strengthened by the Holy Spirit, and now aspire to the one truly "heavenly thing": union of the soul with God. Indeed, the writer forbids his book to be read by anyone less mature.[5] The full title of this work, of which only the opening pages are represented here, is written on the manuscript as follows: *Here bygynniþ a book of contemplacyon, þe whiche is clepyd þe Clowde of Vnknowyng in þe whiche a soule is onyd wiþ God.*

Invocation

GOD, UNTO WHOM ALL HEARTS ARE OPEN, and unto whom all wills are speaking, and from whom no secret thing is hidden: I beseech Thee so to cleanse the intentions of my heart with the unutterable gift of thy grace that I may perfectly love Thee and worthily praise Thee. Amen.

I. The Four States of Christian Life

My spiritual friend in God, to begin with, you should understand that I find, according to my own rough reckoning, four levels or states of Christian life: common, special, solitary, and perfect. Three of these may be both begun and brought to conclusion in this life. The fourth may, by grace, be begun here, but its end is in the bliss of heaven where it shall last forever. And just as you will see how I have ordered them consecutively—first common, then special, followed by solitary and, at the last, perfect—even so I think that in the same order and progression our

---

4. Contrast the *via positiva*, the "positive way" (called "cataphatic" in the Eastern church), which emphasizes affirmation, focuses on the human life of Christ, and tends to describe God in terms of human attributes projected toward an eternal perfection. By and large the *via positiva* is the kind of spirituality which had been dominant in the English tradition, reaching an apogee in the thirteenth century, especially with the Franciscans.

5. In the prologue, not translated here, the author is emphatic and explicit about this, charging the reader not to read, copy, or speak of the work, nor permit anyone else to do so, except "to soche one þat haþ (bi þi supposing) in a trewe wille & by an hole entent, purposed him to be a parfite follower of Criste, not only in actyue leuyng, bot in þe souereinnest pointe of contemplatife leuyng þe whiche is possible by grace for to be comen to in þis present liif of a parfite soule ȝit abiding in þis deedly body." Hodgson, *Cloud of Unknowing*, 1-2.

Lord has, in his great mercy, called you and led you unto Himself by the desires of your own heart.

First, you know well enough that when you were living in the "common" state of Christian life, dwelling in the company of your worldly friends, God, in his eternal love by which He both created you out of nothing and then redeemed you by his precious blood when you were lost through Adam, could not permit you to remain so distant from Him in your condition and manner of life. Therefore He graciously kindled your desire and bound you to Himself by a chain of love-longing, leading you by this means into a more "special" state and form of life, in which you became a servant of his special servants. This was so that you could learn how to live in greater spiritual maturity in his service than before, or than you might have done in the ordinary experience of the Christian life.

Now what will happen? It seems that He will not let you off so easily, for the sake of his heart's love toward you, which He has always had since you were in any way spiritual at all. So what is He doing? Can you not see how delightfully and graciously He has been drawing you toward the third stage and manner of life, which is called "solitary"? It is in this solitary condition and manner of life that you will be able to make those first steps in love toward that ultimate level and condition of spiritual life that is called "perfect."

II. "Solitary" Vocation

So look up now, you poor weak fellow, and take stock of yourself. What are you really, and what have you done to deserve to be so called out[6] by our Lord? How wretchedly weary of heart and spiritually lazy is anyone who is not awakened by the beckoning of his love and sound of his voice calling!

Especially at this point, O wretched man, you should beware of your enemy. Do not begin to think of yourself as holier or better on account of this vocation—your solitary form of life. For in fact you are now all the more wretched and to be blamed if you are not doing all in your power to live a godly life, by grace and good counsel living up to your calling. Accordingly, you should be all the more meek and loving toward your spiritual spouse, in that He, who is Almighty God, King of kings and Lord of lords, would humble Himself so lowly as to meet you

6. The language here alludes to the scriptural account of the calling of Samuel as well as to the traditional metaphor of the shepherd and sheep; it is typical of discussions of vocation in this period.

where you are, and out of all the flock of his sheep graciously to choose you to be one of his special ones, putting you into an enclosed pasture[7] where you can be fed with the sweetness of his love, a foretaste of your inheritance in the kingdom of heaven.

Step forward, then, I pray you, without hesitation. Look forward and forget those things which are behind.[8] Consider what you lack, not what you have already achieved, for that is the readiest means of getting and keeping a spirit of meekness. Your whole life must become an expression of desire for perfection if you are to make effective progress toward it. And this desire must be constantly generated from within your will by the hand of Almighty God and your own consent. But let me assure you of this: He is a jealous lover and will brook no rival. He will not work in your will unless He has your undivided commitment. Nor does He ask for your help; He asks for you. He wants simply that you should look upon Him, and let Him have his way. It is enough that you should be on guard against insects and vermin coming in the doors and windows of your soul; if you are willing for this much, and meekly seek his assistance in prayer, He will soon help you.

To it, then! Let's see how you handle yourself. He is utterly ready, and only waits for you to get going.

But what are you now to do? And how to get started?

III. Focusing Exclusively on God

Lift up your heart unto God in a meek spirit of love, intending that offering for God Himself and not simply out of appreciation for his benefits. To this end be loath to think about anything but God Himself, so that nothing else occupies your mind or will except God. Do everything in your power to forget all the creatures made by God, and their doings, so that neither your thought nor your desire is inclined toward any of them, either in general or in particular. Rather, let these things be, and pay them no attention.

This is the work of the soul that is most pleasing to God. All the saints and angels rejoice in this kind of work, and hasten to help it with all their might. All devils are enraged when you act like this, and try to dissuade you in every way they can. And all people living in this world are wonderfully helped by this spiritual labor of yours, in ways you cannot fathom. Yes, even the souls in purgatory are relieved in their pains by

7. The MS reads *in þe stede of pasture*, i.e., in the special place "instead of" open pasture.
8. See Philippians 3:12-14, a text which lies behind the whole work.

the virtue of this work. You yourself are cleansed and made virtuous by this more than any other type of spiritual exercise—and yet, when a soul is strengthened in conscious desire for it by grace, it is the easiest spiritual work of all, and most quickly accomplished. Otherwise, it is much too hard and too intimidating for you to manage.

Do not give up, therefore, but work at it until you feel this desire. For the first time you try to do it you will experience only a darkness, as it were a cloud of unknowing, something you cannot define except to say that you do feel in your will utterly intent upon God. This darkness or cloud, howsoever you approach it, remains between you and God preventing you from seeing Him in the clear light of your rational understanding, or from experiencing Him directly in the sweetness of love emotionally.[9] Nevertheless, prepare yourself to remain in this darkness as long as you are able for it, evermore crying out for Him whom you love. For if ever you are to see Him or feel Him in this life, it will always be in this cloud and this darkness. And if you will engage yourself diligently as I bid you, I trust in his mercy that you shall come to have this experience.

In order that you should not make any mistake in this matter, or expect things to be otherwise than they are, I should tell you a little more about it as I understand it.

This work requires no great amount of time before it is faithfully realized, though some persons expect otherwise. Indeed, it is the briefest endeavor of all that may be imagined. It is neither longer nor shorter than an atom—the which atom, according to the definition of reliable philosophers in the science of astronomy, is the smallest particle of time. And it is so small that on account of its littleness it is indivisible and well nigh incomprehensible. This is that time of which it is written: "For the time that is given, you shall be asked to give an account how you spent it."[10] And it is a reasonable thing that you should be required to give account of it, for it is neither longer nor shorter than a single impulse of your soul's energy, which is to say, your will. For there may be as many expressions of will or desire in one hour—no more and no less—as there are atoms in an hour. And if you were to be reformed by grace and restored to the first unfallen state of the human soul, then you could continue, with the help of that grace, to be in command of those many desires so that none of them would go astray, but every one of them

9. The MS reads: *in pin affeccion;* the distinction is, as in the writings of St. Bernard and of Franciscans such as St. Bonaventure, between intellect and emotion.

10. A common theme, from Augustine onward, often applied to discussions of Ephesians 5:16 or Matthew 20:1-16.

reach out to that crown of desirable things, the highest object of our will, God Himself.

For by the temperate mediation of his Godhead He meets our souls at their own level, a place where we can recognize Him by virtue of having been created in his image and likeness. Yet He alone, and none but Himself, is sufficient (and more than sufficient) to fulfill the longing of our souls. And our souls, by virtue of his reforming grace, are made fully sufficient to comprehend Him fully by his love, who remains yet incomprehensible by any created intellect or otherwise to any angelic or human soul. (That is, He is incomprehensible by means of the power of intellect, but not incomprehensible by the power of love.)

All reasonable creatures, angels or persons, have in themselves two personal faculties, the principal one being the power of knowing, the second being the power of loving. To the first of these, the intellect, the God who made both is eternally incomprehensible; to the second, the affections, He is fully knowable to each person in his or her particularity. This is so much the case that any given loving soul, by the virtue of love, may know Him fully who is at the same time fully sufficient—and more so than can be measured—to fill up all souls and angels that exist. And this is the everlastingly marvellous miracle of love, which shall never come to an end; for God has always made Himself known in this way, and always will. Grasp this, you who by grace may do so, for the experience of it is endless bliss, while the contrary is endless pain.

If anyone was so reformed by grace as to continue in firm control of the stirrings of the will (since such stirrings are inevitable in ordinary nature), he would never be without some taste of that eternal sweetness, nor denied the full meal in the bliss of heaven. Do not wonder, therefore, if I direct you toward this work. For this is the kind of life, as you shall be hearing, in which man was intended to continue if he had never sinned, and for which he was created, and all other things were created to help him achieve this end. And it is by this means that mankind shall be restored again. Yet for failure to live in this way one will fall deeper and deeper into sin and further and further away from God whereas, by persevering in this alone and nothing else, a person rises steadily higher out of his sin and comes nearer and nearer unto God.

IV. Stewardship of Time

Therefore be careful about how you spend your time. There is nothing more precious. In an instant, as brief a moment as may be, heaven may be won or lost. It is significant of the preciousness of time that God, who is the giver of time, never gives two moments simultaneously, but grants them always in succession. To do otherwise He would have to reverse the whole order and course of his creation. For time is made for man, and not man for time. Therefore God, who is the ruler of nature, will not in his dispensation of time go ahead of the natural impulses of the human soul, which occur merely one at a time. This is so that no one shall have any excuse before God on the Day of Judgment when he gives an account of how he has spent his time. No one can say to Him: "You gave me two times of opportunity at the same moment, when I have but one impulse at a time."

Now you are troubled, and say, "What can I do? If what you say is true, how shall I give account of every single moment? Here I am, twenty-four years old, and I have never paid any attention to time. Even if I were to amend my way in this respect at once, you know very well that by the very argument you have written, neither in the course of nature nor by common grace will there be any extra moments available to me other than those which are ordained to come anyhow to make up for those I have lost. Moreover, I know well enough that by reason of my abundant weaknesses and slowness of spirit I can hardly keep properly one moment in a hundred. So I am utterly done for! Help me then, for the love of Jesus!"

You have well said, "for the love of Jesus," for it is in the love of Jesus that you shall discover your help. This love has such power that it makes all things accessible. Love Jesus therefore, and all that He has is yours. By virtue of his Godhead He is both creator and dispenser of time. By virtue of his humanity He is the one faithful user of time. Because He is both God and man together, He is the best judge of how time ought to be spent. Therefore unite yourself to Him in love and faith, and then by virtue of the knot which joins you shall you be in partnership with Him and with all those who like yourself have been so joined to Him in love—that is to say, with our Lady, Saint Mary, who was full of grace in her investment of time, with all the angels of heaven who never waste time, and with all the saints in heaven and on earth who by the grace of Jesus fully justify their use of time in the virtue of love.

Lo! Herein is comfort. Understand this clearly and profit by it. But let me emphasize this one thing particularly: I cannot see how anyone may claim fellowship with Jesus and his just mother, his high angels and also his saints, unless such a one does all in his or her power, grace helping, to be a good steward of time, so that he can be seen to be doing his part to profit the community, however little that might be, as each of the other persons does his or her part to the same end.

Therefore be alert for this work and its marvellous operation in your soul. For if truly conceived, it comes suddenly and without warning, leaping up to God like a spark from the coals. In a soul rightly disposed an amazing number of such impulses can come in any given hour. In one such moment the soul may completely forget the existence of the outside world. But almost as soon, by reason of the corruption of the flesh, it can fall back again to some thought, or some deed, done or not done. Yet what of it? Almost at once it can leap up again as suddenly as it did before.

V. Transcending Intellect and Technique

Here then, in brief, is how this takes place. It is clear that this experience is far from being a matter of fantasy, false imagination or fanciful opinion—which are not brought in by a spirit of meek and unselfconscious love, but by a proud, curious and inventive imagination; such a proud and curious turn of mind ought always to be put down and trodden underfoot, if this work is to be faithfully conceived in purity of spirit. Whoever hears or reads all this, and thinks that it is something that can be brought about by mental effort (and so tries to figure it out as an intellectual matter, imagining means to counter natural impulses), merely counterfeits the true thing in a manner which is efficacious for neither body nor soul. Truly this person, whosoever he be, is perilously deceived, and so dangerously so that, unless God of his great goodness intervenes with a miracle of mercy and makes him stop what he is doing and humble himself before the counsel of mature spiritual persons, he shall fall into other frenzies, or else into other great mischiefs—spiritual sins and deceptions of the devil—through which he could easily be lost, body and soul, for all eternity. So for the love of God be careful, and do not attempt to achieve this experience intellectually. For I tell you truly that it may not be had by this sort of effort. Therefore leave such things alone.

And do not think that because I call it a "darkness" or a "cloud" that I refer to the sort of cloud you see in the sky or the sort of darkness that falls over your house at night when the candles go out. That kind of cloud you can imagine, conjuring it before your eyes on even the finest summer's day, just as in the darkest night of winter you can imagine a clear and shining light. These analogies are entirely misleading, and not at all what I mean. When I say "darkness," I mean an absence of understanding, or knowing, just as anything you do not know, or else have forgotten, is "dark" to you in that you cannot penetrate it with your inward eye. For this reason it is called not a cloud of the sky, but a "cloud of unknowing" that stands between you and your God.

VI. Transcending Created Things

If ever you are to come to this cloud, and live and work in it as I am recommending to you, just as this cloud of unknowing is above you, between yourself and God, even so you should put a cloud of forgetting beneath you, between yourself and all created things. You may think that you are very far from God, in that this cloud of unknowing is between you and Him, but surely if the matter is rightly construed, you were a lot further from Him when you had no cloud of forgetting between yourself and all created things. And whenever I say "all created things," I mean not only the things themselves, but all the activities and circumstances associated with them. I make no exceptions whatsoever to this, whether good or evil; to put it simply, everything must be hidden under this cloud of forgetting.

For though it is sometimes profitable to reflect upon the circumstances and actions of certain special creatures, nevertheless this activity profits little or nothing. For remembrance of or reflection on any creature that God has made, or upon any of their deeds, is a type of spiritual light; the eye of the soul is turned in that direction, and even fixed upon it, as is the eye of the marksman glued to his target. And I tell you this, that everything you are concentrating on is for that time, as it were, above you, standing between you and your God. And insomuch as you are further from God, it is because there is something else in your mind other than God Himself.

Indeed, if it be courteous and seemly to say so, in this work it profits us little or nothing even to reflect on the kindnesses of God, or upon our Lady, or on the saints and angels in heaven, or even on the joys of heaven, if you are doing this in the expectation that this will feed and increase your spiritual purpose. I believe that for this purpose it will be of no help at all. For though it is entirely good to reflect on the kindnesses of God, and to love and to praise Him for these things, it is far better still to direct your thoughts toward Him in his Being, and to love and praise Him for Himself.

from
The Orcherd of Syon

The Orcherd of Syon, a Middle English translation from the *Dialogo* or *Dialogue* of Catherine of Siena, was prepared for the first generation of Birgittine nuns at Syon Abbey between 1415 and 1420. Though it survives in only three English manuscripts, extracts are to be found in other collections of fifteenth century spiritual writing. The orchard of the title signifies a kind of garden, not merely the literal enclosure of the Abbey but the *hortus conclusus* or "enclosed garden" of the Song of Songs; it also refers to the spiritual conversations which transpire there between *sponsus* and *sponsa*, bridegroom and bride. Its dialogue format recalls models such as St. Augustine's *Confessions*, except that here, unlike in that work, the material is presented as "revelation": God is assumed to be doing most of the talking. The passage translated here is a speculative exposition of chapters 12–16 of John's Gospel.

Jesus Our Bridge

I

The Lord Speaks

"DAUGHTER, FORASMUCH AS I SAID TO YOU that I have made a bridge of my Son, I will not have you be ignorant that the way of my beloved Son was broken off by the disobedience and trespass of Adam, so that no one could come to eternal life. And your first parents gave no thanks to me, as they ought to have done, and so had no part in that great goodness, for which blissful rejoicing I made them and shaped them after my own image and likeness. Because they did not thus possess the good which I had ordained for them, my abiding purpose was not fulfilled. The truth of my purpose is this: that I created that same humanity in order that they should have everlasting life with me, and taste and savor my eternal goodness and sweetness. But they, through their offense, forfeited their place in my will, so that my eternal purpose for them went unfulfilled. All this mischief occurred because that [original] sin had shut up heaven against them and closed the gate of my mercy. And it is this same sin which engendered and spread abroad brambles and thorns and all too many tribulations, with infinite attendant griefs. Almost at once these creatures, in a manner consistent with their revolt against me, turned to rebellion against themselves. Flesh debated against spirit, so that, losing the noble state of innocence, they became like irrational beasts. All [lesser] creatures now rebelled against them, whereas before they were fully in obedience—as long as humanity persevered in that innocence in which it was created. But since they would not be content in that state but trespassed disobediently, therefore they have earned everlasting death both in soul and in body.

"From this trespass and sin came forth a turbulent flood which constantly buffeted them with its waves, multiplying their sorrows, so that many were the labors and great the weariness which had to be borne on account of self, the world and the devil. You would all have perished, for no one could ascend to eternal life, even by the means of great personal righteousness. Wherefore I desired to ordain a remedy for your great distress, and have given you a bridge in the person of my own Son, so that in passing over the torrent you might not perish. This torrent is the tempestuous sea of your present wretched life.

"Do you not see, daughter, how much my creatures are beholden to me, and yet how blindly ignorant, willing to slay their own souls, rather than to take the remedy I have ordained and offered?

"Open now the eyes of your intellect[1] and you will see myriads of mortal men blinded with ignorance, as well as some imperfect servants and still others who follow me in perfect truth, so that you may sorrow over the damnation of the wretched and grieve for their ignorance, and yet rejoice, too, in the perfection of my beloved children. You shall see, moreover, the diverse customs observed by some persons who walk in the light, and also the habits of those who walk in darkness. But first I want you to consider the bridge of my Son, and for you to behold the greatness of that bridge, which stretches from the heights of heaven down to earth, so that the 'humus' of your humanity[2] might be joined to the magnificence of the Godhead.

"This reunification which I have brought about in human nature was, I have said before, necessary for the reformation of the road broken off, so that you might once again come unto life, and pass out of the bitterness and wretchedness of this sorry world. The bridge could not be made only of earth if it was to be sufficient to arch over the torrent and

1. An invitation, though this is in the form of "revealed discourse," to a thoughtful reflection, such as is pertinent to the essentially theological character of this part of the treatise.

2. Middle English *erpe of ȝoure humanyte;* the original makes an indicative pun on the words *humus* and *humanitas.*

reach to everlasting life. For the humus of human nature was not suffi-cient to atone for the sin that was done, nor to do away with the origi-nal sin of Adam, the dishonesty and wickedness of which have brought all humankind into thralldom, anxiety and bitterness, and drawn out from these conditions much foul, rotten and stinking filth, as I have al-ready declared. Therefore it is needful for human nature to be joined to the height of my own eternal nature in the Godhead, so that satisfac-tion may be obtained for all humankind. In this it was the nature of man which would suffer the pain, and the divine nature joined to it the means by which I should accept the sacrifice of my Son offered for you, that it should take you up from death and give you life.

"So the very summit of the Godhead humbled Himself down to the ground and, joining your humanity with his Godhead, mercifully made the bridge and thus graciously built up[3] and made new again the way which had been broken off. And why should He thus make Himself to be the way, except for the intent that you should come into his abiding purpose and rejoice eternally with the angels. And yet the fact that my Son is the bridge is not enough to ensure you this life, unless you actu-ally do walk across upon Him."[4]

The Daughter Replies

Then this soul, so enriched by love, began to speak to our Lord, and said, "Oh Lord, inestimable charitable Love, who is not so influenced by this great love that, on account of it, he may keep his heart from breaking? You, Lord, who are the very fount of charity, seem to have such great delight in your creatures—as if you could not live without them! And yet you have no need of us; you are our Lord and our God. And inasmuch as you are unchangeable, nothing is added to you through our goodness. Moreover, in the heights of your eternal good-ness you are untainted by our evil. Ah, good Lord, who is it that moves you to so much mercy? It is love that moves you, Lord, and not any need that you have of us, who are after all to you just like so many bad debts. O, Eternal Goodness, if I consider myself properly, I myself am a briber, I am a thief. Your Son, Lord, was crucified upon the cross-tree for me, wretch that I am, and I behold your Son there, nailed to the cross. Of your Son you thus made a bridge to me, as a revelation of your good-ness on my behalf, who am your wretched servant. Wherefore, if it be

3. ME *edified*, "built up," is used here in its literal rather than its later metaphori-cal sense.

4. The force of this extension of the metaphor radicalizes here the extremity of Christ's "laying down his life"—literally a "bridge over troubled waters."

acceptable to your goodness, I desire that of that goodness you would reveal to me those who cross over by the bridge, and those who do not."

II

The Lord Speaks

Then the eternal, almighty God, the more to stir up this soul and encourage her to labor more fervently for the salvation of souls, answered her and said, "Before I show you what I will, and also those things you ask of me, I will first impart to you some understanding of the nature of the bridge.

"I said to you before that the bridge stretches from heaven to earth; this is through the conjunction I have made in mankind, whom I formed out of the gritty moisture of the earth. This bridge, my only-begotten Son, has three ladders in his person, of which two are formed by the sorrowful tree of his holy cross, and the third represents his experience of great pain and bitterness when they gave Him gall and vinegar to drink. By these three ladders you should understand three conditions of the soul, which I shall explain to you shortly. The first ladder is at the level of your feet, signifying the soul's affection and desire; for just as the feet bear up your body, so your desire and affection bear up your soul. The nailed feet of Jesus become ladders for you, steps by which you may attain or reach up to the [second ladder, the] wound in his side, through which wound you may then discover the secrets of his heart. After you have ascended up by the feet of your soul's desire, then the soul begins to taste the love of his heart, gazing with the mind's eye upon the heart of my dear Son, wherein the soul shall find completed and perfect love. I say 'completed,' for he loves you for no profit of his own, since you cannot [on your own merit] be of profit to Him, in that He and I are one and complete.

"This soul then sees how much God loves her, and is thus all the more charged with love. Furthermore, when the soul has ascended by this second ladder, then she reaches up to the third, the place of his holy mouth, by which she finds the peace she has longed for, and refuge from wars and battles that she had endured on account of her sins. For on the first rungs of affection and desire, by which she raises her feet up above this earth, she removes herself from the darkness of iniquity. By means of the second ladder she is filled with virtuous love. In the third ladder she tastes a fullness of peace. And so you see how the bridge has three ladders, in order that when you ascend the first and second of them you will come in blessedness to the third and final stage.[5]

"This bridge is lifted up on high so that the water raging beneath might not do it damage, for in Him was no stain of sin. This bridge is raised up, and yet it does not leave the earth; you well know that when He had raised Himself up, as in his torture on the cross, his divine nature did not separate Him from the lowliness of your humanity. Therefore I said to you that when He was lifted up on high still He left not the earth, by way of declaring that He was truly knit and coupled to your human condition. And until He was lifted up, no one could go up that bridge.

"Therefore He Himself said, 'If I be lifted up, I shall draw all things unto me' (John 12:32). I, seeing in my goodness that you might not be drawn up to me in any other way, sent Him to be lifted up by the wood of the holy cross. Accordingly, I made, as it were, a spiritual anvil upon which I forged the Son of Mankind, so that by Him mankind should be washed and cleansed from the mire of his eternal abyss and clothed with enduring life by his singular grace.

"And so my Son draws all things to Himself in this fashion, that He may exhibit his great and unspeakable love toward you and all humankind, for the human heart is drawn by love. He could show you no greater love than to lay down his life for you. Therefore, it is by the strength of his love that any person may be drawn up, unless he resist inwardly and not permit himself so to be drawn up.

"It is for this reason that I said that when my Son should be lifted up from the earth He would draw all things unto Himself. That is truth. But it may be grasped in two manners. One is the sense in which a human heart may be drawn by the desire of love with all the powers of the soul—that is to say, with memory,[6] intellect, and will. When these three faculties are in one accord gathered together in my name, all other operations which the individual performs, in thought or deed, are drawn up toward me and pleasantly unified in the desire of love, raised up in following and pursuing that love which my Son demonstrated on

5. The metaphor of the *scala* or ladder is widely used in medieval literature, from spiritual writing such as Hilton's *Ladder of Perfection* to the *Scalacronica* of Sir Thomas Gray of Heaton, a work of Christian historiography. The metaphor derives from Jacob's ladder, of which Alan of Lille, in the preface to his *Art of Preaching*, says, "The ladder represents the progress of the catholic man in his ascent from the beginning of faith to the full development of the perfect man." Lille, *The Art of Preaching*, ed. Gillian R. Evans (Kalamazoo: Cistercian Publications, 1981), 15. See also the Introduction, 23-25.

6. ME *mynde*.

the cross. So then, my abiding purpose expresses itself truly when it is said, 'I shall draw all things unto myself if I be lifted up,' for when the human heart and all powers of the soul are drawn toward me, all its other works or deeds shall be drawn along.

"But these words, 'I shall draw all things unto myself,' may also be understood in another sense. All things are made and formed for the good of persons, to serve the needs of rational creatures. But the rational being himself is not made for the sake of an irrational creation, but only for me, that he may serve me with all his affections and whole heart. Observe, then, that mankind being so drawn up, everything else in creation is drawn up at the same time, because everything else has been made for mankind. It was necessary, therefore, that the whole bridge should be lifted up on high, and that it should contain three ladders, in order that you might more easily cross over it.

"This worthy bridge is [protectively] walled with stone, covered so that great rains should not wash it out and impede travelers. These stones are true and abiding virtues. But the stones were not laid in place nor the walls built up before the time of my Son's Passion. Even those who attempted to make it to the journey's end by the path of virtue were prevented from arriving because until that time heaven had not been unlocked with the key of his precious blood, and the rain[7] of righteousness would suffer no one to pass across. But once those stones could be laid and set in place upon the body of my holy Son, He built up the wall of stones, and cemented it with mortar mixed and slaked with his precious blood; that is to say, his human blood was mixed with the divine cement, the strength of his divinity fusing with the great fire of his love.

"The stones of the virtues were thus built into the bridge by my power—for there is no real virtue except as it is grounded in Him, and all virtues draw their life from Him. Wherefore no one can have these virtues which should characterize the life of grace unless they come from Him—that is, without receiving his doctrine and following in his footsteps. For He is the one who built up the wall and lived the virtues, and He it is who planted them in their place with his holy blood, as living stones, in order that all faithful persons might freely pass over without any fear of the great rain of righteousness of the Godhead. Such persons are covered with that great mercy which came down from heaven in the incarnation of my beloved Son, who opened the way to heaven with the key of his holy blood. And this is the way in which you

7. ME *reyn,* a pun alluding to both *reign* and *rain.*

ought to think of this bridge, as both built and also covered by the Great Mercy.

"The enclosed garden of my holy church stands and fights for this bridge, and it has also the bread of life, and ministers refreshing drink, his holy blood, so that my own creatures, who are wayfaring pilgrims, will not perish on their way. To that end my love has provided the body and blood of my faithful, perfect Son, who is both God and man, to be ministered unto you.

"Now when someone has crossed over the bridge, then he will come to the gate, which door is part of the bridge and by which all of you must enter. Wherefore my Son said, 'I am the way, the truth, and the life. . . . Whosoever follows after me walks not in the darkness, but in light' (John 14:6; 12:35). And he said further, 'No one comes to the Father, but by me.' And that is a truth you may depend upon. And if you remember well, I have been here showing you already why He said, 'I am the way, the truth, and the life,' and illustrating to you this way, in the likeness of a bridge.

"He said also, however, 'I am the truth,' or, the 'abiding faithfulness.' And this is true because He is joined unto me, who am entirely the character of faithfulness. Whoever follows Him walks in faith, in the guarantee of that truth.[8] He is also life, and whoever follows in this full-ness of faith goes into life. And whoever follows Him will not perish in the darkness, for He is the very light of truth and far removed from all that is not truth. For He destroyed with his truth all the untruth and lies of the devil, such as were exemplified in the tempter's false suggestion to Eve, and by which deception he broke off the heavenly way until Truth made it new again by the means of his glorious blood. Those who follow in this way are the children of abiding truth, for they follow steadfastly in that truth. And when they pass over by the gate of this persevering faithfulness then they come into me who am the place of peace, joined unto this gate and way—united to my dearly beloved Son who *is* eternal faithfulness and abiding truth.

"But whoever departs from this way of necessity makes his way along the brink of the torrent, which path is not protectively walled up with stones, but only bounded by the raging water. And since water has not the power to bear up and sustain, no one is able to pass across the tor-rent alive, but must unavoidably be drowned. So, by sinfulness and pur-suit of worldly pleasures has come about the sorrowful condition of our world. Because the desire and affection of these people is not fixed upon

8. ME *soothfastness.*

the living rock, the stone wherein is life, but rather on misgoverned loves, solely or chiefly on material things or vanities, and because they persevere in loving these things without reference to me, then for them everything becomes like this rushing water. Just as the water rushes by, so runs out the life of a person who sets his heart on such things, even when through his blindness they seem to him to be good and not vain at all. Whoever discovers himself slipping out in the swift current, swirling down toward a certain death, wants to hang on and keep his grip—that is to say, to maintain his life and property and the things he loves, that they might not pass away. But these things do fail; they do pass away, either by death or by my righteous ordinance, until everything is at last stripped away for all to see. And this is the end of those who follow the way of untruth and deception, who walk in the way of the lie. They are then children of the father of lies, offspring of the devil. And since they go by way of the gate of falsehood they are punished with everlasting damnation.

"You will see now that I have shown you something both of my abiding truth and also of the lie—my way, the high way of faithful, steadfast truth, and also the way of the fiend, which is the essence of deception and falsehood.

"Here then are the two roads, and whichever way one goes there are difficulties to be met with. Consider therefore what ignorance and blindness is within the heart of man, that even when a certain path has been made for him and he has been shown it, still he wants to plunge into the torrent. The way that has been provided and revealed is so delightful to those who take it that all bitterness of the journey is transformed to sweetness, and each heavy burden made light. And those who are in physical darkness find here a great light and those who while yet here live encumbered by their mortality discover there a life of health. For those who savor the light of holy faith by the desire of love for it discover already in this life the experience of steadfast and abiding truth, which abiding truth promises to anyone that labors for it refreshment and comfort at my hand, who am generous and alert to the needs of those who serve me. Also I am righteous, granting to each person according to his works in righteous judgment (Revelation 2:23; 22:12). Wherefore it is said, 'There is no evil unpunished, and no good deed unrewarded.'

"Your language is incapable of describing the mirth and gladness of those who walk in this way; indeed no ear may hear it nor eye behold it, yet even in this life those [who obey me] taste it already, and enjoy already in that a foretaste, part of the goodness which is ordained and made ready for them in that life which lasts forever. Well may a person then be called a fool who avoids such good, and chooses rather in this life to taste the proceeds or similitude of hell, going by the lower way with infinite effort and without any comfort or refreshment. It is by their own choice and default that such persons are utterly deprived of me, who am the highest and eternal good. Therefore, my will is that you and my other servants live in a constant awareness and bitter sorrow on account of the wrongs done to me, and also that you have compassion for the ignorance and self-destruction of those who injure me grievously.

"Now then, you have seen and may comprehend what is meant by this bridge, which is now, according to your wishes, more fully explained to you."

III

"... And thus I said, I have made a living bridge of my Son, whose conversation was first with humankind. But when this living bridge of perfect teaching was taken from you, the bridge and the way of my teaching and power of the Father remained, still joined and knit together with the wisdom of my Son and the mercy and pity of the Holy Spirit. This power gives strength to those who follow in the way; the wisdom of the Son gives light by which they may discern truth on the way; the Holy Spirit gives them love, which love drives away and obliterates the poison of one's own self-will, causing only the love of virtues to remain in its place. He is still the way of faithfulness and life, by his doctrine as well as by his actual life, which doctrine is the bridge leading you and bringing you to the height of heaven. Therefore it was truly expressed when my Son said, 'I came down from my Father, down into the world. I leave the world again, and go unto my Father' (John 16:28). That is like saying, 'My Father sent me to you, ordaining that I serve as your bridge that you might escape over the torrent and come to eternal life.' But He said also, 'I shall come to you again. I shall not leave you as fatherless children, but shall send you Comfort' (see John 14:16-17)—that is, the Holy Spirit. It is as though my Son said, 'I shall go now to my Father, but return to you again as his Holy Spirit, who is called the Comforter, who shall show you more clearly all things confirming the way of faithfulness' (see John 14:26). This is the most perfect doctrine I have given you. When He said 'I shall come again to you,' that is exactly what He did, for the Holy Spirit does not come alone, but bears the power of the Father, the wisdom of the Son, and the mercy of the Holy Spirit.

"See then how He returned—not physically, but in power—

strengthening the way of his teaching, which may never fail nor be taken away from one who wishes to follow that doctrine; for inasmuch as it came from me, who am not changeable, it is strong and stable. Therefore you should do everything to follow in the way of that doctrine, without any cloud of doubt, but with the light of real faith already given to you in principle in your holy baptism.

"Now, daughter, I have declared and shown plainly to you the actual, living bridge, and his doctrine, which is one and the same thing. I have said also that there were apostles, evangelists, martyrs, confessors, and holy doctors of theology ordained and set before you as lanterns in his holy church. I have showed you also how my Son, having returned to me, nonetheless returned again to you—not in his bodily presence but by virtue of his power, when the Holy Spirit came upon the apostles. For He shall not come again in his body until the last day, the Day of Judgment, when He shall come again in my majesty and my divine might to judge the living and the dead, and to give rewards to the good, rewarding them in body and soul for their labors. But He shall also apportion great suffering to those who have lived their life here in this world wickedly.

". . . And now I speak to you who are my dear children, that you be zealous to travel by the bridge, and not detour under it. For you will not find there the way of righteousness, but rather the way of lies and deceit. This is the way that wicked persons are going, of whom I have more to say. These are those sinners for whom I beg you to pray to me fervently, that they may come to health and salvation. I ask of you both tears and labors, that they also may yet receive my abundant mercy."

from

The Revelations

St. Bridget of Sweden, or Birgitt as she was called in England, was born about 1303 a few miles from Uppsala, where her father was governor of Upland. She began to have visions at the age of seven; when she was ten she had, following a sermon on the Passion of Christ, a powerful dream in which Christ seemed to speak to her directly, and she began to imagine for herself a cloistered life. But when she was thirteen years old, her father had her married, against her wishes, to the eighteen-year-old son of a nobleman friend. She bore him four sons and four daughters before he died in 1344. A few days after her husband's death, Christ appeared to her in a vision, she writes, declaring that she was now to be his "bride." She turned her estate over to the administration of others, took up a strict religious life, and, in 1346, left for Rome where, save for a pilgrimage to Jerusalem, she remained until her death in 1373. She had a great reputation for spiritual intensity and for fearlessness; in her *Revelationes Extravagantes,* she pilloried Magnus Erikson, king of Sweden, for the self-indulgence and dissipation of life in the court, but she also made a point of coming to deliver her assessment in person.

Bridget's Latin *Revelationes* began to circulate in England even before her death, and many manuscripts of translated versions were available there in the fifteenth century. A brief representation of her work in this volume owes principally to the fact that King Henry V of England decided to found in her honor the Birgittine Order. Syon Abbey was commenced in 1415 in London, and it is this community to which the English translator of Catherine of Siena dedicated *The Orcherd of Syon.*

Many of Bridget's mystical "revelations" now seem, indeed, "extravagant." They were, however, very influential. An example of the way in which they were adapted as spiritual counsel follows here and indicates something of her "prophetic" style.

The Judgment of Christ[1]

I SAW A GREAT PALACE bathed in heavenly light, in which was a great host of heavenly chivalry, knights beyond number like motes of dust shining in sunlight, gleaming as brightly as sunbeams themselves.

1. A Middle English version of the text, Princeton University Library Deposit 1397 (formerly MS Phillipps 1366) has been edited by W. P. Cumming for the Early English Text Society, O.S. 178 (London, 1929); it corresponds to the Latin *Revelationes,* 7.30.

Within this palace there was a marvellous throne in which it seemed there sat the person of a man of incomprehensible beauty, in manner like a lord of great power, whose clothes were magnificent and of indescribable luminescence. And a virgin stood before Him who sat on the throne that was brighter than the sun; all those who were of that heavenly chivalry worshiped her reverently as queen of heaven.

Then He who sat on the throne opened his mouth and said, "Hear ye, all my enemies living in the world (for I do not now speak to my friends, who are following my will)—

"Hear ye, all theologians, archbishops, bishops, and all those of lesser station in the church—

"Hear ye also, all you religious people, regardless of what order or community you are in—

"Hear ye also, you kings, princes, and judges of the world, all you sovereigns and servants—

"Hear ye also, you women—princesses, ladies, wives, maidens, all you people of whatsoever condition of estate, great or small, who dwell in the world.

"Hear these words which I myself who made you speak now unto you:

"I am lodging a complaint—that you have gone far away from me, and given your allegiance to the fiend, my enemy. You have forsaken my commandments, and you follow the suggestions and wishes of the devil. You are paying no attention to the fact that I, unchangeable and eternal God, your maker, came down from heaven to a virgin, taking of her a human body, and have entered into conversation with you. Nor do you consider that I in my own person there gave you counsel and made plain the way by which you should go to heaven.

"I was naked, scourged and crowned with thorns, and so savagely stretched over the length and breadth of the cross that all the sinews and joints of my body were as if burst asunder. I heard all manner of reproach and suffered a most despicable death as well as bitter sorrow of heart for the sake of your healing.

"O my enemies, to all these things you pay no attention, because you are self-deceived. Therefore you bear the yoke and the burden of the devil with a misleading feeling of pleasure, and you neither grasp nor have any feeling for these things until eternal sorrow is well nigh upon you. Sometimes even then these [facts of my suffering] are of no consequence to you. In fact, in this respect your pride is so great that if you could find a way to ascend above me you would gladly do it, and the sheer lust of your flesh is so great that you would rather be entirely without me than forego your inordinate pursuit of pleasure. Your greed is insatiable, as bottomless as a sack cut open at both ends; for there is nothing that can satisfy your covetousness.

"Therefore I swear in my Godhead that if you die in the state in which you are now you shall never see my face, but on account of your pride you shall be drowned so deep in hell that all the devils shall float over you and torment you without respite. On account of your obsession with sex you shall be filled up with the horrible poisons of the fiend, and on account of your greed you shall be filled with sorrow and anguish, becoming partners to every evil that is in hell.

"O ye mine enemies—inhuman, discourteous and unnatural as you are—I seem to you no more to be feared than a serpent hibernating for the winter. So you do whatever you feel like, and you have your prosperity. But I shall arise in the summer, and then you will fall silent. And you shall not be able to flee from my hand.

"Nonetheless, o ye mine enemies, since I have bought you with my blood and I am seeking for nothing less than your souls, therefore turn yourself once again toward me with meekness and humility, and I shall receive you gladly as my children. Shake off the burdensome yoke of the fiend, and remember my charitable love. Then you shall see and confirm in your conscience that I [by contrast] am easy and mild." Amen.[2]

---

2. The Middle English version originally ended at this point—thus the Amen. Several additional folios were subsequently appended to it, but these were by another hand.

JULIAN OF NORWICH

from
The Showings

Dame Julian of Norwich was probably born in 1342 or 1343, and she seems to have made her profession as a nun several years before the time of her remarkable request of God for special revelations and her subsequent experience of them, an account of which follows. After her illness and her first revelation on May 13, 1373, she became an anchoress—one who leads a solitary religious life as distinct from one who lives in a community. The date of Julian's death is unknown, but she was still alive as late as 1416.

Until the seventeenth century her work had little circulation, surviving in comparatively few manuscripts, but interest grew after the English Benedictine Serenus Cressy published a modernized version in 1670. In our own time, Julian is perhaps the most widely known of English medieval mystics, largely because of her importance for the feminist concerns of many contemporary theologians. Her fourteenth revelation and the chapters which follow, of which a significant representation is translated here, develop her image of the second person of the Trinity as "Christ Our Mother" (see Part III of the selection below). Prior to this recent interest, Julian had also attracted the attention of T. S. Eliot, who quotes from one of her earlier chapters ("A Vision of Consolation"—see Part II below) the statement that "all things shall be well."

Julian's writing is more difficult than that of almost any other writer represented in this volume, and few readers are likely to find her as practical as Walter Hilton, as devotional as the author of *The Cloud of Unknowing*, or as evangelical as St. Catherine in *The Orcherd of Syon*. While she is more conventional than Margery Kempe (who visited her for counsel on one of her travels), her book is nevertheless a kind of speculative theology, claiming as its authority the witness of personal mystical vision.

Two texts of her *Shewings*, or *Revelations*, were prepared in Julian's own lifetime—a short text composed some time after the visions and a longer, elaborated (and somewhat edited) text finished in 1393. The selection that follows comes from both texts: Parts I and II are from the short text, and Part III is from the long text. The selection is introduced by a scribe or curator and then begins abruptly with Julian's description of her prayer for "three graces."

A Showing of Love

HERE IS A VISION which, in the goodness of God, was revealed to a devout woman by the name of Julian, a recluse at Norwich. In this year of our Lord 1413 she is still alive. Her vision is filled with words of comfort, inspirational reading for all those who desire to be lovers of Christ.

I. The Request for a Special Revelation

As a gift from God, I desired three graces. The first of these was to have put before my mind the Passion of Christ. The second was to experience physical sickness; the third was to have as a gift from God three wounds. The first of these desires came to me in devotion; it seemed to me that I had a profound response to the Passion of Christ, yet still I desired by the grace of God to have more. I thought I would like to have actually been present with Mary Magdalene and the others who were lovers of Christ, that I might have seen the actual Passion of our Lord that He suffered there for me and that I might have entered into that suffering with Him as did those others that loved Him.

Already I believed firmly in the magnitude of Christ's suffering which Holy Church reveals and teaches, as in the paintings of crucifixes, for example, which are made by God's grace and in accordance with the teaching of Holy Church to represent Christ's Passion insofar as the human imagination can conceive it. Notwithstanding this credal belief I desired to have an actual bodily vision in which I might obtain more knowledge of the physical pains of our Lord and Savior, as well as of the compassion of our Lady and all his faithful lovers who were entering into his suffering with Him both at that time and later, for I wanted to be one with them and to suffer with them. I desired no other vision or revelation of God until my soul should leave this body, for I believed confidently that I would be saved. My intention in this request was only that by the means of such a revelation I should have a more accurate impression of Christ's Passion.

As to the second [request], it came to my mind in contrition, freely and without any seeking for it on my part, a purposeful desire to obtain as a gift from God some physical illness, and I wanted it to be that this might be so severe as to be a sickness unto death, so that in the extreme of that sickness I might take all the rites of Holy Church, expecting myself to die, and so that everyone who saw me should believe the same thing, for I wanted to draw no comfort from physical, earthly life. In the course of this illness I desired to experience all manner of pain, both physical and emotional, such as I should experience if I really was dying—all the threats and tumults of devils and all sorts of other distress right up to the point of the actual exit of my soul, for I hoped that all this might be an expedient for me against the time I should actually die, because I desired to be quickly with my God.

These two desires, concerning [a vision of] the Passion and my illness, I asked for conditionally, since it seemed to me that they were beyond the category of common prayers. So I said, "Lord, you know what I want. If it be your will that I have it, grant it to me. If it is not your will, good Lord, be not displeased, for I want nothing which is out of your will." And I wanted, in my mind, to have this sickness when I was thirty years of age.[1]

The third desire arose when I heard a man speak of Holy Church by means of the story of St. Cecelia, and from his exposition I understood that she received three sword strokes to the neck, from which she suffered death. Moved by this account, I conceived a powerful desire, praying to our Lord God that He would grant me three wounds in my own lifetime—that is, the wound of contrition, the wound of compassion, and the wound of a longing of my will after God. And although I had made my first two requests conditionally, I asked for the third without condition. The first two desires then passed from my mind, while the third occupied me continually.

Now when I was a half year more than thirty winters old, God sent me a physical illness in the grip of which I lay for three days and three nights. The fourth night I received all the last rites of Holy Church, and expected not to live till daybreak. Yet I continued to suffer for two days and two nights, and on the third night expected to pass on at any moment; those who were gathered about me thought the same. This made me keenly unhappy, however, and I became loath to die—not for the sake of anything on earth that I was reluctant to leave behind, nor on account of fears of the unknown, for I trusted in God. But it was because I wanted to live to love God better and for a longer time, in order that I might by the grace accruing to such a life have a greater knowledge and love of God in the bliss of heaven. It seemed to me that the whole span of my life here was very little and short in comparison to an eternity of joy. So I reasoned in this way: "Good Lord, is my continued life no longer to your glory?" And I was answered in my reason and in the experience of my suffering that I was to die, and I assented completely with all my heart's intent to accept the will of God.

Thus I endured till daybreak, and by then it felt to me as though my body were already dead from the waist down. Then I asked to be sat up, with my head propped up with bedclothes, so to have more freedom of heart to await God's will, and to think on Him while my life

1. Analogously with the life of Christ, she seeks an inception to ministry.

should last. Those who were with me sent for the parson, my curate, to be present at my ending. He came, and a child with him, and brought a cross; by that time my eyes were fixed and I could not speak. The parson set the cross before my face and said, "Daughter, I have brought before you the image of your Savior; look upon it, and comfort yourself in reverence of Him who died for you and for me." It seemed to me that I was well enough set as I was, for my eyes were fixed upward into heaven, where I trusted to come. Nevertheless I assented to set my eyes upon the face on the crucifix if I could, in order to extend a little longer the time till my ending, for it seemed to me that I could hold out a little longer with my eyes fixed straight ahead rather than looking up. After this point my sight began to fail, and it grew completely dark around me in the room, dark as night, except that ordinary daylight remained on the image of the cross, I never knew how. Everything else except the cross was ugliness to me, as if the space were filled up with devils.

After this the upper part of my body also began to die, and sensation left it. My hands fell down on either side of me, and I was so weak that my head lolled over to one side. The greatest distress I felt was in a shortness of breath and ebbing away of my life. It was at that instant that I truly imagined myself to be at the point of death. Suddenly, just at that moment, all my pain left me, and I was as sound—particularly in my upper body—as ever I was, before or since. I marvelled at this change, for it seemed to me that it was a secret working of God and not a natural thing. For all that, even the release I experienced was not complete release to me, because I thought I would far rather have been delivered from this world, that being what my heart had been set upon.

Suddenly it came to me that I should ask now of our Lord's grace the second wound as a gift, that He would fill my body with an imaginative experience of his blessed Passion as I had prayed before. For I wished that his sufferings could be my own, with such compassion as would lead to a longing for God. So it seemed to me that I might by grace have his wounds, as I had wished before,[2] but this I never wanted as a physical encounter nor as any similar type of revelation from God, but only as the compassion which it seemed to me a kindred soul might have with our Lord Jesus who, for the sake of his love, was willing to become a mortal person. I desired to suffer with Him, living in my mortal body according as God should give me grace.

At this I suddenly saw red blood trickling down from under the crown of thorns [of the crucifix], all hot, freshly and heavily flowing as if living blood, just as I had imagined it must have been at the time when

2. Cf. the stigmata of St. Francis of Assisi.

the crown of thorns was thrust down on his blessed head. It was just in this way that He, both God and man, suffered for me. I conceived, truly and powerfully, that it was Himself that showed this to me, without any intermediary, and then I said, "*Benedicite dominus!*" This I said with reverent intention and a loud voice, and I was greatly astonished for the sheer wonder and marvel I had there, that He would make Himself so humbly present to a sinful creature still living in this wretched body. At the time I assumed that our Lord Jesus, out of his courteous love, wished to show me some comfort before the beginning of my own temptation—for I anticipated that I might well be permitted by God, and with his protection, to be tempted by devils before I died. With this vision of his blessed Passion, and with the Godhead I saw in my mind, I saw that this was strength enough for me, yes, and for all living beings who are to be saved from all the devils of hell and from all their spiritual enemies.

And at the same time as I saw this physical sight our Lord showed me a spiritual sight of his familiar love. I saw that He is to us all things which are good and comfortable for our help. He is our clothing, for his love wraps, enfolds, embraces us and completely shapes us, covering us for the sake of a love so tender that He may never be apart from us. And so in this vision I saw that He is all things that, to my understanding, are good. . . .

Everything that I saw myself I intend to be understood as having been experienced for the personal benefit of all my fellow Christians,[3] for I have learned in the spiritual revelation of our Lord that this is how He intends it should be. And therefore I beg you all for God's sake, and I counsel you here for your own profit, that you believe[4] the vision of

---

3. The Middle English has "Alle that I saw of my selfe, I meene in the persone of alle myne evyne cristene. . . ." Her point here is to argue that she has been chosen for these revelations as a representative set of eyes for the whole of Christendom; she has been "chosen" to convey special revelation. Here she is making her case for authenticity and authority.

4. See n.3; this sentence was removed from the long text. Edmund Colledge and James Walsh, whose superb two-volume edition, *A Book of Showings to the Anchoress Julian of Norwich* (Toronto: Pontifical Institute of Mediaeval Studies, 1978), is the standard modern edition of the long text, have also done a translation of this, the shorter, text (*Julian of Norwich: Showings*, Classics of Western Spirituality [New York and Toronto: Paulist, 1978]). This latter translation is less satisfactory, in my opinion, than the earlier translation by Walsh alone (London: Burns and Oates, 1961). The more recent translation, for example, translates *leve* here inconsistently and misleadingly as "disregard." The direction of the chapter as a whole makes it clear, however, that the more usual translation, "believe," is correct; *leve* is used this way elsewhere in the chapter.

this wretched worm and sinful creature unto whom it was shown, and that you with all your strength wisely, lovingly and meekly behold God, who of his courteous love and endless goodness was willing to reveal this vision generally, for the comfort of us all. And you who hear and see this vision and teaching, which is from Jesus Christ for the edification of your souls, it is both the will of God and my own desire that you accept it with as much joy and pleasure as if Jesus had shown it to you as He did to me.

For the revelation itself does not make me good unless I love God the better for it, and so may and ought each person do likewise that sees and hears it with good will and the right intention. Accordingly it is my desire that it should be for each and every person the same profit that I desired for myself and to that end was moved by God the first time I saw it—for to the degree that we are "all one" it is a common and general revelation, and I am certain that I saw it for the profit of many others. Certainly it was not shown to me because God loves me better than the least of souls in a state of grace. And I am sure that there are very many people who, though they never had a revelation or vision except only the common doctrine of Holy Church, love God better than I do.

If I focus exclusively on myself, I am in fact nothing, whereas in the generality I am in unity of charity with all my fellow Christians. In this unity of charity stands the life of all mankind who are to be saved. For God is the sum of all that is good, and has made everything which is made, and God loves all that He has made. If any person withdraws love from any of his fellow Christians, he does not love anything, since he fails to love everything. And so when this happens he is not saved, for he is not in peace, while one who loves his fellow Christians generally loves every creature. For in those of mankind who shall be saved is comprehended all—that is, all that is made and the Maker of all—for God is in mankind, and so in mankind is all.

Thus, one who loves all his fellow Christians on a general principle loves everything, and whoever loves in this way is saved. This is the way I choose to love, and thus I do love, and thus I am saved. For I want to be understood as the representative of my fellow Christians, and the more I love of this loving while I am here, the more my experience is like the joy I shall have in heaven eternally—[ecstasy in the knowledge] that God out of his everlasting love would become our brother and suffer for us. And I am sure that whoever sees it this way shall be truly taught and mightily comforted, if comfort is what is needed.

God forbid, however, that you should say or assume that I am a teacher, for that is not now, nor was it ever, my intention; I am a woman, ignorant, weak, and frail. But I know very well that what I say I have as the personal revelation of Him who is the Master Teacher. It is charity, rather, that prompts me to tell it to you,[5] for I want God to be known and my fellow Christians to prosper, even as I would wish for myself that there may be in me a greater hatred for sin and loving of God. And just because I am a woman, ought I therefore to believe that I should refrain from telling you this goodness of God, since I saw at the same time that it is his will that it be made known? And that you shall soon see for yourself in the continuation of this matter which follows, if it be well and truly accepted. Then you will soon forget about me (who am a wretch) and proceed in such a way that I do not hinder you, and so behold Jesus, who is the teacher of us all. I am speaking of those who shall be saved, for at this time God showed me no one else. But [be assured that] in everything I believe as Holy Church teaches, for in all of its details I beheld this blessed revelation of our Lord as unified in God's sight, and I never understood anything in it which either bewilders me or keeps me from the faithful teaching of Holy Church.

II. A Vision of Consolation[6]

And thus our good Lord answered all the questions and doubts I could think of, saying most comfortingly something like: "I will make all things well, I shall make all things well, I may make all things well, and I can make all things well; and you will see for yourself that all things shall be well." Where He says that He "may" [make all things well] I understand the Father; when He says He "can," I understand the Son; where He says He "will," I understand the Holy Spirit; and where He says He "shall," I understand this to apply to the unity of the blessed Trinity, three persons comprised in a single Truth. And where He says "You will see for yourself," I understand by this the union of all mankind who shall be saved in the blessed Trinity.

And in these five words,[7] God wishes to be enclosed[8] in rest and in

5. That is, the revelations still to be told.

6. There follows here an account of vivid revelations of the crucifixion and Julian's questions about details and their implications, including the question of why an all-knowing and all-powerful God should have permitted sin in the first place.

7. I.e., phrases, as in the "seven last words" of Christ.

8. There are a number of places in the text which make one wonder whether there is a Latin text behind it; the writer certainly uses words in rhetorical conjunction which are satisfactory puns in Latin but not in English. Here *enclosed* in rest, followed by the notion of the satisfaction (*end*) of the spiritual thirst of Christ for his Bride may derive from a play on *hortus conclusus*, the enclosed anagogical garden of the Song of Songs in its typical allegorical reading.

peace. Thus the spiritual thirst of Christ has an end. For this is the spiritual thirst, the love-longing, and persists and ever shall until we see that sight on the Day of Judgment, for we who are to be saved and who then shall be Christ's joy and bliss are still here, and shall be until that day. His thirst, therefore, is the incompleteness of his joy in that He does not now possess us completely in Himself as He shall then.

All of this was revealed to me as a vision of [his] compassion, for that will cease on Doomsday. Thus, though He has pity and compassion on us, and longs to possess us, in his wisdom and love He does not permit the end to come until the best time. And in these same five aforesaid words, "I make all things well," I understand a mighty comfort from all the works of our Lord that are yet to come. For just as the blessed Trinity made everything out of nothing, just so that same blessed Trinity shall make well everything that is not well. It is God's will that we have a profound satisfaction in all the deeds He has already done, for He wills thereby that we know all He will do. He revealed this to me in this word which he spoke, "And you shall see in yourself that all manner of things shall be well." This I understand in two ways: first, that I am well provided for in *not* knowing it; second, that I am to be merry and glad because I *shall* know it. It is God's will that we know that in general all shall be well, but it is not God's will that we should know it now except as it pertains to us for the present, and that is the teaching of Holy Church.

III. Christ Our Mother

As regards our [spiritual] substance,[9] God made us so noble and so rich that we always work according to his will and honor. (When I say "we," I mean all those who shall be saved.) For truly I saw that it is us whom He loves, and that we do what is pleasing to Him constantly, without any holding back. And from these great riches and high nobility come commensurate powers into our soul, while it is still knit to our body and we have our sensual being. And thus in our spiritual substance we are complete and in our sensuality we fall short, which failure God will restore by the operation of mercy and grace abundantly flowing into us out of his own natural goodness. And so this natural goodness makes that mercy and grace to work within us, and the natural grace we have from Him enables us to receive the operations of his mercy and grace.

9. *Substance* still meant, in the fourteenth century, "*spiritual* substance"; it did not come to mean what we think of now until much closer to modern times. It is an awkward problem for the translator; Colledge and Walsh confusingly fail to account for it in their translation, and I have been unable to think of a way to convey it faithfully other than by inserting the adjective *spiritual*.

I saw that our nature is complete in God, in which He makes a diversity of things flowing out from Himself to do his will, and whose[10] nature preserves and mercy and grace restore and fulfill. And none of these shall perish, for our nature in its higher part is knit to God in its creation, but God is knit to our nature, in its lower part, when He takes on our flesh. And thus in Christ our own two natures are united, for the Trinity is comprehended in Christ, in whom our higher nature is grounded and rooted; and the second person has taken our inferior nature upon Him, when human nature was first accorded Him. . . . For in that same time that God joined Himself to our body in the Virgin's womb, He took to Himself our sensual soul, by the taking of which He enclosed all of us in Himself, uniting it to our spiritual substance. In this union He was perfect man, for Christ, having joined in Himself all persons who shall be saved, is perfected man.

Thus our Lady is our mother, in whom are we all enclosed and born of her in Christ, for she who is mother of our Savior is mother of all those who are saved in our Savior, and [yet] our Savior is our true mother, in whom we are eternally born,[11] and out of whom we shall never come.

Abundantly, fully and sweetly was this revealed; and it is spoken of in the first [of my revelations] where it says that we are all enclosed in Him and He is enclosed in us.[12] And it is also spoken of in my sixteenth revelation, where He says that He sits in our soul, for it is his delight to reign in our understanding blessedly, sit in our soul restfully, and dwell in our soul eternally, drawing us entirely into Himself. In this work He wants us to be his helpers, focusing all our intention upon Him, learning his laws, keeping his doctrine, desiring, as He does, that everything be done by us, truly trusting in Him—for truly I saw that our spiritual substance is in God.

God the blessed Trinity, everlasting Being, just as He is eternal and without beginning, even so purposed eternally to make mankind, which fair nature was first prepared for his own Son, the second person [of the Trinity]. When He wished to, by full accord of the whole Trinity He made us in an instant. In our creation He knit and joined us to Himself, by which union we are kept as pure and noble as when we were created. By that virtue in each precious union we love our Creator and enjoy Him, praise Him, thank Him and endlessly rejoice in Him.

10. Colledge and Walsh, *Julian of Norwich: Showings*, 291, note that the MSS read either *whose* or *whom* here; they find "neither attractive" and supply instead *which* in their translation, but this leads to other interpretative problems.

11. Here *born* has the value of a pun, meaning also "carried."

12. See n.8.

And this is the work which is being wrought continually in every soul that shall be saved, which is the godly will already mentioned.[13]

And thus in our creation God Almighty is our natural Father, as God All Wise is our natural Mother, with the love and goodness of the Holy Spirit all together one God, one Lord. And in the joining and union He is our true Spouse and we his beloved bride and fair maiden, with whom He was never displeased. For He says, "I love you and you love me and our love shall never divide in two."[14]

I beheld the work of all the blessed Trinity, in which beholding I saw and understood these three properties: the property of the fatherhood, the property of the motherhood, and the property of the sovereignty, in one God. In our Almighty Father, we have our sustenance and our joy with respect to our natural substance, which is given to us in our creation from eternity; and in the second person, in knowledge and wisdom we have our sustenance[15] and, with respect to our sensuality, our restoration and salvation, for He is our Mother, Brother and Savior; in our good Lord the Holy Spirit we have our renewal and return for our living and labor, endlessly surpassing all our desires in the marvellous courtesy of his high, generous grace. For our whole life consists in these three. In the first we have our being, in the second our growth and in the third our fulfillment. The first is nature, the second mercy, the third grace.

With respect to the first I saw that the high power of the Trinity is our Father, the deep wisdom of the Trinity is our Mother, and the great love of the Trinity is our Lord, all those we have in nature and in the creation of our spiritual substance. Furthermore, I saw that the second person, who is our Mother, and in the spiritual substance the same most lovely person, has now become our Mother in the sensual aspect, because we are "double" in the nature God has given us, having both "spiritual" and "sensual" nature. Our spiritual substance is the higher part, which we are given in God the Father Almighty, and the second person of the Trinity is our Mother in the creation of our spiritual nature, in whom we are grounded and rooted, and He is our Mother of Mercy in taking on

13. The reference is to an earlier section not reproduced here in which Julian makes the point that God's love for us had no point of beginning—that we were loved from eternity.

14. The author of *The Cloud of Unknowing* also says this, but he adds a conditional—"except by mortal sin." See *Deonise Hid Diuinite*, ed. Phyllis Hodgson, Early English Text Society, O.S. 231 (1955; reprint, London: Oxford University Press, 1958), 56.

15. ME *kepying*—which is unaccountably translated by Colledge and Walsh in this instance as "perfection."

our sensual nature. And so our Mother is that to us in a diversity of ways, in whom our own [two] natures are undivided. For in our Mother Christ we profit and increase, and in mercy He reforms and restores us, and by the power of his Passion, death and resurrection has united us to our spiritual substance. This is the way our Mother works in mercy toward all his beloved children who are submissive and obedient to Him. And grace cooperates with mercy, especially in two properties, as it was shown, which working belongs to the third person, the Holy Spirit. He works in rewarding and giving [gifts]. His rewarding is a gift of trust and assurance that the Lord gives to them who have labored [in his service], and his giving of gifts is a courteous act out of free grace, fulfilling and surpassing anything that [his] creatures merit.

Thus in our Father God Almighty we have our being, and in our Mother of Mercy we have our reformation and our restoration, in whom our [split] natures are united and made complete and perfect man, and by the fruits and gifts of the Holy Spirit we are fulfilled. And our spiritual substance is in our Father God Almighty; it is in our Mother God All-Wisdom, and it is also in our Lord God the Holy Spirit All-Goodness, for our spiritual substance achieves its totality in each person of the Trinity, which is one God. And our sensual nature is only in the second person, Christ Jesus, in whom dwells the Father and the Holy Spirit; in Him and by Him we are mightily delivered up out of hell and out of the wretchedness of this earth, gloriously brought up to heaven, and joyously united to our spiritual substance, our substantial nature, increased in riches and nobility by the full power of Christ and the working of the Holy Spirit.

And all this bliss we have only by mercy and grace—which kind of bliss we never could have had and known unless that quality of goodness which is in God had been opposed.[16] For wickedness had been permitted to rise up in opposition to that goodness, and the goodness of mercy and grace opposed the wickedness and turned it all into the good and honor of all those who are to be saved. For it is that property in God which opposes good to evil; thus Jesus Christ, who does good against the evil, is our true Mother; we have our being of Him, where the ground of motherhood has its beginning, with all the sweet sheltering of love which flows from it without ceasing.

As truly as God is our Father, so truly is God our Mother—and this He revealed in everything, and especially in those sweet words where He says, "I am it," which is to say "I am—the strength and goodness of

16. This refers to the *felix culpa*, the blessedness of redemption which could not have been known, of course, unless the fall had first occurred.

fatherhood; I am—the wisdom and kindness of motherhood, I am—the light and the grace which is entirely blessed love; I am—the Trinity; I am—the unity; I am—the high sovereign good behind everything that is; I am—the one who makes you to love and to desire; I am—the everlasting fulfillment of all true desires." For where the soul is highest, most noble and most worthy of honor, still it is lowest, meekest, and most mild.

From this foundation in our spiritual substance we have all the faculties which are sensual as a gift of nature, and by the assistance and furthering of mercy and grace, without which we are not able to profit. Our heavenly Father, Almighty God, who is Being—He knows us and loved us since before the beginning of time. Out of this knowledge in the full and marvellous depths of his love by the foreseeing eternal counsel of the blessed Trinity He wanted the second person to become our Mother, our Brother and our Savior. From this[17] it follows that as truly as God is our Father so truly is God our Mother. Our Father wills, our Mother works, our good Lord the Holy Spirit confirms. And therefore it is our duty to love our God in whom we have our being, thanking Him reverently and praising Him for our creation, mightily praying to our Mother of Mercy and Pity, and to our Lord the Holy Spirit for help and grace. For in these three is our whole life—nature, mercy and grace from which we have mildness, patience, pity, and hatred for sin and wickedness—for it is appropriate to the virtuous to hate sin and wickedness.

And so Jesus is our true Mother in the nature of our first creation, and He is our true Mother in grace by his taking on our created nature. All the beautiful activities and sweet natural offices of most lovely motherhood are appropriated to the second person, for in Him we have this goodly will, whole and safe forever, both in nature and in grace, of his own character of goodness.

I understand three ways of looking at motherhood in God. The first has its origin in our natural creation, the second is [his] taking on our nature, the third is motherhood in action. And therein is a spreading forth of this same grace in length and breadth, height and depth without end—and it is all one love.

---

17. *This*, the premise, is Julian's special revelation of which she speaks in the previous sentence; obviously it takes some liberties with Scripture and the magisterium of the church.

MARGERY KEMPE

from
The Book of Margery Kempe

Margery Kempe was born sometime after 1370 and was married in 1393 to John Kempe of King's Lynn, in Norfolk. In 1414, following a series of visions and a decision to live in chastity apart from her husband, she undertook a pilgrimage to the Holy Land. Returning to England the following year, she established herself as an "ecstatic" of controversial style and reputation. The dominant manifestation of her spiritual intensity was sudden, vociferous, and prolonged bouts of public weeping—behavior which probably contributed to her being persecuted as a Lollard (Wycliffite), although the charge seems to have been entirely unfounded. She was supremely confident of her private revelations, however, and, by her own account, unhesitatingly challenged established authority, including that of two of the most prominent churchmen of her day. One of these, Philip Repington, had once been an active follower of Wyclif; his fortunes had much improved, however, subsequent to his public abjuration of association with him. Thereafter he had risen through the ranks from abbot to Chancellor of Oxford until, at the time of his confrontation with Margery Kempe, he was Bishop of Lincoln. The other notable target of Margery's campaigning was no less than Thomas Arundel, Archbishop of Canterbury.

Illiterate, Margery seems to have dictated her autobiographical book to successive scribes, first to an Englishman living in Holland who apparently produced a jumbled copy which could hardly be read in either language. The second attempt, entirely frustrated, was begun by a favorite priest, who gave up the task after four years. He then directed Margery to a ghostwriter, who also gave up in confusion, although he nonetheless took a large commission for the work. At length Margery came back to the priest, who was evidently a Carmelite, or White Friar. Despite numerous difficulties, including serious eye trouble, he at length finished his labors—a kind of command performance—in 1436.

Margery Kempe is not among the most significant English spiritual writers of this period: indeed, the authenticity of her revelations was sometimes doubted even among those closest to her, including her spiritual directors. A selection of her writing is included here for the sake of greater inclusiveness, and also for the sake of illustrating a type of spiritual experience which has not been extensively represented in this anthology.

The selection which follows comes from near the end of the first and longest section of *The Book of Margery Kempe*, much of which is taken up with the account of her dramatic efforts to vindicate her spiritual experience to others and to demonstrate a unique relationship with Christ.

Throughout, the scribe refers to her in the third person, as "this creature."

Visions and Visitations

An angel shows her the Book of Life. She has visions in her sleep.

ONE TIME, as the aforesaid creature was kneeling before an altar of the Cross and saying a prayer, her eyes were closed tightly as if she were going to sleep. Finally, she had no choice, but dozed off into a little nap in which there appeared most realistically before her an angel, all clothed in white as if he was a small child, but carrying a huge book before him. Then said this creature to the little child, or angel, "Ah! This is the Book of Life." And she saw in the book a picture of the Trinity, all illumined in gold.

Then she said to the child, "Where is my name?" The child answered and said, "Here is your name, written at the foot of the Trinity," and with that he vanished, she knew not how.

Soon afterward our Lord Jesus Christ spoke to her and said, "Daughter, be careful now to be true, steadfast, and of good faith, for your name is written in heaven in the Book of Life. This was indeed an angel that gave you comfort. Therefore, daughter, you must be right merry, for I am busy both morning and afternoon to draw your heart unto my heart, in order that you should keep your mind altogether on me, and so greatly increase your love toward God. For, daughter, if you would follow after God's counsel you must not do amiss, for the counsel of God is that you should remain meek, patient in charitable love and in chastity."

Another time, as the creature lay in her contemplation in a chapel dedicated to our Lady, her mind was occupied with the Passion of our Lord Jesus Christ, and she actually thought she was in her spiritual vision seeing our Lord in his human form, with his wounds bleeding as freshly as if He had been scourged there before her. At that she wept and wailed with all her physical strength, for if her sorrow had been great before this ghostly sight, it was much greater after it, and her love toward our Lord increased still more. And then she was taken with great wonderment that our Lord should so become man, and suffer such grievous pains for her who was so unkind a creature to Him.

Another time, as she was in the church of St. Margaret, in the choir, being in a state of great sweetness and devotion and with a great plenteousness of tears, she asked our Lord Jesus Christ how she might best please Him, and He answered to her soul, saying, "Daughter, consider your own wickedness and reflect on my goodness."

Then she prayed, many times and oft, these words, "Lord, in thy great goodness have mercy on all my wickedness, for surely I was never so wicked as Thou art good, nor may I ever be so, even if I wanted to be, for thou art so good that it is impossible thou shouldst be better. And therefore it is a great wonder that anyone should be parted from thee eternally."

Then, as she lay still in the choir, weeping and mourning for her sins, suddenly she fell into a kind of sleep. At once she saw with her spiritual eyes our Lord's body lying before her, and his head, as she thought, closest to her, with his blessed face turned up—the handsomest man that ever might be seen or imagined. But then someone came into her view with a dagger and cut that precious body all along the breast. At once she wept with amazing intensity, having more memory, pity and compassion for the Passion of our Lord Jesus Christ than she had known before. And so every day her consciousness and love of our Lord increased, blessed may He be, and the more her love increased the greater was her sorrow for the sin of the people.

On another occasion the aforesaid creature was in a chapel of our Lady, weeping heavily in memory of our Lord's Passion and such other graces and goodness as our Lord ministered to her mind. Suddenly, she knew not how, she was in a manner asleep. At once, in the vision of her soul, she saw our Lord standing directly over her, so near that she thought she took his toes in her hands and felt them, and to her feeling it was as if they were actual flesh and bone. And then she thanked God for all, for through these spiritual visions her affection was completely drawn into the humanity of Christ and the memory of his Passion, right unto the time that it pleased our Lord to give her understanding of his incomprehensible Godhead.

As has been written before . . . these types of visions and feelings were her experience soon after her conversion, once she had fully committed herself to serving God with all her heart, according to her power, and had fully left the world, actually staying inside the church both morning and afternoon, especially during Lent, and also once she had, with great insistence upon it and with much prayer, obtained her husband's permission to live chastely and purely, and had done great physical penance before going to Jerusalem. But afterward, once she and her husband had mutually agreed upon the vow of chastity, as is written earlier, and she had been to Rome and Jerusalem, and suffered much despite and reproof for her weeping and crying, our Lord of his high mercy drew her affection toward his Godhead. This she experienced in greater fervency of love and desire, yet it was more subtle of understanding than was her sense of Christ's manhood.

Nevertheless, the fire of love increased in her, and her understanding was more enlightened and her devotion more fervent than it had been before when her meditation and contemplation was focused only on his humanity. Yet she no longer had the same violence in crying as she had before, but rather a manner more soft, subtle and easy for her spirit to bear. But it was still as plenteous of tears as ever.

Another time, as this creature was in a house of the Preaching Friars, within a chapel dedicated to our Lady, while she was standing at her prayers her eyelids closed together momentarily in a kind of sleep and she saw, she thought, our Lady in what was the fairest of all her visions, holding a beautiful white kerchief in her hand, and saying to her, "Daughter, would you like to see my son?"

At once, forthwith, she saw our Lady hold her blessed son in her hands and wrap Him ever so gently in the white kerchief so that she could readily see how she did it. The creature had then a new spiritual joy and a new spiritual comfort, which was so marvellous that she could never tell it as she felt it. . . .

PART SIX

The Spirituality of Everyday Life

GENTILESSE

Reproduction of a funerary brass (1416) from Felbrigg Church, Norfolk, showing a couple from the time of Wyclif, Sir Simon Felbrygge and his wife Margaret. The iconography indicates his dedication to being a *miles Cristi* (the lion represents courage or *fortitudo*) and her faithfulness (the little dog symbolizes faith or *fides*).

WALTER HILTON

from
Epistle on the Mixed Life

This passage comes from Hilton's famous letters (c. 1370) to a layman who, following a conversion or renewal experience, was thinking about taking up the contemplative life of a monk. It is clear that he was not only a married man but a lord with responsibility over estates and tenants, and Hilton's letter sets out to curb and redirect his enthusiasm toward responsible spiritual development of his ordinary life. What Hilton proposes is a "mixed life," a life in the world which, when accepted as a matter of God's calling, is sanctified in a heart truly prepared to work for a profound deepening of spiritual experience. The text which follows is from the beginning of the second letter, as found in the Vernon MS.

The Mixed Life

Prologue

THE GRACE AND THE GOODNESS of our Lord Jesus that He has shown to you, withdrawing your heart from love and affection for worldly vanity and indulgence in physical sins, and turning your will entirely toward his service and good pleasure, now also encourages my own heart with many new reasons to love Him in his mercy. Moreover, it greatly induces me to endeavor to strengthen you for the godly purpose and good working that you have begun, to bring it toward a good end if I may, principally as unto God, but also in gratitude for the tender affection and love which you have shown to me, even though I am a wretch and unworthy of it.

I. Why godly desire needs to be ruled by discretion, and works of stewardship wrought in the order of charitable love.

I know well the desire of your heart, that you greatly covet to serve our Lord in spiritual occupation entirely, without distraction or hindrance of worldly business, so that you might, by grace, come to a greater knowledge and experience of God and spiritual things. This desire is good—and as far as I can tell, of God—for it grows out of a charitable love set particularly on our Lord Himself.

Nevertheless, this good desire needs to be shaped and governed by discretion in its outward expression, according to the state in which you find yourself, for charity unruled sometimes turns into vice. Therefore it says in Holy Writ, "Our Lord gave to me orderly charitable love, that the end of charity should not be lost through my own indiscretion" (Canticles 2:4, Vg.). Just so, this charitable love and desire that our Lord of his mercy has given you requires appropriate governance for your pursuit of it. In order that you may perceive the appropriate measures, you should ask yourself certain questions concerning your own position in life, the manner of living that you have been used to, and the grace of virtuous life which you now have acquired.

My purpose is to urge you to resist simple extremes.

Do not utterly follow your instinct to leave off all occupation and business of the world, for these are necessary, in fact, for your self-governance and provision for all others who are under your keeping. I mean, do not give yourself entirely to spiritual preoccupation in prayers and meditation, as if you were a monk or friar or any other man not bound to the world by children and employees as indeed you are. If you were to ignore these obligations, you would not in fact be keeping to an ordinate and charitable love.

On the other hand, if you were entirely to forgo spiritual occupations, ignoring the grace that God has given to you, setting yourself completely to secular business and attending only to the active life with a totality of absorption like one who never left his devotions, what then? You would here also lose the proper order of charitable love. For your state, as a layman, asks that you attend to *both* occupations, each in their proper time.

II. How the life of Mary and Martha, mingled together, is appropriate to those that have leadership responsibilities.

You ought to mingle the works of an active life with spiritual endeavors of a contemplative life, and then you will do well.

For you should at certain times be busy "with Martha" in the ordering and care of your household, children, employees, tenants or neighbors. If they do well, you ought to comfort and help them in this; if they do badly, then teach them to amend themselves and correct them. And you should oversee and wisely keep yourself informed as to how your property and worldly goods are being administered, conserved or intelligently invested by your employees, in order that you might, with the profits, more bountifully perform deeds of mercy for your fellow Christians.

At other times you should, "with Mary," leave off the business of this world and sit down meekly at the feet of our Lord, there to be in prayer, holy thought and contemplation of Him, as He gives you grace.

And so you should go from one activity to the other in maintaining your stewardship, fulfilling both aspects of the Christian life. In so doing, you will be keeping well the priorities of charitable love. Yet, that you may not be in doubt of what I am saying, I shall develop these points now in more careful detail.

III. To whom the active life is most proper, and to whom the contemplative.

You will recognize that there are three manners of life: one is "active," as in business, another "contemplative," as in spiritual service, and the third is made up of both and so called the "mixed" life.

Active life by itself is the province of laymen and women who are secular, worldly, and who tend to be superficial in their knowledge of the spiritual life. Nominal in their devotion, they seem not to feel as much fervor in love as some others do, almost as if they cannot get the knack of it. Nevertheless they fear God and dread the pains of hell, and therefore flee sin, desiring to please God and come to heaven, and generally are in good will toward their fellow Christians. Now it is necessary and expedient for such persons to employ works of the active life as busily as they can, in help of themselves and their fellow Christians, for they cannot do anything else.

A purely contemplative life is the choice of men or women who, for the love of God, forsake all occasion of sin in the world, and of the flesh, and all obligations, responsibilities and care of worldly goods. By making themselves poor and naked, down to the barest needs of the bodily sort, they flee from the governance of other men into the service of God. For such persons it is appropriate to labor and occupy themselves inwardly in order to obtain through the grace of our Lord cleanness of heart and peace of conscience through the rejection of sin and nourishing of spiritual virtues. For these reasons, then, they come to the contemplative life, the special purity of which may not be had without both great exercise of the body and continual travail of the spirit, in devout prayer, fervent desire, and meditation.

IV. How the mixed life is especially appropriate to pastors as well as to those with responsibilities of secular governance.

The third kind of life, which is mixed, is appropriate to men of Holy

Church such as priests and others with pastoral responsibilities, who have care and governance over others—with respect not so much to their bodies as to their souls. For such people it is necessary at times to employ attributes and endeavors of the active life, in help and sustenance of themselves and others. At other times, however, it is necessary for them to leave off all excessive business and to devote themselves for a period to prayer, meditation and the reading of Holy Scripture, as well as to other spiritual occupations, as they feel themselves so inclined.

But this life is also generally appropriate to certain laymen who have positions of leadership by virtue of considerable possession of worldly goods, and also have, as it were, a kind of lordship over others to govern and sustain them. Analogous responsibilities pertain also to other relationships, such as the governance of a father over his children, an employer over his employees, or a landlord over his tenants, assuming that these have likewise received as a gift of our Lord's grace a sense of devotion, and some inkling of spiritual calling. To these folk also belongs this mixed life, that is, both active and contemplative. We may see that if such persons, placed in and charged with responsibilities they have undertaken, were to abandon entirely the business of this world (and the very abilities which ought skillfully to be employed in the fulfilling of their responsibilities), offering themselves exclusively to contemplative life, they would not be doing well, or keeping to the priorities of charitable love. For charity, as you know, lies both in love of God and love of our fellow Christian, and therefore it is only reasonable that he who has charity should focus on *both* objects of that proper love, not exclusively on one or the other.

He who for the love of God in contemplation turns away from the love of his fellow Christians and does not care for them as he ought—especially those in relationships to which he is bound—does not fulfill the law of love. On the other hand, whoever obtains such great satisfaction from works of the active life and business in the world that, while claiming concern and love for his neighbors, he turns entirely away from the life of the spirit to which God has called him—such a person does not fulfill the law of love either.

V. How our Lord Jesus Christ and godly men in positions of authority have given us examples of a mixed life.

Our Lord, in steering some of us toward this mixed life, put Himself in the place of such persons, both those who would be pastors and those who are disposed to positions of secular responsibility, and gave them examples by his own manner of life that they should be able to pursue a mixed life as He did. At times He communed and mixed with people, showing to them his deeds of mercy. He taught the simple by his preaching, He visited the sick and healed them of their illnesses, He fed the hungry, and He comforted those that were in sadness. At other times He broke away from the conversation of all worldly folk, and of his disciples also, and went alone into the desert, or upon the hills, and continued there all night in prayers, as the Gospel tells us (Luke 6:12).

This mixed life was thus modelled by our Lord Himself as an example for those who take up the estate and calling of a mixed life. What his life suggests is that such folk should give themselves to their worldly business in reasonable measure, and to works of the active life such as may profit the people who are under their care. His life also suggests that they should make time for giving themselves entirely to contemplation, in devotion, prayer, and meditation.

This life has been the pattern for holy bishops and leaders of the Church, who had responsibility for both the care of men's souls and the administration of temporal affairs. For these holy men of God did not abandon utterly their appropriate administration or stewardship of worldly goods, nor give themselves entirely to contemplation, despite the rich grace they had in such contemplation. No, they often broke away from their own spiritual rest and refreshment, when they would far rather have still been so occupied, and for the love of their fellow Christians engaged in the demands of worldly business for the benefit of those in their charge. Truly, this was charitable love.

Thus, wisely and discretely, they divided their habits of life into two emphases. In the one, they devoted time to the lower part of charity by works of the active life, since they were bound thereto by the obligations of their ordination; in the other they devoted themselves to the higher part of charity in contemplating God and turning their mind to spiritual things by prayer and meditation. And so, they had fully charitable love toward God and their fellow Christians, both in the affections of their souls within and in the expression they gave outwardly through bodily deeds and endeavors.

Others, who were contemplatives only, and free from all such responsibilities, could have a fullness of charitable love toward God and their neighbors, but it was restricted to their souls' affection and not able to have an outward expression. It often happened in such cases that the more intense the spiritual inwardness, the less was their capability for outward deeds—for they needed not to do this since it was not part of their calling.

VI. To whom a mixed life is most suitable; to whom a contemplative is most productive.

But these godly persons of whom I speak, both those who were ordained and those who were laymen, have had the blessing of a fullness of charitable love in affection within and also in outward working of their devotion. This is the distinctive character of the mixed life. And truly, for one who is in a position of spiritual leadership, such as a pastor, or for one who has a position of secular authority, such as a leader in business or government, I believe that this mixed life is the best and most fruitful, as long as one is committed to it.

For others, who are free and bound neither to temporal administration nor to spiritual ministry, I imagine that a contemplative life alone, if they come to it faithfully and in truth, would be best and most fruitful, most fair and expedient. If they make such a commitment, it is my expectation that they should not then leave it of their own free will for works of the active life—unless, of course, there is a great need for the comforting of others in distress.

VII. Here is shown what life accords most to the one for whom this book was made.

By what I have said thus far you may in part, at least, understand the character of the various styles of life commitment, and determine which accords most to the state of your own life. And truly, it seems to me, this mixed style of life is the one most suitable to you. For our Lord has ordained you and set you in a position of authority over others in considerable degree, and lent you an abundance of worldly goods to administer and sustain, especially on behalf of all those who are under your governance and your lordship, as you act in strength and wisdom. He has also, therewithal, afterward by his mercy granted you grace to have some knowledge of yourself and a spiritual desire and recognition of his love. I think, then, that this life which is mixed will be the one best for you and most appropriate.

What it calls for is a wise apportionment of your life into two dedications, so that you spend some of your time with one, some with the other. You know very well that if you were to leave the necessary business of your active life and be reckless, taking no proper care of your worldly goods, how they are kept or invested, and if you were to have no concern for those who work for you or your colleagues, just because you want only to give yourself to spiritual occupation, then you could not expect to be excused when calamity came. If you were to behave like this, clearly it would not be very wise.

What are all your works worth, whether they be bodily or spiritual, unless they are done properly and reasonably, to the worship of God and at his bidding? *Absolutely nothing.*

ANONYMOUS

Our Daily Work: A Mirror of Discipline

This treatise, once associated with Richard Rolle of Hampole, was more probably written by an unknown Yorkshire pastor of the mid-fourteenth century. It is concerned with the ideal that everything in our daily life should be offered up to God as a part of grateful stewardship. This theme—the sanctification of ordinary work—is one that received strong encouragement in the early work of St. Francis and his lay followers. It indicates, as does the emphasis on meditation on the life and Passion of Christ, how the writings which emerged from the Yorkshire "revival" may be seen as a link between Franciscan spirituality and the preaching of Wyclif and his followers.

Part I of this work, through development of the motif of Christ's vineyard parables, characterizes faithful work as the proper stewardship of men and women redeemed by grace. Work is therefore not simply a burdensome curse resulting from the Fall, but a joyful opportunity for redeeming the time. Fervency of spirit, which for this author was ideally an *ecstasis* of contemplative devotion, is described in Part II as the center of a godly life. Prayer, worship, meditation (focusing on the cross and on the life of our Lord), and habitual circumspection are each discussed as profitable spiritual disciplines. But the author returns us, in Part III, to the practical business of working out our life in Christ, urging us to understand that serving the Lord is also a matter of perseverance (see Romans 12:11).

The style of this text is reminiscent of other instructive spiritual writing, which often quotes "authorities" to support a point. Chief among these is Scripture itself, of course, but writers then (as now) were also fond of citing secular authorities when they seemed to agree with the Bible, and of supplementing Scripture's witness with "tradition," usually material from the lives of the saints and the early church fathers. This writer quotes, with and without acknowledgment, much more than Hilton or Rolle did and is especially fond of illustrative anecdotes and stories. The text translated here is from the Thornton Manuscript, MS Lincoln Cathedral Library A.1.17. A shorter version exists in MS Arundel 507.

THREE THINGS ARE NEEDFUL to everyone who wants to prosper spiritually—God's grace leading and helping him. The first of these, simply, is to be engaged in honest work, without wasting time. The second is to conduct one's prayer life with a freedom of spirit, with respect both to place and to time, whatever one's employment. The third is that one's outward bearing, whatever the circumstances, be so honest and becoming that praise to God and a general encouragement to pursue good work is inspired in all those who look on; as the Apostle urges us: "Let all things be done decently and in order" (1 Corinthians 14:40).

I. Not Slothful in Business

From the beginning, we see that one ought to guard against squandering his short time, or spending it mistakenly, or in idleness letting it pass away. God has sent to man his time in order that he might serve Him, and to gather with good works his grace to attain to heaven. For not only do these brief minutes fly from us, but so also does the time allotted to us in life: as the wise man says, "Our life swifts away" (Job 9:25). St. Gregory puts it this way: "Our life is like a man in a ship—it makes no difference whether he sits, stands, sleeps, or keeps awake—steadily he is carried on where the ship is driven with the force of the weather. So we, in this short time, whatever we do with it, are driven on toward our end."[1] And our enemy Death follows us ever at our back, bearing a sharp spear to strike us through. It is no wonder then, that Seneca says, "Life flies, death follows," and St. Augustine, "Life is nothing else but a swift running to the death."

By this token we see that the issue is not how long a man lives, but how well. For this brief life is all too uncertain. Job therefore says, "I know not how long I may endure, and whether after a short space my Maker may take me away" (Job 32:22, Vg.) and St. Gregory, reflecting on these same words, says, "I know nothing about the length of time I shall dwell here, nor when I shall be taken away to judgment." We are reminded, as St. Jerome says, that "Nothing so much provokes a man as the fact that he does not know how long his uncertain life will last." And yet the same person will hope for a long life for himself, as if he might, by his own force of will, drive Death back. It is in this way that the rich man spoken of in the Gospel of St. Luke, chapter sixteen, was deceived. For riches fail and are not kept by any one, but glide away like a phantom. When the rich have assembled goods together, either by rightful means or with wrongs and poor men's curses, then suddenly they have to leave their goods—unless, of course, their goods take leave of them before that.

1. Gregory the Great, Bishop of Rome in the late sixth century, was most valued in the Middle Ages for his remarkable book *On Pastoral Rule* and for his extensive and often brilliant commentary on the book of Job.

Holy Scripture tells us that "the world passes away and the lusts thereof" (1 John 2:17). A man who falls into the stream and through the force of water is borne away from the shore can, if he can get hold of anything that is well fastened like a root or a stake, prevent the water from bearing him altogether away. But if he latches on to anything that floats along beside him he cannot secure himself. Truly, whether we like it or not, in this life as if in that water, we are ever passing along with the goods of this world, and there is nothing in this world to fasten ourselves to so as not to be swept past. As the Wise Man[2] says, "We shall all die, and like water slip away into the earth." And therefore Job speaks, as if to say, "Of riches and friends I had plenty, but they could hinder me neither from going forth nor from coming again."[3]

And by what path each person shall go the prophet Isaiah shows us when he says, "All flesh is grass, and all the glory of it as the flower of the field" (Isaiah 40:6). Human flesh is like hay, and all of his joy and splendor as the flower of the meadow. Hay is first green grass, and soon after brings forth flowers. A while after that the flowers dry and fall; after that it is mown down with a scythe, dried and taken to a house to be food for cattle. So it is with everyone: in childhood we spring up and wax full as does the grass; afterward we come to adulthood and flower in fairness, strength, intelligence and the possession of worldly goods; afterwards we draw toward old age as our flowers fade—fairness, strength, intellect and other powers. Finally we are stricken down with the scythe of Death, and afterwards taken to a house to become food for beasts—that is to say, dug into the earth to feed worms. Therefore it is said, "When a man dies he shall dwell with serpents and beasts." Indeed, a dead person is so disgusting to our physical senses that one cannot let him be in his literal house three days together, but bears him forth so that the body offends no one with the stench of death.

We begin to see the point. Now is the time to work, for the time will come when there is no time to work, but only to receive rewards for that already done, for as in Revelation the angel has sworn that time will be no more (Revelation 10:6). Let us then do now as the Apostle says: "As we have opportunity, let us work good toward all men" (Galatians 6:10). And as the Apostle counsels us he did himself, for it is said that from the

2. In late medieval authors, a reference to the "Wise Man" may mean Solomon, whom they thought to be chief author of the book of Proverbs as well as the Song of Songs. It can also, however, suggest the "teacher" or "preacher" to whom Ecclesiastes is ascribed, or the author of another of the Wisdom books.

3. The author here conflates portions of Job 16:11 and 16:23 (Vg.), slightly altering the first phrase in v. 23.

first hour of the day until the fifth he worked with his hands to win his food; from the fifth to the tenth he preached to the people; from the tenth until evening he served the poor and pilgrims with such goods as he had; by nightfall he was at prayer, and thus he spent his time.[4]

There are three ways in which one loses his time. The first of these is in idleness; the second is in work that no real good can come of; the third is in good works which are not ordained as they should be.

Wasted Time

Against idleness Solomon says, "Idleness teaches much evil" (confl. Proverbs 19:15 and Ecclesiastes 10:18) and Holy Scripure advises us that whoever follows idleness is most foolish. Whoever does not desist from what harms him is a great fool, the more so since thereby he wins himself no reward. This foolishness is apparent most of all in the pain that it creates. On this account God blames the idle, saying, "Why do you stand all day idle?" (Matthew 20:6). For idleness wastes goods that are prudently gotten, and ends by enticing Satan into the house—for as by good employment the devil is hindered from entering into man's heart, so surely idleness opens the door to him. Even Seneca says that "he lives not to his own benefit who lives for his stomach and the ease of his flesh at every opportunity." Job reminds us that "Man is born to labor" (Job 5:17, Vg.) and it is clear enough that mankind was bound to work after he had sinned, commanded so by God who said: "In the sweat of thy brow shalt thou eat thy bread, till thou returnest unto the earth from whence thou wast taken; for dust thou art, and unto dust thou shalt return again" (Genesis 3:19).

Therefore shall you work stalwartly and not faintly, for He bids you work, with the sweat on your face, even until you are returned to the earth—that is, that in all your lifetime you should lose no time in idleness. Idleness smites a man, as if he were in paralysis, and makes his limbs atrophy till he cannot work. It is with this kind of character in mind that the Psalmist says: "They have hands and do not use them; feet and they do not walk, mouths have they but they speak not, eyes and see not, ears and hear not" (Psalm 115:5-7), for the limbs of such

4. This expansion of the life of St. Paul (and the work habits suggested by Acts 18:3 and 2 Thessalonians 3:7-12) owes to traditional histories and biographies. References to "the Apostle" in this period are invariably to Paul; it should be noted, however, that he was at this time still thought to have authored the Epistle to the Hebrews.

people are so bound in sin that to all good things they are as good as dead, while to evil things they are easy prey.[5]

Idleness is nurse to all the vices, making one reckless about not doing what he is beholden to do. And it is certain that Satan, when he finds anyone idle, puts into that person's heart foul thoughts of fleshly filth and other follies that may bring him to sin; after that he prompts that person actually to perform his fantasies until he entirely contradicts the Apostle's bidding: "Neither give place to the devil" (Ephesians 4:27). Finally, then, the idle person makes himself unfit to dwell in any place but hell. For such a one can hardly dwell in heaven, since heaven is the full reward of those whose time here has been well spent in stewardship they hope has been pleasing to Christ their Lord.

Great shame it is to be idle in this time of grace, in which we are, as servants in the vineyard, hired to work—for if we labor as we ought a great reward awaits us. God gives us in Himself our highest model for a proper approach to work, for as the Apostle says:

> He made Himself of no reputation, and took upon Him the form of a servant, and was made in the likeness of men; and being found in fashion as a man He humbled Himself, and became obedient unto death, even the death of the cross. Wherefore God also hath highly exalted Him, and given Him a name which is above every name, that at the name of Jesus every knee should bow, of things in heaven, and things in earth, and things under the earth; and that every tongue should confess that Jesus Christ is Lord, to the glory of the Father. (Philippians 2:7-11)

Overproud, then, and over-delicate is the servant who in the midst of battle will rest, watching his Lord assailed and sore-wounded by his enemies. No, we ought to work diligently in this time of grace, for we are God's own purchased bond-servants, bought with the price of His dear-worthy blood to work in his vineyard. And yet He promises us a payday, if we do with good will that which, in fact as a debt, we owe Him to do.

Remember that to his chosen friends, before the time of grace, God promised only earthly goods if they did well; to us is promised the bliss of heaven. They endured a long wait before coming thereto, for they went to Sheol and abode there—some a thousand years, some two,

---

5. This passage suggests a conflation (and perhaps a confusion) on the author's part of the *idols* described by the Psalmist and the *idle* of whom he himself is speaking here. He may well be recalling the scriptural passage from having heard it read aloud.

some three—before they came to heaven.[6] But now many people in only a little time gain heaven: if, for example, they die in the state of innocence soon after they are christened; or, if they do full repentance for their misdeeds and turn to God again; or, if they are martyred for God's love. This is the time of the supper that the gospel of St. Luke speaks of, to which God bid his servants call all those who were invited. This is the time of grace, now, when all is made ready, so that there is nothing else to do but wash and go to dine—that is, for people to be cleansed of their sins that they have committed since they were born.

Vain Enterprise

What a terrible loss of time it is to worry over things from which can come no profit! We ought to travail only for the sake of our worship of God, and for our own soul's health. Do not admire the person who has simply lived long enough to go about with a cane, stooping and grey-haired, but deem him as worthily old as he has lived well. There is a story about a student named Josapath who asked of his teacher Barlaham how old he was: "I am," quoth he, "45 years of age." "But Master," replied the student, "methinks you must be of 60 years and more." Then said the teacher, "Ah, since I was born it has been all of 60 years; but those years that I spent in idleness and sin before I took me to this New Life, I hold as years of death. But all those I call years of life in which I have served Jesus Christ my Lord, through his dear-worthy grace." Accordingly then, whosoever would reflect on the amount of time that steals away from him while he or she dallies over eating and drinking, or in excess of useless works, idle speech and foul thoughts, useless jests and other vanities by which people amuse themselves, may rightly understand that though he or she may be old in years, typically all too little of that time has been lived in the manner it ought to have been; for such persons have lived not to their profit nor won a true reward, and peradventure may have even brought on themselves much pain on account of their loss of precious time.

It would be an astonishing thing if a person who gives himself to business of the world more than is necessary had no experience of being hindered in prayer, or in rest of heart, in faithfulness of works, and in

6. This passage reflects the understanding common in the early and medieval church that before the Atonement God's faithful elect of Israel who had died in their faith had been sent to Sheol, the abode of the dead. There they awaited deliverance to their ultimate glory in heaven until Christ, by his resurrection, set them free from the bonds of death.

the perfection of good endeavors. Yes, and it would be a wonder if such a one had no experience of being hindered even in the love he or she ought to be expressing toward God and fellow Christians.

Accordingly, holy men of God in times before our own, knowing something of their propensity to be so hindered, fled the world and its vanities as if it were accursed. For it seemed to some of them that they could not lead a righteous life in the world. Therefore, they went out into the wilderness, and there committed themselves to serve God in peace. Thinking of them, one is reminded of Seneca, who said, "I have become more avaricious, cruel and inhuman, from living among men."

Good Work Compromised

Three types of impediments to spiritual living which are to be avoided come here to mind: useless, vain chattering, raking about in other folks' business, and excessive care about worldly things.

Against useless vain chattering Solomon says, "The beginning of strife is as when one letteth out water" (Proverbs 17:14), which he intends as an uncomplimentary parallel to our abandonment of control over the tongue. No one may come to a knowledge of God—or of himself—who lets his heart be dissipated with much useless speech. This merely makes a way in for the devil.

For this reason Solomon, in another remark, likens such a person to a city without a wall: "He that hath no rule over his own spirit is like a city that is broken down and without walls" (Proverbs 25:28). And St. James adds, "If any man among you seem to be righteous, and bridleth not his own tongue, . . . this man's religion is vain" (James 1:26). St. Gregory in his *Dialogues* makes this useful comment, that "As near as our mouth is to the world's speech, so far is it from God when we speak to Him and pray to Him; for in this state we call Him and He withdraws Himself; for our breath stinks to Him of the idle speech and chatter that has filled us up." Therefore, whosoever wants God's ear to be near his mouth when he prays to Him, let him draw his heart from vain and useless chattering of the world.

There is so much impediment to good work in too much talk that, as St. Ambrose says, philosophers typically bind their disciples to silence for the first five years. Another man, a virtuous abbot named Agathon, writes that he went about with a stone in his mouth for three years to keep himself quiet.

The second impediment concerns those who are always trying to feed their wits with vanities and lusts. One remembers the story of the angel who taught holy Abbot Arsenius, telling him: "Arsenius, you flee the world and all its desires and keep yourself in peacefulness; bridling your tongue that it doesn't get away from you in quarreling or idle speech." Another story tells of an Abbot who for fully twenty years sat in his study, and never once lifted his head above the pages in front of him so much as to see the roof.

Against those who care too much about worldly possessions, Solomon says: "Vain is their hope and their labor without fruit, for they can carry nothing away of all their labor" (gloss on Ecclesiastes 2:21-22). We verify this every day in observing the dead, who, be they ever so rich, take away with them nothing but graveclothes.

Here is a thought for those rich folks who "play" with the world, amusing themselves, and also for those covetous persons who get rich on the backs of the poor, raking together all they can without regard to whom they get it from, rich or poor, or what those persons have left. For all that they deal with is but phantom and dream.

It is just the same with a rich man who satisfies here on earth his appetite for gold, silver and other fleshly things (wherewith the world deceives him as an unworthy wretch) as it is with the poor man who so sorely hungers and thirsts that he almost dies. After long hunger has tortured him, this poor fellow falls into delirious sleep, and he dreams that he is bidden to a great banquet. There he is set at the high table, and all the dainties he can imagine are set before him, wine and *piment*[7] in fair cups.

He eats and drinks his fill, and makes himself glad. All those who stand about him are anxious to do his will.

After he has eaten what he thinks good, the tablecloth is withdrawn and he with great grandeur is directed to the Guest Chamber. There he eats spices, and drinks more wine. Afterwards he is escorted to bed, as if he were a prince, and wrapped in rich robes trimmed with the fur of mink and squirrel.

But when this wretch wakes up he feels his legs all cold. He thinks on the grandeur that he was in, and of all the rich splendor he thought was about him in bed. Frantically, he gropes about him trying to find anything of those rich clothes he thought were upon him, but he feels nothing else besides his own poor tatters and rags. Suddenly he hungers and thirsts more than he did before. Then he knows for a fact it was but a dream. False phantoms—ghosts of the imagination—made him believe he was at a feast.

It is just so that the world's false riches provide the rich, making them

7. *Piment* is spiced wine with fruit juice, usually served heated in the cold months.

believe that all is true that the phantom teaches them. Riches drug them, making them forget themselves, and belittle those who really earned those riches. They make feasts of goods they bilked from the poor, and everyone, for fear of their power, is careful to do what they want. But when death shall waken them from that baleful dream, they shall find all that they believed real to be a mere phantom.

There is a third kind of folk who lose their time. They are those who have a desire to do good, but because they fail to do it in the manner which is appropriate lose their reward. For when good intent is missing in any deed, the reward that should fall to it is not forthcoming. And this can happen in four ways.

First, this can happen on account of a wicked spirit behind the action, as in the offering of Cain. For though he offered to God something of the new fruit, God would not look favorably on it. Rather, he was favorable to the offering of Abel, his brother. St. Gregory's comment on this is that "by the heart's will of him that offers is the gift received by God or rejected. God was not pleased with Abel on account of his offering, but pleased with the offering on account of Abel, who in all of his works was being true and good. But on Cain and his offering God would not look, since he who made the offering displeased God by his poor intentions." If our own offering or service we perform that is in its own nature good nevertheless displeases God, there is a reason. The prophet shows us, presenting God's voice: "When ye make many prayers I will not hear: your hands are full of blood" (Isaiah 1:15).

A second way that some folk lose their reward for good endeavor is a spirit of vanity which has motivated the endeavor in hope of praise. For vainglory makes evil out of good: if alms or charitable deeds which are good in themselves are done for the sake of praise, they amount only to sin.

A third thing that snatches away reward for a good deed is boasting by the one who has done it, after the fact, as the Pharisee did, of whom God said to all those that stood before Him: "Truly, this man has lost his reward for all his good deed" (Luke 18:10-14). It is necessary therefore that a person do all the good he can and yet not pride himself on it in thought or in word, for he has not by himself, nor of his own deserving, achieved these good things.

The fourth thing that snatches from a person a reward for good endeavor is when he or she does it with the intention of being esteemed better than other folk, or to lessen the good deeds of others, or to outdo them if they can. Of such a motivation St. Gregory tells us a little story in his *Dialogues:* Once upon a time a holy bishop, Fortunatus by name, by the grace he had of God, was given the power to banish devils from some folk who had been possessed by them. And so it happened one time that on a certain evening Fortunatus chased a devil out of a man who had been possessed. As soon as he was chased out, the fiend presented himself in the likeness of a pilgrim, and went through the city where the bishop was, weeping and yelling like a poor wretch or beggar, as if he wanted shelter for the night. And then he began to cry, loud enough for the whole city to hear: "Look! See what your bishop has done to me, who you all think is so good and holy! When I had taken myself a lodging and believed myself to be at rest, along came your bishop to my house and put me out by force. Now, as a poor wretch, all I want is a place. I need lodging, and none of you will take pity on me!"

A man of that city heard him speak in this way and thought, "Hm! Here is a good opportunity." So he took him into his house, set him by the fire, and eased his condition with the usual hospitality. But when the man had begun to speak to the supposed pilgrim, inquiring after tidings from far-away places (as men often do of pilgrims), the fiend suddenly leapt over to the child in the cradle, quickly wrung its neck, threw it in the fire, and vanished away. And so, at his departure, the fiend requited the man for his attempt to do a good deed.

To this little story St. Gregory adds a commentary: "Many deeds seem to be good that are not good because they are not done with a good will. This man that harbors a devil disguised as a pilgrim did not do it for any particular pity he felt for him, but only because he spoke ill of the bishop. He called him into his house so that his neighbors would think him a better man and more merciful than the bishop, imagining that he would appear as the good chap who harbored a poor wretch turned out by the bishop." This comment applies the story to many whose motivation for doing good is chiefly to detract from the good work of others, and even to destroy their reputation.

In the same manner, a good deed is lost if the one who does it covets by that means to have riches, position, or honor or worldly goods. Through the defiling of this sin the personal good is lost, and, as Scripture says, "Who sinneth in one thing loses many good things" (James 2:2-10, Vg.), that is, unless he amends himself and repents fully of his actions.

II. Fervent in Spirit

The second part of this book offers us some instruction in how to do the good work that falls to us with freedom of spirit, in place and in time, as is appropriate to each of our endeavors. For we are not to work as if we are compelled, nor are we to do it with anger, nor with a dead heart.

For Holy Scripture says "God loves a cheerful giver" (2 Corinthians 9:7); God loves the one who gives Him anything, however small, with a glad heart. Certainly this applies to endeavors that are consecrated to his praise and honor, and to the health of men's souls; prayer, holy thoughts, and a clear-mindedness about God and his deeds are examples, if they are well intended and followed through to action.

Prayer

Prayer is a sacrifice that greatly pleases God, if it is offered in the manner it ought to be. God asks prayer of us as a kind of debt due Him, as when He says, "God created the nations for His praise and His glory" (cf. Isaiah 43:7), and "The sacrifice of praise shall honor me" (Psalm 50:23). And the Apostle encourages us: "We ought always to pray and not to faint" (Luke 18:1). Therefore, it is good for us to "pray without ceasing" (1 Thessalonians 5:17).

That person prays without ceasing who is always doing good. And certainly people of faith are bound to worship God with prayer, as are persons with a vocation in Holy Church. After all, they live by the tithes and offerings of others. All the community labors to bring them what they need, so that they may serve God without distraction, and with their fervent prayer seek reconciliation between God and man. Also maidens and widows who have taken an oath of chastity have, more than others, a duty to pray.

One who wants to please God with his prayer, offering it up with a free will and a loving heart, will prepare himself in advance, as Solomon counsels: "Before prayer, prepare thy soul, and be not as one that tempteth God" (Ecclesiasticus 18:23). Whoever does not earnestly desire to win that for which he prays, or who despairs of achieving it, is tempting God. The same is true if, as he prays, he pursues a sinful and evil life. Of such folk St. Gregory remarks: "Of what wonder is it if our prayers are answered slowly by God, when slowly or not at all we answer to his commands?" And Isidore adds, "One who is slothful about God's commands, and takes pleasure in the remembrance of past sins, cannot have certain confidence in his prayers."

Whoever seeks results from his prayer, let him do the good he may, flee sin, recall his heart from the world and hold it at home as the Gospel teaches: "When thou prayest, enter into thy closet and shut thy door, and pray to thy Father" (Matthew 6:6). "Enter your bedroom," he says; call your heart home from the world. Then, "shut the door"—that is, keep silent, hold your own counsel, so that nothing may go out.

For it is but pious folly to pray God to come to us poor needy wretches, to give us benefits of his dear-worthy grace, and then not abide his coming, but turn our backs on Him. St. Isidore points out that our souls must be cleansed from the stain of active sin and our hearts withdrawn from the provocations of the world in order that we can pray to God without distraction. For the person whose prayers are mixed with worldly thoughts, however much he or she prays, is far from God. Therefore the Psalmist says: "Be still and know that I am God" (Psalm 46:10).

Here is something that ought to stir us up to pray with great dread and careful consideration, for we are to be speaking to Almighty God when we are but poor, sinful wretches. Even Abraham, who was called a friend of God, said, "I speak to my Lord, which am but dust and ashes" (Genesis 18:27). Isidore comments, "We ought to pray with sighings and tears, in remembrance of our grimy sins, and of the many bitter pains we shall suffer for them unless we repent and Christ shall have mercy on us."

Also, we ought to be very hopeful of success in what we pray, for Christ Himself says, "All things are possible to him that believeth" (Mark 9:23). Therefore we should pray to God as to our Father, and certainly hope to have a response concerning that for which we pray to Him. For Christ says to all his family, "Whatsoever ye shall ask the Father in my name, he will give it to you" (John 16:23).

There are six useful things to know about prayer: how a person should prepare himself in advance; to whom we should pray; for whom we should pray; what we should ask in prayer; what hinders prayer; and, the power of prayer.

The first of these is really what I have been writing about already, beginning at my first comments on prayer and continuing to this point.

We may then take up the second question: to whom shall we pray? Truly, before all, to God Almighty. As the prophets tell us, "Be subject to God and pray to Him." And in the Gospel we read, "Thou shalt worship the Lord thy God" (Luke 4:8; Matthew 4:10). Saints we honor, not as givers of goods, but as friends of God who offer us spiritual guidance in winning from Him the proper object of our prayer. Therefore let us believe in God with all our heart, and certain hope, and perfect charity: it is our Lord God who is to be loved.

Third, for whom ought we to pray? One great scholar has said, "Every Christian is a living member of Christ's holy church; therefore he is bound to pray for all. But especially we ought to pray for those who have responsibility in the church: the Pope, the cardinals, bishops, pastors, and all who have the care of human souls. Also, we ought to pray for all our enemies, and all our friends, for all who are in deadly sin, that they may rise up out of it, for all those departed for whom God's mercy awaits, and for all those who have a trade or a position of community responsibility."

St. Gregory suggests that one who prays for all shall be the sooner heard and answered in his prayer. St. Ambrose adds, "If you pray for everyone, everyone will pray for you." And St. Jerome says, further, "Necessity binds a man to pray for himself, but charitable love for his brethren stirs him to pray for all. And charity, more than necessity, stirs God to hear."

The fourth question is: what ought we to ask in our prayer? Certainly, we should ask for grace in this life, and lasting joy in the life to come. For this is what God teaches us to ask when He says "Seek ye first the kingdom of God and his righteousness, and all these things shall be added unto you" (Matthew 6:33). God makes Himself debtor to those who are righteous, to find them what they need of earthly goods. For righteousness makes people God's children, and a father by his nature is bound to provide for his children.

Earthly possessions ought not to be asked for in prayers, for they have done harm to many. Solomon says, "How long, ye fools, will ye desire those thing which are hurtful to you?" (Proverbs 1:22, Vg.). Therefore everyone should petition with fear, asking the Lord that, if He sees the request as necessary and reasonable, He will fulfill it and that, if it proves to be inappropriate, He will withdraw it. For what may help and what may harm us the Doctor knows better than the one who is sick.

Yet one of these two things may we trust to have through our prayer—either that which we ask for, or that which is better for us.

The fifth question is: what hinders our prayer from being heard by God? Well, at least six things I can think of.

The first, already suggested, is the sin of the person who is praying. As David admits, "If I regard iniquity in my heart, the Lord will not hear me" (Psalm 66:18). And the prophet says, "Our sins have hid his face from us" (Isaiah 59:2). Or consider the Gospel: ". . . Now we know God heareth not sinners" (John 9:31).

A second impediment is the unworthiness of that for which we pray. We see that there are things for which God, through his prophet, forbids that there be prayer: "Pray not thou for this people, neither lift up cry nor prayer for them . . . for I will not hear" (Jeremiah 7:16). It is told in *The Life of the Fathers* that a certain person who was bound in sin came to the reverend abbot, St. Anthony, and said, "Have mercy on me and pray for me," to which the abbot replied, "I will have no mercy on you unless you also help yourself and leave off your sin."

A third impediment is foul and idle thoughts that prevent us from concentrating on our prayers. Of such falsified prayers God says through his prophet: "These people honor me with their lips, but their heart is far from me" (Isaiah 29:13; Matthew 15:8; Mark 7:6). It constitutes a great wickedness indeed if we sinful wretches, when we speak in prayer to Almighty God, are not even fully aware of what we are saying.

Truly, we are bound to displease God when we ask Him to hear our prayer and we will not even hear it ourselves. But it is still worse to employ prayer time for foul and idle thoughts. Remember Abraham who, when he made a sacrifice to God, birds of the air lighted upon it and would have defiled it. He promptly cleared them away, so that none dared come close until the proper time was come and the sacrifice made (Genesis 15:9-11). Let us do as much with our own erratic and flying thoughts, which defile the sacrifice of our prayer.

Our sacrifice of prayer and thanksgiving is agreeable to God when it comes from a clean and loving heart. God is asking us to offer prayer to Him, and He shall send us grace, and He tells us that whatever we do for Him, that will He not forget.

A fourth hindrance to prayer is hardness of heart. It takes two forms. The first is hardness of heart against the poor, to which the Scripture says, "Who so stoppeth his ears at the cry of the poor, he also shall cry, but shall not be heard" (Proverbs 21:13). The other is that hardness in those who will not forgive those who have done them wrong. Such folk Solomon advises, "Forgive thy neighbor who has injured thee while he appeals to thee, and thy sins shall be forgiven" (Ecclesiasticus 28:2). And the Gospel says, "And when ye stand praying, forgive, if ye have aught against any: that your Father also which is in heaven may forgive you your trespasses" (Mark 11:25).

A fifth matter that hinders our prayers from being heard is too little desire after the proper objects of prayer. St. Augustine says, "God stores things up for you, that you may desire with your whole heart. For He will not give to you hastily, in order that you may learn to desire great things with a great ardor." And St. Gregory adds, "If with our mouth we are praying after the joy of heaven, and we do not yearn for it truly in our heart, we are merely moaning."

A sixth thing which can hinder prayer is foul and idle speech on our lips. If you give a great nobleman something to drink in a slutty cup, however good that drink, he will feel disgust and throw it away no matter how dry his throat. So God does with prayer from a foul mouth; he does not appreciate it, and turns away. Accordingly, St. Gregory comments, "The more our lips are defiled with foolish talking, so much the less are we likely to be heard by God in prayer."

Finally, I come to a consideration of the power of prayer. Those who lived before the present age, and who kept themselves steadfast, speaking nothing idle, won from God what they prayed for. . . .[8] St. Gregory speaks to this point:

> Because God's servants withdraw themselves from traffic with the world and its works, they cannot finally speak uselessly. So some bind themselves to silence, daring to say hardly any word unless it be in teaching others or praising God. Therefore, when they ask anything of God, He is likely to grant it at once. But we woeful wretches, dealing with the world and chattering all day long like magpies, what of us? Now we lie, now we twist the truth, now speak evil, now quarrel, backbite, and swear great oaths. Surely these things defile our prayer and hinder its being heard, for our mouth is as far from praying to God as it is near to the world in idle speech.

Remember, prayer is so powerful that if it is granted its due it masters the fiend our adversary, and hinders him from doing his will. . . .

Worship and Meditation

When you have gathered home your heart and its spiritual wits, and have destroyed the things that might have hindered you from praying effectively, winning to yourself that devotion which God alone can send you through his precious grace, quickly rise up from your bed at the sound of the bell. And if you are not within the sound of either a bell or a rooster, let God's love awaken you, for that response pleases Him.

The zealous heart, rooted in love, wakens before both rooster and bell, and has washed her face with sweet love-tears. Her soul within has joy in God with deep devotion and affection, and eagerly bids Him good morning, and utters other sounds of heavenly gladness which God sends to his lovers. Blessed are they above others whom God wakens, for they have already many joys while others sleep. And they find that gladness waiting for them, no matter how early they rise. God Himself says, "Those that seek me early shall find me" (Proverbs 8:17).

Be then a waker, an early riser. Rise up quickly and heartily thank the Lord your God for the rest you have had, and the care of the angels while you slept. A knight takes great pleasure in being called to come and to speak with the king, especially when he knows it will be to his great profit. With much greater reason ought God's knight—that is,

8. This treatise is often repetitive; it seems, moreover, that it has been written over and augmented by at least one copyist. From this point on, I have eliminated some of the redundancies.

every Christian—be ready at the calling of his Lord, who calls him for his great benefit and nothing else.

Soberly then, rise up in good cheer, imagining that you are hearing God call you with these words, "Arise My love, My fair one, and come and show me thy face: I yearn that the voice of thy prayer may come to my ears" (cf. Song of Solomon 2:10, 13).[9] Remember, in your rising, that many persons have perished during that night, some in body and soul. Some burned, some drowned, some died suddenly in their sleep without having repented, and their souls have been drawn by demons into hell. Some of these who died had fallen into deadly sin, into lust, gluttony, theft, envy, manslaughter—all manner of sin. And from all these perils God has delivered you, of His goodness, not of your merits.

What have you done as unto God that He should care for you, and suffer so many others to be lost? You may well have been less deserving than they were. If you consider what God does for you, even though you have not served Him well, you will find that despite all He is as busy to do you good as if He had nothing else to do. It seems almost as if He had forgotten the whole world, and thought only about you.

When you have reflected on this, lift up your heart to God and pray in this fashion: "I thank you, dear-worthy Lord, with all my heart. It is you who have cared for me this night, so unworthy a sinner; it is you who have permitted me to have life and health, and so to meet this day. I thank you, Lord, for this good, and for so many others that you have done unto me, though I have been unkind and an unworthy sinner far more than others. Yet you have showed me such kindness despite the evil I have done."

And commit yourself and all of your friends into God's hands, and say something like this: "Into your dear-worthy hands, my Lord, I yield my soul and body and all my friends, kin and acquaintances, and all who have done me good, either bodily or in spirit, and all who have received the spirit of Christ. I pray that you, for love of your mother, that most worthy maiden, and for the sake of the prayers of all your saints, keep us this day and night from all perils of body and soul. And keep us from all deadly sins, from the tempting of the fiend, and from sudden death and the pains of hell; cause us to have proper fear of these things. May you sanctify our hearts with the grace of your Holy Spirit,

9. This is an instance of the author's memory including not only the Scripture itself (from the Vulgate) but also a "gloss" or moral interpretation, such as is often found in the margins of medieval Latin Bibles.

and cause us here, in whatever we do, to do your will; and may we never separate ourselves from you, Dear Lord. Amen."

When you have prayed in this way, wend your way to a church or chapel; and if you can get to neither, make your bedroom your church. In church it is usually easiest to obtain most devotion to pray, for there God is on the altar, hearing the one who prays and ready to grant what they ask or better. And there, in the presence of his departed saints, and worshiping in a sanctuary, you may be surrounded by angels who also are there to serve your Lord and you—for their office is to speed your prayer, bearing it up to God, and to minister to you His grace in return. As St. Bernard says, "Rise then quickly, at God's call, and put from yourself all heaviness, and answer the Lord with the words that Samuel replied to God when He called him in the night: "Speak, for thy servant heareth" (1 Samuel 3:10).

Here are eight thoughts to prompt our early wakening and our pursuit of doing good: this short life; the narrow path we have to walk; our good deeds that are so few; our sins that are so many; death that we are sure is coming but we don't know when; the strict, hard judgment of that Last Day, when each idle thought shall be revealed and each foul word and sinful work be indicted. For God says that every careless word shall be recalled. St. Anselm puts the question to us: "What will you do in that day when all the time which has been entrusted to you is required, an accounting of how you have spent it, even to the smallest thought." A seventh thought to prompt our getting up and about our work is the harsh torments of hell; an eighth is the joys of heaven.

After you get up, then, pray for the souls that are in torment and imagine that you hear them crying out to you in the words of Job, "Have pity on me, have pity on me, O ye my friends; for the hand of God hath touched me" (Job 19:21). And help them by praying the *De profundis* (Psalm 130:1-8) and *Absolve* (Psalm 32:5). Afterward, greet our Lady with the *Salve regina*. Go then, as I suggested, to the church [or where you may] and, bidding your vain thoughts and business of the world to hold themselves outside the doors, say to your soul as you make entrance there: "Enter thou into the joy of thy Lord, that thou mayest hear his voice and see his temple." For in this sense, Christ's Holy Church is the entrance to heaven.

Afterward, fall down before the cross and honor Him, because for your sake He was put on the cross, and say, "We adore thee, O Christ, and bless thee, because by thy holy cross you have redeemed the world." And then, before you stand up, take a moment just to reflect on how intensely that love did burn in Him who died for you on the cross.

At that point prepare to begin your morning prayers. Crossing your lips, say, "O Lord, open thou my lips, and my mouth shall show forth thy praise" (Psalm 51:15). That is, "Lord, open my lips that have been shut all night from praising you, for I cannot open them unless you help me."

Then say *Deus in auditorium* ("Lord, hear my cry"). With these words get out your heart before God, telling Him, "Lord, thou art my eternal judge, before thee I stand. Avenge thou me of those who hinder me [from serving you]; I shall be overcome unless thou comfort me." At the words of the *Gloria Patri* ("Glory be to the Father" etc.), bow down and say within your heart, "Lord, for your blessing I beseech you." Turn then, as if to the angels who surround you to comfort and guard you from your foes, and say to them, "Come, let us praise the Lord with joy!"

Now fix your eye on some spot and hold it there as you pray: it will help you to focus your heart. In your imagination paint there your Lord as He was on the cross; think of his feet and hands that were nailed for you to the tree, and think of that wide wound in his side, that terrible pathway to his heart. Thank your Lord withall, and love Him for his gift in Jesus; for here all who will be won to Him find the treasure of his Passion and love.

Imagine also that you are able to see his wounds streaming with blood and running down to the earth. Fall down in your heart to that blood shed for you, sweetly, with tears kissing that earth for remembrance of so rich a treasure shed for your sins, and ask yourself within your heart: "Why does this blood lie here as lost? Dare I drink this rich wine[10] that my Lord pours out to me, and hear what God is saying— "Let him who thirsts come and drink. Taste and see how pleasant is the Lord, how gentle and how merciful" (see Revelation 22:17; Psalm 34:8).

In the midst of such meditations angels come to the soul. And God is there, and says to the one who truly loves Him, "What would ye that I should do for you?" And you answer, "Lord, it is enough for me, sinful wretch and outcast from my people, if you will only look upon me, granting me Lord, sinful wretch that I am, to praise and love thee as much as I am able, for I ought so to do."

If you can attain this kind of spiritual thinking in your prayers, you shall have such amazing gladdening of your heart that it will almost seem painful to you to think of anything else. St. Bernard, for the enormous desire he had from such stirrings of his heart in prayer, wished that matins, the time of morning prayer, might last until doomsday!

10. The sense of *piment* (see n.7) or mixed wine is strong; the reference is, of course, to the Eucharist.

Imagine, where you stand or kneel in prayer, that you see Jesus Christ come with all the company of the angels and saints, the angels bearing before Him baskets full of fragments left over from the feasting of his saints who dwell with Him in glory. Imagine that God has bidden that the fragments be gathered up to feed the poor, that they not be lost. These fragments are meat to us poor sinners, who should perish in default, except that God has had mercy on us.

Imagine that you hear God cry out: "Whoever has need of food, put forth your hand and take some." And then bow your head in humility before God, admitting your poverty to Him, and say: "There is no bread in my house" and say also to Him that you have been without a meal so long that you shall die for hunger if you have not his mercy, admitting that nothing can preserve your life but the food that He has provided.

Stir yourself, then, in remembrances of this nature, and others which may kindle your devotion, raising your heart to him always, until you imagine hearing Him say, "Open your mouth, and I will fill it." Then you shall, by God's grace, feel some portion of the heavenly nourishment that feeds all the saints, and you may with feeling sing the Maiden's song: "My soul doth magnify the Lord, and my spirit hath rejoiced in God my Savior" (Luke 1:46ff.).

When God sends you this sort of ardor through his grace, turn yourself toward the angels which have been worshiping with you, and say in your heart: "I pray you as my guardians, sent to me by God, that you also thank our Lord for me!" And finally, turn yourself to the altar, as truly to God Himself, and say "Verily Lord, how great is Thy mercy, that Thou showest to me."

With such love-stirrings God comes to his lovers, bidding you not that prayers be made, but rather pressing in Himself, in the midst of your love and worship, and softening the languishing soul with a dew of heavenly sweetness. And these tears and sighs are harbingers of God's presence. Happy are those who thus mourn and languish before God, for they shall never be separated from Him, but always be near to Him when they desire.

God, when He comes to those who love Him, gives them some sweet taste or apprehension of his fullness, but before they may fully grasp this it is as if He departs, as an eagle spreading his wings and rising up from them. It is as if He is saying that having tasted some part of his goodness we must now "fly up" after Him, lifting our hearts up to where He sits at his Father's right hand, where alone we may be fulfilled in our joy of Him.

God comes to his friends to comfort them. He parts from them that they should become more humble, and that they should not be drawn into pride in themselves for achieving such an elation in his coming to them. For if your Spouse were always with you, you might impute this to nature and not to grace. Therefore, through his grace, He comes when He will, and to whom He will. Also, He withdraws when He chooses, so that by a long intensity of his presence we do not under-value it, but after that intensity has passed He is more yearned for, and sought with all the zeal of our love in sighing and in tears.

But, friend of God, be aware of this: though your Spouse withdraw Himself from you awhile, He sees all that you do, and you can hide nothing from Him. And if He sees that you love any but Himself, except for His sake, or if you make any semblance of love to another than Him-self, He will soon distance Himself.

Your Spouse is a jealous God; sensitive, noble, and rich in all things. Seven times brighter than the sun, in beauty and power He surpasses all others. Whatever He wills is done, in heaven, in earth and even in hell. If He sees any blemish in the one who should be his bride, He soon turns away, for He will look upon no uncleanness.

Therefore be chaste. Be truly humble and mild of heart. With love-longing yearn for Him above all things. And when God withdraws that special intensity of his heavenly affection and sweetness from you, as is sometimes necessary in this mortal life, do not give yourself to carnal lusts and appetites of this world. Rather, give yourself to prayer, medi-tation, the reading of Holy Scripture, or to honest work.

But don't be embarrassed to mourn after your Love, even as a little child who misses its mother. For those who, after having had such a knowledge of God's power and indwelling sweetness, then turn their back on Him to pursue sin have no defense against the consequences of that sin.

It is an unhappy and troublesome thing to leave the fellowship of God and his angels and all the saints and serve the devil, following his counsel with appetites, urges and works of sin. That heart which was hallowed, sanctified through the Holy Spirit to be a temple of God, and which was raised up far above its nature to have heavenly pleasures and joy with God, becomes all too soon, with foul thoughts, loathsome and foul itself. Those same ears which heard words which none are al-lowed to speak[11] now open themselves to backbiting, slander and other profitless speech. Those same eyes that so recently were baptized with tears of repentance and joy open themselves to see mere vanities. That

---

11. The author is referring to those words, in Scripture and in the liturgy, which God speaks of himself.

tongue which just now spoke to God in prayer, all too soon curses, breaks promises, slanders, and speaks foul words. Pray we God of his goodness that He keep us from these vices!

Of the coming of God's spirit many folk will know, by virtue of certain evidences. St. Bernard says, "When you are stirred up by someone in outer or inner spirit to care for righteousness, and to stand up for it; or when you are moved to be meek and patient, to love your brothers and sisters in God, to be open-hearted toward your superiors, to love chastity and cleanness in body and in spirit, take it as a token that God Almighty comes to visit your souls."

If you are able to accept godly chastening from your friend for matters of sin, or words that will move you to virtue and good habits, this is both a sign of God's coming to your heart and a pathway. Then if you put from yourself sluggishness and heaviness, and with a yearning after God learn to appreciate such admonitions and counsel, then your Lord and God will hasten to you. Why? Because the yearning that God Himself has toward you kindles your desire to entertain words of this kind, and brings you to repent bitterly of your sin and to amend your life.

At his in-coming He wakens the soul, stirs it, softens it, washes its wounds with wine and softens them with oil. That is, He stirs up your soul bitterly to repent of what it has done wrong, and softens it with the hope of mercy and forgiveness.

He tears up sin by the roots, as a gardener does the evil weeds in his garden, and grafts in that soul virtues and good habits, good seed where the weeds once grew. What was dried out He moistens with grace. What was black and murky He makes white; what was tangled up He loosens; what has grown cold He makes warm with his love.[12]

By these stirrings you may know that your Lord is coming: by stirrings in your heart, repenting of sin, withdrawing from carnal appetites, amending your life, repenting of misdeeds, all of which signal, in general, the beginning of a "new man" in God, each day, more and more.

And by this you may know when He is withdrawing from you: your exuberance wanes, you become spiritually dry and heavy as a stone, love cools in your heart like a boiling pot that has been removed from the fire. In this case the soul needs to be in a state of longing until He comes to revive it again.

---

12. The reference to Christ as a gardener refers not only to Eden but also to Isaiah (e.g., chaps. 10 and 11), the Song of Songs, and the first resurrection appearance of Christ to Mary Magdalene (John 20:15), when Mary imagines him to be a gardener.

If foul thoughts ever prod you to leave your good God, be sure to ask yourself, "Whose is this image and superscription?" If the answer is "Caesar's"—that is, that of the prince of this world—assume it to be the devil's temptation. Tell it to go away with its false coin, and take it with it to hell. Say, "For my gates are shut. My Lord dwells here; therefore I have no leisure to deal with the likes of you."

Do you remember that holy greeting that Gabriel made to the maiden Mary in Nazareth, and how joyful she was in body and soul in that time? With that greeting, and by her assent to it, she was filled with grace such as won might and power in heaven, earth and hell. Upon her obedience hangs all the world's health, and the restoration of those who had fallen.

Think on the birth of her Child; how she bore Him without the normal consequences of that travail, and she was a virgin. Remember when He was born that they laid Him in a crib before an ox and ass;[13] he had no other cradle. There were no attendants there to wait upon Him with the light of torches, as people do before guest lords of this world. Therefore there came light from heaven to light the place where He was, in Bethlehem, and angels came to sing the child asleep with merry voices.

Think how the three kings came from far lands, guided by a star, and offered Him gold, frankincense and myrrh. Imagine how sweetly the Child must have smiled on them, and looked at them with his lovely eyes. And think how poorly his mother was clad when the kings kneeled before her; for as scholars tell us, she likely had nothing but a white smock, and that more for modesty than for style.

Remember how Jesus' mother came with Him to the temple to make the offering of cleansing, and that they would have bowed there together as if they both were sinful. Think how the old priest Simeon took the child in his arms and blessed God; for there through the inspiration of the Holy Spirit he saw that between his hands was the Savior of all the world. And so he prayed that he might pass out of this world, "for mine eyes have seen thy salvation, which Thou has prepared before the face of all people" (Luke 2:30-31).

Think of that other time at the temple, and the sorrow that his mother had when she missed Him and sought Him three days, then found Him among the rabbis and teachers, listening and probing into points of the Law. Remember how He came to be baptized by St. John; how the Holy Spirit descended on Him in the likeness of a dove; and the Father at that moment affirmed in his own voice that He was his Son.

---

13. The familiar medieval paintings of the Nativity, as well as the literary recollection of it, derive in part from a typological reading of Isaiah 1:3: "The ox knows its owner, and the ass its master's crib. . . ."

Consider how He hallowed wedlock in the house of the governor of the feast, and there, to reveal Himself as Almighty God, changed the water into wine. In the wilderness He fasted forty days without food, yet overcame Satan when he tempted Him there three ways: with gluttony, covetousness and vainglory.[14]

Remember how all were amazed at his preaching, because all the words that He spoke to them were full of grace. Consider how He healed the sick, raised the dead, gave the blind sight, the dumb speech, the lepers healing with a touch of his hands, and how He cured many other sicknesses incurable in their nature.

Think how when He was weary with long traveling He rested Himself at the well, and there asked one to give Him to drink, for He was extremely thirsty. And after all this, then open up your heart to the Lord with tender feeling and think on his Passion, and the torments that Jesus Christ suffered for you.

Circumspection

One may ask God for grace, and securely trust to receive it, who rouses himself up to good endeavors and so garnishes them with heartfelt love and devotion that they may become a savory offering to his beloved Lord. Works of penance, such as fasting, keeping awake, wearing rough clothes,[15] restraining carnal appetites, doing charity and other actions done with devotion and affection to the Lord, ought to be done also with a glad heart and with freedom of spirit.

True devotion is a worthy love-service[16] that God sends to the heart of one who loves Him to make it glad. But one who will make no dwelling place in his heart for this gift is unworthy to have it. We seek what is above us with our faith, but when our heart is closed we cannot appreciate it, for we grow so full of earth that we lose our taste for the things of God.

14. Luke 4:1-13: Satan tempts Jesus, after his fast, by appealing to the bodily appetites (urging Jesus to turn a stone to bread); by tempting him with worldly power and eminence (with all the kingdoms of the world); and by taunting him to perform a vainglorious miracle (to cast himself down from the pinnacle).

15. Uncomfortable rather than luxurious: rough wool or woven hair as opposed to linens and silks.

16. There were relatively few cash payments of rents in the fourteenth century. Love-service, in medieval terms, was the nonmonetary way in which a steward or tenant could yield up due rent—by goods in kind, but especially by "tithing" a percentage of his work to the lord under whom he served. The analogy with the vineyard parables and with spiritual life in general was natural. See David L. Jeffrey, "The Friar's Rent," *Journal of English and Germanic Philology* (1971): 600-607.

Why do so many folk feel sensations forged by the devil, and suffer their enemy so often to throw them over? I see that nothing makes this possible but the lack of grace. Above all other things I believe we grieve God most in that we will not labor to win this grace from God. He promises this grace to all who will seek it, provided that their vessel be clean and empty so as to receive it. St. Bernard says, "The heart that is suffused with covetousness of the world can have nothing of devotion or affection for God. For solid truth and vacuity, lasting things and perishable ones, spiritual things and bodily can not be together at one time."

So worthy a thing is the comfort of God that it will not abide in a breast which is content with other comforts. So unique is affection toward Him that it does not accord well with other affections. Whoever is always yearning after other comforts witnesses against himself that he is resisting the grace of God, unless, of course, it is merely a matter of honest creature comforts betimes, whereby he may cheer his natural being the better to serve God.

After you have spent what time you can in prayers, godly thought and good work, in holy fear of God, prepare yourself to eat what may strengthen your corporal nature so that it does not give out on you. And to this purpose every Christian should feed and clothe his body that it may better serve the Lord in whatever it does. With sobriety, thoughtfulness and moderation go to your meal. Think at your meat to praise the Lord, and after, for He has fed you. And also before you begin, for all the good deeds that He has done for you. . . .[17]

Of three things beware. First, beware that the spirit of devotion to the Lord you have through grace stirring within you be not advertised to others. Hide these things so far as you may, in intention and action, for fear of being vainglorious.

Second, don't presume to think that it is in your power to have such devotions and stirrings of the Spirit whenever you feel like it, but only by God's grace, when He will send these experiences to you.

Third, don't overly esteem yourself because you have had these experiences, nor think therefore that you are especially dear to God. Don't presume to deem some other person unworthy, just because he does not do exactly as you do. Rather, when you have done all as well as you can, think truthfully to yourself and admit it in so many words: "It is worth nothing Lord, what I do, for I am but an inadequate servant." If you will lose no reward, judge no other (Matthew 7:1). Rather, hold yourself unworthy, for if you think you fast or pray more than someone

---

17. Again, I have omitted some material, this time on dietary suggestions and general guidelines for abstinence.

else, it may be that he far surpasses you in humility, endurance, and love.

Therefore, think of your weaknesses, and not only of your strengths. God has good reasons for wanting you to remember the graces and benefits He has bestowed on you: to remind you of your indebtedness to Him so that you serve and love Him more fervently, or, if you be in personal anguish, to gladden your heart.

Sometimes it happens that one who is generally thought to be evil is better, in God's eyes, than one who is judged to be good. Many folk are honest without and unclean within. Some appear to be worldly and dissolute, and yet within they are sanctified and friends of God. And there are those who bear themselves like angels in the sight of men while in God's sight they are befouled and stinking with sin. Some of these folk who seem sinful to us are dear to God Almighty because their inward bearing is heavenly.

Therefore, let us judge no one but ourselves. And let us, for ourselves and all others, pray to Jesus Christ, the son of Mary, who for us was nailed on the cross, that whoever is bound in mortal sin will be set free. And pray we also that those who are living a good life before Him may be granted perseverance to the end.

Imagine that two messengers have come to tell you tidings. One of them is called Fear, and he comes from hell to warn you against your peril. The other is called Hope, and comes from heaven to tell you of the bliss prepared for you if you continue to live faithfully.

Fear tells you that he saw in hell so many sinners being tormented that if all the wits of mankind were rolled into one head, still he might not recount them all—gluttons, robbers, lechers, thieves. He saw rich men who hurt and took advantage of the poor, along with their functionaries. "There were," he says, "men of the Law who would not make a judgment unless it was for personal gain; treasurers who supported wrong-doing by their subtlety; local justices who condemned law-abiding people and acquitted patent criminals; workmen who worked dishonestly and took whatever the trade would bear; tenant-farmers who tithed dishonestly of their productivity. I saw pastors and churchmen who, having the cure of souls, neither chastened nor taught. Indeed, I saw all kinds of people who have worked improperly, and each one was paying a high price for it."

Fear continues: "There I saw a complete absence of all goodness, but plenty of torment and sorrow. There was hot fire ever burning, stinking brimstone, and greedy devils, like dragons, with mouths gaping wide. Hunger and thirst were there insatiable, adders and toads gnawed on the carcasses of the sinful. Such weeping and wailing and gnashing of teeth did I hear, that for fear of it I nearly lost my mind. There was such a murky darkness there you could grip it with your hand; so bitter was the smoke that it made the poor wretches shed glistening tears.

"I heard them bitterly curse the day they were born. Now they yearn to die and they cannot: death, which once they hated, they would rather have now than all the goods of this world. And so I give you this warning: unless you repent and amend yourself of your sins, and have a steadfast will to leave them forever, I saw a seat waiting for you there in hell. It is made of burning fire, where devils shall torment you without ceasing."

The other messenger that comes to you is called Hope. He says he has come from heaven to tell you of the unspeakable great joy of God's friends, saying that "to tell it accurately may no earthly person do, though his tongue were made of steel. For there is a gracious fellowship of God's friends. There they are, with all the hosts of angels, and the saints; and above them God Almighty gladdens them all. Of all imaginable goodness I saw plenty—beauty and wealth that will last forever. There is honor and power that shall never fail, wisdom, love and everlasting joy."

"There I heard the bright angels make melody and song. So worthy is that joy, and so great in all these things, that whoever might taste, as it were, one blessed drop of it, should be ravished forever into the loving of God. Such a person would have such profound yearning to win his way to that glory that all the joys of this world would seem painful to him. He would be overcome with such great yearning after that happiness, that a hundred times more effectively than any fear of the pain of hell it would stir him to love virtue and flee sin."

"And I tell you truly," he says at last, "that if you will leave sin behind, and obey God and love Him as you ought, God has prepared for you there a rich and beautiful seat. And there you shall dwell with Him eternally."

III. Serving the Lord

The third and last part of this book teaches us to so conduct ourselves—wherever we come in life and whatever we are given to do—that it be praise to God and an example of good to all that see us. For the Apostle counsels that in all that we do, we should do it honestly and in good order (1 Corinthians 14:40).

So, at the first, let each lover of God see to it that he yearns not to mix himself up with the world, which hinders and deceives all those who deal with it, preventing them from much good that they might do. As for those who will not be at peace, but are always raking about, their eyes look upon many things, and these eyes, in turn, send messages to the heart. Things that are so imprinted do not come out easily.

St. Bernard complains of the inward damage he experienced in the world while he was still in it, feeling that the world surrounded and besieged him, wounding him on every side. He laments: "Through the portals of my five senses the world shoots at me, wounding me sorely, and through these wounds death presses in to slay my stricken soul. My eyes behold, and my thought changes, kindling sin within me. My ears hear and my heart bows to the sounds; I smell with my nose and it titillates my mind. With my mouth I speak, and in speaking I find beguiling amusement. And with just a little overly soft feeling, lust is kindled in my flesh. How does Satan, my foe that I cannot see, stand ever against me with his bow drawn and bent!"

Therefore, when necessity draws us into the world, where the enticements to sin are so many, we should go with great caution, as into a battle to fight against our foes. A person needs to be well armed against the darts and arrows of his foes that bitterly shoot at him. And he may well fear them the more because he cannot see them. With foot-traps and snares his pathway is made deadly. Accordingly, let anyone who goes out into the world arm himself with a holy fear of God.

Jesus warned his disciples to be wary of the world when He said to them, "Verily the world shall resist you with sore temptations" (John 15:18-19; 16:33). Therefore, if you have to go out into the world, either for your own profit or that of others, don't color your business dealings with any shade of misrepresentation, as if to feign for yourself occasions for dallying with the world for pleasure or advantage, or simply to be known in the councils of powerful people.

People who do this make a show with clever words, and take on affectations in their wish to be regarded as holy by all who observe them. But they are really giving themselves to dabbling, dallying more than they need in buying, selling, or bargaining over worldly business. Indeed, all of their outward bearing so accords with the world itself that it is as David says: "They mingle with the worldly who have no knowledge of God; and such works as they see them do, so do they also" (Psalm 106:35).

So, when you need to undertake some business, bless yourself with the holy name of Jesus, who died for you on the cross, for then you are more secure as you tread. See that your outer clothing be neither overly hideous nor overly fancy, neither in its cut or its color. Keep your limbs to the office they were made for, nor cast your eyes over everything like a child. Don't play with your hands, or bounce about on your feet. When a man's heart is out of its proper keeping, his limbs sometimes fail in their proper office.

And as you ordain your outer bearing in going forth on your business, also see that you are devout in spirit within, especially in praying to your Lord and praising Him. If for the press of your activities you cannot pause to make your prayers, go at a little easier pace.

Many things may hinder you from praying while you work—weariness of your body, people whom you meet who speak with you, the senses of the body getting out of control—until your devotion in prayer cools. When you are walking along, and have already said the prayers you are bound to pray, lift up your heart unto the Lord and just pray to Him in your thoughts with a happy mind. Think on all of the good things God has done for you, and shall do if you serve Him truly. Think on his commandments, and perform them indeed in as much as is in your power. For God so bids us when He says, "Let these my words that I command thee be in thine heart; recount them to thy children; meditate upon them in thy house; walking on thy journey, sleeping and rising" (Deuteronomy 6:7, Vg.).

Or else, when you are traveling, tell pleasing tales to your fellows or something from the Holy Scriptures, that may lighten your journey and gladden your heart in the Lord. And sometimes recite the "Seven Psalms" (Psalms 6, 32, 38, 51, 102, 130, 143) for the quick and the dead, that God may grant grace to the living and peace to the dead.

When you come into a town, there to take rest when you may, according to your state seek a decent place to stay where you may pass the night in peace, and where you may turn that time most to profit for yourself and others. Don't let your carnal appetites or vanity draw you to places which appeal to those things, but look around to see where there may be any who love God, and go there.

Don't look to see where you may be best fed, for in such a place are likely to be many temptations to sin. And don't take lodging with any woman, unless you have for a long time known her to be a good person.

When you have come to the house in which you are to rest, keep your thoughts to yourself in godly circumspection. Let it be that your outer bearing is so ruled by grace that you may stir to good all whom you visit, and through God's grace cut through any murkiness of sin in that place. So doing, fulfill the teaching of the Lord, who urges us, "Let your light so shine before men, that they may see your good works, and glorify your Father which is in heaven" (Matthew 5:16). And St. Gregory commends, "Neither is it greatly praiseworthy to be good with the good, but rather to be good with those that are not good. For even as it is more blameworthy not to be good in the company of the godly, so is it more honorable to have stood for what is good among those who are evil."

Watch where your eyes wander when you come into a new place, and guard yourself from all things that may kindle sin. Look straight ahead as did the wise man who said, "I make a covenant with my eyes lest I think upon a maid." After sight comes thought, and after that deeds.

Jeremiah says, "Mine eye hath laid waste my soul" (cf. Lamentations 2:11). When so holy a prophet can lament over his eyes, surely may another man complain who too often sins in that way. Augustine admonishes you and me, "A shameless eye is messenger to a shameless heart." Gregory adds, "It is not lawful to gaze upon that which is not lawful to desire." And David pleaded with the Lord, "Turn away mine eyes from beholding vanity" (Psalm 119:37).

Be careful, too, that you avoid hearing things that stir you to sin, such as unclean words, backbiting gossip, false judgments, great oaths, controversy, arguments and other such vices of conversation.

When you eat, compose yourself in an orderly manner, and hold yourself in reasonable measure. Don't be looking for extravagant delicacies, but be pleased with common fare. When you are speaking at table, consider to whom, what, when, how, of whom and where you speak. Have your conversation so orderly that you are not like others of the world, but fulfill instead the words of the Apostle: "Be not conformed to this world . . . for your conversation is in heaven" (Romans 12:2; Philippians 3:20).

Though our body is in this world, like a little clod of clay, it is desirable that our spirit, redeemed as it is by the precious blood of God Almighty, be with mind and will in heaven. Let it not soil itself here with sinfulness, like a pig in the ditch!

And whatever you do, and wherever you go, do as the Apostle teaches: "show thyself to all men as an example of good works" (Titus 2:7, Vg.) for through a godly example God is worshiped and praised, and men and women are helped, taught, and strengthened in their belief. Comport yourself so that the people who live with you may say of you as was said of the Apostles Paul and Barnabas: "The gods are come down to us in the likeness of men" (Acts 14:11).

And to God be thanks and praise.

Enabling Grace

This little treatise, *De Gracia Dei,* is attached in the Thornton Manuscript to *Our Daily Work.* But it is clearly a kind of evangelical tract which stands on its own. Immediately following the title there is an explanatory rubric in medieval English: "Of Goddis grace stirrand and helpand, and that na thing may be done with-owtten grace." The writer's main point is that in all our endeavors to serve God, we may finally do only as much as he enables us for by his "stirring and helping" grace. He also indicates that, if we do "our daily work" in a spirit of utter commitment to our Lord, then instead of the "wages of sin" (Romans 6:23) we will receive the reward God has laid up for us in Christ Jesus. Grace is thus for us both means and end: the enabling grace of our Lord permits us to serve him and, in steadily growing measure, it is our reward for that service.

GRACIA DEI VITA ETERNA: these are the words of the holy apostle St. Paul, which we translate into English as "the grace of God is eternal life" (Romans 6:23, Vg.).[1] The Apostle sets before us grace as our proper motivation, for without a knowledge and stirring up of grace within us none of us could hope to attain eternal life. For as St. Augustine comments in this connection, "We can do no good for which He has not prepared us by his enabling grace"—for otherwise all our good deeds are like counterfeit money which can buy us nothing.

Accordingly, we ought not to expect to do anything truly good without grace, or even to have a good intention, for no matter how good it may seem, nothing that we do is actually good unless it is prompted by God's grace. To this the prophet witnesses by God's Holy Spirit when he says: "I know well, Lord, that the good ways of man are not of his own doing in order that he may walk in paths of your leading" (cf. Psalm 17:5; Jeremiah 26:13). For we are likely to turn into a path of the devil's beguiling if we expect to do any good on our own, without grace leading us and enabling us beforehand. To [underscore] the truth of this God gives us the words of his prophet: "I have lost you to your own devices, Israel; yet in me was your help" (cf. Hosea 13:9). Of yourself, He suggests, you are bound to be lost; without his enabling you can never hope to be saved.

---

1. *Charis,* "grace" or "gift," is rendered in the Vulgate by *gracia.*

It is God's grace coming into us which works in us the redirection by which we may obtain the salvation He has provided. For in his first examination of us He found only that which would cause us to be condemned before his righteous judgments.

I. Varieties of Grace

There are three kinds of grace which we find spoken of in the Holy Scripture.

The first of these God gives to all creatures to sustain them, and this is referred to as God's help freely given to all creatures, great and small. Without this gift creatures cannot prosper, or even survive. Just as water is made hot by fire but cools down again when the fire is withdrawn, so, as St. Augustine says, "all creatures that are made from nothing are worth nothing in a very little time, unless God sustains them in his grace." Therefore the Apostle can say, "Through the grace of God I am what I am" (1 Corinthians 15:10). This is as much as to say: "That I am alive, that I feel, speak, hear or see, and all that I am I owe to God's grace!"

The second degree of grace is more special. It is this which God gives freely to every good and reasonable creature. And this grace stands ever at the door of our hearts, and knocks, and asks that of our own free will we let Him in. We hear Him saying: "Behold, I stand at the door and knock: if anyone hear my voice, and open the door, I will come in to him, and sup with him, and he with me" (Revelation 3:20). And this grace, too, is freely offered to us before we have deserved it. Therefore, we ought to ready ourselves to receive this gift of the Holy Spirit, which always is stirring us to good purposes and calling us away from ill uses of our free will.[2]

The third type of grace is special grace—special because it is not given to every rational creature, but only to those who have received the second type of grace and who, with their free will, have fulfilled that grace in deed, being able to say with St. Paul: "The grace of God was not vain in me" (1 Corinthians 15:10). St. Augustine adds that God, working specially in us at last fulfills all that in his grace He began in us. For without his help we can neither do good to ourselves nor please Him. As God says in his word: "Without me, thou canst do nothing" (John 15:5). God's grace goes before our good will, stirring it up to do what is good and to turn away from sin.

2. Compare the use of Revelation 3:20 in the Parson's Sermon of Chaucer's *Canterbury Tales*.

II. Grace and Free Will

Now, two things are necessary to our soul's health. The first is this grace of which I have just spoken; the second is our own free will according with it. And without these two corresponding no one can do what is necessary to the health of his soul. For neither free will, without this enabling grace, nor this grace without the assent of our free will, can do anything to please God. Therefore, as St. Augustine says, "He who made thee without thee will not justify thee without thee"; that is, He who made you without your help will not make you complete or righteous unless you also help yourself. And though the free will of man cannot create the grace of God in man, nevertheless let a person do what is in him to do, that he may be ready and able to receive that grace when it comes.

If you were to find yourself in a pitch dark house one day with its doors and windows shut up, and you would not make any move to let the sun come in, whose fault would it be if the house remained dark? So, do not blame anyone but yourself if you are without the experience of grace. For as St. Anselm says, "Man does not lack this grace because God fails to give it to him; he has it not because he has not made himself ready to receive this grace as he should have done."

God is not stingy with his grace, for He has it in super-abundance, and though He distributes it ever so freely, and to so many, yet He has never the less. All He asks is clean vessels into which to pour it. So St. Augustine says that "God through vast freedom and abundance of his grace fills all creatures to the limit of their ability to receive."

If anyone opens his heart to this grace when God sends it, it shows up in his life and work; do not doubt it. The Apostle, when he had received this grace of our Lord, said, "The grace that God has given me is not in vain," for he demonstrated always in his work the grace which He was given.

We fellowship with God in his grace, almost as merchants do that have common enterprise. For God sets his grace beside our endeavor to effect his transactions with them both. But in repayment for his contribution He wishes to have nothing but our praise and thanksgiving; all other profit that may arise He wishes to be ours. Yet there are those who would cheat God out of his portion, and would themselves be praised by men for their good deeds. But God has said: "I will not give my glory to another" (Isaiah 42:8); that is to say, "Praise and worship that belongs to me I will give to no one else."

III. Sin and Grace

There are three states of human experience: before sin, after sin, and after confirmation of grace—finally, that is, when we have departed from this mortal life and come unto that joy which shall never end.

In the first place, before man sinned, his will was so truly free that He could sin or not sin. It was entirely within his own free will to do good or not. In the last state, in which we have been fully confirmed in grace and are in heaven, we shall sin no more. But in the second state, it is not only that we *may* sin, but that we cannot avoid it. In fact, our will is disposed to ill choices until it becomes strengthened by grace. When grace leads our will, only then is it free to work what is good.

Before mankind sinned, there was no hindrance to doing good, nor any necessity of doing evil. But now has sin joined itself in fraternity with our flesh in what St. Paul calls "the law of the flesh," so that it is master of the flesh and withstands God's law in every way that it can. This hinders our will from assenting to what is good, and stirs it up to such mischief that it cannot work any good unless grace assists us and eases us out of sin.

Everyone, before he sins, has a free will to do good or ill, but when bound to the devil through sinful living, is helpless to come out of these fetters by his own power. Then he is like a ship tossed in a tempest, bereft of all those who could help it steer, and cast from wave to wave wheresoever the tempest drives it. Just so, one who lacks God's grace on account of having fallen into mortal sin is not able to do what he would, but always wavers from one side to the other, at the devil's whim. And except God grants that person grace to rise out of his sin, he shall be tossed in sin till his life's end, and afterward be lost, body and soul, and drowned in endless sorrow.

And you may see this principle at work in worldly affairs. No one can make himself king, but rather the people of the realm choose themselves such a king as they would like. But once he is chosen by the people and confirmed in his sovereignty, then he has power over those who chose him, and however vicious he might be to them there is nothing they can do about it except perhaps through some other yet more powerful person. And this situation is entirely of their own choice, so that they have to suffer whatever he may do to them.

By the same token, mankind before sin had a choice whether to serve under God or under the devil. But when, by exercise of free will we chose to serve the devil, we could not afterwards, when we wanted to, come out of that bondage. So then, worldly people who are bound in sin, when they are counselled to amend their lives, say: "Fain would we rise . . . but cannot." No, through their own strength they cannot. But through the enabling grace of God they can!

IV. The Visitations of Grace

Grace, when first it comes to visit a human soul, wakens it as though out of a deep slumber and asks it three crisp questions: "where are you?"; "where have you come from?"; and "where are you going?"

First Grace says, "where are you?"—as if saying indirectly, "Look at yourself, you miserable wretch, into what a rotten state you are cast down and in what peril! On account of your sin you have fallen into the hands of the enemy, who above all things covets to do you misery, and nothing may deliver you out of his hands but Almighty God, your good Lord, whom you have forsaken."

Next Grace says, "Where have you come from?" This is as if to say, "You poor wretch, look how you have wasted your life in sin. You have come, in fact, from the devil's tavern. Where are all the provisions God has given you to help yourself and with which to worship Him? Sorrily have you lost them. Your Lord made you rich, and now you have become a pauper."

Then Grace asks: "Where are you going?" "O woeful wretch, you are heading toward a terrible judgment, to which God condemns those like yourself, for as you have served so also shall you be served in judgment. So terrible shall you find God there that you will be out of your mind with terror, and cry with an awful voice to the mountains and hills to fall upon you and hide you, that you not see his face. O miserable wretch, if you continue to travel as you have begun you are heading straight into hell, where you shall find fire so hot and raging that all the water in the sea, though it were poured into it, should not slake a spark of it. And because here on earth you stink before God in the foulness of your sin, there you shall be in everlasting vile odor; because here you loved darkness, always to be in sin, there you shall know darkness so thick that you can grip it in your hand; and because here you revelled in sinful pleasures against the will of God, there you shall shed more tears than there are flecks of dust in a sunbeam. A thousand thousand years shall you suffer, pain upon pain, ever renewing your sorrow."

When God's grace has wakened a person up and got his attention with these three questions, and has made him aware of what peril he is in, he is likely to take fright at the thought of God's terrible judgment. Thereupon, he begins to repent of his sin, and yearns to amend his life through God's arresting grace, which immediately begins to stir him up to flee his sinful living and give himself to good. Then follows enabling grace, to assist his goodwill to fulfill his intention in deed.

For it is clear that though someone has a good will to do what is right by virtue of prevenient grace stirring up his good will, yet he cannot actually do anything about it without God's grace following and helping him. This the Apostle affirms of himself when he says, "Not I, but the grace of God within me" (cf. Galatians 2:20), which is as much as to say, "I may do no good thing except God's grace help me."

Any good that we do is thus prompted first by that grace which stirs us up to exercise our free will, and then, through grace following, we are enabled to follow through in action. Then have we that "grace which goes before," prevenient grace before our exercise of free will, and our free will is as a handmaiden then to God to do his will.

God's grace, whenever it is found, is not idle, but evermore working and growing to increase our reward. Therefore we ought to do as the Apostle counsels and not receive the grace of God in vain. For whoever does not employ in action the grace God sends him, has received it in vain. And perhaps it may be that if we take it and do not use what we have been given, we shall lose it, and not get it back.[3]

Grace can come to us in odd and unexpected ways. Isidore of Seville tells a little story about a tiny bug of a species called saura and in his story it signifies the character of grace stirring beforehand. This kind of bug is said to be an enemy of all venomous snakes, so that whenever it sees any snake slithering toward a person to bite him while he is sleeping in the wilderness, it quickly flies to the person, lights upon his face and gives him a little bite as a warning.

By this saura bug we may imagine the action of grace that God sends along to warn us of the devil and his venomous sting. It cries out to you, like the Apostle, saying, "Awake, thou that sleepest; rise up and Christ shall give thee light" (Ephesians 5:14). But those who are ungrateful promptly act against grace and ruin it, as did Virgil, the man in Isidore's story, in the case of the little bug that would have saved him from death. For as this fellow Virgil lay asleep, along came an adder to strike him, as was its nature. But suddenly one of these little bugs saw the adder and quickly flew down onto his forehead, giving him a little bite. With that he woke up and, feeling a smart on his forehead, without so much as looking about, slapped himself on the forehead and so slew the bug. And thus did he repay for its good service the one that only existed to save him!

3. The allusion may be to putting one's hand to the plow and turning back; it certainly invokes the somber warning that "unto whom much is given, of him much also is required" (Luke 12:48).

Think, then, and do not attack the instrument of God's grace when it comes to you to warn you of harm and stir you up to good. We ought to be glad of God's grace and, when he sends it, to take very good care of so rich a gift. For grace is nothing counterfeit, but earnest money of that lasting joy which is to come.[4] As the Apostle says, "The grace of God is eternal life." That is, God's free gift of grace is both a help and means toward our everlasting life.

Therefore He sets grace before us as the path to everlasting joy, and also as a sign, a covenant,[5] if we keep it well, to foster in us a certainty of endless joy. As the Apostle says, "God has given us the Holy Spirit as a pledge of that which is to come." Let us then hold this heavenly pledge, this covenant by grace, and enjoy it well in all our work, and shape our life accordingly in everything that we do.

In this life we will be well as long as God's grace is leading us. But let us remember that when God's grace is not with us we can only fail to do his will. Therefore, by the help of grace let us destroy in ourselves everything that is against grace, whatsoever it be, great or small. And everything that our reason, fallen though it is, tells us is against God's will—all that is sin or may lead us to sin—let us reject it. And let us then have repentance in our hearts, confession in our mouths, and perseverance, with a firm will never to turn again.

---

4. See Hugh of St. Victor, *Soliloquy on the Earnest Money of the Soul*, trans. Kevin Herbert (Milwaukee: Marquette University Press, 1956).

5. Middle English *wedde*, which is also translated as "pledge" in the sentence following.

SIR JOHN CLANVOWE

The Two Ways

Sir John Clanvowe was one of the most noteworthy figures in the English nobility of his day. He was a layperson—a knight, military man, crusader, lord of a considerable estate, and diplomat. For a number of years he was associated with a group of distinguished laymen who were noted both for a strong commitment to practical Christian faith and for their interest in John Wyclif. These men, sometimes called "Lollard knights," exemplify a widespread response to Wyclif's teaching which resulted in a rejuvenated lay spirituality in the upper classes, emphasizing, as Clanvowe does here, the claims of the gospel on everyday life. This treatise was written by Clanvowe while on his last crusade and was finished only shortly before his death in a village near Constantinople on October 17, 1391.

Introduction

THE GOSPEL TELLS US that during the time when our Lord Jesus Christ was here on earth a man came to Him who asked Him if few persons were to be saved. Christ answered him, saying, "The gate is wide and the way is broad that leads to destruction, and many are going in that way. But how slender is the gate and narrow the way that leads to life, and few are those who find that way" (Matthew 7:13-14).

In the words of Christ we are to understand that the way which leads to the suffering of hell is a broad highway, and the way that leads to heaven is a narrow road. For Christ here calls the pains of hell "destruction" and the bliss of heaven "life." In this light it would be a very good thing for us to shape our lives so as to eschew the broad highway and to go along the narrow road—for otherwise we are moving each day very quickly towards another place, and we never know how soon it may be that we are suddenly out of this world. At the point when we do pass beyond it, whoever is found traveling in the broad highway shall without recourse pass into the pains of hell, but whoever is found at that time traveling by the narrow road shall without hindrance pass into the bliss of heaven. And the joy of that place is so great that "no eye has seen, no ear heard, nor has it come into the human heart to imagine what joy God has ordained for those who love him and who are to come there" (1 Corinthians 2:9). Nor does that joy resemble the joys of this world, for all worldly joys are transient and soon over, as well as foully admixtured with fears, a diversity of diseases, and burdens of life.

But the joy of heaven grows greater and greater. Neither fear, travail, nor disease is found there, nor any lack of such things as the heart may desire; and that it may fulfill these purposes, heaven has no end. So then, whoever is found in the narrow way is well off indeed, when he passes at last out of this world, for he shall then dwell eternally with God in everlasting joy. Yet woe to whatever person is found in the broad highway at the moment of departure from this world, for such a one shall be straightway in the pains of hell, which are unlike any pains of this world. For each pain or torment in this world must come to an end—either by death or in some other manner—but the pain of hell is greater than any heart can conjure and it will never end, but ever and always increase. And whoever is there shall never have the release of death, but live forever among the fiends in darkness and in torments unending.

This is why we cry out to our Lord God, praying that in his eternal mercy He will teach us his narrow way and grant us enabling grace to turn out of the broad highway we are in. But to be effectual in this we must be meek, and cry out to Him from a humble heart, for the prophet[1] says that God will teach the meek his ways (see Psalm 25:9). Therefore we cry to Him with this same prophet who said, "Lord, show me your ways and teach me your paths" (Psalm 25:4). But if God out of his goodness teaches us his ways and we ungraciously depart from them in other directions we are greatly to be blamed and much in need of repentance. There are many who cause great damage in this way; though they know the ways of God they abandon them and go in the ways of the devil for the sake of lusts of the flesh or other worldly appetites. Surely, they are greater fools than one who would refuse to trade his own insignificant baubles[2] for all the king's treasure. For a bauble is a device made from materials of small value, and yet is the sort of thing for which a born fool beats on other persons (and often they in turn on him, so that he both smites and is smitten for the sake of it), and yet it really serves no greater purpose than that it is something a fool thinks he has to possess to be happy. Keeping it always beside himself, he will not give it up for anything, loving it so obsessively that his obsession becomes a kind of proof that he is indeed a congenital idiot. Yet there are far more than just those we recognize as such who are proving

---

1. David is typically styled a prophet by medieval writers because of the messianic psalms.

2. Middle English *babel*, possibly a pun.

themselves fools, unwilling to desist from the very lusts by which they injure other persons and inevitably also themselves. And they will not give up these passions for all the treasure of the King of heaven. In their behavior we may know well that the Word of Christ is verified which says, "The wisdom of this world is foolishness in the eyes of God" (1 Corinthians 3:19).

Therefore, for the love of God and of our own souls let us eschew that folly. When we know the ways of God, let us pray to Him most heartily that He may give us grace to keep steadfastly in his ways, and cry out to Him in the words of the prophet, "Lord, make perfect my outgoings in your paths, so that my footsteps are not moved" (Psalm 17:5). And if we work at this ourselves, even as we pray meekly for God's assistance, then we shall learn his ways and walk in them, receiving as we go the blessing of which David speaks in the Psalter, where he says, "Blessed is every one that fears the Lord and walks in his ways," which is as much as to say, "Blessed are those who go in at the straight gate, and who determine to walk in the narrow way."

I. God's Law

What this narrow way amounts to is the keeping of God's commandments. We may recognize this from the words Christ spoke to a person who asked Him what he should do in order to have eternal life. Christ answered him, "If you want to enter in to everlasting life, keep the commandments" (Matthew 19:17). By these words and many others like them in Holy Writ we must realize that there is no other way to heaven except by the keeping of God's laws; the commandments of God form, in effect, the narrow way that leads to heaven. The "straight gate" is the fear of God through which we are prompted to abandon our sinful lusts, as we may unambiguously recognize by that passage in Holy Writ which says, "The fear of the Lord is the beginning of wisdom" (Psalm 111:10); there is nothing we may do in true wisdom but that which will lead us toward the bliss of heaven. Thus it is in the fear of the Lord that the narrow way to heaven begins. And because it is the beginning and entrance to that way it is called the "gate." So then, we can see that the keeping of God's commandments is the narrow way that leads to life, and that the fear of the Lord is the "straight gate" that opens into that way.

The contrary path may be understood in the same fashion: in the breaking of God's laws is the broad highway that leads to the pains of hell, for, as the prophet says, those who turn away from the commandments of God are condemned (Deuteronomy 11:28). And the wide gate of that broad highway is a determined carelessness in the keeping of God's commandments instead of which we simply follow our own evil appetites and fall naturally into the broad path which leads to destruction. May God of his eternal mercy keep us from this and give us grace to go in at the straight gate and keep ourselves on the narrow way until it be his will to take us into the life that way is leading toward. Certainly, if we are wise we will be pleading with God night and day to grant us that. And we may trust completely in Him that He will indeed grant us all things that are good for us so long as we pray to Him with a faithful heart.

Therefore, let us go in through the straight gate—that is, let us be in the fear of our Lord God, for we have neither existence nor life nor health nor conscious mind except by and through Him, and whenever it suits Him He can take any of these things from us. Also He is—and shall be—our judge. He knows all that we are doing and have done, and there is no place to which we can flee from his judgment, for He rules over all and is all-powerful. We are sinful creatures, moreover, and sin must needs be punished, either in this world or another, and though our Lord God is full of mercy, yet He is also full of righteousness. Accordingly, let us fear Him more than anything else, and that shall make us to leave off our idle occupations and evil appetites, the which we may do away with to great personal profit, if indeed we want to conduct our business wisely.

Consider those persons we regard as wise merchants of this world's goods. No matter how much they love money, any time they see that by putting out twenty pounds they can earn a hundred they are happier to put that twenty to work than to draw in forty or fifty pounds from a less fruitful enterprise. And if a merchant knows that by investment of twenty or thirty pounds he may protect himself against the loss of one or two hundred, he is more glad to put twenty or thirty pounds into that cause than to pick up an easy fifty or sixty somewhere else.

Truly, we ought to be much more glad to do away with our evil lusts and sinful deeds, for in so doing we may without risk or hindrance then win the bliss of heaven and protect ourselves against the pains of hell. If we act in this way we are being wise merchants, while if we do not do this we are fools, no matter how much honor, leisure, or riches we acquire in this world.

II. Enemies of the Narrow Way

When our Lord Jesus Christ spoke of the two ways, He urged his hearers that they should strive to go in by the narrow and straight gate. Sure enough, we must strive too, if we want to go that way ourselves. For we have three powerful enemies who will not let us pass that way if they can prevent it, except by the experience of real struggle. These foes are the devil, the world, and the flesh, and they are always lurking about, hoping to lead us back by the wide gate into the broad highway to hell, and to prevent us from passing by the straight gate into the narrow way that leads to heaven.

The devil is always working to get in our way with falsehoods and clever deception.

Our flesh is always getting at us with its foul lecherousness, its appetites and its frailties.

And the world is ever busy to stand in our way with foolishness and vanity, and this kind of thing is real war.[3]

Nonetheless, we may well take the example of the saints now in heaven (who have already passed by the narrow way into bliss) in dealing with these three enemies. For they have left their word and teaching to show us how we should follow after and withstand our enemies as they did—if we are willing to take the example. And it is, accordingly, a great shame and detriment to us if we fail to keep to the way the saints have trod. For by God's grace we can, if we choose, walk in the way they did. After all, among the saints who have gone before were old men and old women who were physically very frail, as well as little children and some gentle young maidens, while some, of course, were strong folk physically, both men and women, rich and poor alike. And yet out of all these disparate conditions of life they all chose to leave behind their own particular worldly appetites to go in through the straight gate, and because they did this they are now in bliss, and much honored both in heaven and here on earth. But it can be the same for us if we will only love and fear our God, and not be heedless of Him. For the wise man says that "each person ought to turn away from evil for fear of God" (cf. Deuteronomy 13:5; Proverbs 8:13). Also the prophet says that "God is nigh to them that fear Him" (Psalm 85:9).

But as I have said, the devil will do his best to prevent us from having any fear of God. He will suggest to us that we have no need to fear God so much, since God is full of mercy, and with the slightest little appeal for that mercy on our part we will be fully forgiven. And if it looks as if we are likely to live for a long time he will say that we might as well live

---

3. Clanvowe was a nobleman and had inherited substantial wealth as well as obligations and opportunities for political involvement. One senses here that this was an area of significant temptation for him.

in ease and fulfill our appetites until we are a little closer to the end, and then there will be time enough to cry for mercy and have forgiveness. In this way we may have both the fulfillment of our lusts in this world and our place in heaven as well. He also likes to say that there "may be" a heaven and hell such as people speak of, but no one alive knows anything about either of them, so that what we really ought to try to be sure about is our state in this world.

Our flesh puts to us the argument that it isn't really up to very much hardship—that it is, after all, tender and if it doesn't get its various appetites satisfied it will surely not even survive. Besides, these lusts and leisures are "ordained for our use," and we can't really be merry without them. Indeed, says the flesh, "I'd rather be dead than give these things up." And so the flesh nags on in this sort of way.

The world tries to convince us that it is neither profitable nor self-respecting for us to deny our appetites, and tells us that all wise and honorable persons of this world work to get for themselves creature comforts, pleasures, power and great fame in this world. Surely if we did otherwise people would cast aspersions and scorn us, regarding us of no account, says the world, so that it is far more wise and self-respecting simply to conform to the style of the world. After all, by this route one can at least be assured of a livelihood and reasonable estate while living. . . . These are the rationalizations of the world.

Against these enemies, however, we have good, true and sufficient answers which Christ has taught us in his laws, and by means of which we may safely protect ourselves from these three cruel enemies and warriors.

III. Spiritual Warfare

With respect to the devil, St. Peter warns us and instructs us in this way. He says, "Brethren, be sober and alert, for your adversary the devil, roaring like a lion, roams about seeking whom he may swallow up and destroy among those of you who stand against him in the strength of your faith" (1 Peter 5:8-9). What the apostle counsels us here is that we may stand against him by belief,[4] and that is a true counsel, for our belief teaches us that the devil is a liar, and is always lurking around, trying to beguile us with his falsehoods. We, on the other hand, were created

4. Clanvowe sometimes uses *belief* interchangeably with *faith,* and means it in the sense of "creed" or "catechism"—the firm body of doctrine which constitutes what he believes. This is distinct from belief in the sense of personal conviction— "faith"—as we sometimes use the word.

to pray to God, and if we do that and keep his commandments and die in that commitment we shall be partners with Him in glory. Yet if we are disobedient and break his laws and die in that condition we shall go to the torment of hell. And no matter how long a life the devil promises us we shall live no longer than God has ordained; even if we were able to live many thousands of years we should still have at last to die and after that be judged according to the works that we have done in this life.[5] So if we have been living a faithful life it is good that we should persevere in it until the day we die; and if we have been living an evil life now is the time that we should, with our last end in mind, amend ourselves.

The fact that God is merciful and good ought not to give us reason to be bolder in sin, but it should make us the more energetic in keeping ourselves from sin. For as we say, the better a lord is, the better he ought to be served. And certainly there is no lord who would not regard himself as badly served if his servant used him the worse simply because he trusted in the lord's courtesy and meekness. That attitude, in fact, might well make a lord most stern against his servant. As soon as we look at it in this way we know full well that the devil's teaching is false and a wicked attack against our true belief.[6] Therefore, with our true belief we should steadfastly withstand him and his lies.

St. James says, "Withstand the devil and he shall flee from you" (James 4:7), and thus, by God's grace, we shall be able to make this strong enemy to flee. But we need to be on our guard, for if he flees one time he will return with another strategem, for he is full of wiles, and if the flesh and the world are attacking us, the devil will always be right there with them to corrupt us in other ways by himself, or by certain familiar and allied means.

For example, he will often try to lead a person into gluttony, and if he is unsuccessful he will immediately try to lure him or her into excessive abstinence. Some persons he will deflect toward ambition and excessive absorption in worldly affairs; but if he cannot overcome them by this means he will try to lure them toward the opposite sin of sloth. Some he endeavors to drag down in despair, and if unsuccessful he tries to make them sin more boldly on account of their trust in God's mercy. And thus the devil moves from sin to sin, and with many temptations busies himself evermore to draw us down toward the broad highway

5. Matthew 25 had a much more powerful influence upon Christian spirituality in this period than in some others; Christians were typically very concerned about the implications of Christ's standards of judgment.

6. I.e., the body of Christian doctrine.

to hell. Therefore we must constantly be on the alert to withstand him with strong faith.

For with respect to the temptations of which I have been speaking, our belief teaches us that neither gluttony nor excessive abstinence are virtuous, but the way of temperance between these two [extremes] is a virtue—consuming moderate amounts of food and drink such as is needful for our physical well-being. Similarly, ambition to have too much of this world is a vice, and sloth is a vice, while the middle way between these two is a great virtue, and that is simply to work faithfully for those things that people genuinely need, and if there is something left over it ought to go straight into helping needy brethren and neighbors. It is a great sin to despair of God's mercy, but also a great sin to sin all the more because we do trust in God's mercy, yet the middle way between these two is a great virtue, and that is to eschew evil for the fear of God and to do good for the love of God. To this end our belief guides us toward the mean which is a virtue, and which falls between the two extremities, which are vices. The devil wants to draw us from virtue and to lead us into vices, and therefore we must walk in paths of virtue and withstand the devil strongly with our faith, despite these temptations and all others like them, and then, in so doing, shall we have thanks of God and victory over our old enemy the devil.

But we must also struggle energetically against our own flesh, for if we allow ourselves to be led by the appetites of the flesh or to be subservient to its frailties it too will surely lead us in by the wide gate into the broad highway to hell. For as St. Paul says, "The flesh lusts against the Spirit, and the Spirit against the flesh, and these are covetous each against the other" (Galatians 5:17); the works of the flesh are vices and those of the Spirit are virtues. Therefore he teaches us that we should not walk after the flesh but after the Spirit, for the "wisdom" of the flesh is death, whereas the wisdom of the Spirit is life and peace. The "wisdom" of the flesh is enemy to God, nor may it be subject to the law of God, and so Paul says to us that if we live after the flesh we shall die— which is to say that we shall be damned. And yet if through the Spirit we mortify the deeds of our flesh, we shall live—which is to say, we shall be saved.

Let us therefore follow this faithful counsel of the Gospel and mortify the vices of our flesh, for this is what the apostle teaches us. And God of his goodness does not ask that we slay the flesh itself, but rather the deeds of our flesh, which are vices fighting against his Spirit. For God of his great courtesy wills that we permit our flesh to have all its reasonable needs, and so has ordained for us adequate meat and drink and clothing. He wants us to take things in such a measure as is best for us, but when we have been consuming in such a way as does us harm He does not consider Himself well served. As a good physician he does not want a sick person to consume more than will do him good, despite the fact that sick persons often want to take and use things immoderately, even to the danger of life and health. By the same token, if we want to enter in at the straight gate we must rule our flesh in good order, just as if it was a sick person prone to falling into madness, hoping thereby to bring it to health.

For our flesh has congenitally that sort of sickness which is inclined to madness whenever it gets everything that it wants. And when it becomes thus disordered then it would readily do harm to its nearest and best friends, for that is in the nature of insanity. And therefore with a good regulation of the Spirit let us put to death our vicious passions and works of the flesh, granting to the flesh just so much as is good for it and no more, so that it may live and be entirely in health. And so shall we then live evermore in endless bliss, and then shall our good hope of glory lead us to govern our flesh well, restraining it a little from its irrational appetites while we are yet here in this sorry world, in good hope[7] that even the smallest things we purposefully endure here in the flesh shall turn us into the way of much more happiness than we could ever desire for ourselves on this earth. Therefore, through God's grace and through good hope, discipline the flesh: keep it under, and walk after the way of the Spirit in at the straight gate into the narrow way that leads to heaven.

We need also to struggle valiantly against the world which, with its folly and vanity, is always busy to bring us into the broad highway that leads to hell. And to this end we ought to do as St. Paul teaches: for he bids us that we should "savor those things that are above and not those things that are on earth" (Colossians 3:2). Rest assured that if we take care to follow this advice it is a most faithful counsel, for if we do behold "those things which are above" we shall find there our Lord God, his blessed mother and all the saints and angels in utter restedness, joy and peace without end. But if we are beholden instead to things of this earth we shall discover that here is nothing which does not entail travail, anxiety, anger or disease, so that whatsoever is gotten here soon passes away. Therefore, for the love of God, let us not set our hearts so much as we do upon the foul stinking muck of this false, failing world. But we have excellent reason to set our affection on those things that are above, and to love them with all our hearts, for they are good, delightful, sure, and everlasting. Surely we ought then to despise and hate those vain

7. As opposed to *wanhope,* or despair.

things of the world which are evil, disturbing, unreliable and perishable, and which are contrary to the things which are above.

St. John says, "Love not the world, neither the things that are in the world, for he who loves the world, the charity of God is not in him. For all that is in the world is lust of the flesh, lust of the eyes and pride of life, which are not of the Father in heaven but of the world" (1 John 2:15-16). And St. James says that the friendship of this world is enmity with God (James 4:4). How then could we do anything more foolish than to love this wretched world, since we see clearly by the teaching of these saints that the love of this world is bound to draw us away from the love of our Father in heaven and make us his enemies? Let us then pray heartily to our Lord God and heavenly Father that He give us grace to love Him and to despise the world. For assuredly we may not love Him properly as we ought if we are loving the world—a world full of falsehood, vanity, folly and everything that is contrary to God.

Those who put their trust in this world are entirely deceived, whereas those who place their entire confidence in God and in heavenly things above have abiding security and will lack nothing that is good for them. And the world does not have anything to offer its lovers, no matter how much favor they find there. For to those the world loves best it can give nothing but what it refers to as "riches," and the sort of "honors" which are falsely so-called. For if these things were named for what they truly are, they should instead be called "sorrow" and "shame." What people call "riches" entail great labor to obtain and are maintained always in fear; to be parted from riches occasions in the possessor such depression that from the first getting of wealth to its last ebbing away, it is all sorrow. Truly, those that have the greatest wealth in this world are as often troubled, fearful and sick, and as soon dead as those who have none of it, and when they die it more prevents their coming to heaven than helps them. Christ said it was hard for a rich man to enter into the kingdom of heaven (Matthew 19:23-24). Therefore, the muck of this world which people call "riches" should indeed be called "sorrow," for when we have most need of it, it is altogether useless.

Rationally, therefore, we ought to despise such riches and be industrious to lay up for ourselves "treasures in heaven" as Christ bids us—a worthwhile treasure which shall never fail, since earthly treasure is false, transient and unsavory. So as St. Paul says, and I have repeated here already, we ought to savor those things which are in heaven above and, by a taste for them, learn to despise the false unsavory things of earth which, if we carelessly attach ourselves to them, will bring us into the broad highway to hell. The taste for earthly things has led many along that path, as St. Paul testifies when he says, "Those who want to be rich fall into temptation and into the devil's snare, and into many unprofitable and envious desires such as lead people into manslaughter and also bring people to destruction of both body and soul" (1 Timothy 6:9). By this and many other authorities, as well as common sense, we may clearly see that what people call "riches" here are not only not true riches, but actually a negative force preventing people from gathering up for themselves the fair riches of heaven, which alone constitute true wealth. Let us then set our affections on those things which are above, and despise all that is here beneath upon earth which would stand in the way of our pursuing the narrow path that leads to the joy and glory of heaven.

The honors and recognition of this wretched world which individuals so much desire, if we consider them rightly, are not honors at all, nor should they be called "honors." Before God all virtue is honorable, all sin shame. In this world it is generally the reverse. For the world holds those persons honorable who are great warriors or military leaders, who destroy and conquer many lands, pillaging their resources and transferring wealth to those who have more than enough already and who spend what they have outrageously in meat and drink and clothing, in building houses, and living in ease and sloth and many other sins. The world also worships those who are always wanting to take revenge proudly and scornfully for every wrong that is said or done to them. These are just the sort of people about whose exploits men write books and songs, and read and sing about so that their deeds might be remembered the longer upon this earth. Yet whatever the world may judge of such "heroes," we ought to learn well that God alone is sovereign truth and a true judge whose judgment will find them to be shameful in the eyes of God and all the company of heaven, for their lives have been lived entirely in sin, shame, and dishonor.[8]

By contrast, such folk as would fain live meekly in this world and out of the riotous noise and strife of which I have been speaking, subsisting simply, eating and drinking temperately and clothing themselves modestly, suffering patiently the wrongs which others do and say to them and who are satisfied with little enough of this world's goods and desire no great name in the world or eminence, such folk the world regards as "lollers,"[9]—worthless fools and shameful wretches—yet surely God

8. Geoffrey Chaucer's *House of Fame* (c. 1378) had made this same point, with the same standard of ultimate judgment poised against the world's allocation of reputation and honor.

9. Clanvowe here uses the word *loller* in such a way that it conveys both the dismissive ME sense of "loafer" and also the general accusation against anyone who seemed too religious for a licentious era that they were narrow sectarians like the

considers them most wise and honorable, and he will honor them in heaven forever while those whom the world honored are disgraced and suffering forever in hell (unless they have repented and amended themselves before passing out of this world).

Let us therefore take our satisfaction in those things which are good and honorable above, and never worry if the world scorns us or considers us wretches. The world scorned Christ and regarded Him as a fool, and He endured all of that patiently. St. Paul says that in suffering for us, Christ left us an example, that we should do the same for Him, following in his footsteps. And therefore let us follow in his footsteps and suffer patiently the scorn of this world even as He did, and then He will give us grace to come in by the narrow way to the honor and glory in which He reigns. If, on the other hand, we pursue the honors of this world despite the fact that God forbids it, they will readily bring us by the broad highway to the shameful place in which the devil also is found, the torments of hell.

We need to be very much aware of what we are doing, that we do not follow the evil company of this world or conform ourselves to it, for that can easily bring us into the broad highway to hell. It is very common for bad company to lead people into sin when the devil, the flesh and the world themselves might not accomplish this except by the means of bad company; this is the way, for example, that men are often led to go to the tavern to get drunk or to the brothel to engage in lechery. Then they take to brawling and commit all kinds of other sins to please the bad company they run with. Yet if it was not for the pressure put on them by the bad crowd they would not yield to those things—either to temptation of the devil, appetites of the flesh or vanity of the world.

In such cases it seems that bad company can be worse than any of these three typical enemies which have been so far considered, and the devil knows that full well. He behaves just like a fowler, who first takes a watchbird and trains it to sit beside his net and sing. When the other birds hear it sing they all fly down into the net, and the fowler snaps up the net and captures them.[10] Some of them he kills, and others he keeps to make watchbirds of in order to beguile the next lot. Just so the devil,

---

Dutch "lollards" and probably dangerously heretical. It was a charge often brought against those who were sympathetic to the spiritual reforms encouraged by Wyclif and his followers, of which Clanvowe certainly was one, but it was about as undiscriminating in its application as the term *fundamentalist* is in the news media of our own day.

10. See Psalm 91:3; Proverbs 6:5. Satan is often represented in medieval poetry as a fowler.

when he can capture a lecherous person, feeds him full with the foul lusts of his flesh and the world, then takes him and makes him his decoy so that by his enticing and evil example he makes others fall and be caught in the devil's net. So he captures more and more until at last he is able to bring all those he captures to a fowl's death, unless somehow by the grace of God one breaks out of his net and flies up heavenward. It is altogether necessary, therefore, that we pray fervently to God that He preserve us from evil company, lest we fall down with them to be caught by our old enemy just as he caught Adam our first father by the enticing of Eve his wife. Through that overcoming of Adam the devil obtained power over all mankind until the time our blessed Lord Jesus Christ suffered a hard death to redeem mankind again out of his power.

Nowadays it seems that sinful persons who act as decoys of the devil are those the world calls "good fellows." Those who waste the goods God has given them in pride of the world and lusts of their flesh, and who go to the tavern and brothel and stay up late throwing dice, engaging in blasphemous talk and hard drinking, who gossip too much, scorn, backbite, mock, mislead, boast, lie, fight, betray their companions and live entirely in sin—these are the ones regarded as "good fellows." Alas for the world we live in; there is too much of this sort of accursed fellowship, all of which, to be sure, walks in the broad way which leads to loss of both body and soul.

As the Gospel says, few people find the narrow way that leads to blessedness. And yet when those few come amongst those who travel on the broad highway, and suggest to them that they leave it for the narrow path that leads to blessedness, these others set on them, mocking and misrepresenting them and making accusations, keeping all the while to the side of those who maintain their evil deeds, arguing that they are on the straight and narrow themselves. Despite all that, the narrow road is God's way, and the broad way is the way of the devil. The world calls them fools who go in God's way, while the generality of mankind calls those who go the devil's route good and honorable—and so in this world it is the retinue of the devil who are worshiped and praised. It is surely true what St. John says, that all the world is bent upon evil (John 3:19-20). Since that is the reality, we ought to do as St. Paul suggests, who urges us not to desire to be like the world (see 1 Corinthians 5:10-11), and we ought to despise this false and wretched world, mired as it is in evil, and set our affections on those things above which are good . . .[11] and keep to the narrow way by obeying God's commandments.

11. I have here deleted three repetitious lines.

IV. What Are God's Commandments?

The broad highway is paved with broken commandments. We should understand in this regard that there are ten commandments, as follows: first, we shall have no other god but our Lord God of heaven; second, that we shall not take the name of the Lord our God in vain; third, that we shall hallow our holy day; fourth, that we shall honor our father and mother; fifth, that we shall slay no person; sixth, that we shall commit no lechery; seventh, that we shall not steal; eighth, that we shall bear no false witness against our neighbor; ninth, that we shall not covet our neighbor's house; tenth, that we shall not desire our neighbor's wife nor his servant nor his maiden nor his ox nor his ass nor anything he owns.

Of these ten commandments, the first three pertain to the love and honor of God; the other seven follow suit with respect to our fellow-Christians.[12] We ought always, therefore, to pay the utmost attention to these commandments, so that we break none of them.

All those who are in a false belief or who are engaged in any kind of idolatry or witchcraft, or who love or reverence or honor anything more than God are breaking the first commandment.

All those who take the name of God with a false intent or in vain are breaking the second commandment.

All those who do not give themselves, on the holy-day, to the service of God, keeping themselves apart from ordinary worldly business as much as is in their power, or who simply spend the holy-day in worldly business, fleshly lusts or in vain merriment are breaking the third commandment.

All those who do not honor their father or mother, or who do not help them or comfort them in body and soul in their need, as they are able, or those who do not honor their spiritual mother, Holy Church, as they ought, are breaking the fourth commandment.

All those who slay any person—in thought, by word, or in actual deed—break the fifth commandment, unless it be the case of such as are given authority with good reason to put persons to death who have deserved death according to God's law. Otherwise no killing of a person is not a breaking of this commandment.

---

12. ME *even-cristene,* a term which is general in its meaning in Hilton or Rolle, for example, but which is replaced elsewhere in Clanvowe with *neighboure.* (One suspects that Clanvowe's translation follows Wyclif in removing the distinction between "fellow Christians" and "neighbors" at large in this context.)

All those who commit lechery in any degree, naturally or unnaturally, break the sixth commandment.[13]

All those who rob or steal, who confiscate by political mastery or extortion or by any guile or falsehood their neighbor's goods, are breaking the seventh commandment.

All those who bear false witness against their neighbor or slander or backbite against them falsely with malice break the eighth commandment.

All those who covet house, land, or anything their neighbor owns, even just in coveting it break the ninth commandment.

All those who desire their neighbor's wife or husband, servant or maiden, even though they do not actually achieve the object of their desire, are breaking the tenth commandment.

All those who break any of these commandments are in the broad highway that leads to hell until they have repented and are in full intention of keeping all the commandments, as they are enabled, until their lives' end. It is very dangerous to break them, therefore, and most profitable to keep them. Worldly, carnal persons think the commandments are hard to keep. But certainly those who are spiritual and who love God sincerely do not think them too hard to follow. St. John tells us that is the charge of God to us that we keep his commandments (1 John 3:23-24), and they are not too heavy.

V. The Way of Love

Therefore, if we love God as we ought to, we should always obey the ten commandments with a loving reverence of Him as our Father and our Lord, and of our neighbor as ourself. And we know that well from the words Christ spoke to a man who asked Him what was the greatest commandment in the law. And Jesus answered and said, "You shall love the Lord your God with all your heart, all your soul, all your mind and all your strength. This is the first and greatest commandment. The second is like to it: you shall love your neighbor as yourself. On these two commandments depend all the law and the prophets" (Matthew 22:36-40). Since we know then that by loving God and our neighbor we can keep all the commandments of God, we ought not then to consider it a heavy business to keep his commandments, nor in that light should we grouch about having to obey them.

13. *Any degreee*—i.e., in thought, deed, or habitually; *naturally or unnaturally*— heterosexual or otherwise.

Surely it is reasonable, delightful and profitable to love God above all other things, and our neighbor as ourself. It is reasonable, since He it was who made us out of nothing according to his own image and likeness, and has ordained that, if we should cooperate with Him by the action of our own will, we can be made partners with Him in the bliss of heaven. Everything here in creation He has ordained for our help and comfort; everything good we possess He gives us; all that we ask of Him from a faithful heart He grants to us.

And when through Adam's sin we had lost our place in paradise He came, and for the sake of his love for us, took flesh and blood of the blessed virgin Mary and became human like us, being born of that blessed maiden without her having ceased to be a virgin. The time of his blessed birth was in the harshest part of winter, and it took place in a poor lodging and cold. And when He was born his blessed mother wrapped Him in a few poor cloths and laid Him in a manger between an ox and an ass to keep Him warm; there was no fancier adornment there.[14] Thus He came, as poor as this, and as meek as He was wise, into this world in order to give us an example of meekness and a commitment to poverty. The eighth day after his birth he was circumcised, in this foreshadowing already his shedding for us some of his precious blood.[15]

He lived here on earth more than two and thirty winters, and preached and taught the people the right way to heaven, and performed many wonders, healing many persons both bodily and spiritually, suffering heat, cold, thirst,[16] ugly dwelling places, scorn, reproofs, backbiting, chiding, wrongs and many other despites and diseases. And at the last one of his own disciples betrayed Him on account of his goodness. After that they took and bound Him as if He were a thief, led Him to their bishop and there accused Him by false witness, tortured Him, blindfolded Him, mocking Him and spitting on his blessed face as they would have done to a dog.[17] Then He was led before Pontius Pilate, there to be falsely accused and imprisoned, afterward stripped naked,

14. See Isaiah 1:3, from which the ox and ass form a gloss to the manger scene: "The ox knows its owner, and the ass its master's crib; but Israel does not know. . . ."

15. This connection between the doctrine of the covenant and the redemption has a long typological tradition, but it was popularized in the later Middle Ages by the Franciscans.

16. The MS reads *thirst bo wete and drie*.

17. Clanvowe was in the Middle East at the time he wrote this, and he may be reflecting the prevalent expression of disgust toward dogs that he would have observed there.

bound to a pillar and beaten with sharp whips until his whole blessed body ran with blood—his body that never knew sin. Then they set on his blessed head a crown of huge, sharp thorns, and dressed Him up like a fool to mock Him, and after that they condemned Him to death and made Him go between two thieves and—as exhausted and broken down as He was—to bear on his back the cross on which He was to die through all the city streets in the sight of his blessed mother, his kinfolk and all his other friends.

When they arrived at last at the place of common justice they nailed his blessed feet and hands with huge, crude nails to the cross, stretching out his limbs. And yet through all his agony this innocent prayed for his enemies and said, "Father, forgive them this guilty thing, for they do not know what they are doing."

Then they hung one thief on his right, the other on his left side, spiting Him further by placing Him in the middle. When He was in excruciating thirst because of the great loss of blood they gave Him vinegar and gall to drink, and when He had tasted what it was He would not drink it, but bowed down his blessed head and gave up his spirit. Then came a knight called Longinus and smote Him through the heart with a spear, and there came out water and blood.[18] All of this He suffered for us. Finally his blessed body was taken down from the cross and buried. He descended into hell and there fetched out those He loved.[19]

But on the third day after all this He rose again from the dead, to live and show Himself to many men and women in many circumstances! And later on, in the sight of his disciples, He ascended into heaven. Now, of his great goodness, He lives to protect us from many perils, and though we grieve Him deeply [by our sins] each day, yet He spares us, giving us time to repent and amend ourselves. And no matter how greatly we have sinned, the moment we are truly sorry and in full and faithful intention to sin no more He gladly forgives us.

Therefore, when we consider thoroughly all these things which God of his great goodness has done and does every day for us, and on the horrible pain He has suffered on our account, we may well know that it is entirely reasonable that we should love God above everything else, as I have said.

But it is also reasonable that we should love our neighbor as ourself, since it is the will and commandment of God that we do so. Also, our neighbor is of the same form and nature as we are ourselves, and there-

18. See John 19:34; medieval tradition gave the soldier the name of Longinus.
19. This refers to the "harrowing of hell"; Matthew 27:52-53 is understood in the context of Psalm 68:18 and especially of Ephesians 4:8-10.

fore it is only natural that we should each one heartily love the other in the appropriate way.

Moreover, it is a delightful thing to love God above all and our neighbor as ourself. For whoever loves God above all else can have the delightful realization that he is loving Him who surpasses all other persons or objects in goodness, beauty, intelligence and power, and that God of his great goodness will return that love a thousand-fold better than any heart can think or imagine, and that with it shall come the love of all the company of heaven and all God's people on earth, and that this love is not fickle as is worldly love, but shall last eternally—shall never end.

To love our neighbor as ourself is a rich and merry tonic both for body and soul, so that the love of God and our neighbor is full of mirth, and produces more sheer delight than anything else. And it is profitable to love God above all else and our neighbor as ourselves, for whoever does this shall have the bliss of heaven that lasts forever, and that is altogether the greatest profit that may be.

So then, since the love of God and our neighbor is so reasonable, delightful and profitable as is proved by these considerations, we are surely utter fools if we do not do everything in our power to remain in the Law of Love, for it is the narrow way that leads to heaven, to which all I have said has been pointing. Therefore let us pray heartily to our Lord Jesus Christ that of his abundant mercy He may give us grace so to come into that way, and to keep ourselves in it.

Conclusion

There are, of course, many folk who want to say that they are in this way, when it is plainly not so. All sorts of people want to claim that they love God more than all other things. But whatsoever they say, Christ, who cannot lie, says this, "Whoever loves me will keep my words and my commandments, and my Father shall love him and we shall come unto him and make our dwelling with him. And those who do not love me do not obey my words" (John 14:23-24). Christ also says, "He who has my commandments and who keeps them—that is the one who loves me" (John 14:21). And St. John adds that we may determine if we know God by whether or not we are keeping his commandments. "And whoever says that he knows God and is not keeping his commandments is a liar, and the truth is not in him" (1 John 2:3-4). And he says further, "Let us not love in word, nor with tongue, but with deeds and in truth" (1 John 3:18).

We can know, therefore, by these words of Christ and of his apostles, as well as many other authorities in Holy Writ, that no person may come to the bliss of heaven unless he is committed to keeping the commandments of God, the which commandments are fully obeyed by those who love God, and their neighbor as themselves as they ought, as I said before.

So then, all those who truly love God and their neighbor as themselves are in the narrow way that leads to everlasting bliss. All those who do not so love God and their neighbor are on the broad highway that leads to death and torments of hell unending.

Therefore, let us lift up our hearts to our Lord God Almighty who has made us and bought us again with his precious blood, praying to Him that for the sake of his great goodness and eternal mercy He will give us grace to keep clear of that broad highway which leads straight into the grisly pains of hell, and grant us grace to travel in that narrow way which leads to the bliss of heaven, until at last we come into that blessedness which He has ordained for those who love Him.

Amen.

ANONYMOUS

Loving Our Enemies

This brief tract was probably written by a Yorkshire cleric of the mid-fourteenth century, about the time John Wyclif was a student getting ready to go up to Oxford. It is a simple piece, in the form of an epistle or pastoral letter, and may have been part of a collection sent around among parish pastors as inspirational guidance. Walter Hilton incorporated it into his *Ladder of Perfection* in a memorable section on love.[1]

THESE ARE THE TOKENS by which you shall know if you love your enemy, and what example you ought to take from Christ in learning to love him.

What it really comes to is this: if you are not stirred up against such a person in anger while faking an outward cheer, and have no secret hatred in your heart—despising him, judging him, or considering him worthless—and if it be that the more shame and villainy he does to you in word or deed the more pity and compassion you show toward him, almost as you would for someone who was emotionally or mentally distressed, and if you actually cannot find it in your heart to hate him, on account of love being so good in itself, but instead you pray for him and help him out and desire his amending (not only with your mouth, as hypocrites do, but with a true feeling of love in your heart), then it is that you have perfect charity toward your fellow Christian.

This is the sort of charitable love exhibited perfectly by St. Stephen, when he prayed for those who stoned him to death. This is the love Christ counselled to all who would be his perfect followers when he said, "Love your enemies: do good to them that hate you, pray for those who persecute and calumniate you." And therefore, if you will follow Christ, be like Him in power. Learn to love your enemies, and sinful persons, for all of them may be your fellow Christians.

Consider and reflect on the way in which Christ loved Judas, who was both his bodily enemy and a sinful dog: how good Christ was to him, how benign, how courteous, how humble toward him whom He knew to be damnable. He chose him for his apostle, and sent him to preach with the other apostles. He gave him power to work miracles. He showed to him the same good cheer in word and deed, even to shar-

---

1. See Hilton, *Toward a Perfect Love: The Spiritual Counsel of Walter Hilton,* trans. and ed. David L. Jeffrey (Portland: Multnomah, 1986), 89-92.

ing also with him his precious Body, and preached to him in the same manner as He did to the other apostles. He did not condemn him openly, nor did He abuse or despise him or ever speak evil of him (and yet even if He had done all of that, it would simply have been to tell the truth!). And most amazing of all, when Judas seized Him, He kissed him and called him his friend. All this charitable love Christ showed to Judas whom He knew to be damnable—not in any kind of feigning or flattering but in truthfulness of good love and pure charity. For though it might seem to us that Judas was unworthy to have any gift of God, or any sign of love because of his wickedness, nevertheless in God's eyes it was appropriate and reasonable that our Lord should behave toward him as He did.

He is love and goodness, and therefore it is characteristic of Him to show love and goodness to all his creatures, as He did to Judas. Follow after Him somewhat if you can, for even though you are imprisoned within the walls of your bodily dwelling, nevertheless in your heart, where the place of love is, you shall be able to have part of such a love toward your fellow Christians as I speak of. Whoever imagines himself to be a perfect follower of the teaching and life of Jesus Christ, as some persons judge themselves to be—inasmuch as they teach and preach and are poor in worldly goods as Christ was—and still cannot follow Christ in his love and charity, loving his fellow Christians every one, good and ill, friend and foe, without feigning, flattering, despising in heart, or indulging in resentments and melancholious reproof, well, truly that person deceives himself. In fact, the nearer to Christ such a person imagines himself to be, the further away in fact he is. For Christ said to those who would be his followers, "This is my commandment, that you love mutually as I have loved you." Or, as we may also translate it: "This is my bidding, that you love each other together as I love you, for if you love as I have loved you, then are you my disciples."[2]

One who is truly meek, or would be meek, can love his fellow Christians. And nobody else can do it.

2. Hilton, in his use of this passage, expands here on the practical problem of how to love like Jesus loves; this borrowed section in his work fits into a larger discussion of the love of Jesus as the measure and standard of the charity to which we are called.

PART SEVEN

Preaching and Pastoral Care

GEOFFREY CHAUCER
From the text of Thomas Hoccleve's *De Regimine Principium*. Reproduced
from Harleian MS 4866 by permission of the British Library.

JOHN WYCLIF

from
The Duty of Pastors

The selections which follow come from chapters 21, 23, and 24 of the
loose Middle English translation of Wyclif's treatise, *De Officio Pastorali*,
which appeared more or less simultaneously with the Latin version
about 1377. There are some differences between the two versions,
however, owing to their being directed toward different audiences. The
Latin original was part of Wyclif's defense in the academy and church
hierarchy of views for which he had already attracted strong opposition.[1] The Middle English version (MS Ashburnham M.M.)[2] would have
been directed to "lordis" and other educated laymen as well as to priests
at the parish level. These three passages reflect the burden of the larger
work, in which Wyclif expresses his preoccupation with a biblically responsible parish ministry—one which offers a vigorous evangelical critique of contemporary culture and which is uncompromised (politically
or otherwise) in its condemnation of sin and social evils. Readers familiar with the good Parson in Chaucer's *Canterbury Tales* will recognize
some similarities.

The Good Pastor

THE FIRST DUTY OF A PASTOR is to feed the sheep.[3] We learn more about
a pastor from what he gives to his sheep [than perhaps in any other
way]. For we ought to accept as part of what we believe that the Law of
God passes all others in authority, in truth, and in intelligence. It is of
the highest authority in that, just as God surpasses men, so God's law
must take precedence over human conventions; it is on this account
that God commended his apostles not to preach the law of men but
rather to preach the Gospel to all manner of persons. Accordingly, those
whose preaching is a matter of jokes and trivial talk are all the more to
be blamed. For God's Word must always be proclaimed faithfully if it is

---

1. *De Officio Pastorali*, ed. Gotthard V. Lechler (Leipzig and London: Wyclif
Society, 1863).

2. *The Duty of Pastors*, in *The English Works of Wyclif Hitherto Unprinted*, ed. F. D.
Matthew, Early English Text Society, O.S. 74, rev. ed. (1880, 1902; New York:
Kraus, 1975), 405-57.

3. This sentence was omitted from the Middle English version.

to be properly understood. And his Word is more wholesome for people to hear since it is the substance of what we believe and teaches us to follow Christ—which is what everyone must do who wishes to be saved. Therefore, we meditate on this law day and night, both waking and sleeping, for when all other laws have passed away this one shall stand eternally in glory. And the heart of this law is the Gospel of Jesus Christ.

Priests ought to be preaching this "heart" to the people, and teaching them to love Christ, for whoever does not love and follow Him is condemned, as Paul says. Certainly, then, that priest is to be blamed who has such free access to the Gospel and yet turns away from preaching it to telling human fables, for the Law of God condemns a person who chooses the worse and heavier part, leaving the better and lighter, both for himself and with respect to the people [in his charge]. God does not ask for rhetoric or rhymes from one whose duty it is to preach, but simply to divide rightly God's Gospel and his words,[4] to arouse people thereby. And thus curates are not to be excused if they neglect to preach to their sheep, for a man should not even be a curate unless he can understand the Gospel, and he is sadly lacking in intelligence if he cannot thereby teach them. (If a parson makes the case that he is prevented from his preaching by circumstance or an impediment of nature, when before he had preached well, let him teach his flock by a holy life, and God will excuse him.)

The second duty that falls to shepherds is to keep their sheep from wolves, such as false friars that come among people to steal wool and do them harm—Christ calls them "ravening wolves"—and parsons ought to warn the people of this peril. Whatsoever false preachers come and preach to the people are like wolves, foxes, or hounds, and all of these should be chased from the flock.

The third duty that falls to parsons is to anoint those sheep which are diseased and to tell them of the medicine of God's Law whereby they can be healed.

Now if shepherds fail to do these three things, they are mere hirelings or wolves. And here parsons should take heed that they do not spoil their sheep by [consenting to] wrongs asked of them by their bishops. Indeed, they should resign their curacy before [agreeing to these things].

The Good Husbandman

I WANT TO DECLARE HERE that a correct preaching of God's Word is the

4. See the description of Chaucer's Parson in the general prologue of *The Canterbury Tales* (lines 477-528) and also lines 30-60 of the Parson's Prologue, selections from which follow in this volume.

most worthy deed that priests may do here among men. For Christ, who is the standard of all good, made this his principal work here, and taught his disciples to continue in it after he was to go to heaven. Thus, since Christ is our best master, it is a matter of revelation and belief that preaching is the best work one may do.

Also, the goodness of any work is measured by the fruit it produces, and more fruit is produced by preaching than by any other work. For this reason such godly preaching is the best work that a priest does, in that by this activity a priest obtains children for God, and causes them to come at last to heaven. Therefore Paul says to his people, "In Christ Jesus I have begotten you through the gospel" (1 Corinthians 4:15), and therefore Christ praises more the preaching of the Gospel by which his Church is engendered than he does the engendering of his own body [in the Incarnation], even though, of course, they are both the work of God. And so scholars point out that procreation, since it preserves common nature, is of a higher order than nurture which preserves merely an individual member of the species. And Christ remarked in Luke's Gospel to a woman who blessed his mother, saying, "Blessed be the womb that bore you, and the breasts that gave you to suck" (Luke 11:27), replying, "Yea, rather blessed are they who hear the Word of God and keep it" (v. 28). For the same reason, and for many more, those who preach God's Word are blessed by it.

Lord, how worthy a work it is to engender God in the human soul by means of planting the seed of God's Word, for this is what will certainly obtain great reward in heaven, both for the obedience of the one who preaches and for the winning of God's children that it produces. And therefore John the Evangelist records that he had no greater experience of grace here than to hear that his children walk in the truth (see 2 John 4).

If you argue that a priest cannot "father" children in God in this way, certainly you must allow that he may do so by God's help, for otherwise no person should obtain even a natural child, since it is God alone who gives the child its soul, and who could obtain a child if that were not given? St. Augustine's opinion on this is sound, that Christ accomplished greater miracles through his apostles in the conversion of multitudes of heathen people from wicked lives to become children of Christ than He did in the miracles [we usually think of]. And accordingly the apostles concentrated more on preaching than on physical charities.

The more that Christ lends his help to a work the more is it good, and Christ lends his help more particularly to preaching than to other work, and therefore it must be better work, since Christ also brings it to so gracious a conclusion. On this account wise doctors of the Church have said that good preaching is better [for human well-being] than any other kind of work, such as medicine or pharmacy for example. And this is undoubtedly why, though Christ bade his disciples to undertake a variety of good works, preaching was chief among them. For it is in this effort that a priest clothes himself in Christ's person. . . . We may gather, then, that it is a more serious sin to fail in this than in other less valuable activities.

Lord, since the sin of Sodom cried out to God for a great judgment, how shall this sin that leaves this unborn spiritual offspring crying out to God then be avenged?

Corrupt Preaching

IT IS WELL TO RECOGNIZE how these men fall into the sin [of perverted preaching], and what antidote is available to counter it, since the [true] work is so precious. There are three classes of people who commonly contribute to this sin: the priests whose duty it is to preach; the people whose responsibility it is to hear the preaching; and those who permit God's Word to be adulterated.

A preacher may sin in many ways. For example, he may be one who does not sow good seed but merely jokes, idle tales and other trivialities, preventing thereby true preaching of the Word of God. For Luke says that this alone is uncorrupted seed, despite the three inadequacies he describes (Luke 8:5-15) as pertaining to the ground on which it is cast.

In another case a priest who sows good seed may mix in poison with the seed as, for example, when his actual motive for preaching includes vainglory or ambition for material gain.[5] It is on this account that Paul says to his people that we are not to be corrupters of the Word of God, but are to speak of God out of a pure motive, since we are speaking before God in Christ (2 Corinthians 2:17). Would to God that preachers in our own time would learn this lesson from Paul, for then they should speak of God, not of this rotten seed, and speak as if they were in fact before [the throne of] God, observing good manners in the Lord's presence.

Moreover, they ought to preach unto the worship of Christ, and not for muck.[6] For among all the species of simony that Christ ever suffered in the church, this is the most foul. It is often the way of "begging

---

5. ME *coveytise of worldly good.*

6. *Muck* is one of Wyclif's favorite terms for material riches; others include *dung, manure,* and *excrement.*

preachers" who are always gathering up the community's good after they have finished preaching—money or grain or anything they can get their hands on.[7] And the gullibility of the people makes them partners in these beggars' sin, for when they make donations to them they are effectively assenting to their simony. And it is a foul error to argue, as many do on this matter, that they are simply giving out of love for God and that is enough for them to be concerned about, for assuredly our wise Lord asks of us both goods and good living. Now for godly living a person will be rewarded and, if he fails, he will fail to have a reward. So, to destroy this kind of erroneous presumption Christ says in the Gospel according to St. Matthew that there will be some of the damned who shall say to Him on that day, "Lord, did we not cast out devils in your name, and did we not do miraculous works in your name?" But Christ shall say to these persons, "Truly I say unto you, I know you not as children of bliss, for you failed to live a godly life" (see Matthew 7:22-23).

Lord, since these men are to be condemned who preach God's Word in Christ's name and cast out devils and do miraculous things, what reward shall these beggars have who fail even in this, and who lie about Christ, and say that Christ begged in the way they do, in defense of their new organizations?[8]

Christ knew full well that such persons should come, even though He forbad them to go from house to house but [instructed his disciples rather] to dwell in one place and not leave it, and to pack along no bags and satchels to beg with.

7. By *prechour beggeres* Wyclif and his followers meant various kinds of religious traveling salesmen, "merchandisers" of the gospel. These included friars—some of whom traded on their religious vocation to beg from door to door—pardoners, summoners, or others of their ilk, who had become notorious abusers of simple folk's piety for personal gain. Chaucer, Wyclif's contemporary, was intensely critical of the same phenomenon in his *Canterbury Tales*, notably in his treatment of the Friar, Pardoner, and Summoner. The problem, of course, is not without analogies in our own time.

8. ME *ordris*, by which Wycliffite texts usually mean the four orders of friars—Dominican, Franciscan, Carmelite, and Augustinian—the dominant "new" religious organizations of the time.

WALTER HILTON

from
The Ladder of Perfection

From Book 2 of Hilton's *Speculum Contemplativorum,* this call for spiritual discernment constitutes a pastoral warning about false shepherds. It is not at all as polemical as similar writings by Chaucer or the Wycliffites, and its subtlety casts light on an aspect of the issue which is often missing in warnings against deceivers in the pulpit.

The Noonday Demon

BEWARE, NOW, OF THE NOONDAY DEMON[1] that counterfeits light as if it is straight from Jerusalem but is nothing of the kind. For the Fiend sees that our Lord Jesus reveals light to his lovers of truth; therefore, in order to deceive those who are unwise he makes a show of light. It always proves false under color of the true light, yet still he beguiles some. I want therefore to say something about how it is that a soul may recognize the light of truth when it shines from God, and distinguish it from the artificial light of the Enemy.

Let me offer a simple example from astronomy. Sometimes the firmament shows a kind of light which seems to be the sun itself but is not. And, of course, sometimes the true sun is revealed truly. Discerning one from the other consists in this: the artificial sun does not show itself except between two black, rainy clouds. Because the sun is nearby, there shines out from the clouds a light which appears to be the sun but is not. The sun itself is revealed when the firmament is clear, or at least substantially clear, of such black clouds.

Now to our purpose: some people seem as though they forsake the love of the world and intend to come to the love of God and the light of understanding in Him, but they will not come out from the midst of this murkiness of soul that I have spoken of before. They will not recognize themselves for what they have been before and are still, through

---

1. The *noonday demon* is a figure from popular mythology associated with the devil himself. In medieval discussions of sin the analogy is often made between this kind of broad daylight appeal of the lie and Satan's approach to Eve in the garden. Hilton's application of the metaphor to spiritual charlatans is unusual.

sin, nor acknowledge how they remain in their own strength nothing before God. They are not diligent to enter into themselves, forsaking outward concerns so as to slay the wicked turmoil of sinfulness in their hearts—pride, envy, wrath and other sins—through a consistent desire toward Jesus in prayer, thoughtful meditation, silence and repentance, as devout and holy men and women have always done. Rather, as soon as they have begun to forsake the world with respect to external appearances, or very soon afterward, they imagine themselves to be holy and in possession of a spiritual understanding of the Gospel and Holy Writ.

Notably, if they keep the letter of the commandments of God and keep themselves from bodily sin, they imagine that they love God perfectly. And they therefore immediately set out to preach and teach all others as if they had received the grace of understanding and perfection of charitable love through a unique personal gift of the Holy Spirit. And they tend to be much more stirred up about such things than others, supposing themselves possessed of great insight, which they feel is given to them suddenly without study beforehand, and also a great fervor of love, so it seems, to preach truth and righteousness to their fellow Christians. Therefore they count it a grace of God that He visits them with his blessed light in preference to other souls.

Nevertheless, if such folk really look about themselves, they will see that this light of insight and heat of passion that they feel comes not from the true sun, the Lord Jesus; rather, it comes from the noonday demon that feigns light and likens himself to the sun.

This is the way that such counterfeiters shall be recognized. The light of knowledge of insight which is feigned by the Fiend to a murky soul is always revealed between two black and stormy clouds. The over-cloud is presumption, the nether-cloud is the down-putting and under-cutting of one's fellow Christians. Now whatever light of knowledge or experience of fervor shines upon a soul, when it is accompanied by presumption, self-promotion and disdain of one's fellow Christians at the same time it is not a light of grace granted by the Holy Spirit. This is so even when the knowledge in itself is of the truth. No, it is either of the devil if it comes suddenly, or of man's own wit if it comes by study. And it ought to be more widely recognized that this kind of feigned light is not the light of the true sun.

Those who have their knowledge in this manner are full of spiritual pride and do not see it. They are so blinded with a feigned light that they attribute their self-promotion and lack of toleration to the laws of Holy Church, as if they were submitted in perfect meekness to the Gospel and the laws of God. They fancy that pursuit of their own willfulness is freedom of the spirit. Therefore they begin to be like black clouds raining down torrents of errors and even heresies, for the words that they utter in their preaching resound to back-biting, strife, discord, and the pronouncement of judgment on both communities and individuals. Yet they argue that all this is done in charity and a zeal for righteousness. It is not so, for as St. James the apostle says: "Where envying and strife is, there is confusion and every evil work" and "This vision descendeth not from above, but is earthly, sensual, devilish," whereas "the wisdom that is from above is first pure, then peaceable, gentle, and easy to be entreated, full of mercy and good fruits, without partiality, and without hypocrisy" (James 3:15-17). Wherever there is envy and contention, there is instability and all sorts of evil work. And therefore the cunning which brings forth such sins does not come from the Father of Light, our God, but it is earthly, beastly, even of the devil.

By these tokens then—pride, presumption, intolerance, indignation, backbiting and other such sins (for these soon follow after)—the counterfeit light can be distinguished from that which is true. The true sun does not reveal Himself in special visitations, granting his light of understanding or perfect love to any soul unless the "firmament" is first made bright and clear of such clouds. That is to say, first the conscience is made pure through the fire of burning desire toward Jesus, which purges away the mists and impediments of pride, vainglory, ill-temper, envy and all other sins which beset the soul. As the prophet says: "A fire goeth before him, and burneth up his enemies round about" (Psalm 97:3). This may be taken in the sense of which I speak, that the desire of love shall go before Jesus in the soul and burn away his enemies there, our sins.

Unless a soul is first struck down from its height of self-elevation by the fear of God, and is well examined and refined in this fire of desire, purified there from all spiritual filth and dross by long discipline in prayer and other devotional exercises, it will not be able to endure the radiance of real spiritual light nor able to receive that precious liqueur of the perfect love of Jesus. But when it has been thus refined and made discerning through his fire, then it will be able to bear and receive the gracious light of spiritual perception and the perfection of love—which is the true sun.

So Holy Writ says: "But unto you that fear my name shall the sun of righteousness arise with healing in his wings" (Malachi 4:2). The true Sun of Righteousness, our Lord Jesus, shall rise over you who honor Him. That is, where meek souls will humble themselves, considering themselves beneath their fellow Christians, recognizing their own unworthiness and casting themselves down before God, making nothing of their own strengths in reverent fear and spiritual beholding of Him continually, then there will be that favorable climate of perfect meekness in which He shines.

It is unto these souls that the true sun shall arise, illumining their intellects with the knowledge of truth and kindling their affection in flames of love. And then shall they both burn and shine. Through the virtue of this heavenly sun, they shall burn in perfect love and shine in the knowledge of God and spiritual things, for they will then have been reformed in perception and spiritual consciousness.

Accordingly, whoever wishes not to be deceived, I think it might be good for him to avoid prominence and begin by hiding his soul's murkiness from the prying of others, as I have said, trying to forget the pressures of the world altogether so as to follow Jesus in consistent desire, offering himself up in prayer and meditation upon Him. For one who does this the light which follows after the darkness will, I believe, be certain and true, and will shine out of the city of Jerusalem from the true sun. Coming to the soul that travails in darkness while crying out for light, it will show the way and comfort it in its struggle.

I believe that a soul that has truly recognized its own murkiness is not vulnerable to a counterfeit light. That is, when a person truly and unstintingly sets himself to forsake the love of the world, and is enabled by grace to come to spiritual consciousness and self-knowledge, governing himself meekly in that experience, he shall not be deceived by errors, heresies or fantasies. All of these come in by the gate of pride; so if pride is properly dealt with, these shall not likely find much reception. For the grace which a soul experiences in coming to terms with its own darkness in meekness shall teach it truthfulness and reveal to it thereby which profferings come from the Enemy.

GEOFFREY CHAUCER

from
The Canterbury Tales

Chaucer was England's foremost poet in the last quarter of the fourteenth century and the first court poet for more than three centuries to write exclusively in English. His most famous (and longest) work is *The Canterbury Tales*, an unfinished masterpiece combining brilliant narrative and poetic skills with trenchant Christian cultural criticism. Chaucer provided a framework for this collection of revealing moral tales by placing each of his stories in the mouth of a typical representative of contemporary society—a knight, a miller, a merchant, an enterprising professional woman, a lawyer, an alchemist's assistant, a doctor, and several professed adherents of the religious life, including apostates and charlatans as well as our exemplary Parson. It is the Parson who in his sermon gathers up the threads of all the other tales and provides the formal conclusion to the collection as it stood just before Chaucer's death.

The occasion bringing all these storytellers together is a pilgrimage to Canterbury. In the fourteenth century a pilgrimage could be—like a trip to the Holy Land today—merely an excuse for traveling in good company or for taking an exotic vacation. A pilgrimage was recommended, however, as an act of penance for sin, providing a time for recollection and spiritual reorientation and for a meaningful experience of reintegration into the family of faith, the body of Christ. Chaucer's audience was well aware of the proper purpose of a journey such as his characters were taking to Canterbury, and they would also have been sensitive to the dubious motives—ranging from misplaced to outright mischievous—of some members of the group. But the Parson, because of the way he is described and by virtue of the sermon he preaches, would have been readily recognized as an example of the godly shepherd whose job it is to point us all to the reconciliation which alone can bring our life's pilgrimage to a satisfactory end. Here is how Chaucer portrays him in the general prologue (lines 477-528):

> There was a religious man of good reknown
> who was poor, the parson of the town,
> but he was rich of holy thought and work;
> also a learned man, a clerk[1]

---

1. I.e., a scholar or "theologian" to the degree that he was a student of his profession, something not true of all "clerics."

who truly would Christ's gospel preach,
and his own flock devoutly teach.
Gracious he was, wonderfully diligent,
and in adversity most patient,[2]
as had been proven many times.
And he hated to badger after tithes,
but would rather give, whenever in doubt
unto poor folks in his parish round about
out of his own offering and also his subsistence.
Little enough was for him sufficient.
Wide was his parish, with houses far asunder
but he failed not to visit for rain or thunder.
Neither sickness nor mischief prevented his call
to the far reach of his parish; to great or small
he came on his feet, and bearing a stave.
This noble example to his sheep he gave,
that first he lived, and afterwards taught.
Out of the Gospel those words he caught,
and this turn of speech he added thereto;
that "if gold should rust, what must iron do?"
For if a priest be foul, on whom we trust,
small wonder if an unlearned man should rust.[3]
And it is surely a shame if a priest reek—
a filthy shepherd among clean sheep.
'Tis a good example a priest ought to give
by his own clean life how his flock should live.
This man set not his pulpit out to hire,
leaving his sheep meanwhile stuck in the mire
while he ran to London and old St. Paul's
to get himself a chantry job, singing for souls,
or in some brotherhood to get enrolled.[4]
Not him; he stayed and guarded his fold
so that no wolf caused it to miscarry—
he was a shepherd, and not a mercenary.
And though he was holy and virtuous
he was never toward sinners contemptuous,

2. Patience was a virtue of wisdom, as celebrated in Boethius's *Consolation of Philosophy* (which Chaucer translated), and in Chaucer's *Tale of Melibee.*

3. See Lamentations 4:1; the figure is employed by Gregory the Great in his *Pastoral Care.*

4. The first was a soft, and often lucrative, employment that took advantage of the grief (or bad conscience) of the wealthy; the second, serving as chaplain for a guild, was similarly seen as much less demanding work than serving an ordinary parish.

> or scornful of speech, or condescending,
> but in teaching discreet, and always bending
> to draw folk toward heaven by spiritual beauty—
> the good of example—in which lay his duty.
> But in the case of persons stubborn in sin,
> whether of high estate or lower condition,
> he would admonish plainly, without hesitation.
> I know no better priest in all of the nation.
> He didn't flatter himself with pomp and reverence
> or cultivate a phony conscience
> but the whole word of Christ and his apostles twelve
> he taught, after following it first himself.

After Chaucer has shown us all twenty-nine pilgrims assembling at an inn, a "hostelrye," in a suburb of London, he introduces their inn-keeper, or Host, as he is called, who devises a game for their journey: each shall tell a tale, and whoever tells the best shall win a free supper.[5] Beginning with the worthy Knight, the pilgrims commence, one after another, to tell their stories. These tales, we discover, reveal so much about the character of each teller that they become a kind of confession, albeit an inadvertent one in most cases.

The reader is invited to participate in an evaluation of these tales in a way unprecedented in medieval literature; and thus, by learning to reflect upon the character of each teller's intention in his or her narrative, the reader develops a heightened sensitivity to the real value of the story. This, the poet teaches, has more to do with the story's integrity— the truth which binds its words and the will of the one who utters them—than it has to do with any superficial value as entertainment. It is highly significant, then, that just as the poem is drawing to a close, the Canterbury journey is also coming to an end, and an inculcation of values that has been developed all along the road is about to be made explicit in two ways. First, the narrator of the poem steps away from an omniscient perspective and identifies himself with his readers—and characters—as one who needs to confront the implications of his own sinful nature and seek its remedy.[6] Second, he presents us with an authoritative guide to that remedy in the person of a good pastor, whose godly character and consecrated life are both corollary and guarantee of his submission to the highest authority, the "Author and Finisher of our faith." What follows is merely an excerpt; the Parson's Tale, the last in Chaucer's series, is also by far the longest.

5. In fact, *The Canterbury Tales* was never in this sense finished; life began to run out on Chaucer before he had written a tale for every pilgrim. Yet we may take the formal structure, concluding with the Parson's Sermon and Chaucer's own "Retractions," to be a faithful indication of the poet's purpose.

6. See the excellent article by Russell A. Peck, "Number Symbolism in the Prologue to Chaucer's *Parson's Tale*," *English Studies* 48 (1967): 205-15.

A Good Parson and His Sermon

Prologue to the Parson's Tale

> By the time the Manciple had his [sad] tale ended[7]
> the sun from its southern sweep had descended
> so low that it was (not more, in my sight)
> than twenty nine degrees above the horizon in height[8]
> So it must have been almost ten o'clock, I guess,
> since slowly out to eleven feet, more or less,
> my own shadow had grown by this time
> in proportion and measure supine,
> reflecting my body's six feet, surmising
> as under the moon's early rising
> —I mean Libra began to ascend—
> just as we came to a hamlet's end.
> At this our Host, as he was wont to guide
> our group along its pilgrim ride,
> said something like "Gentle folks, each one,
> of tales we were promised, we lack only one.
> Fulfilled is my purpose, and all is in order
> (I believe we have heard from every quarter),
> my original ordinance is almost complete.
> I pray God will make his wit more fleet
> who must now unfold our last tale quicker:
> —Sir priest!" he said, "are you a vicar?
> Or an actual parson?[9] Be honest, I pray,
> but whatever you are, don't break off our play,
> now that all except you have told a tale.
> Unbuckle now, and declare without fail
> —for truly, it seems by your expression

7. The Manciple had told a tale of judgment for sin in which the possibility of redemption was withheld, thus creating a sense of frustration in preparation for what the Parson has to say on that subject.

8. Twenty-nine was also the number of pilgrims at the start of the journey. Peck comments on the allegory of this and the following numbers: 29, like 11, signifies incompleteness and a sinful condition; 6 is the number of the soul; 10 (in most MSS) is a reminder that a time of judgment is at hand. See Peck, "Number Symbolism in the Prologue to Chaucer's *Parson's Tale.*"

9. I.e., one who has not hired out his benefice to a low-paid curate, but who actually serves in the parish and does the pastoral work.

you're just the one to cap this collection.
Tell us a fable straight off, for God's own bones!"[10]
    This Parson answered in measured tones,
"You'll get no fable told by me;
for Paul, in writing to Timothy,
reproved those who, in eschewing faithfulness
tell old fables and similar wretchedness.
Why should I sow chaff, and good purpose lose,
when I may plant good wheat if I so choose?
For which reason I'll say to those who will hear
sound moral words and a message more dear,
and then, if still you will be my audience
I'll cheerfully, yet in Christ's reverence,
make you what lawful good pleasure I can.
Believe me, though, I'm a southern man
and can't spin alliterative verse by the letter,
nor, God knows, can I rhyme much better.
Therefore, if you like, I'll not presuppose,
but tell you a merry tale in prose
to knit up all this feast, and make an end.
May Jesus, by his grace, sound insight send
to show you the way, on this voyage,
to make that perfect, glorious pilgrimage
which leads us to Jerusalem above.[11]
If you'll hearken then, to what I speak of,
I'll begin my tale, on which I pray
you'll give me your opinion—no more can I say.
    Understand that I offer this meditation,
submitting it always to careful correction
of theological scholars. I'm not a critic of matters textual;
I'm concerned only with meaning, believe me well.

---

10. Harry Bailly, the Host from the Southwark inn, is a worldly man. His oath is particularly jarring here, uttered as it is to a priest. But it is also an ironic anticipation of the Parson's own admission of motive or intention in speaking. He does preach for the sake of "God's own bones," the bones of Jesus Christ broken on the cross on account of just such idle blasphemy as Bailly has uttered.

11. The model here is derived from biblical passages such as Hebrews 11:13-16 and Galatians 4:22-27 and is reinforced by the development of the two cities motif in such formative works as St. Augustine's *City of God*. Although the analogy implicit in the pilgrim journey from London (or its worldly suburb of Southwark) to the "spiritual" city of Canterbury would have been apparent to medieval readers, this is the first time that the life journey from "Babylon" to the "Jerusalem above" has been made explicit in the poem.

Therefore I want to make it clear
that I'm willing to be corrected in what I say here."
    Upon this word we were soon agreed
for it seemed appropriate to our need
to conclude with matters of virtuous meaning
and so to give him space and hearing
we bid our Host to say to him
that we all pray his tale to begin.
    Our Host had the words for us all:
"Sir priest," said he, "may blessings fall
on you; declare your intent,
but be quick—the sun will soon set,
so be fruitful, and that in little space.
To do well, may God send you his grace.
Say what you wish, and we will gladly hear."
And with that word he spoke in accents clear:

The Parson's Tale

Jeremiah 6:16. *State super vias, et videte, et interrogate de viis antiquis qui sit via bona, ambulate in ea; et inuenietis refrigerium animabus vestris, etc.*[12]

Our sweet Lord God of Heaven, who wills that no one should perish, but wills that we may all come to the knowledge of Him, and to the blissful life which lasts forever, admonishes us by the prophet Jeremiah, who declares this to us as follows: "Stand upon the ways, and see and ask of old paths (that is to say, of old interpretations) which is the good way, and walk in that way, and you shall find refreshing for your souls," etc.[13] There are many spiritual ways that lead folk to our Lord Jesus Christ and to the kingdom of glory. Among these ways there is a full noble way—and entirely accommodating—which will not fail a man or

12. The Parson's text, translated immediately below, is taken from one of the Scripture readings for the week between Palm Sunday and Good Friday, which culminates the Lenten agon, the most important time of reflection on repentance in the calendar of the church. It helps to remind the reader that Lent is almost over, and that choices are to be made.
13. In a gesture typical of his writing for the court of Richard II, Chaucer's *etc.* makes us try to remember, or look up, the remainder of the verse not quoted: "And they said: 'We will not walk.'" The balance of the passage from Jeremiah describes the Lord's intense displeasure with this disobedience of princes, his rejection of their sacrifices and incense, and his coming judgment. The Parson's injunction is to return to obedience by the path of repentance while there is yet time, and it concludes Chaucer's "court counsel."

woman who, through sin, has gone aside from the right way to the heavenly Jerusalem. This way is called Repentance, concerning which one should gladly incline his ear and enquire after wholeheartedly, in order to recognize what repentance is, why it is called repentance, what are the varieties of repentant actions, how many types of repentance there are and which things pertain to and facilitate it as well as which things prevent it.

St. Ambrose says that repentance is the lamentation one makes for the sins of which he is guilty and, with it, the commitment not to do any longer the sort of thing which needs to be lamented. And another theologian says, "Penitence is the lamenting of one who sorrows for his sin, grieving himself for his misdeeds. . . ." In order that such a one be truly repentant he ought first to contritely bewail the sins he has committed, then steadfastly purpose in his heart to make an honest confession of them and to make amends, never recurring to things which need to be repented of and continuing in good works; otherwise his repentance may be pointless. For, as St. Isidore says, "It is only a mocker and trickster, and no truly repentant person, who will go out right away and do again the very things for which he ought properly to be repentant. Weeping without refraining from the sin will not avail."

Nonetheless, we are entitled to suppose that every time we fall, no matter how often, we may, if we are granted grace, rise up again by means of repentance—but it is certainly a dubious basis on which to proceed. For, as St. Gregory says, "whoever will not rise up out of his sin incurs the heavier charge of making a habit of it." Therefore, repentant people who will quit their sin, and forsake their sin before sin leaves them forsaken, Holy Church regards as secure in their salvation. And while it is true that for one who lives in sin and truly repents at the last moment Holy Church still expects his salvation, let us take the surer way.

And now, since I have explained to you what repentance is, you should understand that there are three occasions requiring penitence. The first of these is when a person is baptised after having lived sinfully.[14] St. Augustine says, "Except one is repentant for his old life, he cannot begin the new, clean life." For certainly, if such a one be baptized without having repented of the sins of which he is guilty, he receives the mark of baptism but not the grace of it, nor remission of his sins, until such time as he is truly repentant. Another necessitating circumstance is when persons commit deadly sin after they have already been received into baptism. The third circumstance is when persons from

14. I.e., adult baptism of a new convert.

day to day fall into venial sins after their baptism.[15] It is with this situation in mind that St. Augustine says the repentance of good and humble folk is the penitence of each day.

There are three categories of penitence: one of these is called "formal," another "communal," and the third, "private." Solemn formal penance is of two types—either as when one is excluded from Holy Church in Lent, on account of the slaughter of children or similar things, or when one has sinned openly in such a notorious way that it is talked about all over the country and Holy Church makes the judgment that he be obliged to do public penance.[16] Communal penance is that type enjoined on groups of individuals by priests in certain cases, and which may involve their going on a pilgrimage thinly clad or barefoot. Private penance is that which people do every day for personal sins, which we also confess privately and for which we undertake a private penitential obligation.

Now you ought to understand what is appropriate and necessary to a true and complete repentance. It depends upon three things: contrition of the heart, confession of the mouth, and satisfaction. St. John Chrysostom says that "repentance obliges one to accept graciously every trial to which he is enjoined, with contrition in his heart, shrift on his tongue and a working out of satisfaction in all humility." And this is a fruitful repentance for three things by which we anger our Lord Jesus Christ—that is, by our sinful pleasure in thinking, by our carelessness in speaking, and by our wicked sinful actions. Standing over and against these wicked things of which we are guilty is penitence, which may be imagined as a tree.

The root of this tree is *contrition*, which hides itself in the heart of a person who is truly repentant, just as the roots of a tree hide themselves in the earth. Up from the root of contrition springs a trunk that bears branches and leaves of confession and the fruit of satisfaction. In respect of this Christ says in his gospel, "Do fruits worthy of repentance" (Luke

---

15. Deadly or mortal sin is any sin with the component of ill will or malice, typically including pride, wrath, envy, sloth, and covetousness. Venial sins, or sins of the flesh, may be committed as reflexes of appetite—typically gluttony and lechery—and if they do not acquire a component of one of the deadly sins, or idolatrous persistence, they are remediable by praying the Lord's Prayer.

16. The public penance which would have been in everyone's mind in this context was that commanded for Henry II after he had ordered the murder of Thomas à Becket in Canterbury Cathedral some two hundred thirty years earlier. The result of this attack on the church by secular power and corrupt clerics was the making of a saint and the establishment of Canterbury as a destination for pilgrimage. The analogy for Richard's court would not have gone unnoticed.

3:8),[17] for it is by this fruit that people may know the tree and not by the root (which is hidden in a penitent heart), nor by the branches, or even the leaves of confession. And therefore our Lord Jesus Christ says, "by their fruits you shall know them" (Matthew 7:20).

Out of this root springs also a seed of grace, which seed is the mother of our assurances, and the seed is lively and quick. The grace of the seed springs from God through remembrance of the Day of Judgment and the pains of hell. Reflecting on this Solomon says that it is in the fear of God that man turns away from his sin (Proverbs 16:6). But the liveliness of this seed is the love of God and desire for joy everlasting. This liveliness and warmth draws our heart toward God, and teaches us to hate our sin. . . .

For truly the Law of God is the Love of God, of which David the prophet says, "I have loved thy law and hated wickedness" (Psalm 119:163); whoever loves God keeps his law and his word. . . . Penitence is a tree of life to those who receive it, and they who keep themselves in a state of true repentance are blessed, as Solomon implies (Proverbs 28:13, 14).

In this matter of repentance or contrition one ought to understand four aspects: what contrition is; what causes ought to move us to contrition; how contrition ought to be expressed; and what is the effect of contrition upon the soul. The brief answer to these is as follows: contrition is genuine sorrow which we feel in our heart on account of our sins, bringing the sober determination to confess our sins, and to do penance, and nevermore to sin. And as St. Bernard puts it, "this sorrow must be unfeigned—heavy and grievous, acutely and poignantly felt in the heart." This ought to be so initially because we have trespassed against our Lord and Creator, more acutely because we have sinned against our Father in heaven, and yet more sharply because we have grieved and injured Him who bought us and by his precious blood delivered us from the bonds of sin, the cruelty of the devil, and the pains of hell.

There are six reasons for being moved to contrition. First, we ought to put ourselves in mind of our sins, acknowledging them. Yet be on guard lest that act of remembering becomes an occasion of illicit delight in any way, when it should be an occasion only for great shame and sorrow over guilt. . . . As Hezekiah says, "I will remember all the years of my life with bitterness in my heart" (Isaiah 38:15). . . . This kind of reflection makes one feel shame for his sins, and no delight, as God says by his prophet Ezekiel: "You shall remember your ways . . . and they shall displease you" (Ezekiel 20:43).

---

17. These words were actually spoken by John the Baptist.

The second reason we ought to loathe sin is that, as St. Peter puts it, "whoever commits sin is the servant of sin" (2 Peter 2:19; cf. John 8:34), and sin puts us in dire bondage. . . .

The third reason we ought to be moved to contrition is fear of the Day of Judgment and the horrible pains of hell. For as St. Jerome says, "every time I think of the Day of Judgment I tremble, for when I am eating or drinking or in whatever I am doing, it seems to me that I am always hearing that final trumpet sounding in my ear, and the words, 'Rise up you who have been dead, and come to judgment.'" O good God, much ought we to fear such a day of reckoning, for we shall all be there, as St. Paul says, and "all stand before the judgment seat of Christ" (Romans 14:10); it will be a general congregation, an assembly of the whole, with nobody absent. No excuses will be accepted. And it is not only that judgment will then be passed upon our faults, but also that all our works shall openly be known. And as St. Bernard says, "no special pleading will avail, nor any nimble tricks; we shall be required to give an account of every idle word." And on that day we shall have to deal with a judge who can be neither deceived nor corrupted. . . .

For, as St. Gregory says, "To the wretched who are condemned will be extended the experience of dying without death, ending without end, injury without demise. For their death will be everlasting, a living death, and their ending evermore a beginning of the end, and their degradation shall not cease." Therefore, says St. John the evangelist, "they shall seek death and not find him; they shall desire to die but death shall flee from them" (Revelation 9:6). And Job says that in hell there is no order or rule (Job 10:22). . . .[18]

The fourth point that ought to prompt contrition in our heart is the sorrowful remembrance of the good that we have here left undone, and also the good we have lost. Good works may have been lost either because they were rendered of no value by our falling afterward into deadly sin, or because we performed them while living in a state of sin. . . . These good works are effectively killed, nullified by our repeated sinning, even good works done earlier while we were still living in a state of charitable love, nor may they be quickened again without true repentance. Of these God speaks by the mouth of Ezekiel, saying, "If the righteous man turn again from his righteousness and work wickedness, shall he live?" (Ezekiel 18:24). Nay—the good works he has done will be remembered no more, for he shall die in his sin. . . . For as

---

18. One of the things the medieval mind found most horrible in contemporary imaginations of hell was the spectre of uncontrolled, random violence—a complete anarchy of perverse passions.

much [as this is so] . . . the person who effectively accomplishes no abiding good work may well sing that new French song: "Jay tout perdu mon temps et mon labour" ("I have lost all my time and effort").

The fifth thing that ought to move us to contrition is remembrance of the Passion that our Lord Jesus Christ suffered for our sins. St. Bernard said, "while I live I shall remember the travails that our Lord had in his ministry of preaching, his weariness in traveling, his temptations when He fasted, his long vigils when He prayed, his tears when He wept with pity over 'good' people, the woe and shame and filth that people spoke to Him, the foul spittle that men spat in his face, the blows that they gave Him, the reproofs and accusations, the nails with which He was nailed to the cross, and all the other aspects of his Passion that He suffered on account of my sins, and for no fault of his own."

And you ought to recognize that in human sin every ordinance of God is turned upside down. For properly God, reason, our senses, and the body of man are so ordained that each one of these is to have lordship over the other. God is to have lordship over our reason, reason over our sense-experience, and this in turn over our bodies themselves. But truly, when we sin, this whole order or ordained pattern is turned upside down. In such a situation then, inasmuch as human reason will not be subject or obedient to God, who is Lord over it by right, it loses in turn the lordship that it ought to be exercising over the senses [and emotions], and also in turn over the body. And why? Because feeling and emotion rebel against reason and reason loses its lordship over feelings and over the body; just as reason becomes a rebel against God, so sensuality rebels against reason, and even the body finally rebels. And it is this disarray and rebellion which most certainly our Lord Jesus Christ paid for very dearly in his own precious body. . . .

The sixth reason we ought to be moved to contrition is our hope of three things: forgiveness of sin, the gift of grace to live in obedience, and the glory of heaven with which God shall reward us for the good deeds [of an obedient life]. And since it is Jesus Christ who of his great generosity and sovereign bounty gives us these gifts, He is called by us "Jesus of Nazareth, King of the Jews."

Now, "Jesus," is to say "savior" or "salvation," on whom we must depend for forgiveness of sins, which is what we mean when we say *salvation* from sin. This is why the angel said to Joseph, "You shall call his name Jesus, for he shall save his people from their sins" (Matthew 1:21). And St. Peter speaks to the same point when he says, "There is no other name under heaven that is given to any man by which a person may be saved, except Jesus only" (Acts 4:12).

"Nazareth" is as much as to say "flourishing," or "is alive," by which anyone shall be assured that the one who has granted him forgiveness for his sins will give him also the grace to persevere [in a faithful life]. For in the flower is the expectation of the fruit in due course, and in forgiveness of sin there is the promise of grace to persevere. "I stand at the door of your heart," says Jesus, "and ask to be let inside. Whoever opens up to me shall have forgiveness of sin; I will enter into that person by my grace and sup with him"—that is, by the good works he does, which are the food of God—"and he shall sup with me" in the great joy which I shall give him (Revelation 3:20). Thus shall we be able to have hope, that because we have taken up the work of repentance God shall give us his kingdom, as He promises us in the gospel.

. . . Therefore, one who sets his desire on these things is most wise, and to be truly consistent should not then presume to turn his life to sin, but give himself body and heart into the service of Jesus Christ, and thereby do him homage. For truly our Lord Jesus Christ has graciously spared us in the midst of our follies, and it is clear that if He had not had pity on human souls it is a sorry song we would *all* be singing.[19]

. . . Then shall mankind understand what is the fruit of penitence; according to the word of Jesus Christ it is the endless bliss of heaven. There joy has no contradiction of woe or grief; there all the injuries of this present life pass out of existence; there is security from the pains of hell; it is there where the blessed company rejoices forever, each one in the other's joy; there the body of mankind, once foul and dark, is made more clear than the sun; there our physical bodies which once were sick, frail, feeble and mortal are made immortal, and so strong and healthy that nothing may injure them; there is neither hunger, thirst nor cold, but every soul is made complete in its vision of the perfect knowing of God. To this blessed kingdom we may purchase our admission by spiritual poverty and the glory of humility, its fullness of joy by hunger and thirst, its rest by labor and its life by death and the mortification of our sins.[20]

19. The second part of the sermon is a brief section on confession; the third part is organized around an examination of the seven deadly sins—pride, anger, envy, sloth, covetousness (or greed), gluttony, and lechery—and the appropriate remedies or "satisfaction" for each in turn. The conclusion to the sermon, which follows here, is followed in turn by Chaucer's own confession or retraction (which is not included here).

20. When the Parson's last words have died away there is as yet no *amen*, no benediction. Instead, Chaucer's own words come before us as an envoy: "Here taketh the makere of this book his leve. . . ." His "leaf" from the book, and his "leavetaking" turn out to be a considered confession of his own, by which he not only indicates his own belief but also repents of anything he has written which may have contributed to someone else's sins. He also prays for a true spirit of re-

pentance, for forgiveness, and for strength to live an obedient life "through the generous grace of Him who is King of kings, and Priest over all priests, who bought us with the precious blood of his own heart; so that I may be one of those who at the day of judgment shall be saved." Thus Chaucer's conclusion is offered in supplication to the correction of his own Author, "qui cum patre et Spiritu Sancto vivit et regnat Deus per omnia secula. Amen."

The modern reader of *The Canterbury Tales* may be wondering who won the contest for the free supper, with which the pilgrimage began. The medieval audience would more quickly have grasped Chaucer's point. The *soper* is the Supper of the Lamb, made possible, as the Parson has said, by the unfathomable self-offering of the Good Shepherd. In the lengthening shadows of the setting sun, as the pilgrims ride into Canterbury, weighing the Parson's words each in his or her own heart, they go toward a supper which none can win by his or her own effort but which stands open to anyone who truly desires it: whosoever will, may come. And the Host who mediates at that table is, of course, himself the meal and the means whereby each, participating in his body, may become one with the body of his people, whereupon all earthly contests cease to have relevance.

NICHOLAS BOZON
Christ's Chivalry

Nicholas Bozon was born in the latter part of the thirteenth century and lived to do most of his writing after 1320. He was a Franciscan friar, famous for his *Contes moralises*—short moral stories and allegories which he provided for sermon materials. He composed verse sermons as well, some of them highly dramatic. The one which follows, from the largest single manuscript collection of his work, MS British Library Additional 46919, affords some sense of the typically courtly audience of a mid-century Franciscan working among those whose first language was French. It is a type of the *sermone semidramatico*[1] employed by continental Franciscans, and it employs chivalric imagery in a fashion favored by St. Francis himself.[2]

Listen, my lords, to a tale of high chivalry,
of a noble knight, who for love of his lady
strove so hard that He gave up his life
to win back his exiled bride,

(that is, the human soul that had been betrayed).
But her gentle lover did not hasten
to her rescue till she realized her folly
and the way in which she had completely debased her life.

He allowed her long to be tormented
so she might see how much she had declined;
yet as soon as she cried for mercy, He took pity on her,
and the more so because she had been led astray.

Alone He took to the field to rescue his love;
though victorious in battle and triumphant over all
(partly by force and partly by strategy),
He was wounded sorely for his jealous love.

---

1. The term is from San Bernardino da Siena; there are numerous English as well as Anglo-Norman examples. See D. L. Jeffrey, "St. Francis and Medieval Theatre," *Franciscan Studies* 43, Annual XXI (1983/88): 321-46.
2. See Walter Hilton, *The Ladder of Perfection*, chap. 72. The idea of Christ as chevalier was developed by the English Franciscans from Alexander of Hale's *Introitus* (7.131, lines 58ff.) to James Ryman's poems in the fifteenth century, but the basic imagery goes back at least as far as the great Anglo-Saxon poem, "The Dream of the Rood."

How handsome was the knight in this test—
who for love of his mistress suffered such wounds!
And well ought she to have hung his shield in her chamber.
These were the bearings on the shield He bore:

He bore a shield of silver, stencilled with gules;[3]
in chief, a crown of sharp thorns,
a fair white border on which were four costly signs,
and in the midst of the field, a rich fountain of blood.

Tall and strong was the steed He mounted that day.
Its coat all over was of four kinds of fur:
cypress for the body, cedar for the hooves,
olive for the back, and the great mane of palm.

On his head the knight wore a helmet of bloody locks;
his over-jerkin was bare skin, pierced through and through;
and his mail-coat of suffering was all split and riven,
but the lance He held in his hand was his deity.

And thus it was He conquered him who had conquered us all.
But to do this He had disguised his identity,
for had his enemy recognized Him,
he would on no account have ridden out to battle.

Our chevalier acted wisely:
he borrowed arms of one of his knights-bachelor,
Adam by name, had them refurbished
and a damsel arm Him with them.

He entered this damsel's chamber
(she was the fairest of all);
He entered so secretly, without word or sound,
that no one knew He was there save she alone.

The damsel then armed Him with borrowed armor:
pure white flesh was the jerkin she gave Him, padded
not with silk or cotton but with blood;
for cuisses and greaves[4] she gave Him groin and thighs.

For chauces[5] of mail she wrapped his legs with sinews,
his leg-plates were well-fitting bones;

3. *Gules:* incised crimson lines.
4. *Cuisses* and *greaves:* leg armor.
5. *Chauces:* chain-mail for the lower legs.

covering all, skin was his silken gamboison,[6]
trimmed all about with veins.

Once armed the knight left the chamber,
nobly offering to do battle for us.
His deceitful enemy sortied from the ranks,
not knowing his true identity.

Taking one look at the armor, he sneered in disdain,
but Jesus let him carry on his vain assault,
awaiting the right moment to raise his hand;
when He was Himself doomed to death, then it was
        He made us whole.

Then He left his armor hanging on a tree,
and took the field as a proven champion.
He found his lady in her vile prison,
and took her away with him to salvation.

6. *Gamboison:* under-armor padding.

JOHN MIRK

from
The Festial

John Mirk (or Myrc) was an Augustinian canon and prior of the Augustinian foundation at Lilleshall, in Shropshire. He was as keenly opposed to corruption in the priesthood as Wyclif was and sought to counter it in a variety of ways. One of these was his *Instructions for Parish Priests,* an English verse translation of a Latin work, the *Pupilla Oculi,* which offers a practical guide to the daily responsibilities of a pastor. This little book was finished about 1399 or 1400, yet as John R. H. Moorman writes, it is "so full of practical common sense that it could be put into the hands of the ordination candidate of the twentieth century."[1] Mirk wrote also a *Manuale Sacerdotum,* designed to encourage a colleague in the performance of parish duties. It contains chapters attacking contemporary clerical abuses, including "The pastor who loves the tavern more than his church," "The pastor as gambler," "The pastor as fornicator," and "The pastor as businessman." Best known of his works is his *Festial,* a collection of sermons for high feast-days of the church year, from which the following sermon, effectively a translation and presentation as well as exposition of the epistle for the day, is taken.

On the Conversion of Saint Paul

GOOD MEN AND WOMEN, it is on this day that we have a high festival in the calendar of Holy Church called in English "the conversion of St. Paul." It commemorates that day on which he was converted from being a cursed tyrant into God's servant, from being a high and proud man into one who was meek and devout, and from being the devil's disciple into becoming God's holy apostle. And so, because this man was turned around from a life of wickedness into all goodness, lending great strength and help to the Church, therefore Holy Church commemorates his conversion, though this is done for no other saint except him. And there are three reasons for this: first, because of the great miracle of his conversion; second, for the great joy of his defending of the faith; and third, for the high example he affords in the amending of his life.

---

1. Moorman, *A History of the Church in England* (London: Adam and Charles Black, 1953), 130-31. See Mirk, *Instructions for Parish Priests,* ed. E. Peacock, Early English Text Society, O.S. 49 (London: Early English Text Society, 1868).

Before he was converted this man was first called Saul. For just as Saul, the king of Jerusalem, pursued David for the purpose of killing him, in like manner this Saul pursued Christ and his disciples and servants with the intention of bringing them to their death. Wherefore, while Christ still walked this earth, Saul would never come near enough to hear his teaching. But as soon as our Lord ascended into heaven he began—because he was learned and knew the Jewish law—to oppose Christ's disciples, disputing against them and pursuing them in any way he could with the express purpose of obliterating the laws of Christ.

Then one day he fell into an argument with St. Stephen, and because he could not overcome him, he plotted how he might bring him to his death, so that he never let up until Stephen was stoned to death. Then, as is the manner of the devil's children when they have done a foul turn (they rejoice over it, and become vain and proud in their hearts and increase in their malice), so was this Saul glad of the death of St. Stephen. And because he wanted to obtain for himself a reputation for such wickedness surpassing all others, he went to those who were charged with administering the Jewish law and got from them letters of warrant, by which to capture and bring back all Christian men and women, wherever he might find them, in bondage to Jerusalem to meet their death. And when he had obtained those letters he had such pride in his position and envy in his heart against Christian people that whenever he heard them spoken of he snorted in derision and frothed at the mouth in anger, threatening and menacing them in so hellish a manner that everybody grew wondrously sore afraid of him.

Then, because he heard that in the city of Damascus there were many Christians hiding for fear of their lives, he at once took his horse and his men and rode off in that direction in all haste. But our Lord Jesus Christ—may He be blessed!—revealed the sweetness of his grace thus: when this Saul was in the full of his pride and malice, and planning to accomplish the greatest possible harm and evil, just about mid-day, when the sun was shining most intensely, then at that moment Christ cast a light of grace around Saul which was brighter by far than the sun. And out of that light He spoke thus to him: "Saul, Saul, why do you persecute me?" He was at once so afraid that he fell down off his horse and in great fear said, "Lord, what are you?" Then said our Lord, "I am Jesus of Nazareth whom you are persecuting." He did not say, "I am God of heaven," nor "God's Son of heaven." No. It was principally because Christians believed that Jesus had risen from death to life that Saul was avidly persecuting them, charging that they put their belief in a dead man. Therefore our Lord Jesus said: "I am Jesus of Nazareth," for that is the name He bore in his humanity.

JOHN MIRK

Then Saul believed on Him, and said, "Lord, what will you make of me?" And Jesus our Lord replied, "Rise and go into the city, and there it shall be told you what to do." His men saw this light at the same time, and heard the voice, but saw no man. But they went to Saul, and took him by the hand, since he was now blind, and led him into the city to the house of a worthy man. And there he stayed, praying and fasting for three days and three nights, unable to see but praying constantly to God because of the fear that had come into him concerning his vision. During this time, the Holy Spirit taught him the law of Christ.

On the third day there came to him one of the disciples of Christ called Ananias, as God had commanded him, and though he was desperately afraid of Saul he spoke to him, saying, "Saul, brother, our Lord Jesus Christ has sent me to you that you shall see again, and [instead of being led] become one who leads."[2] And when Ananias had lain his hands on Saul's head, at once he saw, and there fell from his eyes what looked like the scales of a fish. And when Saul had followed him out, he then called him Paul.[3] When Paul had eaten, he was comforted, and his strength returned, and he remained with the disciples who were there a few days. And then he went into the temple and openly preached Jesus Christ, preaching clearly that Jesus was the Christ, and none other. Everyone was amazed at his sudden conversion and said to himself that it was a supreme miracle of God that he who was so much a living curse should so quickly be transformed into so blessed a man. Thus, good people, you may see and hear how great a miracle God showed us in his conversion of Paul.

Holy Church takes also a great deal of joy in Paul's defending of the faith. It was a source of great gladness for all Christian people to see that he who was before so eager to destroy them was now so busy to increase their numbers. And though he was once glad to shed their blood, and sent about seeking to draw them to their death, now he put himself forth boldly, risking death on their behalf. And whereas no one had before dared to preach God's word for fear of him, afterward, with his

2. Acts 9:17 actually reads "and be *filled* with the Holy Spirit." A citation from memory and the transposition of the Middle English *fulfylled* for *folowed* may suggest that Mirk had used an English translation, though not the Wycliffite version (which has *fulfilled*). In any case, the confusion here illustrates the sort of referential wordplay of which medieval preachers were so fond: as Saul had been blind, and led by others, now as a man of new vision he would lead others; as one who had followed after Christians to persecute them, now for the sake of Christ he would be hounded and persecuted.

3. The text of Acts does not begin to call him Paul until later (Acts 13:9), when it is simply observed that he was "also called Paul."

support, they did not hold back for fear of any king or nobleman, but openly preached the faith of Jesus Christ in each place. And he who was so proud before now fell at the feet of every Christian person whom he had wronged and asked of them mercy and forgiveness out of an utterly meek heart. Wherefore St. Augustine compares him to a unicorn, saying: "The unicorn, according to his nature, bears a horn on his nose, and with his horn slays all beasts he fights with, and is so fierce that no hunter can capture him by any strategy—that is, unless he should spy the path where he walks and set down there a woman who is pure, a maiden. And when this unicorn sees her, he will, also by the laws of his nature, fall down and lay his head on her lap, becoming weak and without strength—and so be captured." Thus, he continues, "Paul, who was at first so fierce and proud that no preacher was able to deal with him, nevertheless when God put before him his maiden—that is, the pure and undefiled faith of his Holy Church—he at once fell down from his pride and became simple and meek and subject to Christ's servants."[4] On this account, Holy Church is glad for his defending of the faith.

Paul is also put before us as an example of a signal correction of life. God is so gracious in Himself that He wishes no person be lost, but desires that all men and women be saved. Wherefore, as a striking example and comfort to all sinful persons, he puts St. Paul before us to look upon. For though a man or woman has committed ever so much sin, or lived ever so accursed a life, if each will apply personally the example of St. Paul—that is, to abandon pride and become meek, cease to do sin and become busy to amend his or her life—then shall that person afford God and all the court of heaven more mirth for their conversion than Holy Church has here on earth now over the conversion of Paul.

The tragic thing is that there are men and women who love their sins more than they love God, who will neither for the sake of the love of God nor for the fear of God and the torments of hell leave off their sin, arguing that surely God is not willing to lose what He has redeemed with his own heart's blood. But you who talk like this, be on guard that you do not lose yourself. For while you are loving your sin more than you love your God, and would rather be the devil's servant than God's, you are damning yourself, and are thus the cause of your own damnation. It is for such persons that God has ordained the tormenting of

---

4. A haughty rider was often a symbol for pride; hence one robbed of his pride could be described as being "knocked off his high horse," a phrase which may in fact derive its force from medieval sermons on the life of Paul.

fiends and, at last, pain without end. For as Gregory says, those who shall be damned begin their sentence here on earth, at least in part, and so after their death merely continue in what they have already begun.[5] By way of illustration I will tell this *ensaumple*[6] which was told to me by one who knows it to have happened:

Narracio

There was a man, sinfully accursed in his manner of living, who was an officer to a certain lord. As he rode one day toward an estate belonging to his lord, he was seized with an attack of derangement,[7] in the throes of which he unbridled his horse, which then carried him to a manor house belonging to the lord. But when he came in, the bailiff there immediately perceived what affliction had overtaken him and at once ordered his servants to tie him to a post in the barn. Then, when this bailiff had eaten his supper, he asked one of his servants to go to the barn and see how the man was doing. When this fellow got to the barn he saw three huge dogs, as black as coal, tearing away at his flesh from every side. The servant was so stricken with fear that he scarcely kept his own sanity, but went straight to his bed and lay there sick long afterward. And on the morrow, when the rest of the men came to the barn they found nothing left of the man but his bare bones with all the flesh eaten away.

Thus, whoever lives a foul life may be sure of a foul end. But even if his ending seems to be pleasant in men's eyes, it will prove right foul in the sight of God and all his angels. Wherefore let each one take the good example, while in this life, of St. Paul, and amend while he has space and time for amending. And whoever does do this shall come to meet St. Paul and to have the joy that shall last forever. To the which joy may God bring us all, if it be his will.

Amen.

---

5. Gregory, *Morals,* on Job 10.15 (Job 11:8 in modern editions).

6. ME *ensaumple,* like the Latin *exemplum* from which it is derived, signifies an apparently secular tale whose moral serves to highlight a biblical passage or exposition thereof to which it is attached. These tales were brought together in numerous formal collections, one of the most popular of which was called the *Gesta Romanorum,* or *Acts of the Roman Peoples,* containing both tales of antiquity and more recent additions. Mirk, like many medieval preachers whose work has come down to us, made frequent use of the *Gesta.* This tale, however, seems to have had an oral basis.

7. ME *fell wod.* This derangement and the subsequent response of the bailiff strongly suggest that the cause was rabies, for which there was of course no cure.

PART EIGHT

Scripture and Translation

JOHN WYCLIF
Portrait by Basire

WALTER HILTON

from
The Ladder of Perfection

From Book 2 of *The Ladder of Perfection*, this passage reflects Hilton's conviction that the lover of Jesus will be drawn to the Scriptures as a means of communion, cherishing them as "love-letters" from Christ.

How We See Jesus in His Word

WHEN THE SOUL OF HIS LOVER experiences Jesus in prayer in the way I have indicated,[1] though that person might imagine that he could never have comparable experience of Him by any other means, it sometimes happens that grace puts vocal prayer to silence, stirring the soul to see and experience Jesus in another manner. And chief among these is the beholding of Jesus in his Word. For Jesus, who is all truthfulness, is hidden there, wound in a silken veil of its beautiful words where He may not be known or experienced except with a pure heart.[2] This is simply because truthfulness does not reveal itself to enemies, but only to friends who love and desire it with a meek heart.

Remember that truthfulness and meekness are true sisters, joined together in love and charity. There is no dividing of counsel between them. Meekness is related to honesty; it does not stand alone. Truthfulness—real honesty—always sustains meekness. So they get on together wonderfully well. To the degree that the soul of a lover is made meek through the inspiration of grace opening his spiritual eyes, it sees that it is nothing in itself, and depends upon the mercy and goodness of Jesus alone, everlastingly borne up by his help and favor. Then it desires only his presence, and so it sees Jesus alone.

In this spirit of approach we will find the truthfulness of Holy Writ wonderfully opened up and revealed, far beyond the powers of study and travail and the intellectual reach of our natural human wisdom.

1. See Hilton's "On Prayer" and "On Meditation" in Parts Two and Four above.
2. The image is borrowed from Augustine (*On Christian Doctrine*), but the point behind it was also made forcefully by Hilton's contemporary Wyclif in his *De Veritate Sacrae Scripturae* and elsewhere. As I have pointed out in the Introduction to this volume, Wyclif was at pains to indicate that the reader's intention is a critical aspect of the relationship of authority and truth in reading Scripture. Hilton is making essentially the same point, though without the theoretical support.

And the understanding which we are given there may be thought of as an experience and perception of Jesus.

Jesus is a well of wisdom, and by a little outpouring of his wisdom into a cleansed soul He makes that soul wise enough to understand all of the Scriptures. This does not happen all at once in a special vision, but through that grace the soul acquires a new capacity and a grace-filled talent for understanding it, especially when its words, hidden in our hearts, are called into remembrance.[3]

This opening up and clarifying of our understanding is brought about by the spiritual presence of Jesus. It is just like the Gospel says of the two disciples on their way to the castle of Emmaus, burning in their desire and talking about Jesus. Our Lord Jesus appeared to them in his physical presence in the likeness of a pilgrim, and taught them the prophecies concerning Himself. And as the Gospel says, "Then opened he their understanding that they might understand the scriptures" (Luke 24:45). In the same way the spiritual presence of Jesus still opens the understanding of his lovers who are keen in their desire toward Him, bringing to their remembrance by the ministering of angels the words and content of Holy Scripture unsought and unprompted, one after another. And then He readily expounds the Word he sends, however difficult or mysterious.

The more difficult the Scriptures and the further from the reach of the human intellect, the more delectable is the true revealing of it when Jesus is Master. In attention to Him it is expounded and declared according to the letter, and in its moral, mystical and heavenly senses as well.[4]

---

3. See Psalm 119:11. For Hilton and his contemporaries, it was a matter of practical necessity that the word be "hidden in our hearts." One might go a long time between opportunities to read a Bible; one could, however, more regularly hear it read, and commit passages to memory. But Hilton's point here goes deeper, suggesting that it is the "hidden word" which is most accessible to the Holy Spirit's ministration to conscience.

4. Hilton is elaborating upon the following rhyming Latin hexameters, learned by biblical students in the Middle Ages:

Littera gesta docet, quid credas allegoria,
Moralis quid agas, quo tendas anagogia.

Wyclif (or one of his students) renders it:

De iiij undirstondynges

þe first is þe story, euene as þe wordis shulden tokne
þe secunde wit is allegoric, þt fyguriþ þyng þt men shulden trew
þe þridde wit is tropologik, þt bitokeneþ wit of vertues
þe fourþe is anagogik, þt betokeneþ þyng to hope in blis

MS Lincoln Cathedral 241 (fol. 265), a theological miscellany.

By the letter, which is easiest and most plain, our bodily nature is com-forted. In the moral quality of Holy Writ the soul is informed about vices and virtues, and given wisdom by which to distinguish one from the other. In the mystical sense the Word is illumined in such a way that we see the works of God in His Holy Church, and learn to apply readily the words of Scripture to Christ our head, and to the Church which is his mystical body. And the fourth sense, called the heavenly, belongs uniquely to the workings of love; this is when all the truth of Holy Writ is applied to Love. I use the term "heavenly" because this really is most like a heavenly experience.

The lover of Jesus is his friend, not because he deserves to be but be-cause Jesus in his merciful goodness makes him his friend in a true ac-cord. Accordingly, as to a true friend who pleases Him in love and does not merely serve Him in fear as a slave would do, He reveals his inti-mate concerns. This is what He was saying to his Apostles: "Henceforth I call you not servants, for the servant knoweth not what his lord doeth; but I have called you friends; for all things that I have heard of my Father I have made known unto you" (John 15:15).

To a soul washed clean, which has its spiritual palate so purified from the filth of fleshly love, the Word of God is a lively food and delectable sustenance. It tastes wonderfully sweet when it is chewed upon by spir-itual understanding. And this is because the Spirit of Life is hidden there and quickens all the faculties of the soul, filling them to overflowing with the sweetness of heavenly savor and spiritual delight. . . . Truly, one needs to have white teeth, sharp and clean, to bite into this spiritual bread. . . .

The mysteries of God's Word are enclosed under a key sealed with a signet on Jesus' finger—that is, the authority of the Holy Spirit. For this reason, without his love and his life no one may enter in. He alone has the key of knowledge in his keeping, as Holy Writ says, and He is Him-self the key, and He permits to enter whoever He will through the in-spiration of his grace, and does not break the seal.

Jesus does not do this for all his lovers in exactly the same degree. But to those specially inspired to seek after the truth of Holy Writ, with sincere devotion, prayer and much diligence in study and preparation He opens up his Word. And all those who seek Him may come to the discovery of Him there as our Lord Jesus chooses.

See now then how it is that grace opens up our spiritual eyes, clarify-ing the intelligence so that it is able to rise wonderfully above the frailty of corrupt nature. Grace gives the soul a new capacity to read God's Holy Word and to listen to it and think it; it enables the soul to under-stand truly and richly, and to interpret concepts and words literally spoken in their appropriate spiritual contexts. And this is no great marvel, for the Spirit who expounds and declares his Word in a clean soul, comforting it thereby, is the one who first made it, the Holy Spirit Himself. You should understand that this grace may be found just as well in illiterate as in educated persons—at least as pertains to the experience of truthfulness and a taste for things of the Spirit in general—even though illiterate folks do not see all the particulars, which are not in themselves in any case ultimately necessary.

When the soul is thus enabled to have access to Scripture and is enlightened by grace, then it likes to be alone sometimes, away from the constraints of community and its conversation, so as to freely test its intellectual faculties in probing the truths contained in holy writing. And then come to the mind enough words, good ideas, and concepts to occupy it fully, ordinately, and in serious reflection for a long while.

What comfort and spiritual delight a soul may then feel in this good spiritual exercise through its various illuminations: inward perception, intimate knowing and sudden graces of the Holy Spirit! And the soul may have these by measuring itself against Scripture and in no other way. I believe that no one shall fall into [doctrinal] error as long as his teeth—his inner faculties—are kept white and clean from spiritual pride or mere curiosity of natural intellect. I believe that David was feeling exuberant delight in this kind of reflection on the Word when he said, "How sweet are thy words unto my taste! yea, sweeter than honey to my mouth!" (Psalm 119:103). That is, "Lord Jesus, your holy words indited in Holy Writ and brought to my remembrance through grace are sweeter to my taste, the affection of my soul, than honey is to my mouth." Truly this is a fair and honest work, without painful labor, which lets us see Jesus so richly.

You will recall that there is one kind of vision of Jesus that I have spoken of before, and that is not as He *is*, but as He is clothed under the likeness of works and words, "in a glass enigmatically" (1 Corinthians 13:12), in a mirror and by a likeness, as the Apostle says.[5]

Jesus is boundless power, wisdom and goodness, righteousness, integrity, holiness and mercy. And yet we know that what Jesus is in Himself in glory no soul may see or hear. By the effect of his working He may, however, be seen in the light of grace. His power is seen in his making all creation out of nothing; his wisdom is seen in creation's ordinate disposition and his goodness in redeeming his creatures; his mercy is seen in the forgiveness of sins; his holiness in gifts of grace; his righteousness in severe punishing of sin; his integrity in true rewarding of

5. Vulgate: *per speculum in aenigmate.*

good stewardship. And all this is expressed in the Scriptures, and this is what the soul sees in Holy Writ, along with all other related things.

Know well that gracious understandings of Holy Writ, as well as other writings, are prompted by grace. The Scriptures are nothing else but love letters, epistles between a loving soul and Jesus its beloved or, as I shall say more truly, between Jesus the true lover and the souls loved by Him. He has a great tenderness of love toward all his chosen, his adopted children who are still enclosed in the clay of this bodily life. Therefore, though He is absent from them, hid high above in the bosom of the Father and fulfilled in the delights of the blessed Godhead, nevertheless He thinks about them and visits them often through his gracious spiritual presence. He comforts them by his letters of Holy Writ, expelling heaviness and irritation from their hearts, banishing doubts and fears, making them glad and merry in Himself. And in his Word He offers true promises to all who are his namesakes and who live meekly in obedience to his will.

St. Paul says, "For whatsoever things were written aforetime were written for our learning, that we through patience and comfort of the scriptures might have hope" (Romans 15:4; cf. 2 Timothy 3:16-17). This is another work of contemplation, to see Jesus in the Scriptures once our spiritual eyes have been opened. The clearer our sight is in beholding, the more comforted will be our affection in the tasting. Even a little savor of Holy Writ felt in a pure soul should make it set a small price on all the knowledge of the seven liberal arts and other worldly subtlety. For the result of scriptural knowledge is salvation of the soul unto eternal life, while the result of the other is mere vanity and passing fancy, unless it is first converted by grace to serve a higher purpose.

JOHN WYCLIF

from
The Authority of Sacred Scripture

Wyclif wrote *De Veritate Sacrae Scripturae,* his major hermeneutic work, from about 1376 to 1377, well after he had become established as Oxford's leading philosopher and most controversial theologian.[1] This was a time of much political and spiritual turmoil in the church, when the concept of a reliable magisterium safeguarding Scripture and tradition had been badly undermined. Particularly distressing was the century-long politicization of the papacy following the removal of the papal court to Avignon in 1309 under Clement V. The papacy had continued there despite great opposition and was about to be split between two factions of cardinals—one French, the other Italian—with popes in both Rome and Avignon. Wyclif and others could see the Great Schism coming (as it did in 1378), and while it was to last only a little less than forty years, it produced an almost metaphysical sense of crisis among European Christians of all classes and callings.

Another, more immediate, motivation for Wyclif's drive to get through the tattered magisterium to an authoritative regrounding of Christian faith and practice in Scripture itself was his sense that the formal study of biblical theology in the universities was suffering from a kind of congestive failure and was on the verge of collapse. Bogged down in methodological disputation, many theologians were simply not concerned about matters of biblical authority. Scholastic in their approach—and dependent therefore on Aristotelian categories of logic and modes of inquiry—they were more concerned with the elaboration and defense of theoretical models than they were with any application of the text to life. What Wyclif sets out to do in the passage translated here is to argue the need for approaching Scripture humbly on its own terms rather than forcing onto it alien linguistic and logical models.

From early on Wyclif was committed to rectifying and reordering confused priorities and to rerooting the faith and practice of the church in Scripture—the *lex Christi* ("law of Christ") as he liked to call it—which alone could be for him the benchmark for theological thinking and spiritual life. It is this concern which led to his significant impact upon English spirituality at the end of the fourteenth century.

---

1. For the entire text see *De Veritate Sacrae Scripturae,* ed. Rudolf Buddensieg, 3 vols. (London: Wyclif Society, 1905–1907; reprint, New York and London: Johnson Reprints, 1966). A translation, with notes and commentary, is currently being prepared by Michael Treschow and David L. Jeffrey; the translations which appear here derive from that larger work.

I. The Character of Scripture's Language

IN EXPOUNDING OR INTERPRETING SCRIPTURE one must learn a new grammar and a new logic, as is made clear through the Blessed Gregory and other saints who, on Scripture's authority, expound new senses of Scripture's terms which are not to be found in books of grammar. Where, I ask, except in the teaching of Scripture, is it found that the earth is hell, a virgin, God, the elements, heavenly life, flesh, protoplasm, and the machine of the world? The same is the case with each and every similar equivocation which are taken now in the literal sense and now in the mystical. So when interpreting Holy Scripture we should reject the childish sense and accept the sense which God teaches in accordance with the words of the apostle in 1 Corinthians 13: "When I was a child, I understood as a child, I spoke as a child, but when I became a man, I discarded those things which were childish."

For this reason the Blessed Dionysius expressly says in the *Divine Names* 4 that:

> It is, I think, irrational and foolish not to attend to the force of the meaning but to the words being used, for this is not the characteristic of those wanting to understand divine things, but of those receiving bare words.[2]

Grosseteste . . . adds to this an example:

> There are sentences in which one finds the noun *ereos* and the verb *ereo*[3] used to designate divine and chaste love. [These words] are as becoming in this love as they are disgraceful in base love. And so those who hear the noun *ereos* placed in divine sentences and understand through it the vehemence of false love, as it is common to do with the force of the word's meaning in common speech, do not attend to what is set in holy sentences but to the words as they are commonly taken, which is foolish and irrational.

. . . It is clear then that ancient theologians strove to understand the Scripture's sense and to dismiss other senses that belong to the unfaith-

---

2. Dionysius the Areopagite (Pseudo-Dionysius), a writer of about the sixth century, was significantly influenced by the Neoplatonists, especially Plotinus and Proclus. He in turn greatly influenced the theologians of the school and abbey of St. Victor in Paris, especially Hugh, as well as major thinkers such as Bonaventure and Aquinas. Many of the mystics also placed great value on his work. See *Deonise Hid Diuinite*, ed. Phyllis Hodgson, Early English Text Society, O.S. 231 (1955; reprint, London: Oxford University Press, 1958), for a Middle English "translation."

3. Robert Grosseteste was Bishop of Lincoln early in the previous century, a kind of spiritual father to the English Franciscans and one of Wyclif's favorite authors.

ful or the "childish." And so just as a child who learns first the alphabet, second to syllabify, third to read, and fourth to understand has in each of those stages his own sense [or understanding] that is distinctly intent upon that which he first learns, so afterwards he throws off his first sense on account of confusion. Similarly a theologian first learns the teaching of grammar; second he learns the grammar of Scripture which, when the first grammar is left behind, accommodates itself to the understanding; third he leaves behind sensible signs and attends to the sense of the author, until; fourth, he sees at last the book of life without a veil. People of every sort have a similar order of progress when they attend to or learn a task, because as they reach toward perfection they abandon the imperfect, since that would confuse them and hold them back from the end to which they move. For since the sense of Scripture that the Holy Spirit imparted is the fruit which is chiefly to be acquired, who among the faithful would doubt that pages and the husk of words should be put aside except insofar as they dispose [one] to this sense by leading to it? For if they lead away [from the Truth] they are to be condemned as poison. And this is the one reason that Christ and many saints did not write anything except in the sense of writing on the tablets of the heart, since this is the place in which Scripture's translation becomes more perfect.

Augustine and other saints teach this thought very often. In his homily on Psalm 120, Augustine alludes to a verse in Isaiah 2, "In the last days the mountain of the Lord will be manifest and established in the top of the mountains" (v. 2) and observes:

> Behold where one is to ascend to. But do not think of something earthly. Though you have heard "mountain," you should not think of the high places of some land, though you hear "stone" and "rock," you are not to understand some kind of hardness, though you hear "lion," you should not think of livestock. He is none of these things in himself, but he became everything for your sake.[4]

Likewise in his comments on Psalm 139:6 ("your knowledge is too wonderful for me"), he expounds a verse from Exodus 33: "You shall see my back parts" (v. 23):

> Far be it from us to conceive of the majesty of the Lord as if he had a face in some part of him and a back in another. For if anyone conceives of God

---

4. *Enarrationes in Psalmos* 120.1.43-49. Augustine's commentaries on Psalms are available in an abridged translation in *Saint Augustine: Expositions on the Book of Psalms*, vol. 8 of *Nicene and Post-Nicene Fathers of the Christian Church*, first series, ed. Philip Schaff (Grand Rapids: Eerdmans, n.d.).

in this way what does it avail him that the temples have been closed? He makes an idol in his heart.[5]

He also says, "There are great mysteries in these words," and he explains the psalm by telling how God spoke through his angel to Moses, the representative of the Jewish nation, and how he saw the humanity of Christ figured in the back parts, but which kept from him the divinity signified through his face.[6]

See how this saint labels people who falsely misapply the Scripture in this way as idolaters. And so in general he nowhere yields up any of Scripture's authoritative figures which he recites in the form in which they were set out; but he also discards anything which appears to be false. He observes this in his comments on Psalm 67: "May God have mercy upon us and bless us":

> God our Father is very aptly called a husbandman; for the apostle said, "You are the God's husbandry, God's building" (1 Corinthians 3:9). But in visible things of this sort a vine is not a building, nor is a building a vineyard. We, however, are the Lord's vineyard, since he tends us for fruit; and we are the Lord's building, since he tends us for inhabitation.[7]

And the conclusion follows: God, however, who can do all things, is our husbandman, and so we are secure. In case someone should want evidence that statements of this sort should be granted, he later adds, "Someone may reply, 'On the one hand you say that the apostles are husbandmen, and then you say that God is our husbandman,'" to which Augustine's response is as follows:

> I indeed say that the apostles were husbandmen, since they said, "I planted, Apollos watered" (1 Corinthians 3:6). If I say it no one should believe it, but if Christ said it, alas for anyone who does not believe it. What then did Christ say? "I am the vine, you are the branches, and my father is the husbandman" (John 15:1).[8]

See how Augustine labels those who denied the statements of Scripture as blasphemers. It appears more devout then to allow the words of Scripture in their catholic sense than to make them impossible by restricting them to a bare literal sense. So Augustine adds a rule at the end of his discussion of the same psalm: "If some similes are given to you, if you find them in Scripture, believe them."[9] And so Augustine often says to those opposing him, "Why do I say this? For this reason: because

5. *Enarrationes in Psalmos* 139.6.37-41.
6. *Enarrationes in Psalmos* 139.6.41-90.
7. *Enarrationes in Psalmos* 67.1.16-21.
8. *Enarrationes in Psalmos* 67.1.42-45.
9. *Enarrationes in Psalmos* 67.10.38-39.

Scripture says so." For example, in his eleventh epistle to Paulinus he writes, "If you ask whether God can be seen, I answer that he can be; if you ask for proof, I answer that in Scripture, which is absolutely true, one reads, 'Blessed are the pure in heart, for they shall see God'" (Matthew 5:8). And the same is the case with the most obscure truths, all of which he very capably drew forth from the witness of the Scriptures. This saint did not fear arguments made on the grounds of similitude, through which God was heard, smelt, tasted, and felt even with regard to his deity, because he understood the analogy between the image of the mind and the image of the body with its members. . . .

II. The Character of Scripture's Logic

Furthermore, Scripture's logic is permissible and useful for anyone, and so it is to be imitated. For it was given to the church of Christ, in that Christ is also the head of the church. . . .

With regard to utility and sufficiency it is clear that the logic of truth that is shown in Matthew 5: "Let your speech be yes, yes, or no, no" (v. 37) suffices for every logical communication necessary to the pilgrim, because in keeping it in its entirety a person would not sin with his tongue and doubtlessly would be perfect. A logic which leads so shortly to such a useful end, and on account of which all knowledge or doctrine exists, is very useful. Furthermore, I cannot help but think that every other sophistical precision beyond that which teaches how to remove "poison" is superflous and harmful, since in and of itself this leads more directly to the ultimate end. So then, "what is more is from evil" (Matthew 5:37). And thus it is not necessary for salvation to pursue dialectical methods;[10] rather, these things are simply a matter of intellectual curiosity. In this we go beyond the ancient saints, since the logic of Holy Scripture is all that is necessary for salvation.

From this we may infer that a Christian should speak Scripture's words on Scripture's authority in the form that Scripture itself displays. When this position is held it follows that Scripture should be imitated in logic, and therefore our conclusion follows suit. The major premise is clear from those priests of Christ who use the words of Scripture in discourse, in the ministration of the sacraments, in preaching, and in the exposition of Scripture. For unless Scripture's logic in the verbal, literal sense were correct both in its historical and sapiential parts,[11] Holy

10. I.e., the normal methodologies of scholastic theology.
11. By the *sapiential part* Wyclif refers to "wisdom literature" in the broadest sense—not only the wisdom books, such as Proverbs or Job, but all "teaching," such as that of Paul in the New Testament or the Law in the Old Testament. Sometimes he also means by this term parables and other figurative discourse.

Scripture would be exceedingly evil, and the minor premise of the argument is evident from this: that Scripture's logic is confirmed in the form of its words and in its mode of speaking. But it has been established that just as the Christian should, on the authority of Holy Scripture, state his thought according to the logic and pattern suggested by Scripture, so he should by the same authority have its form of words, since the highest and most humble authority for this has been given by the best of all teachers. How then would he who puts this authority aside not incur the anger of that Teacher? John of Paris touches on this sin in his comments on Jeremiah 2:13: "The people have done two evils; they have forsaken me, the fountain of living water, and they have dug for themselves cisterns which cannot hold water." He says:

> The knowledge of Holy Scripture, which is divine or heavenly, since it lacks the intermeddling of earthliness, is to be learned before all things because of its authority and usefulness. But the knowledge of human tradition, which on the one hand is troubled with earthliness and on the other hand lacks wisdom and includes blasphemy, is to be ejected like Ishmael.

And the Lord himself complains about this sort of thing in Isaiah 5:24: "They have rejected the law of the Lord." His cause is touched on in Isaiah 8, where He condemns Israel, "because this people rejected the waters of Shiloh which flow on in silence" (v. 6), and in Matthew 15, where Jesus says, "You have transgressed the commandment of God for the sake of your tradition" (v. 6).

In this sense, Scripture's logic has [among contemporary theologians] effectively come under unwarranted judgment, since it gets condemned when Scripture is condemned. Now in fact Scripture's logic would not be adequate but far from it, unless it adequately taught every mode of speech necessary for the Christian. If it should be asked where Holy Scripture teaches logic, I say as I did above, that it does so in Christ's precept, "Let your speech be yes, yes, and no, no." For Christ, the best Teacher, gives this as a principle of logic—and not merely at the level of statements—because at one and the same time it fully instructs the church both in behavior and in the logic of verbal communication, and it is sufficiently basic as a principle that these things must be learned. For whoever keeps this maxim will keep the truth when he speaks within himself and audibly, whether in affirmation or negation. And he will exclude false duplicity if in all things he has kept an agreement of mind and voice. Since then this principle, which contains everything, comprehends the science of the voice and, on the basis of that science, taught this logic [consistent with it], would any faithful Christian charge it with any defect or artifice? It was not, however, Holy Scripture's concern to discuss in particular other private logics for the sake of explaining their imperfections and various distances from the highest purpose of Scripture.

This logic, then, which leads so directly to that highest purpose without tumultuous deviations, is absolutely reliable. An indication of this is that other logics are modish and far too multiple. They are modish since, as is clear in Oxford, each novel or foreign system of logic lasts scarcely twenty years. Instead they change often because through the love of personal pride there are as many varied logics as there are professors of logic.[12] Scripture's logic, however, stands forever, since it is established on unbreakable truth independently of fame or the favor of men.

12. Again, the point is that the center of academic debate in Wyclif's time is controversy between competing systems.

JOHN PURVEY

from
The Prologue to the Wycliffite Bible

Scriptural Authority and Spiritual Authenticity

It is doubtful that Wyclif himself is responsible for a very significant portion of the actual labors of translation in the Wycliffite Bible. The first and largest section of the Old Testament was done by his student Nicholas of Hereford, who was later a canon of the Abbey of St. Mary of the Meadows, Leicester, and finally canon of Hereford Cathedral. John Purvey, another of Wyclif's followers and for a time his personal secretary or assistant, may be responsible for much of the balance of the first version of the Wycliffite Bible, completed by about 1384 (though it is possible that Wyclif himself completed the text while in forced retirement from Oxford at his rectory in Lutterworth.)

The Prologue material here is certainly indebted to Wyclif but was actually written by John Purvey while he himself was in hiding at Bristol. During this time Purvey also completely reworked the early translation, producing a much more idiomatic version. The fifteen chapters of the General Prologue were completed by 1396 as a defense of the whole enterprise, making the case for direct scriptural knowledge as a foundation for faith. The selection which follows is from chapters 12 and 13 of the General Prologue.

HOLY SCRIPTURE CONTAINS ALL PROFITABLE TRUTH, and all other branches of knowledge are hidden in the virtue of its meanings or understandings, just as wine is contained in grapes, ripe grain is contained in a seed, branches are contained in the roots, and whole trees contained in kernels.[1]

Holy Scripture condemns sophistry, and says that one who speaks sophistically, or by sophisms, shall be hateful, and indeed shall be found fraudulent in everything, as we are told in chapter 37 of Ecclesiasticus (v. 23).

. . . By this principle of St. Augustine, and by the four understandings of Holy Scripture, and by a wise perception of figurative language, accompanied with good living and meekness and study of the Bible,

1. The text footnotes Robert Grosseteste, thirteenth century Bishop of Lincoln, an Oxford theologian who substantially influenced both Wyclif and the first English Franciscans. The citation is from his sermon "Praemonitus a Venerabili Patre."

simple persons are able to understand something of the text of Holy Writ, and able [thereby] greatly to edify themselves and others. But for the sake of God's love, you who are simple must beware of pride, vain jangling and chiding against proud seminarians and phony religious, answering meekly and prudently to these enemies of God's law and praying heartily for them that God of his great mercy will give to them a true knowledge of the Scriptures, with meekness and charity. And always be ready, whatever person teaches any of God's truth, to adopt that meekly and with great thanksgiving to God. But if anyone on earth or any angel of heaven teaches you something which is contrary to Holy Writ, or anything against reason and charitable love, flee from him as from the foul devil of hell. Hold steadfastly in life and death to the truth and freedom of the holy Gospel of Jesus Christ, observing meekly the sayings and laws of men only inasmuch as they accord with Holy Writ and good conscience—and no farther, either for life nor death.

Also, Holy Scripture is known better by means of its similitudes and dark sayings. It removes the sense of impediment if, as we ought, we assume and believe that something that is written in Holy Scripture, even though it is now hidden or unknown to us, will prove to be at last something better and truer than we are able at first to understand by ourselves. To the good of our worship and our spiritual healing the Holy Spirit has so ordained Holy Scriptures that in straightforward passages He has placed the remedy for our spiritual hunger, and thus overcome the problem of obscurity [of dark passages]; for almost nothing is said in the obscure passages which is not found plainly said in other places.

Therefore, before everything else it is necessary that we be converted by the fear of God, and next that we become meek in faithfulness, not contradicting Holy Scripture wherever it is understood (even though it smites us at the point of our own sin), or even where it is *not* understood, imagining that we might have a better understanding, or presuming to command or teach a "better" thing. By the gift of reverence and piety I can come then to the next level of knowledge, for which purpose every fruitful and scriptural person exercises himself [in the word]—which is to discover no other thing than how to love God for his own sake and to love his neighbor for the sake of God.

Accordingly, this reverence by which one reflects upon the judgment of God, and the faithfulness by which he must necessarily believe and yield place to the authority of holy books, compels him in turn to be self-critical, in that the Gospel knowledge of good hope prompts a person not to self-promotion but to self-admonishment. By this desire, or good will, one obtains with diligent prayers the comfort of God's help, so as not to be broken down by despair. At this point a person commences to be in the fourth degree of spiritual strength, in which one hungers and thirsts after righteousness.

Next, in the fifth stage of growth—that is, in the counsel of mercy, he purges his soul of its clamor and unquiet covetousness after material things, and he grows to despise that which contaminates the soul, and actively loves God and his neighbors, even his enemies. By this means he ascends to a sixth stage, where he purges the "eye" of the soul, by which "eye" God may be seen, as much as He may be seen of those who are dying to this world, and as much as they are able for. For it is to the degree that they become dead to this world that in faith and love they may see God, and it is to the degree that they live for this world that they do *not* see God.

In this stage of spiritual development, in which a person becomes dead to this world, he prefers neither himself nor his neighbor to the truth of Holy Writ. Accordingly, such a spiritual person shall be so simple and pure of heart that neither to please others nor to protect himself from attack will he draw away from the truth. Such a child ascends to true wisdom, which is the seventh and last degree of spiritual maturity which he occupies in peace and rest. St. Augustine says all this at the beginning of his second book of *Christian Doctrine*.[2] Here is a model for blessed introduction, by these seven stages of maturation, to the knowledge of Holy Scripture in this life, to have here restedness of spirit and afterward complete rest of body and soul, without end.

Alas! What do those proud and self-serving wretches make of Holy Scripture who still pursue the world and carnal pleasures and who will not reform themselves and turn from such cursedness? They deceive themselves, as well as those people who think of them as experts; they are actually empty fools. Thus they deepen their own damnation, as well as that of others who are led by their folly, and they blaspheme God. These worldly fools should know that a holy life is a lantern to bring a person to true knowledge, as Chrysostom says, and that the fear and love of God is both the beginning and the perfection of knowledge and wisdom. But since these fleshly apes and worldly moles neither have the beginning of wisdom nor desire it, why are they expounding

---

2. Augustine's *On Christian Doctrine* was a foundational text for medieval hermeneutics and medieval ideas about language generally. Purvey here alludes to *On Christian Doctrine* 2.7.9-11; he draws heavily on this work throughout his Prologue. Wyclif, throughout his Latin works on Scripture, notably *On the Authority of Sacred Scripture*, follows and champions this work of Augustine. But in his imitation of the Beatitudes as a pattern of exposition Purvey also illustrates Wyclif's own principle that the Christian ought to "speak Scripture's words on Scripture's authority in the form that Scripture itself displays" (see p. 336).

Holy Scripture to their own disgrace and that of others? As long as pride and covetousness of worldly goods and honors is rooted in their heart, they are really making homage to Satan, offering him both body and soul in all their clever "interpretation" and invention.

Such fools ought to realize that spiritual wisdom shall not enter into an evil-willed soul, neither shall it dwell in a body subject to sin. They should know what Jesus Christ says, that the Father of heaven hides the secrets of Holy Scripture from the wise and prudent—that is, those who are wise and prudent by human standards, and in their own eyes—and yet reveals them to meek and humble persons. Therefore, you worldly fools, begin by repenting of your sins and forsaking pride and covetousness. Become meek, fear God in all things; love Him in all things, and your neighbor as yourself. Then you shall profit in the study of Holy Writ.

But alas, alas, alas! The greatest abomination that ever was heard among Christian scholars is now proposed in England, by worldly clergy and pretended religious, and in the leading university in our country, as many reliable persons have been reporting with great protestation. This horrible and devilish cursedness is proposed by Christ's enemies and traitors to all Christian people, that no person should study theology or Holy Writ until he has done his examination in arts—that is, commenced upon his degree and been regent for two years afterward! This adds up to nine or ten years after he has completed grammar schooling before he would be permitted to study Holy Writ, even if he has a good intelligence, has worked very hard, and experienced good results through the nine or ten years since completing his schooling in grammar.[3]

This seems utterly the devil's purpose—that few persons or none should study and come to know the law of God. But God says to us by Amos concerning the three great transgressions of Damascus and the fourth, "I shall not convert them." On this passage Jerome suggests that the first sin is to think evil, the second is to consent to wayward thoughts, the third is to engage actively in sin and the fourth sin is not to repent afterwards, but take pleasure in the sinning.[4] But the name

3. The text here seems clearly to be aimed at an audience which includes academic theologians and clerics in training at Oxford. The proposed change would have the effect of ensuring that the majority of ordinands would get through their university years without firsthand study of Scripture!

4. Cf. Augustine's division of the process of sin into four steps: (1) suggestion, as when the serpent speaks; (2) taking pleasure in sinful thought, as when Eve thinks it over; (3) consent of the rational faculty, as when Adam agrees; and (4) the sin in deed. See *On the Trinity*, 7-12; *On the Sermon on the Mount*, 12.34-35.

Damascus is interpreted "drinking blood" or "spilling blood." Lord! Whether Oxford drinks and spills blood, by the slaying of living persons and by acts of sodomy, thus losing a part of human blood whereby a child might be formed, let them judge which know these things. And whether Oxford drinks the blood of sin, and stirs up others in the land to sin by the sinful boldness of its scholars, let them judge the matter justly who have seen these things with their own eyes and know it by experience.

Look now and see where Oxford is engaged in three horrible sins, and a fourth, concerning which God will not rest until He punishes it. There was a time when children and young arts students were as devout and pure as angels by comparison with these others; now it is said that they are characterized by pride and obsession with fashion, and by envy, covetousness, lechery, gluttony and idleness. There was a time when clergymen and theologians were holy and devout, utterly despising the world and living like angels in meekness, purity, sovereign chastity and charity, and they taught the law of God truly in deed as well as in word. Now it is said that they are as indulgent of their mouths and bellies and as covetous as any worldly persons, and that they flatter and tell lies in their preaching in order both to eschew physical persecution and to gain advancement.

That the first great sin [i.e., preoccupation with evil thoughts] is a general problem in the university is much to be feared and, indeed, may be observed directly. The second horrible sin is sodomy, and the strong protection of sodomy, something which is known to many persons in this kingdom and was a matter raised at the last parliament. Alas! Divines who should surpass other persons in purity and holiness, almost as the angels of heaven surpass frail mortals in virtue, these are the ones most implicated in this cursed sin against nature. The third horrible sin is simony[5] and the breaking of [ordination] vows in the house of assembly,[6] which should be a house of righteousness and holiness where evils are redressed. This business of simony, in all its shades and sordidness, is in fact much worse and more of an abomination than the physical sodomy. Yet from each of these three abominations God will still graciously convert clergymen if they do true penance and give themselves wholly to virtuous living.

But as for this fourth and greatest abomination now proposed, which is to prevent Christians—priests and curates—from freely learning the

5. See Acts 8:9-24. Promising spiritual reward in exchange for material profit was then, as now, a flourishing business.

6. The author reveals his familiarity with the meaning of the Greek word *ekklesia* (assembly), which he here applies to the local church.

law of God until they have spent altogether nine or ten years in the study of arts subjects (which in themselves contain many strong errors of heathen cultures against Christian belief), it seems likely that God will not cease from taking vengeance until this and other things are punished very severely. For it appears that worldly clergy and counterfeit religious persons are doing this in order that ordinary persons of intelligence and insight will not be able to know God's law or preach it generally against sins in the country.

But be advised, you who are worldly clergy and counterfeit religious, that God both can and may, if it pleases Him, quickly enable ordinary people outside the university to know as much of Holy Writ as professors inside it.[7] And perhaps it would not therefore be such a loss if men of good will were no longer poisoned with the errors of heathen men for nine or ten years, but that they should simply live well always and study Holy Writ, aided by [the work of] great commentators[8] old and new, and preach truly and freely against open sinfulness to the day of their death. Look, therefore, at what Jerome says in his commentary on Amos. Where God prophesies evils which are to come, it is in order that people may hear and amend themselves and thus be delivered from the peril which draws nigh, or so that, if they despise his warning, their punishment is the more just.

May God in his mercy grant that clergymen hear the great vengeance [against them] threatened by God, and reform themselves truly in order that God spare them. For if they do not reform themselves, they are evidently heretics hardened in their sins. But see what Jerome in his commentary says against heretics, and by way of recommending Holy Scripture. He says in reference to Amos, "Heretics who serve their belly in gluttony are called with full propriety fat oxes—utterly disgraceful bovines." And he reminds us that "we ought to take Holy Scripture in three manners: first, we ought to understand it literally, and do all things in it to which we are commanded; secondly [we ought to take it]

7. By *worldly clerkis* Purvey probably refers both to academics in the university, where most training for the priesthood was obtained (hence, effectively, "seminarians"), and also to ordained clergy already having parish responsibilities. *Feyned religious* implies principally those who have taken vows in a religious order, usually one of the orders of friars (Franciscan, Dominican, Carmelite, or Augustinian), but who have done so out of ulterior motives (e.g., a teaching position in the university) rather than a true calling or vocation.

8. The original word is *doctours*, which implies the great theologians of the church, typically including in the first rank Augustine, Ambrose, Jerome, and Gregory, and then Aquinas, Bonaventure, and others whose work had become authoritative by that time.

allegorically, that is for its spiritual understanding; and in a third [level of reading], with reference to the bliss of things to come."[9]

Though the commentary of Lyra[10] has only just come to me, see also what he says about the understanding of Holy Scripture. He writes as follows in his second prologue to the Bible:

> John says in chapter five of the Apocalypse, "I saw a book written within and without in the hand of him that sat on the throne" (Revelation 5:1). This book is Holy Scripture, which is said to be written without in respect of its literal understanding, and within with respect to its hidden and spiritual understanding.

Further, in his first prologue [to the Bible] Lyra declares that there are four levels of understanding of Holy Writ, saying as follows:

> Holy Writ has this unique quality, that under one literal sense it comprehends many understandings, for the principal author of Holy Writ is God himself, in whose power it is not only to use words to signify a thing as men do, but also to use *things* which are themselves signified by words to signify other things. Therefore, by the signifying of *words* the literal understanding—historical sense—of Holy Scripture is obtained, whereas by that signifying which is accomplished by *things* is yielded up the privy, or spiritual, understanding which has three modes: allegorical, moral or tropological, and anagogical. If things signified by words [e.g., in the Old Testament] are referred in such a manner as to signify things that we ought to *believe* in the New Testament, they ought to be understood allegorically. If things are referred to the matter of things we ought to *do*, then it is the moral or tropological sense [that applies]. If things are given reference to things that should be *hoped for* as the bliss to come, then it is a matter of anagogical sense. The letter teaches us what has been done; the allegorical teaches us what you are to believe; the moral teaches what you are to do; the anagogical teaches where you ought to go. Of the application of these four senses or understandings a good example may be provided by the name "Jerusalem." Literally, Jerusalem signifies a city which was once the principal city of the kingdom of Judah, founded by Melchizedek and then afterward enlarged and made strong by Solomon. In its moral sense it signifies a faithful soul, which sense is implied in the fifty-second chapter of Isaiah, which says, "Arise and adorn thyself, Jerusalem." By the allegorical sense, it signifies the church fighting against

9. The text refers to Jerome's second commentary on Amos, chapter 4.

10. Nicholas of Lyra (c. 1270–1349), a French Franciscan whose postils (commentaries on the Bible), especially those on the Old Testament, were widely influential. His glosses on the text of Scripture came to rival those of the *Ordinary Gloss,* the standard marginal commentary in the thirteenth century. Lyra knew Hebrew—a fact of some interest to Wyclif—and there is some suggestion that he may have been a Jewish convert who had previously received rabbinical training.

sins and demons, according to which sense it is said in the twenty-first chapter of the Apocalypse, "I saw the holy city new Jerusalem coming down from heaven as a spouse adorned for her husband." By the anagogical sense it signifies the church reigning in bliss, and by this sense it is said in the fourth chapter of Galatians that "that Jerusalem which is above, which is our mother, is free." And as an example is provided by one name, so it might be established in one exegesis, and as in one, so in another.

Lyra says all these things in his first prologue to the Bible.

Nonetheless, all spiritual understandings yield place to and require the literal understanding as their foundation. Just as a building which is bowed away from its foundation is disposed to fall down, so a spiritual exposition that is at odds with the literal sense ought to be regarded as unseemly and inappropriate, or at the least less seemly and appropriate [than one which is not]. Therefore it is necessary for those who would profit in their study of Holy Scripture to begin with understanding of the literal sense, primarily because it is by the literal sense alone and not by the spiritual readings that an argument may be sustained or doubtful matters proven or questions properly framed, as Augustine said in his Epistle to Vincent, the Donatist.

In Defense of Translating Scripture

Chapter 15 of the General Prologue to the Wycliffite Bible includes a technical discussion of problems in translating the Latin Bible into English idiom, but its central concern—represented in this next selection— is to situate the present translation in a historical tradition of translations, and to underscore the status of this translation as provisional.

CHRIST SAYS that the Gospel shall be preached in all the world (Matthew 24:14; Mark 16:15), and David [foreseeing these things] says of the apostles and their preaching, "their sound spread out into every land, and their words went out into the ends of the world" (Psalm 19:4). David also says that "the Lord shall tell in his writings of peoples and princes that were in it"—that is, Holy Church (Psalm 86:6 [Vg.]). Jerome, in his commentary on this last verse observes, "Holy Writ is the Scripture of the people, since it was made for the purpose that all people should know it," and the princes of the church that were in it are the apostles, who had the authority to write down Holy Writ. In the same fashion as the apostles wrote down Holy Scripture by the authority and confirmation of the Holy Spirit, so by the Holy Spirit the translation becomes Holy Scripture for us and the ground of the faith of Christians, although the unique worthiness [of the Apostles' own writing] no one has after them, however holy or knowledgeable he is, as Jerome observes on that verse.[11]

And Christ says of the Jews who cried "Hosanna" to Him in the temple, that if they were to be silent the stones should cry (Luke 19:40). Now by stones is implied those heathen peoples who worship stones for their gods. Now since we English people are descended from heathens, we too, therefore, are implicated in these "stones" that should cry out Holy Writ. And as "Jews," when interpreted knowledgeably, signify clergy who ought to be acknowledging God by their repentance from sin and by their voice praising God, so our own ordinary lay persons,[12] in following the cornerstone which is Christ, are able to be seen as signified by stones which lie firm and steadfast in the foundation. For though covetous clergy are gone mad in simony, in heresy and many other sins, and despise and stop the proclamations of Holy Writ as much as they are able, yet the common people cry after Holy Writ to understand it and keep it at great cost and peril to their lives.

For these reasons and others, and with common charity toward the salvation of all persons in our kingdom whom God desires to have saved, a simple creature has translated the Bible out of Latin into English. First this simple creature had much work to do with various colleagues and helpers to gather up many old Bibles, as well as commentaries and glosses, in order to put together one Latin Bible which would be somewhat accurate.[13] Then, this creature has studied it freshly, the text with the glosses, and with such standard commentaries as he could get hold of, especially Lyra on the Old Testament, which has helped much in this work. Third, I have worked through the text in consultation with old grammarians and old theologians concerning hard words and difficult sayings, to discern how they might best be understood and translated. Then the fourth time through, the translator has worked to translate as clearly as he could according to the sense, and to

11. This is to argue for the preeminence of Scripture and the secondary status of the magisterium. It reflects Jerome's view that all translation is at some remove from the original, and hence that translating Scripture requires active cooperation of the Holy Spirit.

12. The text has *symple men,* which in the Prologue can imply ordinary laypersons but also those who hold themselves to be undistinguished, in which sense the author also employs the term elsewhere, as in the next paragraph.

13. One should remember that one of the hazards of an age of hand-copied books was the inevitability of miscopying and, on that count alone, widespread textual error. The author suggests additionally the possibility of unwarranted emendation or revision of the biblical text to suit diverse purposes.

have many good and knowledgeable colleagues present at the [final] correcting of the translation.

[The reader] ought first to know that the best translation from Latin to English is that which translates according to the sense and not merely word for word, in order that the meaning should be as plain or plainer in English as it is in Latin, without straying far from the literal [equivalents]. When an exact equivalent cannot be found in the translation, let the meaning itself always be complete and accessible, for the words ought to serve the intention and meaning; otherwise, they will be superfluous or false. . . .[14]

At the outset I purposed with God's help to make the meaning as true and open in English as it is in Latin, if not more faithful and accessible than in the Latin. And I pray for the sake of charity and the common profit of Christian souls that if any wise person find any faults in the faithfulness of this translation that he insert the true and plain meaning of Holy Writ [in the text].[15] But see that such a person examines his Latin Bible carefully first, for without doubt he shall find, if he consults many, that a great many Latin Bibles are filled with errors, especially some of the newer ones. The common Latin Bibles, in fact, that I have seen during my own life, have more need of correction than has this English Bible lately translated.

Where the Hebrew—by the witness of Jerome, Lyra, and other expositors—disagrees with our Latin Bibles, I have put in the margin, by way of a gloss, what the Hebrew says and, in some places further, how it should be understood.[16] And I did this most in the Psalter, which of all our books [of the Latin Bible] departs most from the Hebrew, since the church does not read the Psalms from the last translation of Jerome from the Hebrew, but from another [Latin] translation by someone else who had much less knowledge and less holiness of life than had Jerome. In fact, there are few books [of the Bible] which the church still reads from Jerome's translation, as may be proven by the proper originals of Jerome, for which he always provided a marginal commentary.

Whether I have translated as plainly (or more so) in English as does the Latin, let wise men who know both languages well, as well as the content of Holy Scripture, make the judgment. And whether I have

14. There follows here a discussion of special problems in translating Latin into English, along with the translator's resolutions for each in turn.

15. Hand correcting, of course, was much more natural and common in an age of manuscript books.

16. Wyclif's own Hebrew seems to have been largely derivative, and this was almost certainly true of the majority of his university followers. Purvey may have been an exception.

been successful or not, no doubt they, who know well the meaning of Holy Writ and English both and will work at these matters, with God's grace may make the Bible as faithful and accessible, yea and more so, in English than in Latin. And it seems beyond doubt to this simple man that with God's grace and hard work, men might expound the Bible much more clearly and succinctly in English than the ancient great doctors have expounded it in Latin, and much more to the point and on a better basis than many late commentators and expositors have done. But may God of his great mercy give us grace to live well and speak the truth in an appropriate manner, acceptable to God and his people, and not to waste our time, be it short or long, as God ordains.

However, some persons who appear wise and holy are arguing, "If people were now as holy as was Jerome, then they could translate out of Latin into English as he did out of the Hebrew and Greek into Latin; otherwise, they should not make a contemporary translation according to their own notion, on account of their lack of [comparable] holiness and knowledge." Though this argument may seem plausible,[17] it has no good foundation, either in reason or in charitable love. For in fact this argument stands more against Jerome, the first seventy translators [of the Septuagint], and against Holy Church than against simple men who now translate into English. For Jerome was not so holy as the apostles and evangelists whose books he translated into Latin, neither had he such preeminent gifts of the Holy Spirit as they had. To an even greater degree, the seventy translators were not so holy as Moses and the prophets, and especially David, neither had they such great gifts of God as had Moses and the prophets. Furthermore, Holy Church has approved not only the faithful translation of ordinary Christians who are steadfast in their faith, but also of open heretics who did away with many mysteries of Christ Jesus by guileful translation, as Jerome witnesses in one prologue to Job and in the prologue to Daniel.[18] Much more reasonably, then, the church in England may approve the faithful and complete translation of simple men who would not, for any good in earth, by their knowledge or power put away the least truth, yea, or the least little bit or letter of Holy Scripture that carries substantial

17. It could seem plausible because of the great reverence in which medieval people held ancient authorities, and the prevalent notion that since the fall all things tended to be in decline—hence implying a steady weakening of spiritual authority as time went on. The author does not so much challenge this notion as use it to his own purposes.

18. The Wycliffite Bible includes in its prefatory material the prologues of Jerome, which Wyclif held in great regard. These are printed in the Forshall and Madden edition (Oxford: Oxford University Press, 1850).

meaning or commendation. Nor ought they to argue about the holiness of persons now living this mortal life, for they know nothing about it, the matter being reserved for God's judgment. If they know any significant spiritual default in the lives of the translators or their helpers, let them lay blame for the fault in charity and with mercy. And let them not damn something which according to the law of God may be done lawfully—such as wearing a good cloak for awhile, or riding on a horse for a great journey—when they do not know the reasons for this being done. For such things may be done by simple men with as great charity and virtue as some have who are regarded as great and wise, when they permit themselves to ride in a gilt saddle, or to use cushions and beds and clothes of gold and silk along with other vanities of the world. May God grant pity, mercy, charity and love of common profit, and may such foolish judgments that are against reason and charitable love be put away.

Yet certain worldly clergy are asking insistently what spirit makes vigorous idiots to translate the Bible into English now, since the four great doctors of the church never dared to do this.[19] This argument is so vulgar that it requires no answer except silence or courteous scorn. For these great doctors were not English, nor were they conversant among English persons nor could they speak the English language. But they ceased not from their labors until they had Holy Writ in the mother tongue of their people. For Jerome, who was a Latin man by birth, translated the Bible out of both Hebrew and Greek and made extensive commentaries upon it. And St. Augustine and many other Latins expounded many parts of the Bible in Latin for the benefit of the Latin peoples among whom they dwelt. Latin was the common language of people around Rome and beyond into the continent, just as English is the common language of our own people. To this day the common people of Italy speak a corrupt Latin, as reliable men who have been in Italy bear witness. And the total number of translations out of the Greek into Latin passes human reckoning, as Augustine witnesses in the second book of his *On Christian Doctrine*. . . .[20] Therefore Grosseteste says

19. The "four great doctors" are St. Ambrose, St. Augustine, St. Jerome, and St. Gregory.

20. *On Christian Doctrine*, 2.11.16. Augustine's point was that the "infinite variety in Latin translations" forces us back to the original Greek, and that a knowledge of languages is an invaluable tool for the student of Scripture. Purvey, recognizing that the translators of the Wycliffite Bible were working from such a diversity of Latin translations, makes the case for translation by analogy with the "body" metaphor for the church. He takes translation to be a universal (catholic) exercise—that is, a continuous process of resolution of the corporate experience of Scripture into the vernacular language of a community.

that it was God's will that diverse persons should translate, and that a diversity of translations be in the church, for where one speaks obscurely, another will be more accessible.

Lord God, since at the beginnings of faith so many persons translated into Latin and to the great advantage of Latin peoples, let one simple creature of God translate into English for the profit of Christian peoples. For if worldly clergy would look well into their books and chronicles they would discover that Bede translated the Bible and expounded upon it extensively in Saxon, which was the English or common language of this country in his time. And not only Bede, but also King Alfred, who founded Oxford, translated at the end of his life the opening chapters of the Psalms into Saxon, and would have done more if he had lived longer. Also Frenchmen, Belgians and Britons have the Bible and other books of devotion and of exposition translated into their mother language. Why should not the English have the same in their mother tongue? I can give no good reason except the hypocrisy and negligence of clerics, unless it is that our people are denied such a grace and gift of God as a punishment for their past sins. May God in his mercy amend these evil causes, and cause our people to possess, know, and truly obey Holy Writ in life and unto death!

... A translator has great need to study well the meaning both before and after ... and he needs to be living a pure life, and to be very devout in his prayers, not having his wit preoccupied with worldly things, so that the Holy Spirit, author of all knowledge and wisdom and truth, may cover him in his work and suffer him not to err. ... In this way, with good living and great effort people may be able to come to a true and clear translation and a true understanding of Holy Writ, no matter how difficult it seems at the beginning. May God grant us all to know well and to well obey Holy Writ, and to suffer joyfully some pain for it at the last!

Amen.

selections from

The Wycliffite Bible

The first or *A* version of the Wycliffite translation, begun by Nicholas Hereford and probably completed by either John Purvey or Wyclif himself (c. 1384), is represented here by the selection which follows from the epistle to the Hebrews. In *A* the translation is word-for-word from the Latin of the Vulgate, with glosses in italics to clarify the sense. The second or *B* version (1396) is represented by the selections from Paul's first epistle to the Corinthians and the first epistle of John. Here Purvey's reworking tries to free itself from absolute literalism enough to capture the sense of the text. All three passages given are significant for the emphases of fourteenth-century spirituality and will serve to characterize the Wycliffite translations.

Hebrews 4:1-16

THERFORE DREDE WE, BRITHEREN, lest perauenture the biheeste of entrynge into his reste left, *or forsakyn,* ony of vs be gessid, *or demed,*[1] for to be aweye. Forsoth it is told to vs, as and to hem. And the word herd profitide not to hem, not meynt to feith of these thingis that thei herden. Forsoth we that han byleuyd schulen entre into rest, as he seyde, As I swoor in my wraththe, if thei schulen entre into my reste. And sotheli the werkis maad parfyt fro the ordynaunce of the world, forsothe he seide thus in sum place of the seueneth day, And God restide in the seueneth day from alle his werkis. And in this eftsoone, If thei schulen entre into my reste. Therfore for it leeueth, *or is ouer,* summen for to entre into it, and thei to whiche the firste it is told, entriden not for her vnbileue. Eftsoone he termyneth sum day, To day, seyinge in Dauith,[2] aftir so moche of tyme; as it is bifore seid, To day if ȝe han herd his vois, nyle ȝe hardne ȝoure hertis, as in the ilke wraththing. Forwhi if Jhesus hadde ȝouyn reste to hem, he schulde neuere speke of othere aftir that day. Therfore saboth halowing[3] is left to the peple of God. Forsoth he that entride into his reste, and he restide of his werkis, as and God of hise. Therfore haste we for to entre into that reste, that no man falle into the same ensaumple of vnbileue. Forsoth the word of God is quyk, and spedy in worching, and more able for to perse than al tweyne eggid

---

1. *Demed:* "judged."
2. I.e., "in the words of David" (Psalm 95:7-8).
3. The "sanctification" or holy observance of the Sabbath.

swerd, and entrynge, *or strecchinge,* til to departyng of soule, *or lyf,*[4] and spirit, and of ioyntouris and merewis, and departer, *or demer,* of thou3tis and intenciouns of hertis. And no creature is invisyble in the si3t of God. Forsothe alle thingis ben nakid and opyn to his y3en, to whom a word to vs. Therfore we hauynge a greet bischop, that perside heuenes, Jhesu, the sone of God, holde the confessioun, *or knowleching,* of oure feith.[5] Forsoth we han not a byschop, that may not suffre to gidere, *or haue compassioun,* to oure infirmytees, but temptid by alle thingis for lyknesse, withoute synne. Therfore go we with trist to the trone of his grace, that we gete mercy, and fynde grace in couenable help.

1 Corinthians 13:1–14:7

IF Y SPEKE with tungis of men and of aungels, and Y haue not charite, Y am maad as bras sownynge, or a cymbal tynkynge. And if Y haue prophecie, and knowe alle mysteries, and al kunnynge, and if Y haue al feith, so that Y meue hillis fro her place, and Y haue not charite, Y am nou3t. And if Y departe alle my goodis in to the metis of pore men, and yf Y bitake my bodi, so that Y brenne, and if Y haue not charite, it profitith to me no thing. Charite is pacient, it is benygne;[6] charite enuyeth not, it doith not wickidli, it is not blowun,[7] it is not coueytouse, it sekith not tho thingis that ben hise owne, it is not stirid to wraththe, it thenkith not yuel, it ioyeth not on wickidnesse, but it ioieth togidere to treuthe; it suffrith alle thingis, it beleueth alle thingis, it hopith alle thingis, it susteyneth alle thingis. Charite fallith neuere doun, whether prophecies schulen be voidid, ethir langagis schulen ceesse, ethir science schal be distried. For a parti we knowun, and a parti we prophecien; but whanne that schal come that is parfit, that thing that is of parti schal be auoidid. Whanne Y was a litil child, Y spak as a litil child, Y vndurstood as a litil child, Y thou3te as a litil child; but whanne Y was maad a man, Y auoidide tho thingis that weren of a litil child. And we seen now bi a myrour in derknesse, but thanne face to face; now Y knowe of parti, but thanne Y schal knowe, as Y am knowun. And now dwellen feith, hope, and charite, these thre; but the most of these is charite.

Sue 3e charite, loue 3e spiritual thingis, but more that 3e prophecien.

4. B omits *or lyf.*
5. B replaces *feith* with *hope.*
6. The *A* version has in addition *or of good will.*
7. *A* reads *is not inblowyn with pride.*

And he that spekith[8] in tunge, spekith not to men, but to God; for no man herith. But the spirit spekith mysteries. For he that prophecieth, spekith to men to edificacioun, and monestyng, and coumfortyng. He that spekith in tunge, edifieth hym silf; but he that prophecieth, edifieth the chirche of God. And Y wole, that alle ȝe speke in tungis, but more that ȝe prophecie. For he that prophecieth, is more than he that spekith in langagis; but perauenture he expoune, that the chirche take edificacioun. But now, britheren, if Y come to ȝou, and speke in langagis, what schal Y profite to ȝou, but if Y speke to ȝou ethir in reuelacioun, ethir in science, ethir in prophecie, ether in techyng? For tho thingis that ben withouten soule, and ȝyueth voices, ethir pipe, ether harpe, but tho ȝyuen distinccioun of sownyngis, hou schal it be knowun that is sungun, ether that that is trumpid?

1 John 4:1–5:4

MOOST DERE BRITHEREN,[9] nyle ȝe bileue to ech spirit, but preue ȝe spiritis, if thei ben of God; for many false prophetis wenten out in to the world. In this thing the spirit of God is knowun; ech spirit that knowlechith that Jhesu Crist hath come in fleisch, is of God; and ech spirit that fordoith Jhesu, is not of God. And this is antecrist, of whom ȝe herden, that he cometh; and riȝt now he is in the world. Ȝe, litle sones, ben of God, and ȝe han ouercome hym; for he that is in ȝou is more, than he that *is* in the world. Thei ben of the world, therfor thei speken of the world, and the world herith hem. We ben of God; he that knowith God, herith vs; he that is not of God, herith not vs. In this thing we knowen the spirit of treuthe, and the spirit of errour. Moost dere *britheren*, loue we togidere, for charite is of God; and ech that loueth his brother, is borun of God, and knowith God. He that loueth not, knowith not God; for God is charite. In this thing the charite of God apperide in vs, for God sente hise oon bigetun sone in to the world, that we lyue bi hym. In this thing is charite, not as we hadden loued God, but for he firste louede vs, and sente hise sone forȝyuenesse for oure synnes. Ȝe moost dere *britheren*, if God louede vs, we owen to loue ech other. No man say

8. *B* has here a gloss drawn from Nicholas of Lyra, Wyclif's favorite exegete: "to speke in tunge is to speke a thing not vndirstonden; *no man heerith*—that is, vndirstondith the sentence hid withinne; *profecieth*—that is, openith and declarith thingis schewid to him either to othere men; *spekith to men*—that is, to the profit of men."

9. *Britheren,* an inclusive term in this period, is an addition in the *B* text; see also two further occurrences in vv. 7, 11.

euer God; if we louen togidre, God dwellith in vs, and the charite of
hym is perfit in vs. In this thing we knowen, that we dwellen in hym,
and he in vs; for of his spirit he ʒaf to vs. And we sayen, and witnessen,
that the fadir sente his sone sauyour of the world. Who euer knowlechith, that Jhesu is the sone of God, God dwellith in him, and he in God.
And we han knowun, and beleuen to the charite, that God hath in vs.
God is charite, and he that dwellith in charite, dwellith in God, and God
in hym. In this thing is the perfit charite of God with vs, that we haue
trist in the dai of dom; for as he is, also we ben in this world. Drede is
not in charite, but perfit charite puttith out drede; for drede hath
peyne.[10] But he that dredith, is not perfit in charite. Therfor loue we
God, for he louede vs bifore. If ony man seith, that Y loue God, and ha-
tith his brother, he is a liere. For he that loueth not his brothir, which he
seeth, hou mai he loue God, whom he seeth not? And we han this com-
aundement of God, that he that loueth God, loue also his brothir.

Ech man that beleueth that Jhesus is Crist, is borun of God; and ech
man that loueth hym that gendride, loueth hym that is borun of hym.
In this thing we knowen, that we louen the children of God, whanne
we louen God, and don his maundementis. For this is the charite of
God, that we kepe hise maundementis; and his maundementis ben not
heuy. For al thing that is borun of God, ouercometh the world; and this
is the victorie that ouercometh the world, oure feith.[11]

10. B gives a marginal gloss from Lyra: "*as he is*—in heuene, and doth good fro
heuene to just men and vniust men; and *we ben in this world*—that is, we louen
bothe freendis and enemyes for his loue, as he comaundith in v.c. [10:26-28] of
Matheu. *Dreede is*, etc.—that is, seruile dreede is not in perfit charite; *dreede hath
peyne*—that is, peyne is due to seruile dreede, for it makith to eschewe synne,
oonly that it be not punschid, not for the abomynacioun of synne, neither to
eschewe the offence of God."

11. B adds another gloss from Lyra: "beleeuith—bi feith foormed with charite;
that Jhesu of Nazareth is Crist—bihiʒt in the lawe and profetis; *loueth him that gendride*—that is, God; *loueth him, etc.*—ech feithful man; *be not greuouse*—to him that
loueth, for why the loue of God and the hoope of meede makith tho thingis esy,
that ben harde and scharpe of her kynde; *born of God*—bi feith foormed with
charite; *ouercometh the world*—that is, temptaciouns and persecusciouns of the
world."

RICHARD ROLLE

The Song of Hannah

The earliest of Rolle's vernacular works was his *English Psalter*, a verse-by-verse commentary on the Latin text of the Psalms. In the *Psalter*, as in the somewhat later commentaries on texts from Samuel and Isaiah which follow here, Rolle first translated a biblical verse as literally as possible into the Middle English dialect of Yorkshire, then he followed it with commentary, also in English. While Rolle had written an academic commentary on the Psalms in Latin in his youth, perhaps even while still a student, he directed his English commentaries toward less learned readers. Various copies were owned by private individuals as well as by the libraries of religious houses. Some of these copies circulated in the later part of the century with Wycliffite materials, for which they formed a kind of imputed native tradition of vernacular translation.[1]

Exultavit cor meum in domino. . . .
1 Samuel 2:1-10 (Vg. 1 Kings 2:1-10)

My heart has rejoiced in the Lord, and my horn is exalted in my God (v. 1a)

Elkanah, who was the father of Samuel, had two wives, Peninnah and Hannah. By Peninnah, who was first to bear children, is signified the

---

1. Rolle's rationale for translation is much like that employed by Nicholas Hereford in his early version of the Wycliffite Bible. In his prologue to the *English Psalter*, Rolle says:

In this work I seek no affected English, but that which is most natural and commonly used and yet corresponds to the Latin, so that those who do not know Latin may, by means of the English translation, actually come to understand the Latin words. In this translation I follow the Latin literally as much as I am able, and where I can find no proper English equivalent I go by the sense of the word, so that those who read it need not be in fear of erring. In my exposition I follow holy theologians, in case my book should come into the hand of some envious person who, without understanding the text himself, will claim that I didn't know what I was talking about, and so bring harm upon himself and someone else by despising a work which is profitable for both.

See *English Writings of Richard Rolle,* ed. Hope Emily Allen (Oxford: Clarendon, 1931), 7.

synagogue of the Jews;[2] by Hannah, who was at first barren and yet later become more fruitful than the other, is signified the church of Christian peoples. Wherefore Hannah burst forth in praise of God and composed this psalm, by means of which the Holy Spirit now stirs us up to the praise of our Lord, who has lifted us out of the errors of heathen peoples.

At the beginning of her song she shows that her highest delight is in God, and says, in our place, "My heart was gladdened in my Lord who, for the fruit of good works and faithful meditation, had pity on my sterility. And my 'horn'—that is, my spiritual strength by which I now can escape those who scorn me—is raised in my God, not in myself or in the vanities of this world."

My mouth is opened above my enemies, because I have rejoiced in thy salvation. (v. 1b)

"Voluntarily and with a glad heart did I open my mouth in the praise of God, above the din of my foes—those who shamed and despised me before—largely because I rejoiced not in pomp and vainglory, but simply in salvation, that is in Jesus, who has exalted me in virtue."

None is holy as the Lord, nor is there any beside Him; and none is as strong as our God. (v. 2)

None is holy and free from sin as the Lord Jesus Christ because there is no other that is sinless except Him. Only in Him and through Him is any person holy, and no one is as strong to avenge evil deeds as is our God, who punishes the wicked for their evil will. Therefore you scorners and despisers of poor people and honorers of the rich,

Talk no more with such excessive pride and boasting. (v. 3a)

Be unwilling any more to let loose your tongue in proud talk just because you are distinguished in worldly power, for that power actually exists to your sorrow and shame. If you remain proud, rejoicing in your riches, pleasures and lecheries, remember that you shall soon have much more sorrow than joy. For there will be no other heaven for you, unless you spend your riches according to God's express will.

---

2. This example of allegorical reading illustrates the prevalent medieval typology, familiar from the early fathers and modelled on Paul's discussion of Hagar and Sarah (Galatians 4:22-27), which evolved as a comparison and contrast of the Old and the New Covenant (or Testament), the letter and the spirit, law and grace, and so on. *Synagogue*, in this sense, automatically typifies the sterility of the Old Law unto salvation, whereas *church (ekklesia)* typifies the fruitfulness of the New.

Let things of the old life depart from your mouth. For the Lord is a God of all knowledge, and He evaluates your thoughts. (v. 3b)

These "old things" are lies, false oaths, running others down, and curses, which reveal that you are really continuing in your old life. Let these things depart from your mouth, and forget them. Adopt the new language of a new life, for the God of all knowledge, who knows all things and can accomplish all things, is the Lord. And He will be judging your old faults severely. To Him all thoughts are open, and He knows very well what you think and in what you actually take your greatest pleasure. Five things are found in mankind: thought, affection, purpose, work, and speech. Let thought be holy, affection clean, purpose correct, work just, and speech temperate.

The bow of the mighty is broken, and the weak are girded with strength. (v. 4)

The "bow of the mighty" is the hope of rich and grasping people, and they bend it to win honors and lordship over this world. But it is defeated, for Christ shall break it and cast it into the fire of hell. And weak persons, meek and feeble people without presumption or pride in themselves, are supported and strengthened. That is, through spiritual strength they are made secure and constant of mind, and enabled to resist their enemies (for all good persons have a multitude of enemies while in this life).

They that were full before have hired themselves out for bread, and the hungry are filled. (v. 5a)

Those that had been filled with earthly lusts and swollen in pride hired themselves out for loaves, that is, the food of the soul. That is to say, they gave themselves up meekly [at last] to receive the love of heaven. And as a result, the hungry, that is, those desiring righteousness and the word of life, are filled with the sweetness of joy unending (which is just as long as this spiritual bread will last).

Many are born to the barren one, and she that had many children grows feeble. (v. 5b)

The barren, or the church of Christian peoples, which at first was sterile of truth and good works, has now borne many spiritual children to Christ. The synagogue, which had many carnal children, has now · grown feeble. (That is, it is known that it brought no one to perfection, and now it brings no one to salvation.)

The Lord kills and he makes alive; he brings down to hell and he brings back again. (v. 6)

Our Lord slays those who become outrageous in their love of this life, and He quickens those who forsake this world and despise this life by comparison with life eternal. He leads down to hell; that is, He puts the fear of hell into sinful persons and so brings them back once again to the hope of [eternal] life.

The Lord makes poor and he makes rich; he humbles and he exalts. (v. 7)

Our Lord conditions the heart of a poor person, mercifully depriving it of covetousness and earthly affections, while He makes him rich with gifts that will last forever. For He does not make us rich in righteousness until He has first made us poor through his mercy. He humbles the proud as punishment to the devils, while He lifts up the humble to the joy of angels.

He raises up the needy from the dust, and lifts up the poor from the dunghill. (v. 8a)

He raises the spiritually needy through his grace, out of the dust of this evil life blown about by the winds of temptation. One who knows his spiritual need is always asking God that he be not reduced to dust. And out of the fen—which is to say, out of the corruption of the body—He uplifts the one who is poor, who despises this world as a holy lover of Christ.

That he may sit with princes, and hold the throne of glory. (v. 8b)

That is, to the end that such a person may have the reward and rest of the apostles, and in the Day of Judgment hold his place before the throne of judgment.

For the pillars of the earth are the Lord's, and upon them he has set the world. (v. 8c)

The "pillars of the earth" are those persons in Holy Church who have been perfected in faithfulness and love, and through whom others are brought to stability and spiritual maturity. And He set the world upon them in the sense that He made them the foundation of his Church, as wide as it is, spread over the world.

He will keep the feet of his saints, and the wicked shall be silent in darkness: because no man shall prevail in his own strength. (v. 9)

The "feet" are the godly affections and devout yearnings of his saints, those whom He sanctifies and makes pure, and He shall keep them from falling since it is on those feet that they go to God. And the wicked, without pity for their own souls, shall grow silent in the darkness of their ignorance and evil deeds, so that they neither praise God nor honestly confess their own sins. For a person is not strengthened by his own strength, and the saints do not presume upon their own virtue or strength, as do the proud whose "strength" is really the cause of their damnation.

The adversaries of the Lord shall fear him: and he shall thunder upon them from the heavens. (v. 10a)

God's enemies are all those who act against justice or who love falsehood. And if they do not fear Him now, they will at the Last Day, when He begins to judge, thundering terribly over them and saying, "Go ye cursed into the fire without end, which is reserved for the devil and his angels" (Matthew 25:41).

The Lord shall judge the ends of the earth: and he shall give empire to his king, and shall exalt the horn of his Christ. (v. 10b)[3]

The Lord shall judge the ends of the earth, not the beginning or the middle, in that every person shall be judged by God as he is found at the end of his life. And then He shall give empire—that is, all of his chosen people who have lived according to his commandments—unto his king, his Son the King. And He shall raise the horn of his Christ, through which He blew and scattered the might of his enemy.

3. The King James Version has "his anointed" in place of "his Christ." Early typology read this reference as a prefiguration of Christ, and many Latin Bibles simply inserted the name directly into the text.

The Song of Isaiah

This commentary, although it does not insert rhetorical rubrics, is self-consciously organized in such a way as to move from invocation, through declaration and confession of sin, to exhortation, to spiritual growth, to proclamation of the gospel, and finally to praise of the Lord through words and through a sanctified life.

Confiteor tibi Domine. . . .
Isaiah 12

I shall confess to thee, O Lord, for thou hast been angry with me: thy wrath has turned away, and thou hast comforted me. (v. 1)

It is to your praise that I confess my sins, for I shall do it because of your anger with my sinning. I may not please you unless I put down my sin through confession, for in this way your fury is turned away. You have transformed endless suffering into a brief penance, and by that means you comfort me, delivering me from a nagging conscience and filling up my heart with knowledge and a consciousness of your love.

Behold, God is my Savior: I will deal confidently, and not fear. . . . (v. 2a)[1]

All people, behold! Lo, God—Jesus Christ—is my Savior, cleansing me of sin and delivering me from torment. Now that I am turned toward Him He saves me, whom before He blinded while I was still turned to the world. In confidence therefore I shall proceed; that is, I will boldly proclaim that He shall come to judge and render sentence upon every person's mortal life. Nor shall I fear to say it, though I be despised by evil persons for my faithfulness.

For the Lord is my strength and praise: and he is become my salvation. (v. 2b)

He is my strength, in whom alone I am become stalwart enough not to be afraid, since by myself I am very weak. And he is also my praise, whose praise I seek in thought, word and deed, rather than praise for

---

1. Although the Vulgate differs somewhat from the more familiar King James Version in phrasing, especially in v. 2, it is substantially common with it in all other verses.

myself. And He has become my salvation from Adam, who brought me into the sickness unto death. Now, you who would enter into this conversation,

You shall draw waters with joy out of the Savior's fountains. And you shall say in that day, "Praise ye the Lord, and call upon his name." (vv. 3-4a)

Through charity and meekness you shall draw waters of wisdom from the wisdom of heaven, in joy rendering your service to God. (The wells are the abundant gifts and grace of Jesus Christ.) And you shall say to others in that day—that is, when you drink only from those clear wells and leave off the muddy waters of earthy lusts—"Confess your sins to the Lord! And thus invoke his name and live so that your life shows forth his praise, which can only happen if you call his name into yourself, making yourself his dwelling place."

Make his works known among the people: remember that his name is high. (v. 4b)

"Make known"—that is, preach among the people that they may know his incarnation, through which He established our salvation, and that He is found through charitable love and good works. And "remember Him"—that is, keep Him always in mind, for his name, Jesus, is exalted above all names. Keep that in your thought and you shall not fall into pride, nor itch to play God, as did Lucifer and Adam.

Sing to the Lord, for he has done great things: show this forth in all the earth. (v. 5)

Sing to the Lord in contemplation (for therein is delectable comfort, if the contemplation is genuine), and using your opportunity, honor Him. For He did a mighty thing in accomplishing the salvation of mankind, dying to save such sinful wretches. What could be more magnificent than to render good for evil? Bear witness to that noble thing amongst all people, but especially

Rejoice and praise, O thou habitation of Sion: for great is he that is in the midst of thee, the Holy One of Israel. (v. 6)

You who dwell in Zion—that is, in his Holy Church—and in the contemplation of God, and have been made the dwelling of Jesus Christ, be glad. That is, show yourself well pleased in the good quality of your life, and praise God who has brought these things about in you. For it is He who is great in you, in love and in virtue, He that is the Holy One of Israel—that is, Christ—sanctifying those who are truly "Israel," who in truth and charitable love are seeing God.

ANONYMOUS

Exposition of the Ave Maria

While once confidently attributed to Wyclif himself, this exposition must now more probably be assumed to come from the pen of one of his followers. It takes the form of a kind of exegetical sketch for a Christmas season homily, in which the familiar Ave provides a counterfoil to abuse, in rich households, of the Christmas celebration.

Heil be þou, marie, ful of grace, þe lord is wiþ þe. blissed be þou among wymmen, & blissed be þe fruyt of þi wombe, ihesu crist. amen. so be it.

THE ARCHANGEL GABRIEL sent from God greeted our Lady St. Mary with these words: "Hail. Be thou full of grace. The Lord is with thee. Blessed be thou among women." And he said nothing more than this, as the first chapter of the Gospel of Luke recounts it (Luke 1:28). But Elizabeth, the mother of St. John the Baptist, said these additional words to our Lady when she had conceived Christ: "Blessed be thou among women, and blessed be the fruit of thy womb," as the same Gospel teaches (Luke 1:42). But Christians add for the sake of devotion the two names: Mary, and Jesus Christ. And it is said that the popes grant much pardon [for saying these names]; however it relates to pardons, though, this adding of the two terms is faithful, for the Gospel does teach us these names and they do indeed stir up devotion.

From this text, men and women—and especially gentlewomen—should learn meekness, chastity, charity, sobriety and humility, and to be ashamed of every evil speech, especially concerning lechery and the evil condoning of sin, ribaldry and villainy. And they should learn here a spirit of holy devotion; then they will properly reverence Jesus their spiritual bridegroom and St. Mary his mother. And if they are living in pride of heart because of their nobility or family connections, rents and riches of this world, and if they despise or are impatient with poor men or women—delighting themselves in lechery to any degree, or in hate, envy, gluttony, drunkenness or boldness to sin, rationalizing these things as they keep them up, living riotously, dancing the nights away and sleeping in the next mornings, forgetting God and the reverence they owe Him, their prayers and devotions—then despite whatever their tongues prattle, their evil lives blaspheme and disdain both Jesus, their noble spouse, and his mother Mary, a treasure of purity and devotion.

If they busy themselves in thought and deed more to be gay in expensive clothes, kerchiefs, pearls, ribbons or other similar vanities, and work diligently to make their bodies fresh and appealing to mens' eyes—coveting these adornments more than they desire to obtain virtue in their souls—they are simply out of charity, and have become the devil's snare whereby he entraps men in lechery and many other sins, keeping them there until he drags both parties into hell. Whatever nobility or dignity such people have had in this world, be they gentlemen or women, on account of living this kind of accursed life they become churls and bondwomen to sin and the fiends of hell, as well as spiritual marriage-wreckers[1] and adulterers, lovers of foul Satan who is viler than any leper in this world. But if they would amend themselves of this worldliness, they would be numbered with those spoken of in the book of Job. Such persons, says God (Job 21:13) lead their days in pursuit of lustful goods and pleasures of this world, and at a certain point they fall down into hell.

Once *courtoisie* and the gentle life were virtuous and honest in word, deed and all manner of good bearing—as sisters in holiness. Now all this is turned to vanity, affectation, tricks and games, and is become a gateway to sin—to pride, ribaldry, sloth, covetousness, gluttony, drunkenness, lechery, the maintenance of sin and whoredom, wrath, envy, boasting, cursed swearing, wastefulness, robbery of the poor, and the destruction of other lands in Christendom.

O gentlewoman, think of the lives of pure and steadfast noble women before you such as, for example, our Lady St. Mary, Mary Magdalene, Susannah, Katherine, Margaret, Agnes, Cecilia and many others, and take what good example you can from their meekness and holiness. For when women are turned fully to good living it is extremely difficult for any man to surpass them in goodness. But it is equally hard for any man to surpass them in sinful living when they are given over to pride, lechery and drunkenness.

In my opinion, young women may occasionally dance (though temperately) for recreation and celebration, as long as they have more thought of their joy in heaven, and therefore love and fear God more in consequence. And they ought to sing honest songs of Christ's incarnation, passion, resurrection, and ascension, and of the joys of our Lady, and learn to despise sin and praise virtue in all their activity. Nowadays, whoever can best play a scene about the devil, sing songs of lechery,

---

1. Wreckers, that is, of the "marriage" between the obedient soul and God.

battles and lies, and holler like a madman, despising the majesty of God and swearing from the heart against the bones and body of Christ is regarded as the merriest sort of person, and obtains the favor of both rich and poor. This sort of stuff is even passed off as celebration of the great solemnity of Christmas! And thus we repay the great kindness and goodness Christ wrought for us in his incarnation by despising Him all the more through such outrages of pride, gluttony, lechery and all manner of harlotry. By this behavior one brings in a season of physical jollity, mirth and pleasure seeking, with the discovery of new sins, instead of holiness and spiritual joy and attentiveness to the word of God in response to his endless charity, meekness, mercy and kindness.

Lord, where are those who work as hard at making their soul beautiful in virtues in the sight of God as they work at dressing up their body for the eyes of men? Alas that so much money and effort is wasted on this rotting body that is worms' meat and a mere sack of dirt, dust and ashes! But the soul made in the image of the Trinity,[2] which Christ bought so dearly with his heart's blood—there is no effort to keep it clean but rather only to increase its sin both night and day. Little do these madmen and women consider the cold and poverty of Christ's mother,[3] or the life Jesus Himself led in this world, despised and sorrowing for our sins, and what a shameful death He suffered at the last. These lords and ladies should not permit swearing, dirty jokes and loose talk in their presence; for if they allowed any of their servants to despise our earthly king much punishment would come to them as a result, and they themselves would be held to be false traitors to the king. O how much more treasonable and false are those worldly lords to Christ the King of all heaven, earth and hell, when they hear such insult done to his majesty and still do not refrain their servants from it. Certainly there were examples of purity, honesty, and holiness which used to come from the courts of lords down to the commons, and in that time a holy life was held in honor among poor and rich alike. But now instead come examples of pride, gluttony, lechery and outright harlotry. And accordingly, sin reigns shamelessly in all walks of life.

Thus the devil blinds people, deceiving them into calling this cursed epidemic of harlotry and sinfulness a great honor to God, and calling devotion to prayers—sober remembrance of Christ's poverty, suffering and death, and of the Day of Judgment—hypocrisy and foolishness.

---

2. The reference here is to the basic Augustinian idea which governs his *On the Trinity*.

3. The allusion is to familiar meditations on the eve of Christ's birth, when Mary and Joseph, poor in this world's goods found their lodging in the cold cave stable.

Good persons are not even permitted to dwell in the courts of lords,[4] lest they drive away the devil and his school of sin and vanity to the displeasure of the young affected fools who gather there, and lest they are the means of bringing Christ into "Christian" people's souls, and his teaching of virtuous living, honest thought, word and deed to the pleasing of God and the salvation of men's souls.

Hail, Mary. That is to say, "may it be well with you, Mary," or "joy unto you, Mary." For just as by one woman came sorrow, pain and woe to all mankind because she did not earnestly trust the word of God but entrusted herself instead to the banter of the devil, coveting overmuch to have knowledge and dignity, so by the earnest faith, meekness and charitable love of Mary came joy and salvation to mankind, for in this spirit she conceived Christ, as the Gospel says.

Therefore, may you also flee falsehood and pride, and hold earnestly to faith in God's word with meekness and charitable love, and you shall have a part in Mary's joy and bliss in heaven evermore. Mary, Christ's mother, was full of grace. St. Stephen was full of grace, as Holy Writ says (Acts 6:8), if less than our Lady, and our dear Lord Jesus was full of grace far surpassing Stephen and our Lady. We may infer by this three levels of fullness of grace, the least abundance of which was in Stephen, the middle amount in our Lady, and most of all in our Lord Jesus Christ.

[*The Lord is with thee.*] The triune God is in all creatures in power, wisdom and goodness, preserving life; otherwise it should turn to nothing.[5] But God is with good persons of virtuous life by grace, approving and accepting the life they offer and helping them in it, rewarding them in eternity and dwelling in their souls now as his temple, causing them to live joyfully in his service and to suffer gladly all injuries and persecution for his name's sake. And God is also in his angels and saints in heaven by a clear revelation of his Godhead to them, making them to know all things and have all things they ever desire without hindrance or pain.

Blessed be thou among women. That is, more than any other woman be blessed, for no other was so sincere in faith nor so good in all manner of holiness, especially in burning love. If you want to have a portion in Mary's bliss and God's blessing, follow Mary in this holiness of life, namely in these seven traits: faith, hope, charity, meekness, chastity, sobriety, and a burning desire for righteousness.

4. Perhaps a reference to the resistance of some noble households to persons of a strict piety (Wycliffite presumably), who must have been seen as a kind of damper on certain types of indulgent merriment.

5. Here perhaps is a more particularly Wycliffian notion, that the "uncreated Trinity" is to be found "in all manner of creatures" (*Trialogus*, 4.27).

And blessed be the fruit of thy womb. That is, Jesus, for by his mercy and grace comes every good thing and especially by his true teaching and voluntary death and eternal power, by which He shall raise all persons on Judgment Day, granting the bliss of heaven in body and soul to those who end their days in perfect charity.

May God give us grace to reflect on Christ's mercy and righteousness, and on Mary's sincerity of faith and meekness, so that we may conclude our own lives in perfect charity.

Amen.

PART NINE

Gospel and Culture

PLOUGHING THE GROUND

This marginal illustration for Psalm 94:20-22 in the *Luttrell Psalter* becomes especially appropriate in the context provided by William Langland. Executed in England about 1340, it is reproduced here from Add. MS 42130 (fol. 170) by permission of the British Library.

WILLIAM LANGLAND

from
Piers the Plowman

William Langland was an obscure clergyman, probably trained for the priesthood in the monastery of Great Malvern not far from his Shropshire childhood home. Born about 1332, he was a slightly younger contemporary of Wyclif and an almost exact contemporary of Walter Hilton. He held no permanent benefice, through lack of family political connections, and served in little places all over the country—at one point living with his wife Kit and daughter Nicolette in a little cottage in Cornhill, where he kept body and soul together by singing commemorative masses for the dead relatives of wealthy patrons. He was tall and gaunt, invariably poorly dressed, and went by the nickname, so he tells us, of "Long Will."

Langland gives us the picture in *Piers the Plowman* of a kind of "vanity fair," a corrupt kingdom from which the governing standard of truth has long since disappeared, where the wealthy and prosperous prey on the poor, and where those entrusted with spiritual leadership corrupt their calling for the same low motives of temporal well-being that governs the robber-barons.

The work is an allegory, resembling John Bunyan's *Pilgrim's Progress* in some respects. It consists of a series of dreams given to the narrator— Langland himself—which, within the conventions of dream vision allegory, allow him to make of his literary self an ignorant and bewildered interlocutor for the allegorical figures such as Holy Church who come to instruct him. It is really the reader who is being instructed in this indirect way. Part of the incentive for such indirection is clearly occasioned by the subversive character of Langland's allegory: the political fable of the rats and mice which follows is a warning to the readers that the work's counsel is necessarily undertaken in a hostile environment.

Langland's narrative does not take the classical Christian format of invoking an interior spiritual journey from the City of this World to the City of God (as does *The Pilgrim's Progress* or even Chaucer's *Canterbury Tales*) but elaborates instead a rambling search for faithful proclamation and application—and thus, defense—of the gospel in a world which seems to the poet to be falling into the power of the Antichrist. An apocalyptic mood hangs over the work, and the dreams are not merely modes of revelation but omens, portents of judgment.

The text of *Piers the Plowman*, whether in Langland's original version (c. 1362) or either of the later two expansions and revisions (c. 1383 and 1390), is extremely hard to translate effectively. This is due in part to the difficult dialect and alliterative character of the language itself, and in part to the fact that this is a text which, for political reasons, is deliberately cryptic—written to disclose and to conceal at the same time.

Langland's use of strategic ellipsis creates problems which go well beyond the grasping of referents for his allegory. An excellent translation of the second or *B* text, with helpful annotations, has been made by J. F. Goodridge (London: Penguin, 1959).

Prologue: The Plain Full of People

IN A SUMMER SEASON, when soft was the sun, I got myself into a woollen cloak as if I were a shepherd, and in the garb of a hermit unholy of works I set out to wend my way into the wide world, hoping to hear of wonders. But one morning in May, among the Malvern hills, a remarkable thing happened to me, as if by the charm of a fairy. I had grown weary in my wanderings and laid myself down to rest under a broad bank beside a brook, and as I lay there, leaning over and looking into the waters, I fell asleep listening to the sound of the stream.

And then there came to me a marvellous dream: I found myself in a wilderness—I know not where—and as I looked toward the east I saw a tower on a hill, reaching up to the sun and splendidly made. A deep gully opened up beneath it, in which there was a dungeon surrounded by a deep, dark moat, dreadful to see.

A fair field thronged with folk I could discern in between, filled with all sort of people, poor and rich, working and wandering about in pursuit of worldly affairs. Some took to the plow, and had little leisure; in cultivating and sowing they perspired heavily, earning what wastemakers would destroy with their gluttony. Others were prompted by pride of appearance and, all dressed up in a veritable parade of fine clothing, went along most curiously disguised. Yet in prayer and repentance there were also many who for love of our Lord lived a disciplined life in hope of the blessed kingdom of heaven; as anchorites and hermits they kept to their calls and were not yearning to be roaming about the countryside to please their bodies with appetitive living.[1]

Still others chose business as a means of getting ahead; it seems in our sight such persons are most like to prosper. Others were providing entertainments as minstrels know how to do, and getting gold by their gleefulness—innocently, I hope! But there were tricksters and jesters, children of Judas, who propounded fantasies and played the part of fools, though they have brains enough to earn an honest living if they chose. What Paul preaches concerning such characters I dare not expound fully here, but surely whoever talks filth is one of Lucifer's henchman.

1. As someone who had no choice but to roam about in poor garb, but who was evidently determined upon his spiritual calling, Langland must have resented these characters as much as he did some of the wealthy and politically powerful.

Panhandlers and beggars went quickly about till their bags and their bellies were crammed full of bread; they misrepresented themselves to get food and fought over their ale. In gluttony, God knows, they go to bed, and rise up in ribaldry, these thieving knaves; sleep and sloth follow them wherever they go. Pilgrims and palmers[2] toured in groups together, visiting the shrine of St. James in Spain and others in Rome. Off they went on these jaunts, gathering many an anecdote and feeling they had licence to tell lies the rest of their lives. There was a band of hermits with crooked staves pilgriming their way to Walsingham[3]—with a gaggle of wenches tagging along. These great long lubbers were the sort that hated to work for a living but got themselves up in pseudo-clerical garb to suggest that they had some kind of legitimate religious calling; they were really disguising themselves as hermits just to have an easy life.

There were friars there too—all four orders of them[4]—preaching to the people to fill their own bellies. They interpreted the Scriptures to suit themselves, misrepresenting it in the interest of fine clothes on their backs; indeed, many of these "masters of theology" can dress as lavishly as they choose, for money and the kind of "merchandise" they peddle usually go together. Now that "charity" has gone into big business and become chief spiritual director of the wealthy, many weird and wonderful things have taken place within just a few years. In fact, unless Holy Church does a better job of holding itself together, the greatest calamity in the world could quickly come upon us.[5]

There was also a pardoner out there, preaching like a parson.[6] He produced a document covered with bishops' seals, and claimed that he

2. A palmer was a kind of vocational pilgrim, a person who made a life's work out of traveling to one holy site or another, professing poverty.

3. A popular goal of pilgrimage within England, second only to Canterbury.

4. Franciscans, Dominicans, Augustinians, and Carmelites. By this time many of the friars had betrayed their calling, becoming itinerant huckster-preachers whose objectives seemed less the multiplication of the kingdom of God than the multiplication of their own incomes. Cf. Wyclif's and Chaucer's criticisms.

5. Langland may have been thinking of a permanent schism in the Western church. The Great Schism of the fourteenth century—with popes at both Avignon and Rome and factions of friars supporting each in bitter antagonism—badly undermined any sense of secure stable authority in the church and threatened to destroy it entirely.

6. Pardoners were another species of particularly distasteful religious huckster. Licensed by one pope or another, and often recruited from the orders of friars, they sold "pardons" or indulgences (as well as dubious relics) on the sly, behind the back of the local parish priest. They also acted as itinerant preachers and typically promised healings or the miraculous increase in the productivity of farms and businesses if one of their relics would be purchased at a handsome price.

himself could absolve everyone from spiritual deception and broken covenants. The ignorant in the crowd liked that idea well enough, and believed his claims, and came up to him, kneeling down to kiss his "documents." Dazzling them, with his papers in their faces, he quickly raked in their rings and broaches with his rolled up scroll.

So we give our gold to support gluttons, and leave it to wastrels with luxurious ambitions. Would that the bishop was blessed with both his ears; perhaps they wouldn't be so brazen in their deception of the people. But it's not by the bishop's leave that these boys get to preach; the parish priest and these rovers are splitting the cash between them— money which should be going to help the poor folk of the parish, and would be if it weren't for these charlatans.

Parsons, parish priests, were out there complaining to their bishops that since the time of the Plague their parishes were too poor to survive in;[7] so they were asking permission to abandon their charges and go to live in London to sing there for simony,[8] because silver is sweet. Bishops and new graduates, masters of theology and theologians with doctorates—to whom Christ appointed the care of souls, and who received the "crown" of their tonsure as a sign that their duty in the church is to do the work of charitable love faithfully among the poor and unlearned—they were all living in London, even in Lent.[9] Some served the court and counted the king's money; others got posts in the Exchequer and Chancellery, where they collected debts from wards of the realm, and obtained the king's rights over unregistered property. Others went into the service of lords and ladies, and became stewards over domestic business. Their masses, daily prayers and chapel hours were handled irresponsibly; indeed, my fear is that at the last day Christ in his judgment will curse many of these folk eternally.

Looking at all this I began to understand something of the power which was entrusted to Peter, to "bind and unbind," as Scripture says[10] and how Peter left it in the purview of Love, as our Lord commanded, sharing it out among the four highest virtues, which we call "cardi-

7. There were four incursions of the bubonic plague during the reign of Edward III, the worst of which was the Black Death of 1348–49, followed by separate epidemics in 1361–62, 1369, and 1375–76. With anywhere from one-third to two-thirds of the inhabitants killed by disease in most parishes, some priests could not collect sufficient tithes for their own support.

8. Money obtained for singing masses for the dead in the side chapels of major city churches, such as St. Paul's Cathedral.

9. In Lent especially, these men were responsible for conducting rigorous programs of catechism in their own parishes, including the preparation of adult converts for baptism and the reconciliation of penitents.

10. See Matthew 16:19.

nal"—hinges upon which swing the gates of Christ's kingdom, to close and open it, revealing the blessedness of heaven.[11] But as for those other "cardinals" at the papal court in Rome, who have assumed the same name and presume that they have the power to make a pope—it is not my place to impugn them here. The election of a pope requires both love and learning; accordingly, I both can and cannot speak more of the papal court.

Now into the field I saw coming a king, led by a troop of knights. The power of the Commons enabled him to reign, and then came Common Sense and provided scholars to counsel the king to protect the people. Then the king, the knights and clergy all three decided that the common people should provide them with revenue. The common people contrived common-sensical trades and for the benefit of everyone plowmen were ordained to till the earth and work it as an honest life requires. The king, the Commons, and Common Sense as a third established law and order so that each person might know his or her responsibilities.

Suddenly, up lept a lunatic, a lean lad to boot,[12] and getting down on his knee before the king he said in sepulchral tones, "Christ keep you, sire King, and your kingdom too. May Love lead you and your people in faithful love, that for your righteous governance you come to be rewarded in heaven!"

Then from up high in the air an angel of heaven swept down to speak something in Latin (for ignorant folk can't jangle in Latin nor interpret it in such a way as to credit themselves; they only suffer and serve); and what the angel said was this:

> "You say, 'I am a king, I am a prince'—
> but in time you may be neither.
> Your duty is to administer the laws of Christ,
> who is *your* king.
> If you are going to do this, you had better be
> as meek as you are just.
> Let justice be clothed in mercy,
> Sow such crops as you hope yourself to reap.

11. *Cardinal* comes from the Latin *cardo*, "hinge." The four "cardinal virtues" were prudence, temperance, fortitude, and justice. The apostate cardinals of the Schism referred to in the next sentence, who warred with each other at Avignon, Amiens, and Rome, had become a major source of spiritual scandal in the fourteenth-century church.
12. I.e., Langland himself.

If you strip justice of mercy, you shall yourself
   be judged by justice alone.
Sow mercy and mercy shall you reap again."[13]

A certain loudmouth—a veritable glutton for words—then taunted the angel, answering back:

"Since a king must rule to have the name of king,
He cannot be a king who doesn't uphold the laws."

And at this all the common people began in one voice to cry out in a tag of Latin, "The king's decrees are as binding upon us as the Law."

The Parliament of Mice and Rats

And all at once the field was filled with a horde of rats, and running with them more than a thousand little mice, all coursing to a Council meeting called for their common profit.[14] For a Court Cat used to come when he felt like it, pounce on them, knock them all about and toy with them mercilessly in whatever way he pleased. "And if we dare complain about his little pleasures," they said, "he will just go after us all the more, clawing at us and trapping us in his paws until we'd sooner be dead before he gives up. If we could only think up a way to resist him, we could be lords of our own domain and live as we pleased."

Then said a big, famous rat who was skilled in speech: "I have observed exalted gents in the cities and towns wearing bright gold chains of office round their necks and fancy collars—both knights and squires. They too are always looking for trouble, laying waste wherever they please. Now if there were a bell on their collars, it occurs to me, people could hear them coming and run away. So," continued the rat, "logic suggests that what we need to do is to buy a brass bell, or one of bright silver, attach it to a collar for our common profit and hang the thing

13. The angel—though the word in Middle English, as in Latin, can also mean "minister" or "messenger"—has been thought possibly to allude to Thomas Brinton, Bishop of Rochester, who preached a similar warning on the accession of Richard II, the "boy king," to the throne in 1377. See G. R. Owst, *Literature and Pulpit in Medieval England* (Oxford: Blackwell, 1966), 577-78. The implication is not primarily that the prophetic judgment rendered in Latin is more authoritative, but that persons of considerable authority—not just folk like the narrator himself—share the same point of view.

14. *Commune profit* was a medieval English term of considerable weight in both moral and economic spheres, and it is a recurring concept in Langland; it has no really apt modern English equivalent. Russell A. Peck speaks of the term as key to the moral philosophy of Langland's contemporary, John Gower, and accords to it

around the cat's neck. Then, whenever he moves about either to riot, to rest, to roam or to play, we can hear him. If he is just in a playful mood we can peep out of our holes even when he is about, but if he is on an angry prowl we can be warned to keep out of his way."

The whole assembly of rodents agreed to this plan. But when the bell was bought and fastened on a collar there wasn't a rat in the bunch who for all the kingdom of France would risk trying to fasten it on the cat's neck, nor to slip it over his head even if the whole of England should be his reward. So they were disappointed in themselves and their feeble plan, and that all of their strategy and labor had been wasted.

Then a clever looking little mouse pushed himself through to the front and, standing before the whole assembly of rodents, spoke as follows: "Even if we killed the cat, another would come to claw us and our tribe, despite our creeping under benches! So I advise that for our common profit he be left to himself, and let's not even think of being so bold as to show him the bell. I heard my father say, seven years ago now, "When the cat is but a kitten the court is in trouble." And we should take the witness of Holy Writ where it says, "Woe to that land whose king is a child."[15] For then no one can rest for the rats at night. While the cat is after rabbits he's not out for our flesh, and while he is stuffed with his own venison we have no cause to defame him. Better a little loss now than that a long haul of sorrows should come amongst us because we were unwilling to lose the odd shrew. Many a man's malt would we otherwise ruin, and you rats would be tearing up their clothes if that Court Cat weren't around to keep one step ahead of you! For if you rats had your own way you couldn't begin to govern yourselves.

"As for me," said the mouse, "if you take my advice you'll leave cat and kitten alone, and forget all about this business of the collar. (I never contributed to it myself, though even if it had cost me plenty I certainly

---

its proper New Testament values when he defines it as "the mutual enhancement, each by each, of all parts of a community for the general welfare of that community taken as a whole." See Peck, *Kingship and Common Profit in Gower's "Confessio Amantis"* (Carbondale: Southern Illinois University Press, 1978), xxi. The modern reader ought to imagine here neither the enforced subordination of personal initiative implied by classical Marxism nor a cloaking of individual license with a sort of piety of civic virtue. In the "body" analogy employed by Jesus and Paul, common profit was taken to be the earthly goal of the body of Christ, even as it was to become its heavenly perfection. Cf. the conclusion of Chaucer's Parson's Sermon.

15. Ecclesiastes 10:16. Richard II acceded to the throne in 1377 as a ten year old; the country was effectually administered by his protector, John of Gaunt (patron of both John Wyclif and Geoffrey Chaucer), who is the cat referred to in this allegory.

wouldn't let on about it.) Let both of them go their own way, leashed or unleashed, to catch what they can. My word to the wise is: let each one keep to his own business."

Now what this little dream means, you merry men, figure out for yourselves, for I don't dare tell you, and that's God's truth.

Now besides all this I have described there stood a hundred men in silk gowns, apparently "servants" who served as lawyers, pleading their cases before the bar for money—not once would they open their lips on behalf of justice for the love of our Lord. You could more easily measure the mist on Malvern hills than get a word from their mouth without producing money.

But barons and burghers and bond-men too all milled in this gathering, as you shall soon hear; bakers and brewers and butchers abounding; wool-beaters, weavers, tailors and tinkers; toll-collectors; masons, miners and others. And all kinds of shoddy workmen—diggers and delvers who did their work ill—whiling away the day in bawdy songs like "God save you now, Mistress Emma," and so on, while cooks with their knaves cried, "Hot pies! Get 'em hot! Fat pigs and geese! Come on and eat! Go to it!" And taverners with them cried more of the same: "White wines of Spain and red wines of Gascony; with Rhine wine and Rochel wash down that roast!"

All this I saw in my sleep, and seven dreams more.

Passus I: The Teaching of Holy Church

Now what this mountain signified, the dark valley and also the fair field of people, I shall plainly show you.

A lovely lady, most learned and clothed in linen, came down from a castle and gently called my name, saying, "My son, are you sleeping? Do you see all these people, how busy they are in milling about? The greatest proportion of people who pass through this earth have their honor in this world; they don't want anything better, nor do they believe there is any other heaven than the here and now."

I was afraid to look at her, although she was beautiful; I said, "Forgive me, Madam, but what does all this mean?"

"The tower on the hill," she replied, "is where Truth lives, for He is Father of Faith, and created you all, with body and countenance and five physical senses that you might turn all to his worship while you are here. To that end He has commanded the earth to assist you all with wool, linen and food as you have need, in such measure as permits you

378

to live in comfort. Of his courtesy He commanded three things in common, all that your body requires: the first is clothing to protect you from the cold; the second is meat to sustain your strength; the third is drink for when you are thirsty—but not out of measure, so you are not the worse for wear when you ought to be working.

"Remember the story of Lot who, when he was living under the influence of drink did with his daughters the devil's pleasure, delighted himself in drink just as the devil wanted, and consumed by lust then lay with them both, and all because of too much wine the deed was done. 'Come,' they said, 'let us make our father drink wine, and we will lie with him, that we may preserve the seed of our father' (Genesis 19:31-38). So Lot was dragged down by wine and women, and there got by gluttony girls that were churls.[16] So you beware how you deal with delicious drink, and you will be the better for it. Moderation is like a medicine, however strong your craving. Not everything your gut asks for is good for your spirit, nor is everything precious to your soul going to gratify your appetites. Don't believe the promptings of your body, because it has been taught by the wretched world to tell lies, and will betray you if it can. And the devil and the flesh are out together to hunt down your soul, and whisper evil in your heart. So that you may be aware of these things I am here to give you counsel."

"Pardon me, Madam," I responded, "I like well enough what you say, but the money of this world that men hang onto so tenaciously; tell me, Madam, to whom does that kind of treasure belong?"

"Turn to the Gospel," she said, "and see what God Himself says about that. When the people who opposed Him brought Him a penny in the Temple, and asked Him whether or not they should worship King Caesar, God asked them if they could say whose name appeared on the coin in letters, and whose image was impressed upon it. 'Caesar's,' they said; 'anyone can see that!' 'Then render to Caesar,' said the Lord, 'whatever is Caesar's, and to God the things that are God's; otherwise you do Him wrong' (Matthew 22:21).

"Right Reason should rule you all in these things, and Common Sense buy your treasure, looking after your money for you, giving you what you need as you need it, for Good Stewardship and these other two go naturally together."[17]

16. Lot's daughters gave birth to sons, but because ME *gerl* can mean a child of either sex, one suspects that Langland here intends *gerlis that were cherlis* to cut both ways.

17. By *Common Sense*, Langland means "moral common sense." *Good Stewardship* refers to the creational mandate to exercise dominion as well as servanthood; the medieval term here is *husbondrie*.

Then I implored her for the sake of Him who made her about "that dungeon in the dale that looks so dreadful; what can it mean, Madam? I beseech you, please tell me."

"That is the Castle of Insecurity," she said. "Whoever goes in there may well rue the day he was born, both body and soul. In it lives a creature called Wrong, the Father of Lies who founded the establishment. He was the one who lured Adam and Eve into sin, and counselled Cain to kill his brother; he was the one who made a fool of Judas with the Jews' silver, and hung him on an elder-tree afterward.[18] He is a preventer of love, and betrays most easily those who put their trust in prosperity, for in that sort of thing Truth will never be found."

Then I began to wonder in my mind what woman this was who quoted me such wise words of Holy Scripture, and I begged her in the name of the Most High to tell me, before she went on her way, who it was had been counselling me so aptly.

"I am Holy Church," she answered, "and you really ought to recognize me for I took you in when you were a baby and taught you your faith. You came to me with godparents, who pledged you to love me loyally all your life."

Then I crumpled to my knees and cried out for her grace, begging her to have pity on me, and to pray for my sins, and also to teach me plainly to believe in Christ, that I might learn to do the will of Him who created me. "Teach me no more about prosperity, then, but tell me just one thing, you who are called 'sanctified': how may I save my soul?"

"When all treasures are tested," she said, "truth is the best, founded securely on the fact that 'God is love' (1 John 4:8); the truth of this you may judge for yourself. It is as precious a jewel as dear God Himself, for whoever speaks the truth and nothing but the truth, and who lives accordingly and does no person harm, is living in a way accountable to the Gospel, both on earth and in the eyes of heaven, and in this much, by the words of St. Luke, is to be likened unto Christ.[19] Theologians who know this ought to be proclaiming it roundabout, for Christians and non-Christians alike are in desperate need of hearing it.

"Kings and knights should, in reason, protect this Truth, riding out into their kingdom to put down transgressors, binding them fast until Truth has determined upon the conclusion of their trespass. That is clearly the proper vocation of a knight—not merely to fast one Friday

18. The elder-tree detail is a feature of medieval tradition, persisting to the time of Shakespeare; cf. *Love's Labor's Lost*, 5.2.599.

19. This statement is not found in Luke's Gospel: it is possibly a mislocation, referring to John 8:12ff. Langland could not have afforded to own a Bible, and his biblical knowledge would have depended on memory.

every hundred years or so, but to stand fast by every man and woman who wants to walk in the way of Truth, and never to abandon them either, for love nor money.

"King David in his time dubbed knights[20] and made them swear on their swords to serve the Truth forever; anyone who failed in that point was apostate to the Order. And Christ our King knighted ten orders of angels, cherubim and seraphim and seven others like them, giving them power of his own majesty, the merrier to be in his presence, and over their serial ranks he set archangels, teaching them all by the power of the Trinity to know Truth, and thus to be submissive to do his bidding; to them it was his only commandment.

"Lucifer too, and all his legions, learned this in heaven; he was loveliest to look upon after the Lord Himself. But he broke the bond of obedience, lost his joy, and fell from that fellowship in the likeness of a fiend into deep, dark hell, there to dwell forever. More thousands fell with him than anyone can number, springing out with him in ugly shapes, for they believed on him who lied to them in this manner: 'I will put my feet above the heaven; I will be like the most high' (cf. Isaiah 14:13-14). And all who hoped it might be so fell out in the likeness of fiends, for heaven could no longer contain them, and for nine days they fell and fell, till God in his goodness stopped their fall, and caused the heavens to close up and stand in stillness.

"When all these wicked ones tumbled out of heaven they fell in various wondrous ways, some remaining in the air, some on earth, and some deep in hell. But Lucifer lies lowest of them all; on account of his pride, his pain has no end. All those who work with Wrong shall follow him on the day of their death, there to dwell with that shrew, but those who live in obedience to the Holy Scriptures and conclude their lives in Truth, which is the best that can be done, may be assured that their souls will go to heaven, where Truth Himself, the triune God, will enthrone them all.[21]

"So I conclude as I began, in the light of these texts of Scripture,[22] by saying that when all treasures are tried, Truth is the best. Teach this to the ignorant—learned persons know it already—that Truth is the only real treasure, the most reliable on earth."

"But I have no natural gift for learning," I protested. "You will have to teach me more thoroughly. By what sort of craft does Truth come into my body, and into what part?"

20. A typical medieval contemporization, possibly referring to 1 Samuel 22:2 or 2 Samuel 23:8-39.

21. Implicitly, in the place vacated by Lucifer and his followers.

22. Matthew 22:21 and 1 John 4:8.

"You poor dimwit," she retorted, "you really are a dull fellow. You learned too little Latin, my lad, in your youth: *Heu mihi, quod sterilem duxi vitam iuvenilem!*[23] There is a natural faculty of knowing that prompts your heart intuitively to love your Lord better than you do yourself, and not to commit deadly sin, even if you should die first.[24] Now this is the inward action of Truth. If anyone can teach you better than it does, permit him to do that and learn as well as you can.

Here is the testimony of God's Word; live according to it. Truth tells us that Love is heaven's remedy. No trace of sin remains in one who is completely given over to Love. All of God's works He does by the power of Love.[25] He taught Moses that it was the most precious thing, most like unto heaven itself, the fullness of peace and most precious of virtues.[26]

Heaven could not contain Love, it was so heavy with Himself, until it had consumed its fill of this mortal earth and taken on of it flesh and blood; then was never leaf on a linden tree lighter, more subtle and piercing than the point of a needle, so that even the toughest armor is no avail against it, nor can the highest walls keep it out.

Love is leader of the Lord's people in heaven, and mediator between the King and the Common—between God and man. Love is our leader; He applies the law, judging mankind for sins and exacting due penalties.

And so that Love can be recognized by natural instinct, it comes to us by the power of the Spirit, and has its center and seat in the heart of man. For every virtue springs from a natural intuition of the heart, derived from the Father who formed us all, looking on us with love great enough that He would let his Son die for our sins, meekly, to make amends for us all, wishing all the while that no harm should come to those who put Him to suffering; in fact, He meekly sought God's mercy on those who were putting Him to death.

"Here you may see the way He exemplified in his own person that He was both mighty and meek, and able to grant mercy even to those who would hang Him on a cross and put a spear through his heart.

"I advise you, then—those of you who are rich—to have pity on the poor. Though you are powerful politically, be meek in your dealings. 'For by the same measures with which you mete out judgment among others, so shall you be measured when you wend your way out of this world' (Matthew 7:1-2).

23. "Alas for my fruitless and misspent youth!"
24. This is a strong idea in Langland, and in most medieval theology, which is notably opposed by the later Protestant doctrine of total depravity.
25. By *Love* here Langland means Christ. Cf. Ephesians 3:17-19; John 1:3.
26. An Augustinian reading of Deuteronomy 6:5-6; 10:12; etc.

"For though you be true to your word and work honestly, and are as chaste as a baby that weeps in church, unless you live faithfully and love also the poor, and truly share such goods as God has blessed you with, you will have no more merit by your masses and devotions than an old crone gets from her maidenhead that nobody wants.

"James the gentle apostle lays down in his epistle that faith without works is more feeble than no faith at all, and dead as a doornail unless one's actions accord with it. Chastity without charity—be sure of it—is as disgusting as a lamp without light.[27] Many chaplains are chaste, but lack all charity; no men are more greedy once they have their chance to get ahead. Ungrateful to their kinfolk, indeed to all Christians, they cannibalize charity and call out for more. Such chastity without charity will be chained up in hell!

"And there are many parish priests who keep their bodies pure, but who are so encumbered with covetousness that they cannot see past it; avarice has such a grip on them that they are closed up like a strongbox. There is no Truth of the Trinity in that, only the treachery of hell, and it teaches ordinary folks to behave in the same way.

"Therefore these words are written in the Gospel: 'Give and it shall be given unto you (cf. Luke 6:38), since I have given you everything you have.' And that is the treasure-lock of Love which, opened, releases my grace to comfort those who are insecure, anxious, burdened, and encumbered with sin. Love is the physician of life, and next to our Lord Himself, and is also the straight gate that leads to heaven. Therefore I repeat the gist of my texts: when all treasures are tried, Truth is best. And now that I have told you what Truth is, and that there is no better treasure, I may tarry no longer with you. Take care now to put yourself into the keeping of our Lord."

27. This allusion, typical in medieval spiritual writers, is to the parable of the wise and foolish virgins.

ANONYMOUS

Of Servants and Lords

This Middle English tract is assigned to a period immediately following the Peasants' Revolt in 1381, when Wyclif and his followers were being discredited by charges of complicity with the leaders of the uprising. The tract makes clear that Wyclif's group disclaimed the association, and that they had sharp criticism for both the unjust rich and those they employed, many of whom argued against government and lords on principle. Whether this work is by Wyclif himself or by one of his followers we cannot be certain; what we may be sure of is that the style of this piece, the courageous ferocity of its social criticism, and the principled biblical standard of its ethics are entirely consistent with all of Wyclif's Latin works on the same subject.

I. The Duty of Servants

FIRST, LET US BE CLEAR that servants ought truly and gladly to serve their lords and masters, and not prove false, idle, grouching or sluggish in their service. Rather, they should consider themselves properly recompensed in their positions, in which God has for their good ordained them to be, and they should keep themselves in humility against pride, and busily work to counter idleness and sloth. For St. Paul urges that if you are called to be a servant then you are not to make an issue of it—that is to say, you ought not to be complaining or despairing on that account (1 Corinthians 7:20-24).

Paul also teaches us in these words: "You servants be obedient to them that are your masters according to the flesh, with fear and trembling, in singleness of heart, as unto Christ; not with eye-service as if you were trying to please men, but as servants of Christ, doing the will of God from the heart; with good will doing service as to the Lord of all lords and not to men, knowing that whatsoever good thing any man doeth, the same shall he receive of the Lord, whether he be a servant, a bond or a free man" (Ephesians 6:5-8). That is to say, there is a reward from God for doing what is good.

Paul also teaches servants in this way: "Obey, ye servants, in all things, your masters according to the flesh. In whatever you do, work from the heart, in wisdom and in intention, as to the Lord and not to men, knowing that it is of the Lord that you shall take recompense, your heritage in heaven. Serve then the Lord Christ. But whoever does wrong or injury shall receive according to the wrong he has wickedly done, and be sure that God is no entertainer or respecter of persons" (Colossians 3:22-25). That is, one person shall not be spared God's judgment on account of his riches or position or noble blood while another poor man is punished for a little trespass, as is true now in this wicked world. No, each person shall be punished according to his own guilt, and each rewarded according to his own good life.

On this point the devil prompts some people to say that Christians should not be servants or serfs under heathen lords, since they are false to God and less spiritually worthy than Christians. They argue further against service to Christian lords, since they are brothers and kin, since Jesus Christ redeemed all who are Christians upon the cross and made them free.[1] Against this heresy Paul writes in the book of God's law: "Let as many servants as are under the yoke count their own masters worthy of all honor, that the name of God and his doctrine be not blasphemed" (1 Timothy 6:1), that is, held wrongfully in contempt or despised. And this word is understood to apply to heathen lords.

"But those servants that have true or Christian lords, let them not despise to serve them because they are brethren both naturally and by faith, but rather serve them more earnestly because those lords are Christians and beloved, partners with us in good works." Teach these things, says Paul to Timothy, both to the learned and the unlearned: "If any man teach otherwise, and does not accord with wholesome words of our Lord Jesus Christ, and to that doctrine which is accorded to mercy,[2] he is proud, knowing nothing, but wailing or languishing over questions and debates about words. Of this is generated envy, strife and blasphemies, which are a kind of despising of God, as well as evil suspicions, disputations among men who are corrupt in heart or soul and destitute of the truth" (1 Timothy 6:2-5).

Paul also teaches in general that Christian men and women ought to be so holy in their living that people who are out of faith will be ashamed, and have nothing evil to say of Christians. And he charges servants to be subject and under the governance of their lords, pleasing them in all things, not being contradictory or fraudulent, but in all things exhibiting good faith—that is, fidelity and honesty—and so

1. The author here refers to a kind of socialist doctrine being propounded around the time of the Peasants' Revolt in 1381.

2. The Middle English word is *pitee* (the word used to translate the Latin *pietas*), which can mean not only "pity" in the sense of "mercy," as I have translated it here, but also "piety." The Authorized Version solves the problem by using the word "godliness."

making their work an act of worship, and all things brighter in the teaching of our God and Savior.

And therefore Peter teaches that Christians ought to possess so clear a conscience and so blameless a life that enemies of our faith who backbite or slander us are confounded, as well as those who falsely challenge our good life in Christ (1 Peter 3:16). And Peter speaks very plainly of this matter, commanding Christians to live well among those that are outside of faith, that in whatever manner they speak against us as if we were doing wrong, they may nevertheless by our good works which they plainly see, glorify God in the time of visitation (1 Peter 2:12).

Some people, without charitable motives, slander poor priests[3] with the charge that they encourage tenants to believe they may lawfully withhold rents and service from their lords when these lords appear to be openly wicked in their manner of life. They tell these lies about poor priests in order to make lords hate them, failing to mention that what they are really teaching is the truth of God's law—for the worship of God, the profit of the realm, and the stability of the king's lawful power in eradicating sin. For it is actually these same poor priests who do most to correct by God's word those who have rebelled against their lords, charging all servants to be subject to their lords, even those who are tyrants. They teach according to St. Peter's admonition: "Servants, be subject to your masters with all fear; not only for the good and the gentle, but also the froward" (1 Peter 2:18), those who detract from a godly understanding.

As St. Paul says, each man ought to be subject to higher powers, that is, to men in positions of governance, since there is no power which is not ordained by God. Consequently, whoever rebels against this power is bound to be condemning himself. And Paul then commands us that we be subject to princes as to necessity, and "not only for wrath but also for conscience sake" (Romans 13:1-5).

Therefore we pay taxes to princes, for they are to be seen as ministers of God. And Paul bids us to pay our debts to all men, tribute to whom we owe tribute, custom duties and tolls—as well as fear, reverence and honor—to whom these are due (Romans 13:6-7).

It is in this spirit that servants should truly and freely serve their lords and masters, and live in quietness, peace, and charitable love, so moving their lords by this example of their patient, open, true lives (for

---

3. *Poor priests* is a term signifying priests who stay within their vocational allowance, not trying to make illegitimate gains from unscrupulous practices or moonlighting. After 1400 the term came to be specifically associated with the Lollards, but in this text it is a more literal and general term of commendation.

even ungodly lords may be so moved) to come themselves to faithful and holy living.

There is a deliberate deception put about [not by poor priests but] by clerics of Antichrist that, if it is lawful for parishioners to withdraw tithes and offerings from clergymen that openly live in lechery or other great sins, not performing their office, then by the same token servants and tenants ought to be able to withdraw their service and rents from lords who openly live an ungodly life.

Well, on the first matter, parishioners have in fact the authority of God's word and human law also: there is no compunction to pay tithes to disreputable clerics. But in the civil matter of withdrawing service and rents from wicked lords it is quite a different thing. Clearly, they are charged by God in the words of Peter and Paul to be subject to wicked lords. On the same point Christ paid taxes for Himself and his apostles to the heathen emperor (Matthew 17:27). We do not read that He or any apostle paid tithes, however, to wicked high priests after the time He began his ministry.

Lords are entitled to powers over men's possessions and bodies to a reasonable degree, and the temporal sword and worldly authority to compel people to do their service and pay their rents (Romans 13:4). But on the witness of the Gospels—Christ's life—and the Acts of the Apostles, priests are not granted such powers to constrain people to pay tithes, especially when they themselves are not fulfilling their spiritual office but are actually harming those under their care by false teaching and an evil example. But even those who perform their pastoral duties well and find persons who will not pay tithes should suffer this meekly and, according to the examples of Jesus, refrain from cursing the offending party (Luke 9:51-56).

II. The Duty of Lords

Let us consider now how lords should conduct themselves in their estate and duties. First they should know God's law, and study and maintain the rule of Scripture, eradicating wrongs and maintaining poor folk in their right to live in rest, peace and charity. They should suffer no officer wearing their colors to extort, abuse people physically, or deprive poor people of their rights, perverting the power of their office.

This is what Holy Scripture has to say in the fifth book of God's law: "When a king is ordained by the choosing of God and of his people, he shall not multiply to himself many horses, he shall not have many wives to draw his heart into carnal appetites, and he shall not hoard out of measure great quantities of silver and gold. Rather, after he has ascended to the seat of authority in his realm, he shall undertake to write out a copy of the book of God's law in a volume, taking instruction from priests and the company of the Levites as he works. And he shall have it with him, and he shall read out of it all the days of his life, so that he learns to fear the Lord his God and keep his words, as these are commanded in the law.[4] And his heart shall not be lifted up in pride above his brethren, and he shall not crook to the right or to the left from that standard, so that he and his children may reign a long time in Israel" (Deuteronomy 17:15-20).

Kings and lords should also be asking God, out of great desire and commitment to a holy life, that they might be granted wisdom in heavenly things and knowledge of earthly things, by which to rule God's people. They should not seek riches or worldly substance, nor worldly glory, nor unreasonable vengeance on their enemies, nor long life in the world. Solomon asked in this way, and so God gave him wisdom and knowledge but also more in material things than any king has had before or after.

Kings and lords ought to be clothed with righteousness and rightful judgment as with a diadem. They ought to be eyes to the blind, feet to the crippled, and father to the poor. With all diligence they ought to seek out legitimate causes not brought to their attention by others, destroying the power of the wicked, snatching the prey from out of their teeth. And when they sit like kings in the midst of their people they should be comforters of those who mourn and those upon whom much misfortune had fallen, and make it their business to deliver the poverty-stricken in their misery, and the fatherless and motherless children who are without assistance. In this way they may be a blessing to those who were on the point of perishing and may comfort the heart of widows. These good actions and many others were the pattern of governance

---

4. This model had been followed by King Alfred (849–899), who composed a code of laws drawing on the Mosaic books and earlier English law codes and including a personal program of translations from scriptural commentary by Augustine, Gregory, Bede, and others. In Wyclif's own time, Queen Anne, wife to Richard II, was the monarch who most nearly approached the ideal described here. When she came to England from her native Bohemia she brought, among her courtiers, a group of young men who studied with Wyclif at Oxford. They provided, at her request, a translation of the Gospels in English, which she kept at her side and from which she read daily. (It is these same students who, especially after Anne's death in 1396, went back to Prague where their many manuscripts of Wyclif's works were so profoundly to influence John Hus.)

for Job, a godly governor, and they are there in the Scriptures for an example to kings and lords (Job 29:12-17).

Also God himself says in the book of Isaiah that we should cease to do evil and learn to do good and seek judgment, helping those who are wrongly oppressed, giving due judgment to the fatherless and motherless, maintaining the widow, helping them in any way that we can (Isaiah 1:16-17).

Therefore Holy Scripture tells us that "Mercy and truth preserve the king; and his throne is made strong by humility and mercy" (Proverbs 20:28), and that "a king that sits in the seat of judgment scatters all evil with the glance of his eyes" (Proverbs 20:8). It pleases God far more that we should do mercy than that we should make sacrifices. On this account, too, Solomon says that those who do wickedly are abominable to the king, for his seat is made secure by righteousness (Proverbs 25:5). And David says that it is the honor of the king to seek judgment; and for the righteous and perceptive judgment that Solomon made between the two common women, all the land of Israel respected him.

Therefore Paul teaches us that rulers ought not to be in fear of good work but of evil, and that one who is established in worldly authority does not have the power of arms without cause, for he is a minister of God to avenge those that do evil (Romans 13:3-4). And St. Peter teaches Christians generally to be subject to all others for the sake of God, and to the king in authority before others, as well as to dukes and ministers of the state who are commissioned by the king to fulfill acts of judgment on miscreants and to commend good deeds and those who do them (1 Peter 2:13-14).

Paul instructs lords thus: "You who are lords, give unto your servants what is right and equitable, knowing also that you have a Lord in heaven" (Colossians 4:1). And he says also in his epistle to the Ephesians: "And you who are lords do to your servants the same things"— that is, as he has already said, good, righteousness, equity from the heart, with good will—"without threatening; knowing that your own Lord and Master is in heaven, and that there is no preferentiality or respect of persons with him" (Ephesians 6:9). That is, be assured that God does not exempt anyone, for the sake of riches, lordship or worldly friendship, from his judgment on sin; nor does he forget, on account of their poverty, to reward the good life of his poorest servants.

Since it is the duty of kings and lords to punish sins and reward good deeds, if lords then abandon this duty and maintain sinful persons and criminals, all the while failing to help the poor obtain their rights, they may well fear that their rule and authority will be taken from them. As the wise man says: "A kingdom is translated from one people and given to another on account of unrighteousness, injuries, wrongs, quarrels, and debates, or on account of guile and deceit" (Ecclesiasticus 10:8).

III. The Wickedness of the Times

With some reason, people fear that unrighteousness against God reigns in our land, for people fear more to displease some miserable earthly wretch in case they should betray their worldly friendship than they fear to offend Almighty God and lose his blessed friendship. There are those who would rather carry out an evidently evil precept of Lucifer's children than perform the most righteous commandments of God, and who manifestly care more for a stinking little heap of worldly goods than they care for the eternal glory of heaven.

For how many are there who make themselves more busy to obtain the muck of this world than to obtain virtue and godly life? And how many are there who show more sorrow over a decline in their worldly prosperity than when they fall from God's grace and charitable love into a multitude of sins? And we see persons who love far more to avenge wrongs and abuses against their own person and authority than they desire to correct wrongs or abuses against the majesty of Almighty God Himself.

Imagine it! It can be that if someone speaks one little word of reproof, or suggests any villainy on the part of a lord or powerful man of this world he will be prosecuted and punished so extravagantly that all the world marvels over it; but if other people speak falsely of our God, saying for example that Christ begged for his living as some now needlessly do,[5] all the while despising his name with cursed swearing, telling filthy stories or gossiping about foul sins in an attempt to blemish the cleanness of Christian souls, these people are not cast out. Oh no. They are cherished and held to be good fellows, some of them even regarded as holy men, all because God's law is not known and so their hypocrisy remains hidden. And thus unrighteousness reigns all around us.

Injury and wrong is done to poor lay people in many ways. Clerics do not teach them faithfully God's law, either in words or by the example of a godly life. And yet these same men of the cloth pronounce a curse upon those of the poorest folk who do not pay them tithes and offerings. Actually, it is these same clerics—fat in their pride and glut-

5. The Wycliffites, along with many others, attacked the friars, many of whom had by this time corrupted the ideal of St. Francis and, despite having grown rich, were begging shamelessly from people who could ill afford to support them.

tony, suffused with the entertainment and banquets of lords and rich men—who should be giving to the poor the material goods that they need rather than taking away what little they have. For their excessive wealth is built on the backs of the poor, who all the while continue in deprivation and wretchedness both of body and soul.

And yet many of these prelates will not even perform the sacraments and their spiritual duties for their subjects, their parishioners—not even the consecration of churches, altars and cemeteries—unless someone is there to pay them a great deal of money. These buyers and sellers in the temple stand condemned by God.

In the same fashion, lords very often do wrong to poor folk by extortion and unreasonable taxes, and requisition the property of citizens, giving them nothing but dubious receipts for it. And they despise those they thus prey upon, threatening and even beating them when they come to collect. This kind of lord devours poor people's scanty means to support his own gluttony, wastefulness and pride, while his subjects perish on account of his mischief, beset by hunger, thirst, and cold, and their little children with them. And if they do not immediately pay their rent, their farm animals are attacked, and they are prosecuted without mercy, no matter how poor and needy or feeble with age or burdened with hard times and having many children to support.

And yet these same lords will not hear the causes of poor men and help them to obtain their rights, but they allow absentee landlords to destroy them, withholding from poorfolk their due, the wages for which they have exhausted their flesh and blood. And so, you might say, they eat and drink the flesh and blood of the poor, and are like cannibals, as God plainly suggests of such tyrants by his prophets. Thus God says through Isaiah (1:15, 23) that such lords are companions to thieves, and their hands are full of blood, so that when they pray aloud and hold up their hands God will not hear them, nor will he receive their offerings that have been wrongfully gotten from the goods of the poor by extortion, ravening and "legalized" robbery.

For all this, men of the law, lawyers and justices who should eradicate such offenses by proper use of their offices, and see to it that each person obtains what is right and reasonable, actually maintain the state of these wrongs for money and fees and robes of honor. Indeed, they often bar poor people from their rights, persuading them that it is better for them not to pursue their cause, however clear the case, than to pursue it and lose still more by their own deceitful ruses, delays, dissembling and prejudicial documents which they employ for their own purposes. And thus wrong is maintained—by "law"!—and truth and human rights outlawed in many states and countries.

The course of honest society in our own country is beset badly by strife, wranglings and debates, as authorities strive with their tenants to bring them into thralldom far greater than they are entitled to by reason or charity. And they snipe and attack, cursing and wearing people down by day and night, those in power maintaining their contestation even into the courts of civil arbitration. Whoever is the stronger party is the one who gets his way, whether right or wrong. And if such people fail at this level, they simply extend their contestation and debate, disseminating it among hundreds and thousands of others, and sometimes over many countries until they get what they want. And by such extension of conflict, propaganda and litigation many lawyers now hold great estates and go about in great trappings and charge incredible fees.

And some lords, no matter how holy and devout they seem in church, in order to protect their own authority, beat down the citizenry and maintain other miscreants and thugs for the purpose, though the people under them in fact are pursuing their rights in a rational and appropriate manner. The churchgoing of these people is the pretense of a liar, and actually just one more expression of their covetousness and pride.

True men of God strive for an understanding of Holy Writ, and say that it is most true and the best standard for the governance of all Christian souls, whatever their estate. But there are hypocrites who say, directly, that Holy Writ is false and new laws concocted by worldly churchmen and academics are better for Christian people than Holy Writ. And therefore hypocrites in the churches study human law and color over the Scriptures by their pride and covetousness. They abandon the Gospel and God's Law,[6] because they condemn the pride and covetousness of worldly ministers and teach humility, the adoption of poverty and dedication to prayer and spiritual occupation.

True clerics, on the other hand, maintain that the order and faith made by Jesus Christ, who was man and God, is most perfect. It is most enlightened, and it is most secure for the power, wisdom and charity of any lord. Hypocrites insist that their "new" style of religion, founded by sinful men and full of errors, and propounded by fools and worldly people—proud and grasping wretches—is best. Therefore they abandon the rule of Christ, and his freedom, binding themselves by their singular profession to a company of sinful fools. Yet Christ and his apostles never taught or employed any such profession.

6. By "the Gospel" Wycliffites typically meant the first four books of the New Testament; by "Goddis Lawe" they meant either the whole of canonical Scripture or, as here, the whole of the O.T. and the balance of the N.T. exclusive of the Gospels.

Many children, alas, have been attracted to such worldly religion for love of worldly pride or welfare of the body more than for any desire to lead a holy life or to serve God in penitence and purity of soul. And some have even been stolen away from their friends and families by these pretenders, and some misled by lies and false promises, and when later they have had second thoughts, they have not been permitted to turn again to a pure and simple faith in Christ. This happens even when some discover themselves entirely unable to accord with these new religions built upon the designs of sinful men. And yet, victims that they are, to the degree that they are aware of what has happened to them they are also in some measure responsible for maintaining the hypocrisy and for repression of their own conscience, as well as for leaving a better thing and wittingiy holding onto something worse.

True clerics set before us the life of Christ and his apostles as a pattern for our living in voluntary poverty, without false and needless begging and without pursuit of worldly lordship. This is the best pattern, the one most perfect in itself, for all pastors, since Jesus Christ, who was God and man, chose this style of life and since He did not err in thought, word or deed.

Despite this pattern, however, some religious hypocrites suggest that it is best to pretend a holy style of poverty in the manner of Christ and his apsotles while all the time living behind closed doors in the lap of luxury, in costly housing rivaling that of great men of the state, and spending as much on clothing, food, drink and politically motivated entertainment.

And this life they keep up by falsely begging money from poor people who can hardly pay their rents, let alone tithes and offerings, who are trying to maintain their wives and children and falling ever into debt, no matter if they work night and day. However poor or deep in debt these poor victims are, such hypocrites will not desist from robbing them through false appeals and begging such as are condemned by the law of God.

Other hypocrites say indeed that it is better for clergymen to have endowments of worldly rents and lordships, and the revenue of parish churches made payable to them entirely in simony,[7] rather than to have to live in simple poverty like Christ and the apostles. And yet when such people assume the role of secular lords they do not govern the people well as lords should, but shrug, saying, "Oh, I am dead to the world." Nor do they then teach the people God's law in word or by example,

7. Simony was understood as the attempt to pervert spiritual authority for material profit. See Acts 8:9-24.

faithfully as they should, but say that it is not their calling to preach. So they do not in any way work for their livelihood, as God first enjoined Adam to do for his penance, and as St. Paul did, who worked with his hands as was necessary for his sustenance. These people live in idleness and gluttony and feign holiness, praying with their mouths and elaborating frivolous ceremonies rather than living according to the Gospel.

Faithful clergymen try to maintain their commitment by following Holy Scripture, rational order and the example of Christ's life and that of his apostles. But these new hypocrites maintain their false pretensions with the support of sinful men, by dissembling, by temporal power and gifts of money, and also by censures—such as suspensions, cursing and imprisoning those who resist them. On this account, there is much strife and debate. For many lords and important persons are deceived by the multitude of hypocrites, and many blinded by gifts of money and worldly profits that they get by means of these hypocrites. Some are misled by carnal affection and worldly friendship. For all of these reasons, few stand with the true clerics, and very few lords or wealthy Christians stand by God's law and make their business the winning of souls to eternal life.

But the true, poor priests are slandered as heretics, simply because they speak the truth of Holy Writ, and they are cast out of their churches, cursed, imprisoned and in every way imaginable prevented from preaching the Gospel, for fear that by Christ's teaching they might warn the people against the deceptions of Antichrist and his proud, worldly and covetous clergy. And thus more strife and debate is occasioned in our land. . . .[8]

So many of the troubles that beset us are a product of deceitfulness. Among lawyers and men of law, deception is the rule, for a deceitful society is to their advantage. Thus they manipulate lords to maintain wrongs and commit new ones even when these lords sincerely hope to do what is right and try to please God. And by their own double-dealing and greed these men of law purchase lands and income property, then extort from the tenants, trampling on the rights of rich and poor alike. And yet they make themselves to appear outwardly so full of pious justice that you might think they were angels from heaven, so able are they to color over their falseness and blind the people.

In merchants as well, guile is everywhere to be found. For they swear falsely by Christ and the Trinity that their merchandise costs more than

8. I have deleted two or three essentially redundant passages from the balance of this work.

it does, that it is so worthwhile and beneficial, and so forth, beguiling the people. Moreover, they are quick to teach young apprentices their crooked craft, and praise most whoever among them is most effective in duping customers. They disguise their usurious practices, using the wiles of the devil so that hardly anyone can find them out and correct them before the day of reckoning.

In servants employed in many occupations there is also a rule of guile: people work quickly while their master is present but then in his absence are idle; they fool about and do nobody any good, all the while swearing and maintaining that it is impossible that they should produce anything more or better than they are already.

But alas, nowhere is deceitfulness more the rule than among the clergy. For they deceive people by their vain prayers, pardons and indulgences. And they know neither how to pray effectively nor the condition of those for whom they pretend to pray. They ought rather to be in mortal fear that they are stirring God up to a terrible recompense for their own wicked lives. What they must understand is that there can be for them no pardon except that which comes from God, and which requires of them godly living and dedication to charitable love as the end of all their endeavors. And this pardon is not the kind that can be bought and sold, despite what many of them are accustomed to nowadays.

Whoever is most in charity will be most readily heard by God, whether a shepherd or a common laborer, whether he be in the church or out in the field. And whoever keeps faithfully the commands of God, that person shall have forgiveness and eternal life; there is no effective pardon from any other creature under God.

And so, as you see, deceitfulness reigns in so many areas of life and in so many people that our land ought to be sorely in dread of being completely conquered—unless, that is, sinful behavior and the rule of deception are chased out, and a rule of truth and charity very soon established.

IV. Practical Measures for Reform

Those who are lords ought now to be aware of their responsibility, and see to it that they do charity and mercy in good conscience to those under their authority; otherwise they shall themselves get no mercy or love from God. For a wrongful oppression of the poor calls for vengeance from God, just as much as does murder. And lords ought to see to it that they govern their servants and tenants well, that they of all people may fear the anger of God, and so flee sin, living virtuously and in truth before God and all mankind.

For those who are lords ought to be setting a holy example of life for their servants and subjects, being more concerned to admonish or punish for wickedness before God than for deceitfulness or despite against their own person or worldly profit. And they ought more to praise, cherish and love their people for a holy life and a truthful bearing than for any flattering behavior or for mere addition to their worldly advantage or profit.

In this way, lords who are virtuous in themselves might nourish virtuous servants and be true both to God and man, reproving and punishing the wicked and treacherous who are a curse on all. And sin amongst themselves might be hurled out, and an honest and virtuous life maintained and nourished.

But to effect these things, lords will need to correct some of their own behavior. To begin with, though secular law and vicious custom of our time permit it, they will have to abandon the use of bad laws which effectively permit exploitation of their servants. For all these laws and ordinances are worth nothing unless they are administered in charity and good conscience. Lords ought to procure good, and rest, and peaceful conditions for their servants as good fathers and helpers, and they ought not to permit any of their stewards or officials to do them wrong. For inasmuch as it is in their power to correct abuses, if they fail to do so they are as much to blame and shall also be punished—even, as St. Paul says, more sharply in many cases, for their maintaining the circumstances of abuse does more [to perpetuate injustice] than the wicked stewards do by themselves (Romans 1:32). Paul says plainly that one who does not provide for his own, especially those of his own household, has forsaken the faith and is worse than a heathen (1 Timothy 5:8).

On this account it seems clear that a lord who does not punish wrongs or extortions performed by officers in his service forsakes a right standard of faith and is worse in this respect than a pagan, for in the sight of God he does more harm to Christians, and contributes to hate, dissension and strife between poor and rich. After all, he might easily enquire of faithful people of the country concerning the conduct of his officers and amend them—if indeed he loved the truth of God and rightful help of poor folk as much as he loved the health of his own body and the wholesomeness of his food. Alas, too many, it seems, have fallen out of charity, loving more their belly and their selfish appetites than their responsibility to honor Christ in their governance of God's people.

Lords ought to warn their officers that if they do wrong to tenants they will lose their positions and place in the community. Then officers of lords would suddenly grow wary of attempting more extortion or abuse.

Lords are badly deceived when they dawdle at home eating, drinking and being merry, saying their morning prayers with their mouths only and not in heartfelt devotion followed up by deeds, all the while permitting the people to be abused by their officials. For God tells us in the writing of Solomon that it is better to do mercy and perform rightful judgments than to offer sacrifices. For the presence of a righteous lord should do more to eradicate wrongs and abuses than many letters and petitions sent to these same evil officials, for as far as they are concerned, each request for action is merely a dead letter.

What is it worth for a lord to cry aloud with words to God, while poor folk are petitioning for righteous judgment against him for extortion and wrongs that he or his officers have caused to be done in his name? For God will sooner hear the righteous complaint of the many poor than he will hear a lord and many hypocrites asking unrighteously for his help in increasing their worldly prosperity. God will not hear sinful men crying to Him in the time of their need if they will not hear poor men when it is in their power to help them out of the wrongs and mischiefs wrought upon them.

There is also a great lack of righteousness among those in authority when they will not correct pride, covetousness and worldly living among those clergymen who are doing so much harm to the Christian community. For if lords would despise the pride of covetous clergymen, and neither condone nor abet their pursuit of worldly positions and their simony—which are openly condemned by Holy Writ and the life of Christ—then these proud and worldly clergy, full of greed, lechery and other sinful behavior, should soon be diminished, and sanctified living and true teaching be brought again to our churches.

But here we are up against the guile and hypocrisy of Antichrist and his clerics again, for they argue that secular lords have no jurisdiction over the clergy, and only ecclesiastical authorities may chastise clergy when they rebel and will not submit to their bishops. But Solomon put out one high priest and ordained another in his place, and outlawed the first without asking help of the priesthood to do it, on account of that priest's treason against Solomon and his people (1 Kings 2:27).

Now treason against Christ and his law and people is more serious than treason against an earthly king, and more deserving of punishment. As Peter and Paul teach us, lords are ordained of God to correct misdeeds and misdoers, and to praise good deeds and their doers. The more serious the sin, the more obliged are lords to punish it; and since the sin of corrupt clergymen is far greater than the sin of other ordinary people, it follows that lords ought more to be concerned with correcting it. . . . And therefore Christ, when He was praised by the people, went into the temple and drove out the simonites, so giving example to our earthly lords to do the same. It is presumably on this account that Peter and Paul do not exempt clergy from the admonition of lords.

Since then God's law allows a general power to secular lords to admonish and correct mischief, why should these lords not punish evil clergymen who are more responsible than anyone for leading other folks into sin and disturbances of the realm? Christ himself suffered patiently an innocent death at the hands of Pilate, who was a secular justice; still more reason why clergymen should be willing to abide rightful punishment of their criminal behavior by secular lords. And Paul expressed himself willing to accept death at the hands of secular judgment if he deserved it; he appealed also to the pagan emperor of Rome. So it seems that clergy who refuse to admit the jurisdiction of secular authorities, or to be amended by them, are willfully contrary to the humility, patience and charity of Christ and his apostles, and have set themselves up above them in devilish pride.

Yet consider how lords can so readily abet these deceitful wrongs, advancing men of lewd life and low learning to benefices, churches with the care of many souls, and take to themselves profit out of these assignments for many years. And some keep many priests in their own chapels simply for the sake of having personal choirs, and they make some priests officers in their own households: some in charge of their kitchens, some accountants and bookkeepers, some their secretaries, some stewards of the court, some councillors and administrators of their worldly business. What have these things to do with the calling of a priest? And they will not permit these "household" clergy to go and teach the souls for which they must answer at the day of judgment, and for which Christ shed his precious heart's blood. Instead, they keep them like packs of wolves in sheep's clothing, always ready to slay the souls of Christians by their sinful example, hindering the acts of mercy in body and spirit; and they are in this way actually cursed traitors to God, and to his true priests, and to God's poor people.

But if there is any really spiritual pastor or priest who lives a good life in meekness and works of mercy among the poor, not wasting laymen's offerings in vain feasts or other means of money-raising, but steadfast in prayer, teaching God's law truly, and diligently striving for a true understanding of the Scriptures, this man is likely to be despised as a dog, or called a pig, hypocrite or a heretic. And this will be true especially if he reproves men for their wickedness and tries to teach them the best way to heaven, in word and in his life. Such a person is likely to be bandied about privately and publicly harassed, and so hated by the comfortable rich that he is likely to lose his church or be forced for shame or oppression to flee the country. And by this kind of wrong many good men are kept from God's service and from the teaching of the truth.

And lords ought to consider how they may do many other wrongs in office. For many waste their time in sloth and idleness, and waste their goods in boastful living, in pride and excess. And whoever lives most extravagantly is likely to be held by worldly people the most successful and worthy of respect, especially if he is powerful enough to get away with some of the injustices of which we have spoken.

And thus when they should be maintaining households and officers who are righteous examples of virtuous life, they are maintaining the very opposite—extortioners, thieves, and predators who destroy their poor neighbors and make the enterprise of such a lord like a den of thieves. Whether they realize it or not, such lords must then take responsibility for being procurators of the devil, maintainers of falsehood and sin, debasers of God's law and of his servants.

What ought to be done? These things: Lords should work diligently to come to a knowledge of the Scriptures, and set themselves to understand and perform honesty and equity. They should maintain the rights of the poor, and guard in peace and tranquility their knowledge and strength, enabling poor folk to labor and build their own livelihood and thus to be able to pay their rents to their lords.

For God says through David, "And now, ye kings, understand; be instructed, ye that judge in the world: serve ye the Lord with dread in your heart; and rejoice yourself in Him with trembling" (Psalm 2:10-11). And the wise man says that the most exacting judgment shall fall upon one who is in authority over others (Wisdom 6:6), and Jesus says that "unto whom much is given; of him shall much be required" (Luke 12:48). May God move lords to eradicate sin and nourish virtue, inspiring a holy life in the clergy and in all their other subjects.

Amen.

GEOFFREY CHAUCER
Gentilesse

Geoffrey Chaucer (c. 1340–1400) was England's poet laureate in the time of Walter Hilton and John Wyclif. Like Wyclif, he was attached to the household of John of Gaunt, Duke of Lancaster. He served as Clerk of the King's Works until 1386, two years after Wyclif's death, and this poem may be taken as a species of "court counsel."

ADVICE TO A GOVERNOR

The first stock,[1] father of gentleness[2]—
whoever claims gentility
his line must trace, and every wit address
to follow virtue, worldly vice to flee.
For virtue breeds nobility,
and not the reverse, you may depend,
whether he wears mitre, crown, or diadem.[3]

The first stock was full of righteousness,
true to his word, faithful in charity,
pure in heart, directing his business
to shun the vice of sloth, in honesty.
Unless his heir loves virtue, as did He,
he is not gentle, though he sport a gem,
whether he wears mitre, crown, or diadem.

Vice can well inherit great prosperity;
but no one yet, as well we see,
bequeaths to an heir true nobility.
That comes not with position or degree
but from the Father of all, in majesty,
who makes those heirs who well please Him
—whether he wears mitre, crown, or diadem.

---

1. I.e., God, the trunk of the family tree of all humanity, the true progenitor of all that is.

2. *Gentilesse*, Chaucer's form of the word, means "nobility" as well as the character of a noble life, i.e., "gentility."

3. *Mitre* signifies a bishop or any high official in the church; *crown* signifies royalty; and *diadem* refers to lesser nobility.

GEOFFREY CHAUCER

Balade de Bon Conseil

TRUTH

Fle fro the prees° and dwell with
    sothfastnesse,°   *crowd / truthfulness*
Suffise unto thy good, though it be smal,[1]
For hord hath hate, and clymbyng tykelnesse,°   *insecurity*
Prees hath envye, and wele blent overal.°   *prosperity blinds*
Savour no more than the byhove° shal.   *profit*
Reule wel thiself, that other folk canst rede;
And trouthe the shal delivere, it is no drede.°[2]   *fear not*

Tempest the noght al croked to redresse,
In trust of hir that turneth as a bal.[3]
Gret reste stant in lytel bisynesse.
Bewar also to sporne ayeyns an al.[4]
Stryve noght as doth the crokke with the wal.
Daunte° thiself, that dauntest otheres dede;   *govern*
And trouthe the shal delivere, it is no drede.

That the is sent, receyve in boxomnesse.°   *generous, humble spirit*
The wrastling for this world axeth a fal.
Here nis non home, here nis but wyldernesse:
Forth, pilgrym, forth! Forth, beste, out of thi stal!
Know thi contree, lok up, thank God of al;
Hold the hye wey, and lat thi gost° the lede;   *spirit*
And trouthe the shal delivere, it is no drede.

---

1. "Let your goods be sufficient for you, even if small."
2. The allusion is to John 8:32: "And you will know the truth, and the truth will make you free."
3. Lady Fortune, who turns her wheel.
4. "To kick against an awl," or, "to kick against the pricks." The allusion is to Acts 9:5.

Envoy

Therfore, thou Vache,[5] leve thine old wrechedenesse;
Unto the world leve° now to be thral.   *stop*
Crie Hym mercy, that of His hie godnesse
Made the of noght, and in especial
Draw unto Him, and pray in general
For the, and eke for other hevenlyche mede;
And trouthe the shal delivere, it is no drede.

5. At first taken to be the French word for cow; subsequently it has been suggested that the reference is to the Lollard knight Sir Philip de la Vache, who, like Chaucer, lost his government job in 1386.

ANONYMOUS

Courageous Witness

This selection comes from a larger work, *The Leaven of the Pharisees*, an antifraternal treatise which forms part of the collection of Wycliffite tracts in MS Corpus Christi College, Cambridge, 296. The work is in general an application of Luke 12:2-8 to the legalism and political opportunism of the friars, which the author sees not only as an offense to the gospel but as a threat to simple Christians, especially those who wish to identify themselves openly with an evangelical (and presumably Wycliffite) persuasion. Such an open scriptural critique and witness could invite serious consequences after about 1382, by which time sympathizers with any position that might be construed as Wycliffite were subject to arraignment.

CHRIST SAYS that "there is nothing covered that shall not be revealed, and there is nothing hidden so secretly that it shall not be discovered and made known. For those things that you have said on your couches or small beds shall be preached from the roof of houses" (Luke 12:2-3).

Here Christ means that people should be alert, and openly speak the truth against hypocrisy. For although such things are hidden now they shall at the last be rewarded, in the Day of Judgment.

But this also applies to cowardice among Christ's disciples, if for the sake of avoiding physical pain and death they spare themselves from telling openly the truth of God's law. On this account Christ says to his disciples that they should fear God and nothing else more. Truly, Christ says, "I say to you my friends, do not be frightened of those who have power to slay the body and have nothing more to do after these things are over; but I shall show you whom you ought to fear. Fear him supremely who, after he has killed the body has power also to send both body and soul to everlasting hell. So, I say to you, fear Him" (vv. 4-5).

Here Christ intends us to understand that we are to fear nothing more than we fear God, and offending Him. For if persons are in fear of physical suffering and death and, on that account, cease to proclaim openly the truth, they are made unable to receive with us the bliss of heaven. Yet if they declare publicly and steadfastly the truth of God, nothing will be able really to harm them, so long as they persevere in peace and charitable love.

To this effect Christ afterward says, comforting his disciples by way of granting them reasons, "Are not five sparrows sold for a half-penny, and not one of them is forgotten before God; but even the hairs of your head are numbered. Therefore you will not be afraid; you are of more value than many sparrows" (vv. 6-7). Christ intends that we understand by an analogy. Since God Almighty takes such great care over little birds that not one of them, even the least of them, is forgotten, how much more shall God keep you, since He is all powerful, all knowing and filled with good will. Nothing may happen without his knowing, therefore, and his ordinance, and thus it shall be all for the best.

And nothing may overturn his ordinance, so we should take what comes our way in patience, and thank Him for it. And when the hairs of our heads are counted so they might not be lost, we will not be lost in body or soul, since each of us is of more value than the hairs of our head! It is as if Christ were saying to us that nothing of ourselves, body or soul, will perish or suffer pain to our [eternal] harm as long as we keep ourselves in patience and charity.

With his final words Christ gives us confidence to die for the sake of his Law so as to be rewarded by the bliss of heaven, when He says, "Each person who acknowledges me before men, the Son of Man shall acknowledge him before the angels of God" (v. 8). Here, Christ calls Himself the Son of Man, for He is the son of the virgin Mary and, accordingly, a human person, and so called a man in the language of Holy Writ.

We see that all these things are said for the sake of a true acknowledgment of Christ. First, we are to acknowledge in our hearts by sincere faith that He is true God and true man, without sin in any degree, whether by thought, speech, or action in any of its circumstances, and to witness in words the truth of the Gospel, how Christ lived most meekly and most poorly and most virtuously before all people, even as the Gospel teaches. Then we need to acknowledge Him in our life, living according to the law of God and being willing to die for it if need be. This is the true acknowledgment and this is what shall cause individuals to be approved by Christ at the Day of Judgment before all the company of saints and angels, and before creatures good and evil, for the way in which they were true witnesses of Christ here on earth before mankind, in full willingness to suffer slander, persecution and death for the love of Jesus Christ and his Word.